CBAP®/CCBA™: Certified Business Analysts Study Guide

 **W9-AJK-759**

BABOK® Guide Version 2.0 Knowledge Areas and Underlying Competencies

KNOWLEDGE AREA	CHAPTER
Business Analysis Planning and Monitoring	
Plan Business Analysis Approach	2
Conduct Stakeholder Analysis	2
Plan Business Analysis Activities	2
Plan Business Analysis Communications	2
Plan Requirements Management Process	2
Manage Business Analysis Performance	2
Enterprise Analysis	
Define Business Need	3
Assess Capability Gaps	3
Determine Solution Approach	3
Define Solution Scope	3
Define Business Case	3
Elicitation	
Prepare for Elicitation	5
Conduct Elicitation Activity	5
Document Elicitation Results	5
Confirm Elicitation Results	5
Requirements Analysis	
Prioritize Requirements	6
Organize Requirements	6
Specify and Model Requirements	6
Determine Assumptions and Constraints	6
Verify Requirements	6
Validate Requirements	6
Solution Assessment and Validation	
Assess Proposed Solution	7
Allocate Requirements	7
Assess Organizational Readiness	7

Sybex®
An Imprint of
WILEY

KNOWLEDGE AREA	CHAPTER
Define Transition Requirements	7
Validate Solution	7
Evaluate Solution Performance	7
Requirements Management and Communication	
Manage Solution Scope and Requirements	4
Manage Requirements Traceability	4
Maintain Requirements for Reuse	4
Prepare Requirements Package	4
Communicate Requirements	4
Underlying Competencies	
Analytical Thinking and Problem Solving	8
Behavioral Characteristics	8
Business Knowledge	8
Communication Skills	8
Interaction Skills	8
Software Applications	8

 The BABOK® Guide Version 2.0 is subject to change at any time without prior notice and at the IIBA's sole discretion. Please visit IIBA's website (www.theiiba.org) for the most current listing.

Sybex®
An Imprint of
WILEY

CBAP®/CCBA™
Certified Business Analysis
Study Guide

CBAP®/CCBA™
Certified Business Analysis
Study Guide

Susan Weese

Terri Wagner

WILEY

Wiley Publishing, Inc.

Acquisitions Editor: Jeff Kellum
Development Editor: Mary Ellen Schutz
Technical Editors: John A. Estrella and James Haner
Production Editors: Dassi Zeidel and Nicholas Moran
Copy Editor: Kathy Grider-Carlyle
Editorial Manager: Pete Gaughan
Production Manager: Tim Tate
Vice President and Executive Group Publisher: Richard Swadley
Vice President and Publisher: Neil Edde
Media Project Manager 1: Laura Moss-Hollister
Media Associate Producer: Josh Frank
Media Quality Assurance: Shawn Patrick
Book Designer: Judy Fung
Proofreader: Publication Services, Inc.
Indexer: Jack Lewis
Project Coordinator, Cover: Katie Crocker
Cover Designer: Elizabeth Brooks

Dear Reader,

Thank you for choosing *CBAP®/CCBA™: Certified Business Analysis Study Guide*. This book is part of a family of premium-quality Sybex books, all of which are written by outstanding authors who combine practical experience with a gift for teaching.

Sybex was founded in 1976. More than 30 years later, we're still committed to producing consistently exceptional books. With each of our titles, we're working hard to set a new standard for the industry. From the paper we print on, to the authors we work with, our goal is to bring you the best books available.

I hope you see all that reflected in these pages. I'd be very interested to hear your comments and get your feedback on how we're doing. Feel free to let me know what you think about this or any other Sybex book by sending me an email at nedde@wiley.com. If you think you've found a technical error in this book, please visit http://sybex .custhelp.com. Customer feedback is critical to our efforts at Sybex.

Best regards,

Neil Edde
Vice President and Publisher
Sybex, an Imprint of Wiley

Good luck to all the planners, crammers, and refreshers getting ready to sit the CBAP® or the CCBA™ business analysis certification exam!
—Susan Weese and Terri Wagner

Dedicated to my family, friends, and colleagues who put up with me spending so much time on this book.
—Susan

Lovingly dedicated to my niece Jenna for her passion for life, generous spirit, and keen analytic skills.
—Terri

Acknowledgments

We'd like to thank Pete Gaughan, Editorial Manager; Jeff Kellum, Acquisition Editor; Dassi Zeidel and Nicholas Moran, Production Editors; Kathy Grider-Carlyle, Copy Editor; Jack Lewis, Indexer; and James Haner, our Technical Proofreader. Without all of their contributions and assistance, this book would never have made it to the presses. In particular, we would like to thank our Development Editor, Mary Ellen Schutz. Her attention to detail, requests for clarity, and questions about what we really meant to say kept us on target to produce the complete study guide you are reading right now. We would also like to thank Dr. John Estrella, our Technical Editor. John held us to the highest standards for representing business analysts and how they get things done—right down to the smallest detail about each requirements modeling technique. Without the professional and helpful folks at Sybex, this book never would have happened.

A big thank-you goes out to the founders and supporters of the International Institute of Business Analysis (IIBA™) and the team who developed the contents of the *BABOK®️ Guide*. We would also like to thank our colleagues and good friends, Ginger Sanchez, Peggy Oglesby, and Phil Bennett, for sharing their wonderful business analysis stories and ideas that became the basis for many tales in this book. Thanks also to Melisa Pearce of Touched by a Horse for sharing her barn project with us.

Each of us has a few folks we would like to acknowledge and thank individually.

ME, if you were here with me I would give you a big hug! Without your herding and nipping during the development process, this book would never have become such a great product. Your Gentle Editing is subtle, targeted, and very effective. Thanks to my husband, Danny, for giving me the kitchen nook table and eating his breakfast standing at the counter while I wrote this book. Terri, thank you for the opportunity to write this book; it was great fun! Little Man, thank you for lying on my computer every morning and helping me think through things. You are the prince of cats.

—*Susan*

Thanks to Susan for taking the helm and navigating these waters. Your dedication, talent, and wisdom never cease to amaze me. I admire your professionalism and cherish your friendship.

—*Terri*

About the Authors

This book is the result of collaboration between Susan Weese and Terri Wagner. Susan authored the book. Terri reviewed text, contributed some practice exam questions, and lent her experience and expertise to the overall project. We hope that you, the reader, will enjoy reading this book as much as we enjoyed writing it.

Susan Weese, CBAP®, PgMP, PMP, PRINCE2, MSPM Susan is a management consultant, curriculum designer, and professional speaker specializing in project management and requirements development process development and implementation for complex information technology projects. She started her work career as a software engineer, designing and developing complex mathematical algorithms for satellite and radar systems. Halfway through her work life, Susan crossed to the dark side of technology and became actively involved with managing programs, projects, large consulting organizations, and business processes. She is still having a blast and has never looked back.

Susan founded Colorado-based Rhyming Planet, Inc., in 2000 to motivate, lead, and enable technical and business professionals to accomplish their program and project goals. Susan is also an adjunct faculty member at Colorado State University and the University of Phoenix, delivering courses on project management and the underlying competencies that make good managers into great managers. She is currently a PRINCE2 assessor for the APMG-US, auditing global training organizations and instructors developing and delivering certification courses in this project management methodology.

Terri Wagner, MA, PMP, CSM Terri Wagner has managed multi-million dollar project management office portfolios for international consulting clients. She has also led teams of project managers, business analysts, process specialists, operational groups, and trainers in the planning, design, development, and deployment of internal system and operational enhancements, as well as client-based solution initiatives. She has been honored as a creative thinker with the ability to successfully apply technology for the advancement of internal and external operational efficiencies and quality. Terri has taught business analysis, project management, portfolio management, business leadership, business acumen, communication, applying emotional intelligence, critical thinking, team problem solving, leadership and interpersonal skills, negotiation skills, general management, earned value management, quality management, time and efficiency management along with other topics to state and governmental agencies, corporate clients, and at the graduate level in the university system, and has developed a coaching program for first line through executive level for a Fortune 500 company.

Terri Wagner is the owner/managing member of Mentor Source, Inc., a Colorado-based coaching, consulting, and training company. She has delivered training, coaching, consulting, and project management in the United States, Canada, the Caribbean, and Europe.

Contents at a Glance

Contents

Introduction

Congratulations on your decision to study for and take the International Institute of Business Analysis (IIBA™) Certified Business Analysis Professional (CBAP®) or Certification of Competency in Business Analysis (CCBA™) exam. This book was written specifically with you in mind. The book also targets individuals who want a set of "tried and true" business analysis best practices and activities to use when performing business analysis work.

The focus and content of this book revolves around *A Guide to the Business Analysis Body of Knowledge® (BABOK® Guide) Version 2.0*, published by the IIBA™ headquartered in Toronto, Canada. We will refer to the *BABOK® Guide* throughout this book and use its contents to drive our discussions on performing successful business analysis work across the project life cycle. In some cases, certain phrases are used verbatim to ensure strict conformance with the *BABOK® Guide*. Both certification exams focus on the contents of the *BABOK® Guide,* and we recommend that you get a copy of the guide to assist you when you are using our book to prepare you for the exams.

The book contains many hints and tips about preparing for and passing the exam and using what you have learned in your everyday work. The first tip for anyone wanting to become familiar with the *BABOK® Guide* is that you need to learn its language. Speaking this language gives you a common business analysis language, regardless of the industry or organization you work in. The terms and definitions found there may be different from the terms and definitions you use at work. So, your first step is to familiarize yourself with the terms and definitions so you are comfortable with *BABOK® Guide*-speak.

This book covers all 16 of the techniques that the *BABOK® Guide* identifies as essential for all business analysts. You will see them introduced as one of the 16 essential techniques when that particular technique is covered in detail as part of a knowledge area chapter. The 16 essential techniques include:

- Acceptance and Evaluation Criteria Definition
- Brainstorming
- Business Rules Analysis
- Data Dictionary and Glossary
- Data Flow Diagrams
- Data Modeling
- Decision Analysis
- Document Analysis
- Interviews
- Metrics and Key Performance Indicators
- Nonfunctional Requirements Analysis
- Organization Modeling

- Problem Tracking
- Process Modeling
- Requirements Workshops
- Scenarios and Use Cases

Your second tip is that you need to be very familiar with the six knowledge areas defined in the *BABOK® Guide*. These knowledge areas divide your business analysis knowledge and skills into six common areas. You will start with the high-level definitions and then drill down into the detailed tasks and techniques that successful business analysts use to get the job done. Let's move on and talk a little bit about the focus and intents of this book.

What You Will Learn

This book helps you prepare to take the CBAP® or CCBA™ certification exams. The CBAP® exam is designed for experienced business analysts, while the newer CCBA™ exam targets people who have less experience in the business analysis profession. We cannot guarantee that reading this book will result in you passing the exam, but we hope that you will find its contents motivating and helpful.

The CCBA™ exam provides less experienced business analysts with their first step toward obtaining the CBAP® designation. This exam targets individuals who are proficient in some aspects of business analysis, are in the process of developing business analysis skills and expertise, and who apply business analysis to smaller scope projects and less complex tasks. The CCBA™ certification expires after five years. The expectation is that you will then apply to take the CBAP® exam when you have gained more business analysis experience. You can also retake the CCBA™ exam if you have not yet met the required CBAP® exam level of business analysis experience.

What Is Covered in This Book

The *CBAP®/CCBA™: Certified Business Analysis Study Guide* follows a simple project life cycle we frequently use as the basis for our projects. The life cycle consists of three high-level phases:

- Controlled start, where you plan for your project's business analysis activities and define the scope of the new solution your project will create
- Controlled middle, where the project work is actually being performed to define, design, and build the new solution
- Controlled end, when you wrap up your work activities and transition the new solution into operational use

We placed the knowledge areas of the *BABOK® Guide* within these three life cycle phases in order to work through the business analysis tasks and techniques from project start to end.

We've included several testing features, both in the book and on the companion CD. Following this Introduction is an Assessment Test that you can use to check your readiness for the actual exam. Take this test before you start reading the book. It will help you identify the areas you may need to brush up on. The answers to the Assessment Test appear after the last question of the test. Each answer includes an explanation and a note telling you in which chapter this material appears.

An Exam Essentials section appears at the end of every chapter to highlight the topics you'll most likely find on the exam and help you focus on the most important material covered in the chapter so that you'll have a solid understanding of those concepts. However, it isn't possible to predict what questions will be covered on your particular exam, so be sure to study everything in the chapter.

Review Questions are also provided at the end of every chapter. You can use these to gauge your understanding of the subject matter before reading the chapter. They can also be used to point out areas where you need to concentrate your study time. As you finish each chapter, answer the Review Questions and then check to see whether your answers are right—the correct answers appear on the pages following the last question. You can go back to reread the sections dealing with questions you got wrong to make sure you understand the material and answer correctly the next time you are tested on the material. If you can answer at least 80 percent of the Review Questions correctly, you can probably feel comfortable moving on to the next chapter. If you can't answer that many correctly, reread the chapter, or the section that seems to be giving you trouble, and try the questions again.

You'll also find more than 100 flashcard questions on the CD for on-the-go review. In addition to the Assessment Test and the Review Questions, you'll find Bonus Exams on the CD. Take these practice exams just as if you were actually taking the exam (that is, without any reference material). When you have finished the first exam, move on to the next exam to solidify your test-taking skills. If you get more than 85 percent of the answers correct, you're ready to take the real exam.

WARNING

The Review Questions, Assessment Test, and other testing elements included in this book are *not* derived from the CBAP® or CCBA™ exam questions, so don't memorize the answers to these questions and assume that doing so will enable you to pass the exam. You should learn the underlying topic, as described in the text of the book. This will let you answer the questions provided with this book *and* pass the exam. Learning the underlying topic is also the approach that will serve you best in the workplace—the ultimate goal of a certification like CBAP® or CCBA™.

Finally, you will notice various Real-World Scenario sidebars throughout each chapter. They are designed to give you insight into how the various processes and topic areas apply to real-world situations.

To get the most out of this book, you should read each chapter from start to finish and then check your memory and understanding with the chapter-end elements. Even if you're already familiar with a topic, you should skim the chapter; business analysis is complex. There are often multiple ways to accomplish a task, and you may learn something even if you're already competent in an area.

Chapter 1: Foundation Concepts lays the groundwork for navigating and understanding the content and intent of the *BABOK® Guide*. This chapter gives you a high-level look at what it means to be a business analyst and reviews the underlying competencies of the business analyst, the key business analysis stakeholders, and the *BABOK® Guide* requirements classification scheme.

Chapter 2: Controlled Start: Business Analysis Planning and Monitoring takes you through planning the business analysis activities for your project using tasks from your first knowledge area. In order to achieve a controlled start to a project or project phase, you must plan what needs to be done, how to go about doing it, and who needs to be involved with the work.

Chapter 3: Controlled Start: Enterprise Analysis steps you through translating your organization's business strategy into a proposed new business solution. During your project's controlled start, you will define and document the business requirements for your project. The business requirements justify why a particular project should be initiated to address a particular business need.

Chapter 4: Overarching Tasks: Requirements Management and Communication focuses on ensuring that the right people are involved with developing, understanding, and approving the project requirements. In addition, your project requirements must be accessible and managed during your requirements development work and throughout the project life cycle.

Chapter 5: Controlled Middle: Elicitation guides you through gathering, organizing, and understanding the necessary information to develop the business, stakeholder, solution, and transition requirements for your project and understanding what your project stakeholders need from the new solution.

Chapter 6: Controlled Middle: Requirements Analysis takes your elicited requirements information and makes sense of it. The tasks in this knowledge area focus on analyzing the stated requirements from your elicitation efforts and building the real stakeholder or solution requirements for your project.

Chapter 7: Controlled End: Solution Assessment and Validation focuses on assessing proposed solutions, allocating requirements to solution components, and validating the solution to make sure that it will meet the business need and deliver value to the organization and its stakeholders.

Chapter 8: Underlying Competencies defines the core framework of business, technical, and domain knowledge possessed by effective business analysts. Your core framework of knowledge is enhanced by your management, interpersonal, business, and structured problem solving skills.

Appendix A: Advice on Completing Your Exam Application examines the required qualifications and application process for successfully completing and submitting your application to sit the CBAP® or CCBA™ certification exam.

Appendix B: Knowledge Areas, Tasks, and Elements lists the knowledge areas, tasks and elements to assist you in your study efforts.

Appendix C: Mapping Techniques, Stakeholders, and Deliverables to Knowledge Areas and Tasks provides you with a coverage matrix mapping business analysis techniques, deliverables, and stakeholders to the knowledge area tasks that use them.

Appendix D: Quick Summary of Business Analysis Techniques provides you with brief descriptions of each business analysis technique in the *BABOK® Guide*.

Appendix E: Quick Summary of Business Analysis Deliverables provides you with brief descriptions of each deliverable produced as a business analysis task output in the *BABOK® Guide*.

Appendix F: About the Companion CD identifies the contents of the companion disk and how to use it.

Glossary: We have also included a Glossary of terms in PDF format on the companion CD.

How to Become CABP®/CCBA™ Certified

The CBAP® and CCBA™ certification exams each address all six knowledge areas from the *BABOK® Guide*. The exams also test your knowledge of sources referenced by the *BABOK® Guide* and your own business analysis experience.

The CBAP® exam is designed for experienced business analysts, while the newer CCBA™ exam targets folks who have less experience in the business analysis profession. You can apply and pay for the exams online using the IIBA™ website. Most people schedule and take the exams in a testing center and complete the questions on a computer. Feedback is immediate as to whether you have passed or failed the exam once you submit your finished set of questions. Let's take a look at each exam in a bit more detail.

More on the CBAP® Exam

The CBAP® exam targets experienced business analysts. The exam contains 150 questions that must be answered within 3.5 hours. The questions you will be facing are based on Bloom's Taxonomy, which is discussed later in this section.

Requirements for candidates sitting the CBAP® exam include 7,500 hours of business analysis work experience in the last 10 years, demonstrated experience and expertise in four of the six knowledge areas, a high school education or equivalent, and 21 hours of business analysis-related professional development in the last four years. You will also be required to provide two references from a career manager, client or CBAP®. These requirements to take the exam are discussed in detail in Appendix A, "Advice on Completing Your Application."

More on the CCBA™ Exam

The CCBA™ exam provides newer, less experienced business analysts with their first step toward obtaining the CBAP® certification. This exam targets individuals who are proficient in some aspects of business analysis, are in the process of developing business analysis skills and expertise, and who apply business analysis to smaller scope and less complex tasks and projects.

Requirements for candidates taking the CCBA™ exam include a minimum of 3,750 hours of BA work, aligned with the *BABOK® Guide*, in the last seven years with at least 900 hours in two of the six knowledge areas or 500 hours in four of the six knowledge areas, a minimum of 21 hours of Professional Development, and a high school education or equivalent. You will also be required to provide two references from a career manager, client or CBAP®.

The CCBA™ certification expires after five years. The expectation is that recipients will then apply to take the CBAP® exam as a more experienced business analyst. There is also an option to retake the CCBA™ exam if you have not yet met the required CBAP® exam level of experience during that time period.

What's on the Exams

The CBAP® and CCBA™ exams each contain 150 questions that must be answered within 3.5 hours. The passing mark for your scored exam is calculated based on psychometric procedures that the IIBA™ does not disclose to the public. The CBAP® and CCBA™ Exam Blueprints indicate the relative weight of each knowledge area by providing you with the percentage of questions from that knowledge area on your exam. The percentages are provided for you in Table 1.1. Due to rounding issues, some of the percentages do not add up to exactly 100 percent.

TABLE 1.1 Exam Knowledge Area and Question Breakdown

Knowledge Area	CBAP® Exam % of Questions	CCBA™ Exam % of Questions
Business Analysis Planning and Monitoring	19.33 %	20%
Elicitation	14%	13.33%
Requirements Management and Communication	16%	16%
Enterprise Analysis	15.33%	15.33%
Requirements Analysis	15.33%	19.33%
Solution Assessment and Validation	16%	16%

All the questions on your exam are multiple choice questions with four possible answers from which to select. There are no penalties for incorrect answers, so remember to attempt to answer every question.

Types of Questions

In 1956, Benjamin Bloom, an educational psychologist at the University of Chicago, proposed his Taxonomy of Educational Objectives, classifying learning objectives into six hierarchical levels: knowledge, comprehension, application, analysis, synthesis and evaluation. This taxonomy drives the structure and style of the exam questions you will be seeing on your CBAP® and CCBA™ exams, as the questions will range across this entire taxonomy. Questions may also have a scenario for reading before the body of one or more questions.

The breakdown of questions across Bloom's Taxonomy is not provided in the IIBA™'s exam blueprint. As a rule of thumb, you should expect to see approximately 70 percent to 80 percent of your questions taken from the easier question types (knowledge, comprehension, application, and analysis) in the taxonomy and 20 percent to 30 percent taken from the more difficult question types (synthesis and evaluation).

If you are able to recognize the type of question you are being asked, you can use this recognition to arrive at the correct answer to that question. Let's have a look at each question type in more detail.

Knowledge Questions   Knowledge questions test your ability to know specific facts and recall information that you have learned. This information may be straight from the *BABOK® Guide*, or it may be something you have learned from another source. These questions are very straightforward, and remind us of the traditional multiple choice questions from exams we took in our younger days. Here is an example of a knowledge question:

Which type of requirement typically describes high-level organizational needs?

    A. Business

    B. Stakeholder

    C. Functional

    D. Transition

This is a "define the term" question, and the correct answer is A. As stated in the *BABOK® Guide* glossary, business requirements describe the higher level business rationale for your project or initiative. Answering this question correctly requires you to recall the definitions for the different types of requirements found in the *BABOK® Guide*.

Exam Spotlight

Notice that the wording of the question and the correct answer may not be word for word from the *BABOK® Guide*. This is something you will commonly see in the certification exams, so be sure that you understand what you are learning versus simply memorizing the information.

Comprehension Questions   Comprehension questions require you to interpret facts and understand meanings. This is a step up from a knowledge question, where simple memorization and recall usually provides you with the correct answer. Here is an example of a comprehension question:

What type of requirements contains the environmental conditions of the solution?

    A. Transition requirements

    B. Stakeholder requirements

    C. Business requirements

    D. Solution requirements

This is a "check your understanding" question, and the correct answer is D. As stated in the *BABOK® Guide* glossary, solution requirements include both functional and nonfunctional requirements for a particular project. This question requires understanding of the requirements types found in the *BABOK® Guide* and the knowledge that environmental conditions are nonfunctional requirements which are a subset of the solution requirements.

Exam Spotlight

Notice that all of the answers in this example deal with the actual classes of requirements found in the *BABOK® Guide*. There are no distracter answers that jump up and tell you they are incorrect. Each possible answer is something you have been studying. Beware of the distracter answers that are good answers, and make sure you know the correct answer for the question you are being asked!

Application Questions   Application questions raise the bar a bit more by asking you to use information to solve problems. These questions take your knowledge and comprehension, combine them and ask you to do something with the result. Here is an example of an application question:

Transition requirements are typically prepared after which requirements document is completed?

A. Solution requirements

B. Stakeholder requirements

C. Business requirements

D. System requirements

This is a "use the information" problem asking you about the logical sequence for developing the types or classes of requirements on a project. Be sure to answer using the *BABOK® Guide* classification scheme and a generic life cycle versus answering from your organization's scheme and life cycle models unless they are exactly the same. The correct answer is A. Once the solution requirements are defined, the transition requirements for the solution can be built.

Exam Spotlight

Watch for the modifiers in your exam questions, such as MOST, LEAST, BEST, or WORST. They add difficulty to the question as they ask you to select the correct answer that falls at the appropriate end of this sliding scale—best versus worst or least versus most. That usually means all of the answers are correct, but some answers may be more or less correct than others.

Analysis Questions   Analysis questions are a bit more difficult to navigate. This question type asks you to recognize patterns and seek hidden meanings in the information you are provided. A very common type of analysis question is looking at and analyzing a series of process or activity-related steps performed by the business analyst. Here is an example of a synthesis question:

To capture the process of provisioning a circuit, the business analyst observed an ordering supervisor for half a day. The resulting information could then be incorporated into all of the following types of requirements EXCEPT:

A. Transition requirements

B. Solution requirements

C. Stakeholder requirements

D. Functional requirements

This question is a pattern question focusing on a recommended series of steps to be followed by the business analyst who is using observation as a technique to elicit or analyze project requirements. The twist is that you are looking for the wrong answer this time around. The correct (wrong) answer is A. A capability of the solution is not usually found in the transition requirements for a solution.

Exam Spotlight

Watch for the positives and negatives in your exam questions, such as NOT or EXCEPT. If you miss the negative, it is very easy to get an answer wrong, even for a question to which you know the answer.

Synthesis Questions   Synthesis questions test your ability to relate facts and draw conclusions based on the information you are given. Here is an example of a synthesis question:

After reviewing the existing process to approve a new cell phone order, Ginger realized that the senior manager is not always available to manually approve the purchase. She documented the capabilities that facilitate a faster ordering approval process relative to the existing situation. She felt that the existing process was inefficient and that it needed to be changed. What would be an appropriate way for Ginger to express the cause of the current cell phone ordering delays?

A. Blame the manual process for the inefficiencies

B. State all of the facts in a neutral manner

C. Express opinions on how to fix the process

D. Insist that approvers adhere to strict deadlines

You are being asked to "draw a conclusion" based on the specific scenario you have been provided within the body of the question. Ginger is being asked to effectively use her underlying competencies as a business analyst to solve a problem. Her best choice is to confront the problem and lay out all the information for the decision makers to analyze and then decide what to do. The correct answer is B.

Exam Spotlight

Watch for too much information. Occasionally (as in the above question statement) more information is given than is needed to answer the question correctly. Don't let extra, unrelated information lead you to select an incorrect answer or waste too much time on a particular question.

Evaluation Questions   Evaluation questions expect you to assess ideas and make reasoned judgments. Take a look at the following example of an evaluation question:

To document why your project was initiated, it is appropriate to include the:

A. Business case

B. Project mandate

C. Solution approach

D. Business goals

This is a "reasoned judgment" style of question based on what you know and the fact that you understand what is required in this particular situation. Typical business analysis documents used to initiate a project are created in the Enterprise Analysis knowledge area and include the business case, required capabilities, solution scope, and business need. The correct answer is A.

Exam Spotlight

When you are taking the exam, make sure you are able to read the questions and possible answers swiftly but accurately. You need to understand what the question is about before you can select the correct answer. Adult readers are notorious for skimming, scanning, and searching when they read. This can cause you to jump to selecting the wrong answer based on what you think you just read. Train yourself out of these bad habits and learn to read the actual question being presented.

Remember that you will face 150 questions of various question types on your CBAP® or CCBA™ exam. You need to navigate these questions efficiently and effectively to achieve a passing score on your exam. Although there is no substitute for knowing and understanding how the *BABOK® Guide* says you should do your business analysis job, your comfort with question types may also be of assistance.

How to Use This Book and CD

We've included several testing features, both in the book and on the companion CD. Following this Introduction is an Assessment Test that you can use to check your readiness for the actual exam. Take this test before you start reading the book. It will help you identify the areas you may need to brush up on. The answers to the Assessment Test appear after the last question of the test. Each answer includes an explanation and a note telling you in which chapter this material appears.

An "Exam Essentials" section appears at the end of every chapter to highlight the topics you'll most likely find on the exam and help you focus on the most important material covered in the chapter so that you'll have a solid understanding of those concepts. However, it isn't possible to predict what questions will be covered on your particular exam, so be sure to study everything in the chapter.

Review Questions are also provided at the end of every chapter. You can use these to gauge your understanding of the subject matter before reading the chapter and to point out the areas in which you need to concentrate your study time. As you finish each chapter, answer the Review Questions and then check to see whether your answers are right—the correct answers appear on the pages following the last question. You can go back to reread the section that deals with each question you got wrong to ensure that you answer the question correctly the next time you are tested on the material. If you can answer at least 80 percent of the Review Questions correctly, you can probably feel comfortable moving on to the next chapter. If you can't answer that many correctly, reread the chapter, or the section that seems to be giving you trouble, and try the questions again. You'll also find more than 100 flashcard questions on the CD for on-the-go review.

Don't rely on studying the Review Questions exclusively as your study method. The questions you'll see on the exam will be different from the questions presented in the book. There are 150 randomly generated questions on the CBAP® exam and the CCBA™ exam, so it isn't possible to cover every potential exam question in the Review Questions section of each chapter. Make sure you understand the concepts behind the material presented in each chapter and memorize all the formulas as well.

In addition to the assessment test and the review questions, you'll find Bonus Exams on the CD. Take these practice exams just as if you were actually taking the exam (that is, without any reference material). When you have finished the first exam, move on to the next exam to solidify your test-taking skills. If you get more than 85 percent of the answers correct, you're ready to take the real exam.

Finally, you will notice various Real World Scenario sidebars throughout each chapter. These are designed to give you insight into how the various tasks and knowledge areas apply to real-world situations.

Also on the CD is a Glossary of terms, in PDF format.

Test Taking Tips And Advice

On your exam day, it is important that you be relaxed, psychologically prepared, and confident. We recommend that you try to be well rested and adequately nourished when you take the exam. Staying up all night before the exam for some last minute studying is not a good idea.

It is a good idea to make sure you know the location of your testing center prior to exam day. We suggest that you do a "drive by" of the location so you know where you are going and exactly how to get there. You can also call the day before to confirm your exam date and time and the hours of operation. A friend, Peggy, showed up at her testing center to sit a certification exam only to discover that the testing center location had been moved the week before. Peggy had to rush to the other location and then begin the exam. Luckily, Peggy was an early bird, so the damage was minimal. The testing center staff told her that she had been notified of this testing center relocation by email, but Peggy could find no message from them in her inbox. Try to avoid that kind of last-minute stress if you can.

When you arrive at the testing center, you will have to lock up your personal belongings in a locker or leave them in your car for the duration of your exam. You cannot take any food or beverages into the exam, so they must be consumed ahead of time or stored in the locker as well. Be sure to give yourself plenty of time to drink that extra-large latte with four shots of espresso in it. The testing center staff will provide you with scratch paper and pencils. They will also take you into the testing area, seat you at your computer, provide you with headphones to muffle the noise, and confirm that the correct exam is being provided to you.

You have some time before the exam must start if you take the tutorial on how to use the exam software. We recommend that you take the tutorial even though you already know how to point and click. You can use this time to jot down any cheat sheet notes on the scrap paper that you have prepared prior to the exam. Of course, these notes and reminders must all be in your head since you can't take your own paper into the testing area.

Be aware that there might be other people in the testing area taking a wide variety of exams, so people may come and go during your testing window. If you are easily distracted, this activity may take your attention away from your exam. You may take a break at any time during your exam; however, the timer keeps going while you are away from your seat.

How to Contact the Authors

We welcome feedback from you about this book. If you have specific questions or comments, please send us a message at cbapccba@rhymingplanet.com. You can also post questions and comments on Susan's exam-focused blog at cbapccba.blogspot.com or www.cpabccba.com. Her blog offers CBAP® and CCBA™ exam advice and support. You can also contact us through our websites. Susan's website is www.rhymingplanet.com and Terri's website is www.mentor-source.com.

Sybex strives to keep you supplied with the latest tools and information you need for your work. Please check the book's update page on the Sybex website at www.sybex.com/go/cbap. We will post additional content and updates that supplement this book if the need arises.

Assessment Test

1. Who determines what *BABOK® Guide* tasks are appropriate for their project?

   A. Portfolio governance board

   B. Business analysis team

   C. Program or project manager

   D. Key project stakeholders

2. Which statement about business analysis stakeholders is FALSE?

   A. They are likely to participate in business analysis tasks.

   B. They are a set of roles that must be filled for the project.

   C. They have a vested interest in the project and its outcome.

   D. They interact with the business analyst in specific ways.

3. What term is used to define an area undergoing analysis, including both an organization and its external stakeholders?

   A. Domain

   B. Solution

   C. Requirement

   D. Scope

4. Which statement best describes the relationship between the lead business analyst (BA) and project manager (PM) when planning the resources and tasks for business analysis activities?

   A. BA manages all stakeholders, PM manages project team.

   B. BA assigns all team roles, PM manages team work efforts.

   C. BA oversees project processes, PM manages overall project.

   D. BA manages business analysis work, PM manages overall project.

5. The business analysis plan is typically _____ with and is a _____ of the overall project plan.

   A. Estimated, element

   B. Managed, subproject

   C. Integrated, component

   D. Produced, subset

6. What output is produced from conducting stakeholder analysis?

   A. Stakeholder summary matrix and chart

   B. Stakeholder roles and responsibilities

   C. Stakeholder RACI matrix and onion diagram

   D. Stakeholder list, roles, and responsibilities

7. Outputs from determining business analysis activities include the Work Breakdown Structure (WBS) and an activity list. What is defined in the activity list?

   A. Activity descriptions and logical dependencies

   B. Resource effort estimates and resource assignments

   C. Detailed descriptions and resource assignments

   D. Resource effort and activity duration estimates

8. What determines the optimal business analysis approach?

   A. Organizational structure

   B. Enterprise architecture

   C. Business analysis process assets

   D. Expert judgment

9. Which knowledge area's activities are often performed as pre-project work?

   A. Solution Assessment

   B. Enterprise Analysis

   C. Requirements Analysis

   D. Business Architecture

10. What describes how the selected solution approach will deliver the defined solution scope?

   A. Implementation approach

   B. Solution scope definition

   C. Major dependencies

   D. Results measurement

11. What describes an organization's business processes, software, hardware, people, operations, and projects?

   A. Business architecture

   B. Strategic architecture

   C. Enterprise architecture

   D. Technical architecture

12. Which task describes how business requirements are allocated for implementation?

    A. Organize requirements

    B. Determine solution approach

    C. Allocate requirements

    D. Define solution scope

13. Which risk response strategy can be used for both positive and negative risks?

    A. Transfer

    B. Accept

    C. Enhance

    D. Mitigate

14. Which technique compares an organization's strategies, operations, and processes against the "best-in-class" strategies, operations, and processes of their competitors and peers?

    A. Decision analysis

    B. Benchmarking

    C. Feasibility study

    D. Brainstorming

15. When does traceability begin on a project?

    A. Business objectives

    B. Business need

    C. Business problem

    D. Business goals

16. Where are the standards located for how and when requirements should be maintained for reuse in an organization?

    A. Business analysis plan

    B. Metrics and KPIs

    C. Organizational Process Assets

    D. Requirements structure

17. You are communicating functional and nonfunctional requirements to the test team. Which communication mechanism is recommended for this situation?

    A. Informal presentation

    B. Structured walkthrough

    C. Requirements workshop

    D. Formal presentation

18. What traceability relationship is used when you are including a requirement that is necessary only if another requirement is implemented?

   A. Effort

   B. Necessity

   C. Cover

   D. Value

19. You are functioning as a temporary apprentice for a day in order to get a hands-on feel for how the current system is being used. This is a variation of which technique?

   A. Interviewing

   B. Observation

   C. Workshops

   D. Prototyping

20. What two outputs are produced when preparing for elicitation?

   A. Elicitation results and supporting materials

   B. Stated requirements and stakeholder concerns

   C. Supporting materials and scheduled resources

   D. Scheduled resources and elicitation results

21. Which two techniques does the *BABOK® Guide* recommend you use to confirm the stated requirements and stakeholder concerns?

   A. Observation or surveys

   B. Interviews or focus groups

   C. Workshops or interviews

   D. Interviews or observation

22. When eliciting requirements, what technique is used to document any stakeholder concerns?

   A. Problem tracking

   B. Issue management

   C. Questionnaires

   D. Lessons learned

23. You are preparing to moderate a focus group to elicit stakeholder requirements. Where do you document the session goals and questions to be used?

   A. Meeting minutes

   B. Moderator notes

   C. Discussion guide

   D. Not documented

24. What key input should be available to the business analyst when they are preparing to elicit requirements?

   A. Scheduled resources

   B. Solution approach

   C. Elicitation results

   D. Solution scope

25. What are the things you believe to be true on your project but that you have not actually verified?

   A. Capabilities

   B. Constraints

   C. Assumptions

   D. Limitations

26. What types of requirements are developed using the tasks found in the Requirements Analysis knowledge area?

   A. Business and stakeholder

   B. Stakeholder and solution

   C. Solution and transition

   D. Business and solution

27. Which of the following tasks is not part of the Requirements Analysis knowledge area?

   A. Verify requirements.

   B. Allocate requirements.

   C. Organize requirements.

   D. Validate requirements.

28. You have decided to prioritize your solution requirements based on a cost-benefit analysis of their relative value to the organization. What is your basis for prioritization?

   A. Policy compliance

   B. Business risk

   C. Technical risk

   D. Business value

29. You are describing the key objectives of organizing requirements to the project manager. The first objective is to understand what models are appropriate for the business domain and solution scope. What is the second objective?

   A. Identify model interrelationships and dependencies.

   B. Influence the results of the overall prioritization process.

   C. Articulate requirements at the right level of abstraction.

   D. Describe stakeholder objectives supported by the models.

30. Which task is an ongoing process to ensure that stakeholder, solution, and transition requirements align to the business requirements?

    A. Allocate requirements.

    B. Validate requirements.

    C. Organize requirements.

    D. Verify requirements.

31. Which knowledge area contains tasks that are performed in order to ensure solutions meet the business need and to facilitate successful implementation of those solutions?

    A. Enterprise Analysis

    B. Business Analysis Planning and Monitoring

    C. Requirements Analysis

    D. Solution Assessment and Validation

32. Which of the following items is not a solution component?

    A. Business rules

    B. Organization structure

    C. Release plan

    D. Software applications

33. Which element is not one of the three elements used to assess organizational readiness?

    A. Stakeholder impact analysis

    B. Technical assessment

    C. Cultural assessment

    D. Business risk assessment

34. Which technique assists you in estimating the value and optimizing your approach for the different ways you might choose to allocate your project requirements?

    A. Functional decomposition

    B. Business rules analysis

    C. Decision analysis

    D. Process modeling

35. Which assessment looks at whether or not the solution is able to meet the business need at an acceptable level of quality?

    A. Solution validation assessment

    B. Stakeholder readiness assessment

    C. Solution performance assessment

    D. Proposed solution assessment

36. Sam has worked for you for eleven months and has commented several times how much he appreciates all the coaching he has received while working for you. He stated that he has learned a lot just by observing your leadership style when working with others in the organization. This is an example of which of the following types of power?

    A. Reward power

    B. Expert power

    C. Legitimate power

    D. Referent power

37. Haley is a junior business analyst who loves learning new skills and techniques to do her job. Whenever possible, she job shadows a senior business analyst on her team to acquire new ideas on how to do her job more efficiently. Haley is best described as which type of learner?

    A. Auditory

    B. Visual

    C. Kinesthetic

    D. Practical

38. Experienced business analysts are familiar with existing solutions and their capabilities within the organization. This allows them to effectively:

    A. Recommend appropriate team members to carry out the solution.

    B. Challenge the "as is" state and create new paradigms.

    C. Identify, assess and implement changes to those solutions.

    D. Document those existing solutions to expedite project delivery.

39. What is the formula for calculating the number of lines of communication in a network?

    A. (n × (2n))/2

    B. (n × (n−2))/2

    C. (n × (n−1))/2

    D. (n × (n−1))/4

40. You are a business analyst applying leadership and facilitation skills to help a larger team reach a decision on a set of solution requirements. You are exhibiting skills from which underlying competency area?

    A. Analytical thinking

    B. Behavioral knowledge

    C. Communication skills

    D. Interaction skills

Answers to Assessment Test

1. B. The business analyst and the business analysis team determine which *BABOK® Guide* tasks and techniques are appropriate for their organization and their projects. For more information, see Chapter 1.

2. B. The list of business analysis stakeholder roles is NOT a set of roles that must be filled for a project or initiative. They are a suggested set of generic stakeholder roles that may play a role in business analysis activities. For more information, see Chapter 1.

3. A. A domain is the area undergoing analysis and may include both the organization and its stakeholders. For more information, see Chapter 1.

4. D. The lead business analyst or the business analysis team needs to develop, define, and manage the roles and tasks associated with business analysis activities in coordination with the project manager. The business analyst is responsible for providing clearly defined requirements deliverables for the project. For more information, see Chapter 1.

5. C. The business analysis plan is typically integrated with and a component of the overall project plan. This is the responsibility of the project manager. For more information, see Chapter 2.

6. D. The output from conducting stakeholder analysis is the stakeholder list, roles, and responsibilities. For more information, see Chapter 2.

7. A. The activity list elements identify a unique number and a description for each activity in the list. The activity description is a verb-noun phrase. Additional information for each activity may include assumptions, logical dependencies, and milestones. For more information, see Chapter 2.

8. D. When planning the business analysis approach, expert judgment is used to determine the optimal business analysis approach. For more information, see Chapter 2.

9. B. Many activities performed by a business analyst are not part of a specific project. Enterprise Analysis activities are often considered pre-project work or an early feasibility phase of a project. For more information, see Chapter 3.

10. A. The implementation approach describes how the selected solution approach will deliver the defined solution scope. It is one of the three elements of the solution scope, along with the solution scope definition and any dependencies. For more information, see Chapter 3.

11. C. The enterprise architecture describes an organization's business processes, software, hardware, people, operations, and projects as well as the relationships between them. For more information, see Chapter 3.

12. D. The Define Solution Scope task in Enterprise Analysis describes how the business requirements are allocated for implementation. For more information, see Chapter 3.

13. B. Acceptance is the risk response strategy used for both positive and negative risks. For more information, see Chapter 3.

14. B. Benchmarking compares an organization's strategies, operations, and processes against the "best-in-class" strategies, operations, and processes of their competitors and peers. For more information, see Chapter 3.

15. A. Traceability begins on a project with the project's business objectives. For more information, see Chapter 4.

16. C. The Organizational Process Assets (OPAs) contain the standards for how and when requirements should be maintained for reuse in an organization. For more information, see Chapter 4.

17. A. Informal requirements presentations are used as an informal check of requirements status (completeness, correctness) to communicate requirements to the delivery team, test team, or affected business areas, and to communicate requirements to other project teams. For more information, see Chapter 4.

18. D. Value is the traceability relationship used when including a requirement that affects the desirability of a related requirement. For more information, see Chapter 4.

19. B. The three variations on the observation technique include the business analyst participating in the work being done to get a hands-on feel for things, becoming a temporary apprentice, or watching a demonstration of how a specific process or task is performed. For more information, see Chapter 5.

20. C. The two outputs produced when preparing for elicitation are the scheduled resources and the supporting materials. For more information, see Chapter 5.

21. D. The *BABOK® Guide* recommends that you use interviews or observation to confirm the stated requirements and stakeholder concerns. For more information, see Chapter 5.

22. A. The problem tracking technique is used to document any stakeholder concerns that are discovered when eliciting requirements. For more information, see Chapter 5.

23. C. As part of preparing to conduct a focus group, the moderator creates a discussion guide containing the goals and objectives of the session and five to six open questions. For more information, see Chapter 5.

24. D. When preparing for elicitation, the key task inputs include the business need, solution scope, business case and stakeholder list, roles, and responsibilities. For more information, see Chapter 5.

25. C. Assumptions are the things you believe to be true on your project but that you have not actually verified. For more information, see Chapter 6.

26. B. Stakeholder and solution requirements are typically developed using the tasks of the Requirements Analysis knowledge area. For more information, see Chapter 6.

27. B. The allocate requirements task is part of the Solution Assessment and Validation knowledge area. For more information, see Chapter 6.

28. D. Business value is a basis for prioritizing requirements using a cost-benefit analysis of their relative value to the organization. For more information, see Chapter 6.

29. A. The two objectives of organizing requirements are to understand what models are appropriate for the business domain/solution scope and identifying model interrelationships and dependencies. For more information, see Chapter 6.

30. B. The Validate Requirements task in the Requirements Analysis knowledge area is an ongoing process to ensure that stakeholder, solution, and transition requirements align to the business requirements. For more information, see Chapter 6.

31. D. The Solution Assessment and Validation knowledge area contains tasks that are performed in order to ensure solutions meet the business need and to facilitate successful implementation of those solutions. For more information, see Chapter 7.

32. C. The release plan is not a solution component, although it is built in order to guide the implementation of the new solution and its components. For more information, see Chapter 7.

33. D. A business risk assessment is not one of the three elements used to assess organizational readiness. The other three elements listed are correct. For more information, see Chapter 7.

34. C. The decision analysis technique assists you in estimating the value and optimizing your approach for the different ways you might choose to allocate your project requirements. For more information, see Chapter 7.

35. A. The solution validation assessment looks at whether or not the solution is able to meet the business need at an acceptable level of quality. For more information, see Chapter 7.

36. D. Referent power is given to you by your subordinates based on their respect and regard. For more information, see Chapter 8.

37. B. Haley is learning new business analysis skills and techniques by observing more experienced people doing the task, making her a visual learner. For more information, see Chapter 8.

38. C. Experienced business analysts are familiar with existing solutions and their capabilities within the organization. This allows them to effectively identify, assess, and implement changes to those solutions. For more information, see Chapter 8.

39. C. The correct calculation for the number of lines of communication in a network is $(n \times (n-1))$ divided by 2, where n = the number of people or nodes in the network. For more information, see Chapter 8.

40. D. Interaction skills include the ability to work as part of a larger team and to help that team reach decisions. This is done through a combination of leadership and facilitation. For more information, see Chapter 8.

CBAP®/CCBA™
Certified Business Analysis
Study Guide

Chapter 1

Foundation Concepts

- ✓ **Describe business analysis and the role of the business analyst.**

- ✓ **Recognize the basic contents, structure, and intent of the *BABOK® Guide.***

- ✓ **Define the *BABOK® Guide* requirements classification scheme.**

- ✓ **Explore the six business analysis knowledge areas.**

- ✓ **Map business analysis activities to a generic project life cycle.**

- ✓ **Understand the content and intent of the *BABOK®* Guide.**

This chapter lays the foundation for navigating and understanding the content and intent of *A Guide to the Business Analysis Body of Knowledge® (BABOK® Guide)*. It is our high-level look at what it means to be a business analyst and how to successfully perform business analysis work. Business analysts can be found in all facets of an organization—projects, programs, strategic planning, operations, or other initiatives. Although the examples in this chapter use projects and the project life cycle to step through the discipline, remember that business analysts do not have to be members of a project team to do their jobs. They can work almost anywhere.

The set of generally accepted best practices defined by the *BABOK® Guide* provides a business analysis framework defining areas of knowledge, associated activities and tasks, and the skills required to perform them. The scope of this standard covers pre-project activities, the full project life cycle, and the final product's operational life.

What Is Business Analysis?

Let's start with an example of how difficult it can be to do *business analysis* work when you are not certain where to begin. New business analysts start their careers in a number of ways. In the past, it was not uncommon for young software engineers to transition into the business side of an organization when their manager called them into their office, saying, "We are short-staffed, and I need you to figure out what the users need this new software application to do." The fledging *business analyst* needed to discover who to talk to, what to ask, how to ask, and how to document the information that they discovered in a way that made sense to the development team and to the business. This was not an easy task the first time around!

In this situation, performing basic business analysis work took a lot longer than it seemed like it should. These unprepared rookie business analysts had great difficulty deciding exactly how to get started. There was no process in place to guide them and no one available to point them in the right direction. They found themselves longing to go back to their cubicles and just write some more code. Luckily, there is no need for business analysts to feel this way today. There are standards, books (like this one), websites, blogs, and tons of experienced folks out there to mentor and guide business analysts in getting the job done right.

Business analysis is the glue that holds successful organizations together. It is a distinct discipline focusing on identifying business needs, problems, and opportunities, and on determining the appropriate solutions to address them. The resulting projects and initiatives may focus on systems development, process improvement, organizational change, or some combination of the three. Business analysis touches all levels of an organization: strategic, tactical, and operational. Business analysts participate across the project and the product life cycles as they look at all aspects of an organization's enterprise architecture, stakeholder needs, business process, software, and hardware.

The set of generally accepted best practices defined by the *BABOK® Guide* make this book an essential resource for every business analyst. You should take this basic business analysis framework and make it work for you and your projects. The areas of knowledge, associated activities and tasks, and the skills required to perform them will give you a valuable starting point for introducing, validating, or improving your business analysis processes throughout an organization. Even better, the scope of the *BABOK® Guide* covers pre-project activities, the full project life cycle and the final solution's operational life.

The *BABOK® Guide* focuses on building underlying competencies that make for a successful business analyst on today's projects. The *BABOK® Guide* defines business analysis as *"the set of tasks and techniques used to work as a liaison among stakeholders in order to understand the structure, policies, and operations of an organization and to recommend solutions that enable the organization to achieve its goals."* Put simply, a business analyst is defined as anyone performing these business analysis activities.

When looking at business analysis in an organization, you need to make sure that you know how the organization views its business analysts. First, what is the role of the business analyst? Second, what is the expected relationship between the business analyst and the project manager? And third, who are the stakeholders with whom the business analyst will be interacting along the way? We will look at each of these topics next.

The Business Analyst's Role

The linchpin of successful business analysis is the business analyst performing the actual work. Their involvement in defining and validating *solutions* that address key business needs and goals is essential to both project and business success. According to the *BABOK® Guide*, "A business analyst works as a liaison among *stakeholders* in order to understand the structure, policies, and operations of an organization, and to recommend solutions that enable the organization to achieve its goals."

So, what exactly is the job description for the business analyst? There have been many job postings lately that came straight from the *BABOK® Guide* role definition. That is a good sign. The adaption and integration of these principles as best practices in the corporate environment will lead to stronger business analysis process, better business analysts, and more credibility and consistency in the role of business analysts today. Here is a short list of the business analyst's job responsibilities from the *BABOK® Guide*:

- Liaises and communicates with project stakeholders
- Elicits, analyzes, and validates project *requirements* for changes to business process, policies, and information systems
- Understands business problems and opportunities in the context of the requirements
- Recommends solutions enabling the organization to achieve its goals

In many organizations, the folks performing business analysis work do not have the job title of "business analyst." The business analyst role can be filled by anyone performing business analysis work regardless of job title. The *BABOK® Guide* lists a number of job roles that may do business analysis work, such as business system analysts, requirements engineers, process analysts, product managers or owners, enterprise analysts, business architects, and management consultants.

Additional Roles: Generalist, Specialist, and Hybrid

The International Institute of Business Analysis (IIBA)'s *Business Analysis Competency Model, Version 2. 0* takes a closer look at the role of the business analyst in today's projects and initiatives. As part of the job profile, they classify business analysts using three categories:

Generalist   The generalist role is effective across a wide range of techniques and is able to adapt to a range of project circumstances.

Specialist   The specialist role uses a limited set of business analysis techniques with great skill and expertise, often working on complex business problems.

Hybrid   The hybrid role combines business analysis competencies with other professions, such as project management or testing.

Essential Skills of Effective Business Analysts

Business analysts must possess a wide spectrum of skills and knowledge. Being a technical expert in a particular area does not guarantee success as a business analyst on a project. In addition to the necessary business, technical, and *domain* knowledge, the business analyst should have management, interpersonal, business, and structured problem-solving skills.

 Real World Scenario

Reviewing Requirements Over a Cup of Coffee

Years ago, Phil was leading a team working on an executive compensation system for top-level management. The team needed input from a small, closed community of senior and executive management customers in order to define the current and future processes. Unfortunately, his key contact from this group felt that the job of customer interface had been given to a young, up-and-coming star who didn't have a clue. This made developing a rapport with the key customer contact almost impossible. However, the project deadlines remained inflexible, as they usually do.

Taking what little input was offered and doing significant research from other sources, the team compiled their draft of the business requirements document. The document was huge. It was single-spaced and double-sided, and it filled a three-inch binder. There was a meeting to step through it. The customer contact was there and took her place at the head of the table. Phil sat at the opposite end of the table.

During the meeting, the customer's demeanor grew increasingly agitated. She hurled the requirements document down the table toward my friend along with the exclamation, "I don't do this kind of menial work." Unfortunately, Phil reacted by returning the document in the same manner. His aim wasn't quite as true, and the document slammed into her coffee cup sending a spray of hot, sugary liquid into her lap. Her color changed from the red of aggravation to the scarlet of rage. She stalked out of the room. So much for creating rapport with the customer! In the end, it all worked out. Both parties apologized and the project (meeting the business requirements that had been approved) was delivered. But how much better things could have been if this situation had been avoided in the first place.

The technical experts on the project team may not be the best choice for the business analyst role. Technical skills and expertise are necessary on the project team, but they are not the skills and knowledge that separate effective business analysts from the pack. Superior business analysis skills are not necessarily derived from a superior set of technical skills.

Soft skills and knowledge support and enable effective business analysis. Knowing what to do and when to do it is a good start for a business analyst, but how you actually do that work makes a big difference! The *BABOK® Guide* refers to these behaviors as the "*underlying competencies*" of effective business analysts. The underlying competencies are in addition to knowing what business analysts produce from a work activity and a deliverable perspective. They encompass the interpersonal skills and additional business and technical knowledge that are necessary for doing the business analyst's job well. These essential skills range from applying structured analysis techniques to issue management to addressing solution usability concerns.

The *BABOK® Guide* puts the essential skills and knowledge of effective business analysts into six categories:

Analytical thinking and problem-solving skills

Behavioral characteristics

Business knowledge

Software knowledge

Interaction skills

Communication skills

Let's take a quick look at each of these categories that are the building blocks for the business analyst's skill and knowledge.

Analytical Thinking and Problem-Solving Skills   Facilitating solutions to business problems would be impossible without a logical mind. Analytical thinking and problem-solving skills enable the business analyst to assess and understand a situation. Once that situation is fully understood, the business analyst assesses and recommends one or more potential solutions to address the business need, problem, or opportunity.

Behavioral Characteristics   Effective business analysts apply personal integrity and strength of character when dealing with people, including the business analysis team, project team, and internal and external project stakeholders. The ability to build strong, lasting working relationships serves both the business analyst and the project well.

Business and Software Knowledge   It is impossible to be a liaison between the business and the technology if you have no understanding of the business. Skilled business analysts understand the internal and external business environment surrounding their projects, and they use that knowledge to make good decisions and recommendations.

Software applications are typically used by the business analyst to develop and manage requirements. This can range from using a word processor to document project scope to using a requirements management tool to develop detailed user and system requirements. Although using a requirements management tool is not a required skill, the ability to master and apply requirements management, word processing, and spreadsheet tools are desirable traits in experienced business analysts.

Interaction Skills   Good business analysts are team players. In large part, this is due to their ability to interact and work well with other members of the team. Leadership and facilitation skills play a key part in defining and agreeing to a solution to a business problem or need.

Communication Skills   The number one reason for project failure is poor communication. Business analysts must have excellent communication skills in order to develop requirements.

The underlying competencies of effective business analysts have numerous pieces and parts. In Chapter 8, "Underlying Competencies," we will discuss them in more depth, and we will add in a few additional skills that you might want to use on your projects.

The Business Analyst and the Project Manager

There is much buzz about the potential for overlap and conflict between the *project manager* and the business analyst. Interestingly enough, many project managers perform business analysis work early in their projects—developing feasibility studies, business cases, scope statements, and business-level requirements as part of project selection, initiation, and scope definition. Many project managers were part of the business analysis team earlier in their careers. As a result, many project managers have business analysis skills to complement and overlap their project management skill set.

The project manager's responsibilities differ from the responsibilities of the business analyst in several ways. The project manager focuses on meeting the project objectives. They initiate, plan, and manage the project. The project manager makes sure the project team delivers a solution that meets requirements, the acceptance criteria, and the customer's quality expectations. The project manager juggles the many constraints present on a project, such as scope, budget, schedule, resources, quality, and risk. On a large project, the business analysis team is only one part of the project resources the project manager is managing.

The business analyst and the project manager typically work closely together on projects and must maintain good communications. There is potential for the project manager and the business analyst to be in conflict with one another. The business analyst works with key stakeholders to understand the structure, policies, and operations of an organization and to recommend solutions. The project manager focuses on planning and managing the project to achieve the project objectives and deliver those solutions to the stakeholders. Where are they going to step on each other's toes? There are two key areas for conflict: stakeholder communication and planning.

The project manager and the business analyst both need to communicate well with key stakeholders. Without planning and discussion, the project manager and the business analyst could easily come to blows about who "owns" the stakeholders, when in actuality the project "owns" the stakeholders. A good project-level communications plan needs to be built and followed to minimize potential areas of political game play and conflict. As far as planning goes, the business analysis team must remember that it is a subset of the project team. As such, any business analysis work plans they put together must be consistent with and roll up into the overall project plan.

Dealing with Key Stakeholders

There is no project without stakeholders. Stakeholders have a vested interest in the project and its outcome, and they are the major source of requirements, constraints, and assumptions for the business analyst. Remember that stakeholder roles are like hats—one person may wear multiple hats and fill more than one role on a project.

There are a number of generic stakeholders that will interact with the business analyst across the project life cycle. While the list in Table 1.1 doesn't cover every possible role, it is a good starting point for who should be involved with your business analysis activities. Many organizations have different names for the same role, so don't get excited if these are not the generic stakeholder roles with which you are familiar. In addition to the business analyst, there are a number of key stakeholder roles involved with business analysis activities. They are summarized in Table 1.1.

TABLE 1.1   Key Business Analysis Stakeholders

Stakeholder	Description
Customer	Uses the products, services, or solutions.
Domain Subject Matter Expert (SME)	Possesses detailed, in-depth knowledge of a particular topic or problem area of the solution scope or the business need.
End User	Directly interacts with the resulting solution when it has been completed and deployed.
Implementation SME	Responsible for designing and implementing potential solutions and providing specialist expertise. Subsets of the Implementation SME role include developers, software engineers, organizational change management professionals, system architects, trainers, and usability professionals.
Operational Support	Helps to keep the solution functioning by providing end user support or day-to-day operational support.
Project Manager	Manages the work performed to deliver the solution.
Tester	Verifies that the designed and constructed solution meets the requirements and quality criteria for that solution.
Regulator	Defines and enforces standards for developing the solution or for the resulting solution itself.
Sponsor	Authorizes the solution development work to be performed and controls the budget.
Supplier	Provide products or services to the organization.

Exam Spotlight

These stakeholder role names and definitions from the *BABOK® Guide* are exactly what you will see in your exam questions. The business analyst is a stakeholder for all business analysis activities and is responsible and accountable for their execution. Remember that stakeholder roles are like hats. One person can wear one or many hats across the project life cycle. The roles are not necessarily the same as their job titles; however, they do indicate the job responsibilities and the level of accountability for the person filling that particular role on a project.

Exploring the Business Analysis Knowledge Areas

The *BABOK® Guide* is based on a set of *knowledge areas* guiding the business analyst when they perform business analysis activities at any point in the project or product life cycle. Knowledge areas define what business analysts need to understand and the *tasks* they should perform. They do not represent project phases, and their activities are not intended to be performed in a linear fashion. Tasks from one or more knowledge areas may be performed in any order (such as in succession, simultaneously, or iteratively), provided that the necessary inputs to each task are available.

Six knowledge areas are defined by the standard. If you are planning to take the Certified Business Analyst Professional (CBAP®) or Certification of Competency in Business Analysis (CCBA™) exam, you will need to memorize the high-level definition of each knowledge area, as well as the more detailed tasks, elements, inputs, and outputs. If you are interested in applying these knowledge areas to your work world, you will need to master the tasks and the skills in order to become an effective business analyst. The six knowledge areas listed here are shown in Figure 1.1.

- Business Analysis Planning and Monitoring
- Elicitation
- Requirements Management and Communication
- Enterprise Analysis
- Requirements Analysis
- Solution Assessment and Validation

Exam Spotlight

Here's a memory aid for the six knowledge areas—BEaRERS.

 Business Analysis Planning and Monitoring

 Enterprise Analysis

 Requirements Management and Communication

 Elicitation

 Requirements Analysis

 Solution Assessment and Validation

Business analysts are the BEaRERS of good news!

FIGURE 1.1   Relationships between knowledge areas

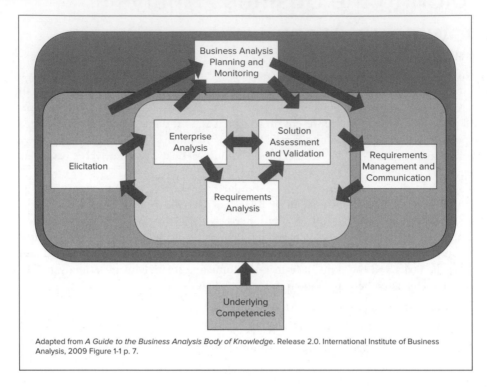

Adapted from *A Guide to the Business Analysis Body of Knowledge*. Release 2.0. International Institute of Business Analysis, 2009 Figure 1-1 p. 7.

Knowledge Area: Business Analysis Planning and Monitoring

Business Analysis Planning and Monitoring is where the business analyst plans how to approach the business analysis effort. The approach is a set of processes, templates, and activities used to perform business analysis in a specific context. The tasks govern and monitor the performance of all other business analysis tasks. These planning and monitoring activities take place throughout the project life cycle. The results of this knowledge area govern the tasks found in the remaining five knowledge areas and set the performance metrics to be used to evaluate all business analysis work. So, what is a business analyst to do? Well, the business analyst's task list for this particular knowledge area consists of:

- Determining the business analysis approach for the project
- Performing stakeholder identification, analysis, and categorization
- Defining the business analysis activities to be performed
- Addressing business analysis communication requirements

- Planning the requirements development and management process
- Managing and reporting on the business analysis effort

Knowledge Area: Elicitation

Elicitation defines how business analysts work with stakeholders to identify and gather requirements and understand their needs and concerns. The business analyst's task list for this knowledge area consists of:

- Building a detailed elicitation schedule for a specific activity
- Meeting with stakeholders to conduct the elicitation activity
- Documenting and recording the elicitation results
- Confirming elicitation results with key stakeholders

Knowledge Area: Requirements Management and Communication

Requirements Management and Communication defines how the business analyst approaches communicating requirements to stakeholders. Tasks and techniques for managing changes, conflicts, and issues related to requirements are also described. Business analysts perform requirements communication activities as part of requirements development work by:

- Managing the solution scope and requirements
- Managing requirements traceability
- Maintaining requirements for reuse
- Preparing requirements packages
- Communicating requirements

Knowledge Area: Enterprise Analysis

Enterprise Analysis focuses on how the business analyst identifies the business needs driving a project by performing problem definition and analysis. In addition to defining and refining these driving needs, the business analyst is responsible for defining a feasible solution scope that can be implemented by the business. This work may also include developing a business case or feasibility study for a proposed project. Typically, the tasks in this knowledge area occur prior to or early in the project life cycle. The business analyst's task list for this knowledge area includes translating business strategy into proposed new business solutions by:

- Defining and understanding the business problem or opportunity
- Assessing capability gaps in the organization

- Determining the most feasible business solution approach
- Describing the resulting solution scope
- Developing a business case for the proposed solution

Knowledge Area: Requirements Analysis

Requirements Analysis describes how the business analyst progressively elaborates and prioritizes stakeholder and solution requirements. In essence, the business analyst takes the elicited information and makes sense of it to derive the real requirements for the project. This knowledge area also focuses on graphically modeling the requirements as well as documenting them. When performing these tasks, the business analyst should ensure the feasibility of the requirements while defining, describing, and refining the characteristics of an acceptable solution. The business analyst's task list for this knowledge area consists of:

- Prioritizing the relative importance of the requirements
- Organizing requirements
- Specifying and modeling requirements
- Defining assumptions and constraints
- Verifying requirements
- Validating requirements

Knowledge Area: Solution Assessment and Validation

Solution Assessment and Validation focuses on assessing and validating proposed, in progress, and implemented solutions before, during, and after the project life cycle. While many tasks in this knowledge area take place later in the project life cycle, some solution-focused activities may occur quite early. The business analyst's task list for this knowledge area consists of:

- Assessing the proposed solution
- Allocating stakeholder and solution requirements
- Assessing organizational readiness
- Defining transition requirements
- Validating the solution
- Evaluating solution performance

We will examine each knowledge area and every task within it in great detail in the coming chapters. You will need this level of knowledge to successfully prepare for and pass the certification exams. You will also need this level of knowledge to be an effective business analysis practitioner in your organization.

How Are the Knowledge Areas Organized?

Knowledge areas divide what business analysts need to know and how they perform their tasks into six common buckets. The business analyst can dip into one or more buckets at any time—in any order—to select a deliverable or perform a necessary task. The knowledge areas are not a road map or a methodology; they simply break business analysis stuff into common areas.

- Tasks
- Inputs
- Elements
- Techniques
- Stakeholders
- Outputs

The content of each knowledge area is defined using the same structure. Let's take a look at this structure now.

Tasks   In order to achieve the purpose of a particular knowledge area, the business analyst must perform a defined set of high-level tasks. Each task has a particular purpose and adds value to the overall effort when performed. The expectation is that each task will be performed at least once during any project.

Inputs   Inputs consist of the information and preconditions required by a task so that task can begin. These *inputs* must be usable by the task that needs them. They are produced externally to the business analysis activities, by a single business analysis task, or by multiple business analysis tasks.

Elements   Elements are the detailed concepts that are necessary to perform a particular task. For some tasks, the *elements* are categories of things to be considered. For other tasks, the elements are subtasks performed by the business analyst.

Outputs   Outputs are the results that are created or changed when a task is successfully completed. One task can have one too many *outputs*.

Techniques   Techniques guide the business analyst in the many ways a particular task might be done. The *techniques* found in the *BABOK® Guide* are considered best practices that are used by many business analysts. However, business analysts can certainly use techniques that are not found in the standard.

Exam Spotlight

When you are reviewing and learning the techniques from the *BABOK® Guide*, make sure you don't miss anything! There are two types of techniques: general and knowledge area specific. The general techniques are summarized in Appendix C, "Mapping Techniques, Stakeholders, and Deliverables to Knowledge Areas and Tasks," of this book and are defined in Chapter 9 of the *BABOK® Guide*. They can be used by any activity, and many are used by more than one. Knowledge area specific techniques are defined as part of the knowledge area task that uses them. They are only used by a single task. The knowledge area specific techniques are addressed in Chapter 2 through Chapter 7 of this book as a part of the discussion of each specific task that uses them.

Stakeholders   All tasks come with a generic list of stakeholders who may be involved in performing that task or who might be affected by the task and its outcome. Interestingly enough, the business analyst is a stakeholder for every business analysis activity found in the *BABOK® Guide*. This makes perfect sense—the business analyst is responsible and accountable for making sure that these tasks are done and done well. Remember that earlier in this chapter we took a look at the key generic stakeholder roles that typically interact with business analysts on their projects.

Exploring Requirements

Projects are successful when what is to be accomplished is clearly stated and agreed upon. For most projects, this statement consists of defining the high-level scope of the project along with its more detailed project requirements. The general definition of a requirement is something wanted or needed. Business analysts in many organizations spend a lot of time developing requirements. This is a good thing. Defining and documenting requirements allow you to quantify and document the needs, wants, and expectations of our project stakeholders.

The *BABOK® Guide* uses the term *requirement* to cover many aspects of the business and its needs. Their broad view of requirements addresses both the current state of the business as well as its desired future state. Requirements may focus on the business, the users, or the systems and subsystems that already exist or are being considered. Requirements range from high-level enterprise capabilities to organizational structure and roles to processes and policies. Information systems fall into the requirements realm, as do business rules. Requirements analysis activities are also quite broad in nature. There is no prescription for the correct level of detail in your project requirements other than what is sufficient for understanding and subsequent action.

Determining the Business Analysis Approach

The business analysis team typically determines both the business analysis approach and the requirements management process for their project. The business analysis approach defines the methodology used for business analysis work on the overall project and each of its phases. It includes team roles, deliverables to be produced, how and when tasks are performed, techniques to be used, and other aspects of the high-level business analysis process.

Defining the Requirements Management Process

The requirements management process is a detailed subset of the business analysis approach, targeting how the team performs requirements development activities for a project. The process should be documented in the requirements management plan. This deliverable defines many things, including:

- How the team will deal with requirements traceability
- The explicit process for developing requirements
- How requirements will be prioritized
- What requirements attributes will be collected
- How changing requirements will be handled both during requirements development and after the requirements are agreed upon and baselined
- Who will review and approve requirements and any requested changes

In addition, the requirements management process defines the types or classes of requirements found on the project. Often, these requirements classes are associated with a particular requirements document. Classifying requirements allows the business analysis team to make sure that their project requirements are reviewed and understood by the correct stakeholders. Requirements classes help you determine the appropriate level of detail and the specificity needed in the project requirements, and they help you decide how many documents you will use to define what is needed.

Requirements classes can be defined using two dimensions: focus and type. Requirements classified by focus tend to be named in a more traditional way:

- High-level business requirements
- User requirements
- System requirements
- Software requirements

Each lower level of requirements defines the level above it in greater detail. This is a form of progressive elaboration, where the characteristics of the solution are determined incrementally and in greater detail as the project moves forward in time. After all, the more information you have, the better your solution definition will become. Solutions are typically defined at a high-level of detail early in a project or initiative, and then refined into more detail over time as additional information is gathered and analyzed.

Classifying Requirements

The *BABOK® Guide* contains its own requirements classification scheme. This is the scheme that we will be using throughout the book as well as the scheme you will see on the certification exams. A requirement is defined as a condition or capability needed by a stakeholder to solve a problem or to achieve an objective. This aligns nicely with the International Institute of Electrical and Electronics Engineers (IEEE) definition of requirements for software-intensive systems. Regardless of your project type, the project requirements must be used to design, develop, and deliver a solution that adds value to the business as a whole.

In order to implement the *BABOK® Guide* requirements classification scheme, you will need to assess and map the levels of requirements to your existing requirements process and the resulting requirements documents. You don't have to use these requirements classes if you don't want to use them. However, you do need to make sure that all of these requirements classes are being addressed by your requirements development approach in some way. The relationship between the *BABOK® Guide* requirements classes is shown in Figure 1.2.

FIGURE 1.2   Classes of requirements

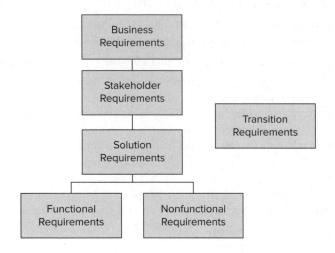

Let's take a closer look at each class of requirements.

Business Requirements   Business requirements are the highest level of requirements and are developed during Enterprise Analysis activities. They define the high-level goals, objectives, and needs of the organization. They also describe and justify the high-level business functionality that is needed in the resulting solution. In order to define a solution, the *business requirements* will be progressively elaborated and decomposed to the next level of detail, the *stakeholder requirements*.

In the *BABOK® Guide*, the business requirements are not contained within a single, standalone document. They are composed of a set of Enterprise Analysis task deliverables, including the business need, the required capabilities, the solution scope, and the business case. (We will look at these deliverables in more detail later when we dig into this knowledge area in Chapter 2, "Controlled Start: Business Analysis Planning and Monitoring.")

Stakeholder Requirements   These requirements define the needs of stakeholders and how they will interact with a solution. Stakeholder requirements bridge between the business requirements and the more detailed *solution requirements*. Many folks refer to stakeholder requirements as high-level user requirements. They identify what is needed from the user's perspective and define "big picture" capabilities that the resulting solution must possess.

Stakeholder requirements are developed and defined as part of the tasks found in the Requirements Analysis knowledge area. Like the business requirements, the stakeholder requirements will be progressively elaborated into the more detailed solution requirements.

Solution Requirements   Solution requirements are the most detailed type of requirements found in the standard. They describe the solution characteristics that will be needed to meet the higher-level business and stakeholder requirements. Typically, solution requirements are subdivided into two specific types: *functional requirements* and *nonfunctional requirements*. They are developed and defined as part of the tasks found in the Requirements Analysis knowledge area.

Functional Requirements   Functional requirements define the capabilities that a product must provide to its users. They are a subset of the Solution Requirements that are developed for the project.

Nonfunctional Requirements   Nonfunctional requirements describe quality attributes, design and implementation constraints, and external interfaces that the product must have. They are a subset of the Solution Requirements that are developed for the project, and they are typically paired up with the functional requirements that they constrain and bound in some way. They would add characteristics to the functional requirements

Transition Requirements   *Transition requirements* define the solution capabilities required to transition from the current to the future state and are no longer needed once the transition is complete. Typically, transition requirements are created later in the project life cycle after both the current and new solutions have been defined. They are developed and defined as part of the tasks found in the Solution Assessment and Validation knowledge area.

 Real World Scenario

Case Study: Palmer Divide Vineyards

You are a team member at Palmer Divide Vineyards, currently defining their new green initiative. The owners would like to conserve energy and water resources, reduce pollution, recycle more effectively, and become a certified Green Business. You have been assigned to lead the team to discover the IT requirements for the project.

Following discussions with the IT group, you learn that the existing information systems will not support the ongoing green initiative research studies. You recommend that Palmer Divide's business requirements include the following statement: *"The vineyard operation shall upgrade existing information systems to support ongoing green initiative research studies."*

Breaking down the IT system business requirement for the vineyard yields the following stakeholder requirement focusing on stakeholder interaction with the system: *"The research team sets up the tracking data for a new green initiative study."* This would be one of many stakeholder capabilities that the upgraded systems would provide.

Next, you look into the solution requirements for the stakeholder study parameter capabilities and recommend that the project solution requirements include: *"The research study leader logs into the system with study leader access privileges. The research study leader defines the set of research study data fields for their research project."* This would be a functional requirement.

A nonfunctional requirement accompanying the previous set of functional requirements addresses the access and authentication parameters for logging in to the system. *"Logging in as a study leader provides read, write, update, and delete capabilities for selected study data."*

Transition requirements included data conversion activities for the upgraded IT system.

Our favorite requirements classification scheme comes from the software engineering standards developed by the IEEE. It focuses on the three Cs—capabilities, conditions, and constraints. According to the IEEE, a *requirement* is a capability needed by a user to solve a problem to achieve an objective. These capabilities must be met or possessed by a product to satisfy a contract, standard, specification, or other formally imposed documentation. Conditions and constraints together equal the nonfunctional requirements classification found in the *BABOK® Guide*. *Conditions* are statements that determine a possible outcome, like the "if" part of an "if-then" statement. *Constraints* are limits or boundary values for a particular function or capability.

Classifying Project Requirements Your Way

The IEEE requirements classes align quite nicely with the *BABOK® Guide* requirements classes. Basically, the capabilities are the functional requirements and the other two classes are the nonfunctional requirements. Functional requirements define the capabilities provided to users and other interested parties, while nonfunctional requirements define conditions of the system or product as a whole as well as any constraints or limits on all or part of the system. You can easily extend the three Cs to focus across the different levels of requirements focus, such as the business, stakeholder, and solution requirements found in the *BABOK® Guide*.

The Requirements State Machine

When you look at requirements across the project life cycle, you will notice that they change as the project progresses. They start as a bunch of information and are analyzed into meaningful requirements. The analyzed requirements are reviewed and approved by their key stakeholders. Following review and approval, the requirements are used as the basis for designing a solution. See the pattern? Requirements development fits nicely into a state machine approach as the requirements change over time—they transition from state-to-state based on actions that have been taken. Many requirements deliverables are modified based on the state that they are in at a particular point in time. This is particularly true for the requirements found in the *BABOK® Guide*.

Exam Spotlight

When preparing for your exam or simply trying to apply the best practices in the book, be aware of states and how they affect where you are in the project life cycle relative to your business analysis work, what has been done, and what should be done next.

You will see these different types and states of requirements used when naming inputs and outputs to business analysis activities. This will help you recognize where you are in the project life cycle and where you are in your requirements development process. You may also see the term *Requirements* with no modifiers attached, or noted as *Requirements [Any]*, indicating any class of requirement in any state. Inputs and outputs from business analysis tasks may use this notation.

Let's say you are developing your project's business requirements. According to the *BABOK® Guide*, the solution requirements include the business need, the required capabilities, the *solution scope*, and the business case. This is the set of deliverables produced by Enterprise Analysis activities. The solution scope defines the capabilities that a solution must possess in order to meet a business need. In addition to modifying your requirements to the specific class of requirements you are focusing on, business requirements, you can also reflect the state of these business requirements at a particular point in time.

When you develop business requirements, you will need to elicit information from key stakeholders about what they and the business actually need. These stated requirements reflect what the users have told the business analyst about what they need. As part of our elicitation results, these stated business requirements will be analyzed, prioritized, validated, and verified prior to becoming the accepted set of business requirements for the project. They would be named Requirements [Stated] in the inputs or outputs for a particular task, indicating that your business analysis team sought information from the users about what they needed.

The requirements state machine is worth watching; it provides the business analyst with guidance and recommendations about what has already taken place and what might be the logical next step in the requirements development process. Table 1.2 summarizes the possible states and may be of assistance when you are navigating the *BABOK® Guide*.

TABLE 1.2   The *BABOK® Guide* Requirements State Machine Summary

Requirements State	Description
Allocated	Associated with the solution component or components that will implement the requirements
Analyzed	Modeled and specified requirements
Approved	Agreed to by stakeholders and ready for use in subsequent business analysis or implementation efforts
Communicated	Shared with and understood by the stakeholders in their current state
Maintained and Reusable	Formatted and suitable for long-term or future use by the organization; may be saved as organizational process assets
Prioritized	Having an attribute describing its relative importance or assigned priority to stakeholders and the organization
Stated	Stated needs expressed by the stakeholders during elicitation
Stated, Confirmed	Confirmed by the business analyst to match both the stakeholders needs and their understanding of the problem
Stated, Unconfirmed	Representing the business analyst's understanding of the stakeholder intentions
Traced	Having clearly defined and identified relationships to other requirements within the solution scope
Validated	Demonstrated to deliver value to stakeholders, are within the solution scope and are aligned with business goals/ objectives
Verified	Requirements have been checked and are of sufficient quality to allow further work to be performed

Keep an eye on the classes of requirements and their current states as you navigate and use all of the knowledge area tasks. They provide valuable road signs to keep you headed in the right direction.

Understanding How This Applies to Your Projects

As you can tell from this first chapter, successful business analysts bring a serious mixture of skills, dedication, and knowledge to their projects in order to solve business problems and meet business needs. It isn't just the ability to execute the business analysis techniques that gets the job done, either. Effective business analysts must also possess excellent interpersonal skills as well as a strong set of business and technical knowledge.

 **Real World Scenario**

The Fledging Business Analyst Makes a Mistake

Everyone has to start somewhere. Phil's first formal solo assignment as a fledgling business analyst was to aid in the automated tracking of key performance measurements for one of the operating departments in a large telecommunications firm. The process was manual and senior management felt that it was time to make it computer-based. Phil left his software engineering role behind, put on his business analysis hat, and went to figure out exactly what was required.

Phil followed the rules for being a business analyst on this new assignment. He interviewed the client and captured every word. He parroted back the key elements of the conversations. He carefully documented the current processes as described. He obtained sign-off from the client sponsor. Phil was proud of following the rules and getting this complex manual algorithm explained in concise and well-understood terms.

When programmed (by someone else), the automated results didn't come close to what the manual process reported. Phil proceeded to put his technical hat back on and spent days pouring through reams of manual data, comparing that data with the automated results. After consulting with the client sponsor (along with his reams of data), Phil discovered that he had missed an unrevealed rule about how the data values were tracked on a daily and monthly basis. Because he understood the math, the business, and the technology of the automated system, he was able to ripple this new requirement and deliver a solution that met the client's requirements.

It's okay for Phil to wear multiple hats on his projects, as long as he realizes which hat he has on at any particular time. People often find it difficult to leave the technical work behind and think about the business when they are wearing their business analyst hat. Doing so can lead the fledging business analyst into trouble, resulting in incorrect or incomplete requirements and project problems downstream. Phil was lucky that he was able to put his technology hat back on and address his requirements problem sooner rather than later.

Business analysts must also be able to map the proven principles, best practices, and deliverables of the *BABOK® Guide* across their organization's project life cycle. This allows them to create a flexible framework for the essential work activities of the business analyst. The standard allows you to build a business analysis methodology providing an integrated framework of elements for successful business analysis work that can be tailored to the project environment.

Exam Spotlight

This generic life cycle model is not on the exam. However, if you plan to use the *BABOK® Guide* as the basis for your business analysis work activities, you have to make it work for your organization. Mapping to your existing life cycle model is the first step in integrating these best practices into your own projects.

Different business analysis skills, techniques, and knowledge are used at different places in the project life cycle. To implement the contents of the *BABOK® Guide* on your projects, you will need to map what needs to be done to when you would like to do it. If you have an existing project life cycle in your organization, this is the time to dust it off and use it. If not, it's time to build one. Our generic project life cycle consists of three parts: controlled start, controlled middle, and controlled end. When you think about your projects, one way to keep track of what needs to be done is to know "when and where" you are in this simple model (see Figure 1.3).

Don't confuse the six knowledge areas of the *BABOK® Guide* with the phases of the project life cycle. The *BABOK® Guide* is not a methodology or a road map for business analysis. Instead, it is a set of best practices that can be used to build a framework for business analysis activities supporting the activities and deliverables defined by an organization's project life cycle. The organization is responsible for mapping these best practices to their selected project life cycle.

FIGURE 1.3 Mapping the *BABOK® Guide* to a generic life cycle

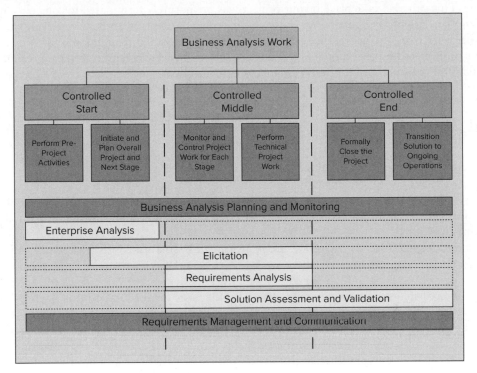

Controlled Start   The controlled start to a project includes the pre-project activities where you determine if this is a viable and worthwhile project for the business. It also covers the project initiation, where you do more detailed planning for our overall project and for the next detailed project stage. At the end of the controlled start activities, you should have your project scope finalized, business justification in place, and the high-level project plan built. The project team should be ready to get to work. Numerous tasks and deliverables from the Enterprise Analysis and Business Analysis Planning and Monitoring knowledge areas are used at this point in time with a little Requirements Management and Communication work thrown in for good measure.

Controlled Middle   The controlled middle of a project is where the technical work gets done, one stage or phase at a time. The project manager uses the plan to measure and monitor project performance and to control what takes place. This is Management by Walking Around (MBWA), where you are into everything—regular status, informal conversations, checking the health of the project, dealing with stakeholders, forecasting future performance, and dealing with issues and risks. The business analysis work is a subset of this plan, and business analysis work performance is also managed and controlled during this time. Business analysis tasks typically include those from the Elicitation, Requirements Analysis, Solution Assessment and Validation, and Requirements Management and Communication knowledge areas.

Controlled End   A controlled end to a project is when you are wrapping up a job well done. This can also take place if your project was prematurely terminated for one reason or another, hopefully a rare event. You take stock of achievements, report on the effort, ensure objectives and acceptance criteria are met, and transition the final product of your project into its operational life. There are specific tasks in Solution Assessment and Validation that focus on this part of the project life cycle.

Summary

You covered a lot of content in this chapter! You learned that business analysis is an essential part of every organization. Successful business analysts bring a serious set of skills and knowledge to every project or initiative in order to liaise among the stakeholders to address business needs and solve business problems. Business analysis is more than just asking questions!

You looked at how the *BABOK® Guide* provides a business analysis framework defining areas of knowledge, associated activities and tasks, and the skills required to perform them. The scope of the *BABOK® Guide* covers pre-project activities, the full project life cycle, and the final solution's operational life. It is also the basis for the CBAP® and CCBA™ certification exams, and it provides the backbone of this book.

The *BABOK® Guide* contains its own requirements classification scheme. This is the scheme you will see on the certification exams. A requirement is defined as a condition or capability needed by a stakeholder to solve a problem or to achieve an objective. Classifying requirements allows the business analysis team to make sure that their project requirements are reviewed and understood by the correct stakeholders. Requirements classes help you determine the appropriate level of detail and the specificity needed in the project requirements, and to decide how many documents you will use to define what is needed.

The six business analysis knowledge areas were visited as a part of our chapter tour. These knowledge areas guide the business analyst when they perform business analysis activities at any point in the project or product life cycle. They define what business analysts need to understand and the tasks they should perform. They do not represent project phases, and their activities are not intended to be performed in a linear fashion.

In order to use the *BABOK® Guide* at work, you will need to map its business analysis tasks to your own Project Life Cycle (PLC) or Systems Development Life Cycle (SDLC). This will allow you to create a business analysis methodology that supports your project and product-focused life cycles and will help you to keep the lights on. This book uses a very simple project lifecycle as the basis for a map. It has only three phases: controlled start, controlled middle, and controlled end. Most life cycles are far more complex!

Because many of you are planning to use this book in your preparations to take the CBAP® or CCBA™ certification exams, the content and structure of the exams are covered here. It takes a lot of work to successfully prepare for and pass these exams—they are not intended to be easy! The CBAP® exam is designed for experienced business analysts, while the newer CCBA™ exam targets folks who have less experience working as business analysts. The questions in each exam are built using Bloom's taxonomy, and they can be quite straightforward or rather difficult.

Exam Essentials

Be able to list and describe each knowledge area.   The names and high-level descriptions of each of the six knowledge areas are required knowledge for you as you prepare to take your exam. As you dig deeper into each knowledge area, learn to also list the tasks and their key inputs/outputs/techniques as part of your exam preparation repertoire. The six knowledge areas are Business Analysis Planning and Monitoring, Enterprise Analysis, Elicitation, Requirements Analysis, Requirements Management, and Communication and Solution Assessment and Validation.

Be able to recognize the underlying competencies every good business analyst should possess.   The six high-level categories are analytical thinking and problem solving skills, behavioral characteristics such as trustworthiness, business knowledge, software knowledge, interaction skills, and communication skills.

Be able to describe and relate the requirements classes in the *BABOK® Guide.*   Starting at the highest level of detail, they are business requirements, stakeholder requirements, solution requirements, the functional and nonfunctional subsets of the solution requirements, and the transition requirements.

Be familiar with the key stakeholder roles.   The exact role names and definitions from the *BABOK® Guide* are what you will see in your exam questions, so make sure you know each of them. Remember that the stakeholder roles are like hats, and one person can wear one or many hats during a project life cycle.

Be able to navigate your copy of the *BABOK® Guide.*   Tabbing your copy of the *BABOK® Guide* helps you find exactly what you need to know. You might find it helpful to use multiple colors of durable tabs to mark the chapters in your book, the glossary, the index, and any other information that you think will be useful.

Key Terms

This chapter introduced the knowledge areas from the *BABOK® Guide* that you will be using as a business analyst on your projects and other initiatives. You will need to understand how to apply each of these knowledge areas at the right spot in the project life cycle in order to be an effective business analyst. Additionally, you will need to know each knowledge area by name and definition in order to be successful on the CBAP® or CCBA™ exams. Each knowledge area will be discussed in greater detail in the chapters to come.

Business Analysis Planning
    and Monitoring

Enterprise Analysis

Elicitation

Requirements Analysis

Solution Assessment and Validation

Requirements Management
    and Communication

You have learned many new key words in this chapter. The IIBA has worked hard to develop and define standard business analysis terms that can be used across many industries. Here is a list of some of the key terms that you encountered in this chapter:

business analysis

business analyst

business requirements

domain

elements

functional requirements

inputs

knowledge areas

nonfunctional requirements

outputs

project manager

requirements

solution requirements

solutions

solution scope

stakeholder requirements

stakeholders

tasks

techniques

transition requirements

underlying competencies

Review Questions

1. A business analyst is currently defining a set of changes to the current state of an organization that allows the organization to take advantage of a business opportunity. What is most likely being defined?

    A. Project scope

    B. Business need

    C. Solution scope

    D. Business domain

2. In what knowledge area is the business analyst MOST likely to be scoping and defining new business opportunities?

    A. Enterprise Analysis

    B. Solution Assessment

    C. Requirements Analysis

    D. Enterprise Assessment

3. What project role focuses on understanding business problems and opportunities?

    A. Business architect

    B. Project manager

    C. Project sponsor

    D. Business analyst

4. A capability needed by a stakeholder to achieve an objective is also called a:

    A. Strategy

    B. Requirement

    C. Solution

    D. Process

5. Your project implementation plan defines 12 capabilities of the planned systems solution that will not be needed once the new solution is operational. What type of requirements are these?

    A. Functional requirements

    B. Nonfunctional requirements

    C. Reusable requirements

    D. Transition requirements

6. Who is primarily responsible for achieving the project objectives?

    A. Program manager

    B. Project manager

    C. Business analyst

    D. Project sponsor

7. Inputs to a specific business analysis task may be externally produced by:
    A. Requirements
    B. Preconditions
    C. Techniques
    D. A single task

8. In order to determine solutions to business problems, the business analyst applies a set of:
    A. Activities and tasks
    B. Inputs and outputs
    C. Tasks and techniques
    D. Practices and processes

9. Knowledge areas define what a business analyst needs to understand. They do NOT define the project:
    A. Scope
    B. Techniques
    C. Phases
    D. Resources

10. All of the following are part of the business requirements, EXCEPT:
    A. Solution scope
    B. Business need
    C. Required capabilities
    D. Business goals

11. What knowledge area contains the next MOST logical steps after the business analyst has built a business case and gained management approval for a project?
    A. Solution Assessment and Validation
    B. Business Analysis Planning and Monitoring
    C. Requirements Management and Communication
    D. Requirements Analysis

12. All of the following are knowledge areas EXCEPT:
    A. Solution Assessment and Validation
    B. Requirements Planning and Monitoring
    C. Requirements Management and Communication
    D. Enterprise Analysis

13. The business analysis team has put together the elicitation results documenting their understanding of the user needs. What types of requirements have they developed at this point in time?

    A. Maintained and reusable

    B. Communicated and confirmed

    C. Validated and confirmed

    D. Stated and unconfirmed

14. Identifying key roles and selecting requirements activities is done as part of which knowledge area?

    A. Requirements Analysis

    B. Requirements Development

    C. Business Analysis Planning and Monitoring

    D. Requirements Elicitation

15. Requirements gathering activities are also known as requirements:

    A. Planning

    B. Development

    C. Analysis

    D. Elicitation

16. What represents the information and preconditions necessary for a business analysis task to begin?

    A. Activity

    B. Input

    C. Output

    D. Technique

17. You are a business analyst measuring alternatives against objectives and identifying tradeoffs to determine which possible solution is best. You are most likely engaged in what activity?

    A. Problem solving

    B. Systems thinking

    C. Creative thinking

    D. Decision making

18. What defines the business analysis team roles, deliverables to be produced, and tasks to be performed?

    A. Requirements process

    B. Project management plan

    C. Solution approach

    D. Business analysis approach

19. When does the business analyst ensure the feasibility of the proposed requirements to support the business and user needs?

    A. As part of building a business case

    B. During Requirements Analysis

    C. When organizing business requirements

    D. While planning and monitoring tasks

20. The system users have stated their needs for revised online order entry system capabilities. Her team needs the ability to perform online, remote order entry when they are traveling worldwide. What class or type of requirements best describe this need?

    A. Functional requirements

    B. Business requirements

    C. User requirements

    D. Transition requirements

Answers to Review Questions

1. C. A solution is a set of changes to the current state of an organization made in order to enable the organization to meet a business need, solve a problem, or take advantage of an opportunity. It is the basis for the project scope that implements the solution and its components.

2. A. Enterprise Analysis contains pre-project or early project activities such as assessing feasibility and building a business case for a potential business initiative.

3. D. The business analyst is responsible for understanding the business problems and opportunities in the context of the requirements.

4. B. One definition for a requirement is a condition or capability needed by a stakeholder to either solve a problem or to achieve an objective.

5. D. Transition requirements describe capabilities that a solution must have to facilitate transitioning from the current to the desired future state. They are not needed once the transition is complete and cannot be created until both the current and new solutions have been defined.

6. B. The project manager has primary responsibility for achieving the project objectives.

7. D. Inputs represent information and preconditions necessary for a task to begin. They are produced externally by a single task.

8. C. Business analysis is a set of tasks and techniques used to identify business needs and determine solutions to business problems.

9. C. Knowledge areas define what a business analyst needs to understand and the tasks they need to perform. They do not define a methodology or indicate project phases as tasks may be done in any order as long as their inputs are available.

10. D. The deliverables produced by the Enterprise Analysis tasks that make up the business requirements include the business need, the required capabilities, the solution scope, and the business case.

11. B. Building a business case is typically done as part of Enterprise Analysis activities. The next most logical knowledge area applied after Enterprise Analysis is completed would be Business Analysis Planning and Monitoring where requirements-related resources and tasks are defined.

12. B. Requirements Planning and Monitoring is not a knowledge area. The six knowledge areas are Business Analysis Planning and Monitoring, Enterprise Analysis, Elicitation, Requirements Analysis, Solution Assessment and Validation, and Requirements Management and Communication.

13. D. The stated, unconfirmed requirements represent the business analyst's understanding of the user needs or intentions.

14. C. Business Analysis Planning and Monitoring defines requirement-related resources and tasks throughout the requirements development process.

15. D. Requirements gathering or requirements collecting activities are also known as requirements elicitation.

16. B. Inputs are the information and preconditions necessary for a business analysis task to begin. They may be generated outside of the scope of business analysis or generated by a business analysis task.

17. A. Problem solving involves measuring alternatives against objectives and identifying tradeoffs to determine which possible solution is best.

18. D. The business analysis approach defines the methodology used for business analysis work on the overall project and each of its phases. It includes team roles, deliverables to be produced, how and when tasks are performed, techniques to be used, and other aspects of the high-level business analysis process.

19. B. The business analyst is responsible for ensuring the feasibility of proposed requirements when defining, describing, and refining the characteristics of an acceptable solution as part of Requirements Analysis activities.

20. A. Stakeholder requirements are statements of stakeholder needs, describing how that stakeholder will interact with a solution. This need from a class of users is best described as a stakeholder requirement. Solution requirements could also be a correct answer to this question, although they were not one of the potential answers provided.

Chapter

2

Controlled Start: Business Analysis Planning and Monitoring

CBAP®/CCBA™ EXAM TOPICS COVERED IN THIS CHAPTER

- ✓ Select the business analysis approach for the project.
- ✓ Perform stakeholder identification, analysis, and categorization.
- ✓ Plan work activities performed by the business analyst.
- ✓ Address business analysis communication.
- ✓ Plan the requirements management process.
- ✓ Manage and monitor the business analysis effort.

Now that you are more familiar with the discipline of business analysis, you are ready to address planning the business analysis activities for a project or initiative. You have learned the basic pieces of the discipline: the underlying competencies of the business analyst, the key business analysis stakeholders, and the *BABOK® Guide* requirements classification scheme. Using this foundation, you will begin to apply business analysis tasks and techniques as we walk through the first knowledge area, Business Analysis Planning and Monitoring.

The first skills you will put to use are analytical thinking and problem solving. After all, before you can begin a project or project phase, it's a good idea to know what work you need to do. In order to achieve a controlled start to a project or project phase, you must be methodical and consistent in your planning, definition, and decisions. This is the first step in planning the business analysis work effort for a project. Figure out what needs to be done, how you will go about doing it, exactly who needs to be involved with the work, and how involved they should be.

Business Analysis Planning and Monitoring

The Business Analysis Planning and Monitoring knowledge area focuses on laying the groundwork for successfully defining, planning, and completing the business analysis work for a project. The business analyst builds the business analysis work plan by executing the knowledge area tasks. The business analysis tasks that the business analyst puts in the work plan depend on what needs to be done for the time period of the planning effort. Typically, the business analysis work plan becomes part of the project management plan.

The tasks in this planning-focused knowledge area generate several key business analysis deliverables. They include the:

Stakeholder list, roles, and responsibilities

Business analysis approach

Business analysis plan

Requirements management plan

Business analysis communication plan

We will cover each deliverable in more detail in this chapter.

The Business Analysis Planning and Monitoring knowledge area also addresses monitoring and reporting on the business analysis work being performed on a project once the planning is complete and the work efforts are underway. This ensures the project's business analysis effort produces the desired outcome and that the business analysis work is done right.

The Business Analyst's Task List

The business analyst has six tasks to perform in the Business Analysis Planning and Monitoring knowledge area. We will look at each of these tasks in greater detail later in this chapter. The task list from the *BABOK® Guide* includes:

Planning the business analysis approach

Conducting stakeholder analysis

Planning business analysis activities

Planning business analysis communication

Planning the requirements management process

Managing business analysis performance

These tasks focus on planning how the business analysis team will approach a specific effort. The business analyst is responsible for developing, defining, and managing the roles and tasks associated with this work. We will step through each of these tasks in greater detail later in this chapter. The goal of the project is to define, develop, and deliver a solution that addresses a business problem, need, or opportunity. To achieve that goal, the business analyst must have detailed knowledge of each task, be able to apply the recommended techniques, and produce high-quality deliverables as a result.

Exam Spotlight

Exam questions in this knowledge area are organized and presented using this list of tasks. It is your job (and ours as well) to make sure you know when this work is done and how you go about actually doing it!

When Does Business Analysis Planning and Monitoring Take Place?

"Begin at the beginning," the King said gravely, "and go on till you come to the end; then stop."

—*Lewis Carroll, Alice in Wonderland*

The tasks in the Business Analysis Planning and Monitoring knowledge area occur throughout the project life cycle. Many of these tasks are done as a part of pre-project activities as the basis of a project's controlled start. The business analysis deliverables created at the beginning of a project are used to define, govern, and monitor the performance of all other business analysis tasks across the project life cycle. The plans and approaches developed for the overall project may require updates and additional details as each subsequent phase of the project life cycle is planned.

The controlled start to a project includes the pre-project activities where teams determine if this is a viable and worthwhile project for the business. Controlled start also covers project initiation activities, where you do more detailed planning for the business analysis effort on a project and any associated project stages or phases. At the end of a controlled start:

- The *solution scope* is finalized.

- The *business case* and justification are in place.

- The high-level *business analysis plan* has been built.

- The business analysis team should be ready to get to work.

Numerous tasks and deliverables from both the Enterprise Analysis and Business Analysis Planning and Monitoring knowledge areas are created and used during a controlled start. Tasks in the Business Analysis Planning and Monitoring knowledge area allow you to decide how to go about the business analysis work that is required to define, develop, and deliver a solution. Tasks from the Enterprise Analysis knowledge area focus on defining the business requirements and justifying delivery of the solution scope for the project. We will take a detailed look at the Enterprise Analysis tasks in Chapter 5, "Controlled Middle: Elicitation." Right now, we are concerned with planning how to do the business analysis activities versus actually doing the work.

 Real World Scenario

What Exactly Am I Supposed to Be Doing?

Russ discovered early in his career as a project manager that all plans are not created equal. He was a replacement for the project manager on a fairly complex data center consolidation project. Russ stepped in near the end of the first major phase of project work, which was developing the user requirements for the new data center.

One of his first tasks was to review the current project plan and evaluate the progress to date. Russ noticed that the requirements development work was shown as a single two-week task in the project plan with no additional details about the requirements process itself. Because the resulting user requirements document was shown as a completed deliverable and this task was marked as 100 percent complete, he decided to look at the new capabilities the project would provide to the business and its users. So he did.

After reading the first four pages of the document, Russ knew there was a problem. He finished reading the user requirements document, closed the file on his computer, and reached for the phone to call the lead business analyst for this effort into his office. When Mary arrived, he asked her, "What exactly is this document supposed to be? Is this just a high-level concept that we need to now go out and define?" Mary replied that the document was the final, approved user requirements document. All the business analysis team had to do now was give the document to the developers. The developers would figure out the rest.

Russ asked Mary to explain the process she and her team had gone through to produce the deliverable. She explained that she had worked in tandem with the development director to elicit, analyze, and specify the user requirements for the project. Basically, the key users had not been involved or consulted at all. As Mary was quick to point out, "That wasn't in the plan so that wasn't how I did the work." Basically, the user requirements work had to begin all over again and had to be done correctly the second time.

Russ worked closely with his business analysis team to plan the requirements development work in far greater detail. This time around, the team gave themselves adequate time to elicit and analyze the requirements and planned the time to validate the requirements when everything was complete. Completing the rewritten user requirements took five additional weeks of work. Funny enough, this didn't impact the scheduled end date. The original requirements would have been impossible to use for the design and construction of the data center.

Remember that your focus is on planning and monitoring the business analysis work for a project, not on planning and managing the whole project. That is the responsibility of the project manager. However, in either case, the plans need to be built and implemented at the appropriate level of detail.

Plan the Business Analysis Approach

The first task in the Business Analysis Planning and Monitoring knowledge area is to plan the business analysis approach. There are many ways to approach business analysis work on a project. In order to get the business analysis work started on a project, you must first decide how to go about doing it. The overall business analysis process for performing work consists of:

- Deciding how and when business analysis tasks will be performed
- Agreeing on the techniques to be used
- Defining the deliverables to be produced

Figure 2.1 summarizes the inputs, outputs, techniques, and associated tasks for building the business analysis approach for a project. The best business analysis approaches are based on the organizational environment where they will be used. The business analysis approach is a subset of the overall project approach. It defines the set of processes, templates, techniques, and activities used to perform business analysis on a project or initiative. When documented, the business analysis approach creates a formalized and repeatable methodology. In comparison, the *project approach* describes the way all of the project work will be approached.

Once the business analysis approach is established for a project or initiative, it is not expected to change significantly through that project's life cycle. However, the business analysis approach should be revisited at each phase of the project to ensure that it is being followed and that no changes are required for the work that will be started or based on business analysis performance to date.

FIGURE 2.1   Task summary: Plan business analysis approach.

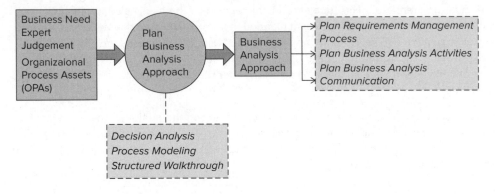

Plan-Driven Versus Change-Driven Approaches

When you define your business analysis approach, you must decide where it falls across the spectrum of *plan-driven approaches* and *change-driven approaches*. Plan-driven approaches focus on ensuring that the solution is fully defined before its implementation begins. Change-driven approaches are used on projects where many small iterations are defined and developed en route to the final result. Hybrid approaches combine aspects of both types, and may require additional tailoring and scaling of the business analysis approach to combine them well. Most organizational environments and their management teams are likely to be more comfortable with one approach over the other.

Real World Scenario

The Project Has Two Faces, Part 1

Introduced into the exciting realm of online payment processing on a consulting assignment, Ginger discovered that projects can successfully incorporate both plan-driven and change-driven approaches to get the job done. She was brought on board by a financial services firm to lead their efforts in launching their new online payment processing system. Of course, before it could be launched it had to be defined, designed, and built from the ground up.

Early phases of this effort focused on building the actual system. Ginger recommended that the project team use a plan-driven approach. This would ensure a system that would be scalable as more customers came on board. The architecture and infrastructure capabilities for the new system would be thoroughly documented and well understood. The system's payment processing capabilities would be well-defined, and all key stakeholders in the organization would know what the final system looked like and what services the product would provide. Senior management agreed with this approach, and the work began.

Once system development was well underway, it was time to look for new customers for this soon-to-be operational product. Ginger was asked to lead the implementation team responsible for on-boarding new customers. This was the point where the game changed. Previously, her focus was on a well-designed and well-defined online payment processing system. Now, her focus was on marketing the product to and acquiring new customers as quickly as possible. The goal was to complete each customer implementation in less than 30 days.

To achieve this goal, Ginger recommended a very different approach from the development team's plan-driven project. She and the team decided that a change-driven approach was the only way to get each implementation done swiftly and accurately. The team developed requirements templates to use as the basis for setting up each customer's portal into the payment processing system. The information in these templates was gathered by telephone. Of course, billing information for each customer was also collected. Customers had their own data repositories and a customized front-end for their shopping carts.

Use of the streamlined requirements templates enabled each implementation manager to quickly walk their clients through the process of getting the online payment processing system up and running on their websites. Management was ecstatic when the money started flowing in from happy customers. And Ginger the consultant was invited to the celebration when everything was complete.

Plan-driven business analysis tries to minimize your up-front uncertainty (or risk) and maximize your control over the business analysis activities on your project. This is a more traditional style of development, such as the waterfall model of software development or what you find in straightforward business process reengineering initiatives. The biggest issue with plan-driven approaches is whether or not the solution requirements can actually be well defined prior to commencing the overall solution delivery efforts. In effect, plan-driven approaches use structure to control project risk.

Another way to think of plan-driven versus change-driven business analysis approaches is to call them traditional versus agile development methodologies.

Change-driven business analysis approaches target rapid delivery of business value. In order to achieve that goal, they accept greater uncertainty (risk) relative to the overall solution delivery. This is an exploratory approach to finding the best solution, using short iterations to incrementally develop components of the solution. Change-driven approaches that you may be familiar with include agile development methods and many continuous process improvement projects being done in organizations. One key feature of change-driven approaches is that they use flexibility to control project risk.

Do not confuse today's plan-driven business analysis approaches with the traditional, linear models of the past. Today's plan-driven approaches are flexible and adaptable, using time-boxing, iterative development, and multiple releases to help folks get the job done. The traditional linear models of the past typically use the draft-walkthrough-revise-final-approve cycle.

Plan the Business Analysis Approach

Now let's get to the task at hand, which is planning the business analysis approach. Every task has inputs, outputs, elements, and techniques. This task is no exception. Let's start with the inputs. Inputs are either informational in nature or outputs produced by other business analysis tasks. Inputs are acted on by the task elements and techniques, producing one or more task outputs. Let's take a look at the task inputs used when planning a business analysis approach:

Business Need   The business analysis approach is impacted by the business need that is driving the project. This makes sense. Both the project approach and the business analysis approach will be impacted by the problem or opportunity it is addressing. The business need for the project is defined during Enterprise Analysis.

Expert Judgment   Expert judgment is used to evaluate and build the optimal business analysis approach for your project. Your team will rely on individuals or groups with specialized knowledge or skills in business analysis and other aspects of the domain to assist in defining the approach.

Organizational Process Assets   Organizational process assets are an organization's policies, guidelines, procedures, plans, approaches, and standards for conducting work. A subset of these assets may directly define or indirectly govern business analysis work on a project. Organizational process assets can include existing business analysis approaches already in use by the organization, corporate standards, templates, change management methods, and requirements tools. They also can include historical information from previous projects, such as risks, performance measures, schedules, and other data. When you discover a business analysis asset treasure trove at one of your clients, it means you don't have to reinvent the wheel.

Table 2.1 summarizes the inputs needed to plan the business analysis approach for a project and also lists the task that was the source of the input (if applicable).

TABLE 2.1   Inputs: Plan Business Analysis Approach

Task Input	Input Source	Source Knowledge Area
Business need	Define business need	Enterprise Analysis
Enterprise Architecture	—	—
Organizational Process Assets (OPAs)	—	—

The experienced business analyst spreads their attention across eight elements when they consider the contents of the business analysis approach. The results of each element are formally documented as part of the business analysis approach for the project. The detailed elements necessary to plan the business analysis approach include:

- Determining timing of business analysis work
- Deciding degree of formality and level of detail for business analysis deliverables
- Selecting methods for prioritizing the requirements
- Building an appropriate change management approach
- Planning and integrating the execution of business analysis activities
- Creating an approach to stakeholder communications
- Identifying any requirements analysis or management tools to be used
- Considering project complexity

Exam Spotlight

Remember that selecting and defining your project's business analysis approach is situational. It depends on a number of factors, such as organizational needs, business analysis team skills, and solution complexity. Combining practices from plan-driven and change-driven approaches could result in a stronger business analysis approach.

Let's step through each of the elements involved in deciding on and building a project's business analysis approach.

Determine Timing of Business Analysis Work   It is critical that you determine when the business analysis work will take place throughout the project. This includes identifying not only the tasks to be performed, but also the business analysis resources that will perform each task. Requirements development time is a traditionally heavy period of work for the business analysis team. You need to know if these efforts will align with specific project phases early in the project (plan-driven), or if the work will be done iteratively throughout the project (change-driven).

Decide Formality and Level of Detail   All expected business analysis *deliverables* across the project life cycle should be defined in the business analysis approach. If you forget a particular deliverable that is due later in the life cycle or change your mind about one that has already been defined, you can always revisit the business analysis approach and make the necessary changes. Plan-driven approaches are usually quite formal and produce very detailed document sets requiring formal approval. Change-driven approaches can be quite informal, often limiting the documentation to a bare minimum. Project work and business analysis deliverables are approved informally though team interaction and feedback.

Select Requirements Prioritization Methods   The business analysis approach also determines how the project requirements will be prioritized. There are numerous ways to prioritize all levels and types of project requirements. We will look at them in detail when we get to the Requirements Analysis knowledge area in Chapter 6, "Controlled Middle: Requirements Analysis."

Exam Spotlight

Remember that change-driven business analysis approaches must have well-prioritized requirements because a prioritized requirements list may well be the only required project documentation.

Build a Change Management Approach   Change management for business analysts tends to focus on how changes impact the project requirements. It is almost impossible to define requirements for a project that do not change. Change is one of the constants in the project environment—the stakeholders change their minds, the project budget changes, or perhaps the technology you assumed you would be using for the solution is different. Many organizations have a formal change control process in place that addresses these and many other aspects of dealing with change. If there is no organizational-level or project-level process, the business analysis team is responsible for creating a process for the business analysis aspects of their project.

Plan and Integrate Business Analysis Activities   The business analyst must decide on the process to follow for planning a project's business analysis activities. This requires coordination and communication with the project manager, because this business analysis work plan is typically integrated into the higher-level project plan. If there are planning standards to follow for the project, the business analyst should use those standards when planning the business analysis work. These standards could include guidelines for estimating or specific planning and scheduling tools to be used. If the business analysis work plan is not consistent with the project plan, it will be difficult to integrate into the overall effort.

Address Stakeholder Communications   The business analysis plan for stakeholder communications is a subset of the project-level communication plan. Planning the business analyst's communication with project stakeholders requires serious coordination with the project manager. The business analyst is responsible for selecting the appropriate communications technologies or for reviewing the project-level plan and making sure it will work for the business analysis tasks. The primary focus is on making decisions and approving business analysis deliverables. Remember that these communications can be formal or informal, written or verbal.

The effectiveness of a business analyst depends on the corporate culture. Working in a large organization seems to require more formal written communications. We have worked in large organizations with so many layers of management that the business analysts almost never speak directly to a decision maker. On the flip side, many business analysts working in smaller organizations find that formal written communications almost never occur. In this situation, stakeholder communications are almost always verbal and informal in nature.

Identify Any Tools to Be Used   Often, business analysts are expected to use requirements analysis or management tools during a project. If this is the case on your project, the business analysis approach is the place to define what those tools are and how they will be used on your current effort. Requirements tools can impact many aspects of business analysis work, including the techniques selected for performing tasks the notations that are used in requirements development and the way requirements are packaged for stakeholder review and approval.

Consider Project Complexity   Project complexity impacts the business analyst in a number of ways. In general, the more complex the project is, the more complex the business analysis effort is as part of the project work. Complex projects may result in a greater number of formal deliverables and stakeholder review points. Complex projects can also be riskier for everyone—the business, the project team, as well as the business analysis team and its business analysts. Situations with a complex solution should be addressed with more up-front modeling and planning work. Examples of complex projects include building an airline reservation system or creating a telecommunications circuit ordering and provisioning application.

Exam Spotlight

Be sure you remember the six factors that increase the complexity of business analysis work. The rule of thumb is that as these factors increase, so does the project complexity. They are:

- The number of stakeholders

- The number of business areas affected

- The number of business systems affected

- The amount and nature of risk

- The uniqueness of requirements

- The number of technical resources required

There are a number of techniques that you might choose to apply when building a business analysis approach for your project. We recommend that you use the decision analysis technique in order to consider alternative business analysis approaches before making your final decision. Let's take a look at that technique in greater detail.

Recommended Technique: Decision Analysis

Decision analysis is a required technique in the fundamental knowledge base of an effective business analyst. So let's take a closer look at what this technique actually is and how you might apply the technique on your projects. It allows the business analyst to examine and model the consequences of different decisions before actually making or recommending a particular decision. The business analyst's goal is to make or recommend a well-informed decision. This is typically done using some form of mathematical modeling to assess possible outcomes. In many cases, decision analysis involves creating very complex models, using sophisticated software applications.

Effective decision analysis requires the business analyst to understand all aspects of the decision in order to effectively structure the decision problem and process. They need to be aware of any relevant values, goals, and objectives and should clearly understand the nature of the decision that must be made. It is essential to identify the areas of uncertainty affecting the decision and the consequences of each possible decision. Uncertainty often results in calculating the expected value of outcomes versus knowing the actual values by computing the percentage chance of each outcome taking place and multiplying the numeric value for the outcome by that percentage.

Decisions and their resulting outcomes can be financial or nonfinancial in nature. In either case, the business analyst may choose to use financial models to estimate or value a particular decision in financial terms. This is done to provide a method for gauging the outcomes in a comparable fashion. Common financial valuation techniques that the business analyst might use can be found in Table 2.2.

TABLE 2.2 Common Financial Valuation Techniques

Technique	Description
Discounted Cash Flow	Calculate the future value of money using specific data such as an interest rate
Net Present Value (NPV)	Convert the future value of costs and benefits to today's value
Internal Rate of Return (IRR)	Calculate the interest rate (or discount rate) when NPV = 0
Average Rate of Return	Estimate the rate of return on an investment across a specified time period
Payback Period	Determine the amount of time it takes for an investment to pay for itself without considering the time value of money
Cost-Benefit Analysis (CBA)	Use a ratio to quantify the costs and benefits for a proposed solution where benefits typically equal revenue

Decision analysis may also involve trade-off decision making that involves evaluating and valuing multiple objectives. The *BABOK® Guide* recommends two methods for trade-off decision making, elimination of dominated alternatives and ranking objectives on a similar scale. Dominated alternatives are options that are clearly inferior to other options being considered when rated against the objectives. Objectives are ranked by proportional scoring, where the best outcome is scored as 100 and the worst is a zero with everything else scored in-between.

One of the simplest methods used in trade-off decision making is performed using a decision tree. This allows the business analyst to determine the *expected monetary value (EMV)* to assist them in weighing decision alternatives and evaluating the monetary impact of these potential decisions. Starting at the far right of the tree on the smallest branches, you multiply the probability assigned to that outcome by the expected monetary impact for each branch. EMV is also called actuarial value.

Real World Scenario

Inside or Out?

Imagine that you are a coffee vendor dealing with the weather prediction: There's a 50 percent chance of sun today, a 35 percent chance of some clouds, and a 15 percent chance of rain. You have two options for where you place your coffee cart on this particular day: inside a downtown office building or outside on the sidewalk. You use a decision tree to evaluate the potential outcomes of both decisions based on your estimated financial gains and losses. You will examine two related factors: the selected location (inside or outside) and the weather prediction for today (sunny, cloudy, or rainy). After comparing the monetary outcomes, you will decide which location is the best place to set up your coffee cart.

Based on your previous experience, you assign a monetary value for your expected earnings based on the type of weather and your location for the day. A positive number means that you think you will make money and a negative number means that you expect to lose money.

You start to set up your decision tree. Regardless of where you set up your coffee cart, the weather prediction tells you that the probability of sun today is 50 percent, the probability for clouds is 35 percent, and that there is a 15 percent probability of rain. For each of your possible locations (inside or outside), you note these numbers. Make sure that all three probabilities add up to 100 percent so that all options are covered.

Now you factor in your previous experience. When you set up your coffee cart outside on a sunny day, you typically make about $300 in profit. You note that value beside the sunny option (a 50 percent chance) on the outside branch of your tree. Now you calculate the estimated values for your net earnings on the other two possible days with your coffee cart set up outside. Selling coffee outside on a rainy day (a 15 percent chance) equals a net loss of $100. Last but not least, being outside selling coffee on a cloudy day (a 35% chance) yields an estimated $200 profit.

You do the same for your alternative location, setting up your coffee cart inside the office building. Setting up your cart inside requires you to pay a fee, which reduces your profits somewhat. You complete the other "branch" of the tree. Inside on a sunny day (a 50 percent chance) has an estimated $250 profit. If it is a nice day and you are inside, many of your customers will not come inside to look for you. You figure that being inside on a rainy day (a 15 percent chance) equals a $225 estimated profit and that having your coffee cart inside on a cloudy day (a 35 percent chance) equals an estimated $250 profit.

Now you multiply the probability and the value of each "branch" on your tree so that you can compare your likely profits and make a well-informed decision. The Expected Monetary Value (EMV) tells you the weighted value of setting up your shop in one location or the other. You calculate this by multiplying the probably times the expected outcome. So, setting up your shop outside generates the following values:

- EMV (coffee cart outside on a sunny day) = 0.5 × $300 = $150
- EMV (coffee cart outside on a rainy day) = 0.15 × –$100 = –$15
- EMV(coffee cart outside on a cloudy day) = 0.35 × $200 = $70

You then do the same calculations for setting up your shop inside given the weather prediction:

- EMV (coffee cart inside on a sunny day) = 0.5 × $250 = $125
- EMV (coffee cart inside on a rainy day) = 0.15 × $225 = $33.75
- EMV(coffee cart inside on a cloudy day) = 0.35 × $250 = $87.50

In order to compare both options (inside or outside) across all possible weather conditions (sunny, rainy, cloudy), you must add up all of the possible outcomes for each option. Setting up your coffee cart outside has a total EMV of 150 – 15 + 70 = $205. By comparison, the overall EMV for setting up your coffee cart inside the office building is 125 + 33.75 + 87.5 = $246.25. Given this data for comparison, you would select the option with the higher EMV. That means you would choose to set up your coffee cart inside today.

The graphical decision tree shown next is a structured decision-making approach for whether or not you should set up your coffee cart inside an office building or outside on the street based on the weather predictions for that particular day.

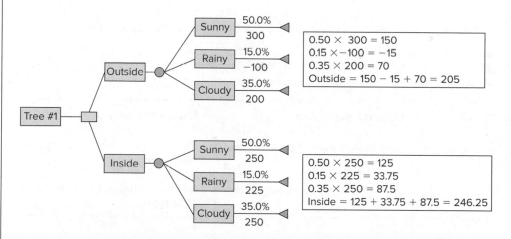

You can use the graphic to calculate what we just stepped through manually. The EMV (outside) = $102.50 and the EMV (inside) = $46.00 for each node (the small circle). Based on the probabilities and the values you assigned to the outcomes, the best decision would be to put your stand outside today (and hope that it doesn't rain).

Additional Techniques to Consider

The *BABOK® Guide* lists some additional techniques that may be used when building the business analysis approach for a project. They are summarized for you here.

Process Modeling   Process models are often used by the business analyst to document the steps of the business analysis approach or process for a project. Think of graphically depicting a series of business analysis process steps on a whiteboard with arrows between them to show the sequence of events. That is a simple process map that can be used to build and decide on a business analysis approach.

Structured Walkthrough   Experienced business analysts use a structured walkthrough to validate the business analysis approach for a project with key stakeholders and team members. This is a meeting with a tour guide. Your destination is the business analysis approach, and your meeting agenda will walk you through the possibilities in order for the group to decide on the approach that is right for their project.

Once you have chosen one or more techniques, you are ready to create your business analysis approach. We'll discuss that next.

Create the Business Analysis Approach

The business analysis approach specifies how the business analysis team plans to perform the business analysis work on their project. Essentially, this approach is the business analysis methodology for the project. If the approach is documented and saved as a business analysis process asset, it can be revised and reused on subsequent projects in the organization. Once the business analysis approach is complete, it is used as an input by other business analysis tasks that are summarized in Table 2.3. They include planning business analysis activities and planning the requirements management process. Both tasks are also part of the Business Analysis Planning and Monitoring knowledge area.

TABLE 2.3   Output: Plan Business Analysis Approach

Task Output	Output Destinations	Source Knowledge Area
Business analysis approach	Plan business analysis activities	Business Analysis Planning and Monitoring
	Plan requirements management process	Business Analysis Planning and Monitoring

The recommended contents of the business analysis approach include:

- Team roles and responsibilities
- Business analysis deliverables

- Business analysis techniques
- Timing and frequency of stakeholder interaction
- Elements of the business analysis process

A number of stakeholders are involved with planning the business analysis approach for a project. Some stakeholders should participate in building all or part of the approach; others are only affected by the approach. As previously mentioned, the project manager must make sure that the business analysis approach aligns with the project approach. In a similar vein, testers must ensure that the approach facilitates appropriate testing of the resulting solution.

Stakeholder availability and involvement across the project life cycle may impact the contents of the business analysis approach. Key stakeholders involved with this deliverable include:

- Customers
- Domain SMEs
- End users
- Suppliers
- Sponsors

It is also important that the business analysis approach be compatible with the development or implementation life cycle being used by the implementation team. Once the business analysis approach is complete, the team needs to think about who will be involved with the business analysis work on the project and determine the level of their involvement. You figure that out during stakeholder analysis, which we will talk about next.

Conduct Stakeholder Analysis

Think of the business analysis stakeholders on a project as members of a professional sports team. Each stakeholder has a particular position to play as a member of the team. Some of your stakeholders are starters and play for the whole game; others substitute in and out during the game and play intermittently. There are stakeholders on the team who don't play the game but might coach the team, bring water out onto the field, or cheer for the team from the stands. Just like players on a sports team, some of your stakeholders will play better than others. The business analysis team needs to know these stakeholders and the role or roles they play in the project.

Effective business analysts recognize the importance of knowing, understanding, and involving your project stakeholders. Stakeholder analysis should begin early in the project life cycle when the business requirements are being developed. The resulting stakeholder information is then revisited and revised throughout the project life cycle. Without up-to-date stakeholder analysis information, it is not easy to elicit, validate, or approve project requirements with the appropriate individuals or groups.

The business analyst initially performs stakeholder analysis during the controlled start phase of a project, or as part of the pre-project activities. Analysis activities at this point in time focus on key stakeholders who are impacted by the business need and the proposed solution. The initial stakeholder list, roles, and responsibilities are enhanced and revised with each subsequent project phase as the business, stakeholder, solution, and transition requirements are developed for the project. Figure 2.2 summarizes the inputs, outputs, techniques, and associated tasks for conducting stakeholder analysis in accordance with the *BABOK® Guide*.

 Real World Scenario

Losing the Sponsor's Support

The initial stakeholder analysis helps the business analyst evaluate the attitudes of the stakeholders regarding the project at hand. Savvy business analysts also perform analysis periodically throughout the project to track changes in stakeholder attitudes. This is particularly true when institutionalized processes are the target of change. If you are not aware of changing attitudes among your key stakeholders, there could be trouble ahead for your effort.

This happened to Phil on a project that had been divided into three phases. The first two phases were relatively inexpensive commitments that were easily implemented. However, the third implementation phase involved much higher vendor involvement at a much higher cost.

When the time came to begin the third phase of this effort and the vendor's work estimates, which added up to several hundred thousands of dollars, was presented to the project sponsor, the sponsor's support for the effort vanished. The sponsor's recollections of support for the previous two project phases also disappeared. Adding insult to injury, the sponsor made a point of disparaging the entire effort in the next executive staff meeting.

What was going on? Was there anything Phil could have done to prevent this? Phil was fortunate that he had the signed project approval documents to protect himself and his team from imminent doom. This is a worst-case example. Effective business analysts have learned to keep a finger on the pulse of their key stakeholders, especially in long-term projects. This often provides early warning signals of potential problems.

FIGURE 2.2 Task summary: Conduct stakeholder analysis.

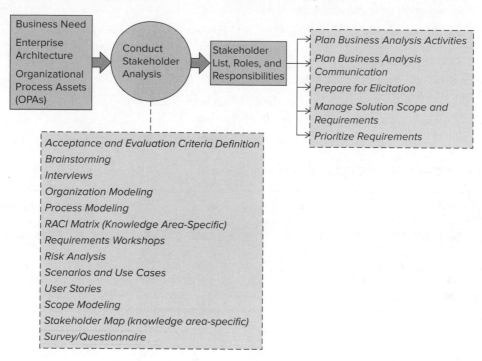

 Remember that stakeholder roles are like hats. Some individuals may be called on to play a variety of stakeholder roles on the same project, as well as different roles in different projects. A stakeholder may wear many hats and play multiple team roles in your project. A job position title is typically defined and assigned by the organization and does not necessarily correspond to the team role an individual may play in a project. Team roles are defined project-specific roles and responsibilities. Team roles may occur intermittently or throughout a project.

As discussed earlier in the chapter, inputs can be informational in nature or outputs produced by other business analysis tasks. Inputs are acted on by the task elements and techniques, producing one or more task outputs. Let's take a look at the task inputs used when analyzing our project stakeholders:

Business Need   In this task, the focus is on the stakeholders who will be affected by the business need that is driving the project. Over time, you may discover and analyze new stakeholders that the business analysis team was unaware of at the beginning of the project. You also need to beware of the stakeholders who change their position as the project progresses. The business need for the project is defined during Enterprise Analysis.

Enterprise Architecture   Looking at the organization and how it is sliced and diced assists the business analyst in stakeholder analysis activities.

Organizational Process Assets   Organizational process assets are an organization's policies, guidelines, procedures, plans, approaches, and standards for conducting work. The business analyst should seek out and use any existing policies, procedures, methods, and templates as part of stakeholder analysis.

Table 2.4 summarizes the inputs to the Conduct Stakeholder Analysis task and also lists the task that was the source of the input (if applicable).

TABLE 2.4   Inputs: Conduct Stakeholder Analysis

Task Input	Input Source	Source Knowledge Area
Business need	Define business need	Enterprise Analysis
Enterprise Architecture	—	—
Organizational Process Assets (OPAs)	—	—

Business analysts performing stakeholder analysis at any point in their projects should apply four detailed elements as they build their stakeholder list, roles, and responsibilities. The detailed elements necessary to analyze stakeholders and document meaningful information about them include:

- Identify stakeholders.
- Analyze complexity of stakeholder group.
- Assess stakeholder attitude and influence.
- Define stakeholder authority levels over business analysis work.

Let's take a look at each element in greater detail.

Identify Stakeholders

How do you figure out who needs to be involved with the business analysis activities for your project? It can be fairly straightforward to find the key business analysis stakeholders for a project. Because business analysts tend to spend a lot of time developing project requirements, identifying and analyzing stakeholders is an absolute must. It can be quite painful to miss a significant stakeholder early on and then discover them later in the project. There can also be indirect or hidden stakeholders out there who are waiting to be found.

Stakeholder identification should occur at both the overall project level and each project phase. Business analysts should perform this task when a business need is identified and revisit and revise the results for as long as business analysis work continues on the project. The business analysis stakeholders are an important subset of the project stakeholders, so communication and coordination with the project manager is required.

Stakeholders may have varying levels of responsibility, authority, and participation. Their involvement can, and often does, change over the course of the project life cycle. Business analysis stakeholder responsibilities and authority can range from occasional contributions to the effort to having full responsibility for the project and its outcome.

Identifying stakeholders late in the project is risky. This can lead to new requirements late in the project life cycle, revisions to existing requirements, solution rework, and possibly even new solution work that was not scoped out or planned. Many stakeholders who are not involved at the appropriate time in a project tend to be dissatisfied and often do not buy into the resulting solution.

Analyze Stakeholder Complexity

The more business analysis stakeholders there are, the more complicated dealing with them can become. Complexity factors that the business analyst should consider include the number and variety of end users for the solution, as well as the number of interfacing business processes and systems. This data is initially discovered as a part of stakeholder analysis and factors into the subsequent planning activities for both business analysis work and business analysis communications.

Assess Stakeholder Attitudes and Influence

Business analysts are responsible for assessing the positive and negative attitudes and behaviors. When doing this, they need to consider a number of factors. Stakeholder attitudes toward the project must be assessed and then managed across the project life cycle. At a minimum, attitudes need to be looked at relative to the business goals, objectives, and solution approach for the project. Additionally, attitudes must be assessed from a people perspective, considering things like the stakeholder's perception of the value of business analysis work, collaboration, and the sponsor and other key team members.

Understanding the nature of influence is essential when building effective stakeholder relationships and trust. The business analysis team should assess the influence of key stakeholders at the project and organization levels. The amount of influence required for a successful project should be analyzed relative to the amount of influence possessed by the key stakeholders. Informal stakeholder influence with the other stakeholders cannot be overlooked, as having informal project champions is a gift to the business analyst.

Define Stakeholder Authority Levels

The business analysis team needs to know exactly which stakeholders have authority over the business analysis work and deliverables. This includes reviewing and approving deliverables (such as requirements), requesting and approving changes, and vetoing proposed requirements or solutions.

There are a number of techniques that you can use when you are analyzing your project stakeholders. There are three techniques that we highly recommend you use when analyzing business analysis stakeholders:

- Organization modeling
- A RACI matrix
- Stakeholder maps

We usually start off our stakeholder analysis efforts with the organizational modeling technique to get a sense of "who goes where" in the organization relative to a project. Then we start building a RACI matrix to define who decides what. We also like building stakeholder maps to view our key stakeholders relative to different aspects of our projects. Let's take a look at these three recommended techniques in greater detail.

Recommended Technique: Organization Modeling

Most of us have seen an organization chart showing the hierarchy. This is an example of an organizational model. The model defines the purpose and structure of an organization or an organizational unit. When you use this technique for business analysis, you basically build an organization chart that shows the organizational units, lines of reporting, the roles, and the people in those roles.

When you are working with a new client, one of the first things you should ask for is a current organization chart. This will allow you to evaluate who sits where in the food chain and to decide who you might initially involve in your business analysis efforts. This is an excellent way to identify business analysis stakeholders.

Recommended Technique: RACI Matrix

This grid technique is used when conducting stakeholder analysis, and it is defined as part of this specific task in the *BABOK® Guide*. A RACI matrix is used to define business analysis stakeholder roles across four designations: Responsible, Accountable, Consulted, and Informed. The matrix may be created for the entire business analysis effort, a particular business analysis task, or a specific business analysis deliverable, such as the business analysis approach you learned about earlier in this chapter.

Responsible   Business analysis stakeholders are responsible for the work that they are tasked to perform.

Accountable   Accountability lies with the sole decision maker who makes the required decisions for the business analysis effort task or deliverable.

Consulted   Relevant stakeholders should be consulted prior to the work being done if their inputs or advice is needed.

Informed   This is usually an "after the fact" role as these stakeholders are notified of the outcome after work is complete.

An example of a RACI matrix can be found in Table 2.5.

TABLE 2.5   RACI Matrix

Palmer Divide Vineyards Requirements Development

Tasks	William	Ginger	Hector	Sawyer	Dan	Hattie	Taylor
Elicitation	I	I	R, A	R	R	I	R
Analysis	I	I	R, A	R	R	I	R
Specification	A	I	R	C	C	I	C
Validation	I	I	R, A	R	R	I	R

Recommended Technique: Stakeholder Map

This graphical technique is used when conducting stakeholder analysis, and it is defined as part of this specific task in the *BABOK® Guide*. A stakeholder map is not the same thing as an organization chart. While an organization chart shows people and how they fit into the organizational reporting and common structure, a stakeholder map looks at how these stakeholders will be involved with the resulting solution. This takes the concept of an organizational model one step further by visually relating the identified business analysis stakeholders to the solution, as well as to one another.

There are two basic types of stakeholder maps: a stakeholder matrix and an onion diagram. A stakeholder matrix provides a two-dimensional look at stakeholder influence versus their level of interest in your efforts. By comparison, an onion diagram depicts stakeholder involvement with the resulting solution. Figure 2.3 shows an onion diagram.

FIGURE 2.3   Onion diagram

Impacted External Stakeholders:
Our Customers

Organization Management and SMEs:
Dan, Sawyer, William

Impacted End Users:
Hector, Sawyer

Solution Delivery:
Taylor,
Ginger

Additional Techniques to Consider

The *BABOK® Guide* lists some additional techniques that may be used when analyzing your business analysis stakeholders for your project. They are summarized for you here.

Acceptance and Evaluation Criteria Definition   As part of stakeholder analysis, the business analyst must determine the specific stakeholders possessing the authority to either accept or reject the resulting solution based on the defined and agreed-upon acceptance criteria. It can be difficult to get sign-off on your final solution when you haven't defined what makes that solution acceptable to the customer and key end users of whatever you have built.

Brainstorming   Brainstorming is an excellent technique to use when the business analysis team is generating a list of all possible stakeholders for the business analysis effort. Generating ideas about who the business analysis stakeholders are could reveal hidden stakeholders that should be involved with your efforts.

Interviews   When interviewing business analysis stakeholders, the business analyst should always ask the interviewees to identify additional stakeholders.

Process Modeling   Anyone involved with the business processes that are affected by the proposed solution should be identified as a stakeholder. Process models can assist the business analyst with that identification, as they show the related processes and systems.

Requirements Workshop   When conducting requirements workshops on any project topic, the business analyst should always ask the participants about any additional stakeholders.

Risk Analysis   The results of stakeholder analysis may contribute to the risks for the business analysis effort and to the project. The people involved with your efforts can be the source of possible risks, and they can also help the team identify additional risks that may be important downstream.

Scenarios and Use Cases   Identified stakeholder roles can be used as the basis for actors and roles if the business analysis team has selected the scenarios and use cases modeling technique.

User Stories   Identified stakeholder roles can be used as the basis for actors and roles if the business analysis team has selected the user stories modeling technique.

Scope Modeling   Scope models can show the business analysis team the set of stakeholders external to the solution scope who interact with the solution in some way.

Survey/Questionnaire   Business analysts may use this technique to identify shared characteristics of a particular business analysis stakeholder group.

Build the Stakeholder List, Roles, and Responsibilities

According to the *BABOK® Guide*, the following information about your business analysis stakeholders should be included in the stakeholder list, roles, and responsibilities:

- Names
- Titles
- Category
- Location
- Special needs
- Authority levels
- Number of individuals in each role
- Description of stakeholder influence and interest

Remember that there are two discrete sets of information that a business analyst needs to collect as part of the stakeholder list, roles, and responsibilities. First, you have the administrative data, such as names, departments, contact information, locations, roles, responsibilities, authority, and expertise. Second are the actual results of the stakeholder analysis. This is where the business analysis team assesses and records stakeholder influence, interest, expectations, involvement, and any key requirements the stakeholders might have for the business analysis efforts and the overall project.

Once the initial stakeholder list, roles, and responsibilities information is complete, it is used as an input for a number of other business analysis tasks summarized in Table 2.6. They include tasks from a number of knowledge areas such as Business Analysis Planning and Monitoring, Elicitation Requirements Analysis, and Requirements Management and Communication.

TABLE 2.6   Output: Conduct Stakeholder Analysis

Output	Output Destinations	Destination Knowledge Area
Stakeholder list, roles, and responsibilities	Plan business analysis activities	Business Analysis Planning and Monitoring
	Plan business analysis communication	Business Analysis Planning and Monitoring
	Prepare for elicitation	Elicitation

A number of stakeholders are involved with conducting stakeholder analysis for the business analysis activities of a project. Remember that the responsibility for analyzing business analysis stakeholders is shared with the project manager. This means that any stakeholder analysis results should align with the project stakeholder analysis results in both structure and content.

Key business analysis stakeholders may be able to recommend other stakeholders to include in the stakeholder analysis results. This includes the domain SME, testers, sponsor, regulator, and implementation SME.

 **Real World Scenario**

Case Study: Palmer Divide Vineyards Stakeholder List

Business analysts often like to use a spreadsheet to capture stakeholder information and keep it in a single location. Table 2.7 provides a populated template for the initial stakeholder list, roles, and responsibilities at Palmer Divide Vineyards. You can collect the data shown here or add information to your list based on your organization and the nature of your project.

TABLE 2.7   Template: Stakeholder List, Roles, and Responsibilities

Name	Position	Role	Responsibilities	Location	Influence	Interest
William	Vineyard co-owner	Project sponsor	Governance and funding	CO	High	High
Ginger	Product manager	Project manager	Project scope, schedule, budget	CO	Moderate	High

Name	Position	Role	Responsibilities	Location	Influence	Interest
Hector	Marketing director	Lead business analyst	Requirements development	CO	Moderate	High
Sawyer	Vineyard manager	Cultivation lead	Domain SME- biodynamic farming	CO	High	High
Dan	Winemaker	Domain SME	Domain SME - enology	CO	High	High
Hattie	Admin. assistant	Coordinator	Project administration	CO	Low	Moderate
Taylor	IT director	IT lead	Implementation SME	CO	Moderate	Moderate

Plan Business Analysis Activities

Business analysis activities must be planned for the overall project and for each project phase. The resulting business analysis plans are the road map for what needs to be done, when it needs to be done, and who is responsible for actually doing it. Planning for and measuring the progress of business analysis work is typically done by the business analysis team. The resulting plans also govern performance of all business analysis tasks and define the roles and responsibilities coming along for the ride.

Exam Spotlight

The *BABOK® Guide* planning activities focus ONLY on business analysis tasks and deliverables.

Experienced business analysts recognize that successful planning for the business analysis efforts is really a Planning 101 type of exercise. The process they follow is not much different from what the project manager does to plan the project; it is simply focused on business analysis work and deliverables. The business analyst needs to describe the scope of business analysis work, build a *Work Breakdown Structure (WBS)* and an activity list, estimate each activity, allocate and optimize resources, and figure out how to deal with the inevitable changes that will come their way. If all goes well, the plan enables the business analysis team to work well with the project manager and to engage the project stakeholders.

Business Analysis Planning Checklist

We always use templates and checklists to help us get our business analysis work completed. Here is a checklist of things to consider when building your business analysis plan:

- Define the scope of work.

- Plan the activities or tasks.

- Generate a task list.

- Develop the WBS.

- List task attributes and characteristics.

- Devise acceptance criteria for tasks and deliverables.

- Construct task dependencies.

- Identify critical and slack paths.

- Make resource and scheduling decisions.

- Assign resources.

- Assess resource requirements.

- Derive the BA-focused schedule.

- Calculate the budget.

- Integrate with the project plan and schedule.

The primary goal of business analysis planning is to identify and schedule requirements-related activities and resources. The resulting project requirements define the capabilities of the solution to the stated business problem, opportunity, or need. To do this, the *BABOK® Guide* recommends the use of *rolling wave planning*. Rolling wave planning allows the business analysis team to create a high-level plan for the overall business analysis effort, and then build detailed plans over time, addressing near-term activities. This method works well for both plan-driven and change-driven business analysis approaches and projects. Planning for each project phase as you approach its start is a one common way to slice and dice the more detailed near-term planning.

Remember that a plan is a model of what needs to be accomplished for a particular effort. Plans are frequently updated to reflect what is known at a particular point in time. An initial business analysis plan often requires revision based on issues that the team encounters, lessons learned while work is being done, or changing business drivers and strategies that impact the project. Figure 2.4 summarizes the inputs, outputs, techniques, and associated tasks for planning business analysis activities in accordance with the *BABOK® Guide*.

Planning for business analysis work also requires coordination and communication with the project manager. The business analysis plans should be consistent with the project-level plans. Given that the business analysis work plans are typically integrated into the project plans, the business analyst should use consistent project planning standards guidelines and tools. This planning-related information is defined in the business analysis approach.

FIGURE 2.4   Task summary: Plan business analysis activities.

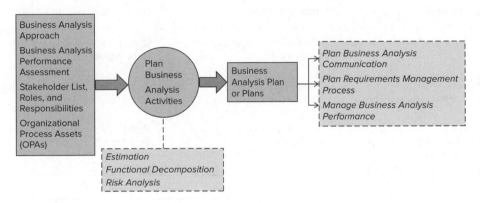

Several key inputs used to plan business analysis activities are key outputs produced by other business analysis tasks, including the business analysis approach and the stakeholder list, roles, and responsibilities. These two govern how the planning is done and who is involved with the work to be performed. Let's take a look at the task inputs used for planning business analysis activities:

Business Analysis Approach   The business analysis approach governs planning activities, as it defines the planning process and the development lifecycle. Knowing if the business analysis approach is plan-driven, change-driven, or a hybrid is essential to the business analyst. Each approach has different priorities, timing, deliverables, and tasks that will need to be part of the business analysis plans.

Business Analysis Performance Assessment   Previous business analysis work performance data on an earlier phase in this project or on previous efforts should be used as part of the current business analysis planning activities.

Stakeholder List, Roles, and Responsibilities   Understanding the preferences of key business analysis stakeholders will shape the resulting business analysis plans to some degree. Stakeholder roles and levels of involvement need to be understood, especially for requirements development activities.

Organizational Process Assets   Organizational process assets are an organization's policies, guidelines, procedures, plans, approaches, and standards for conducting work. The business analyst should seek out and use any existing policies, procedures, methods, and templates as part of planning business analysis activities.

Table 2.8 summarizes the inputs to this task, and it lists the source of the input (if applicable).

TABLE 2.8   Inputs: Plan Business Analysis Activities

Task Input	Input Source	Source Knowledge Area
Business analysis approach	Plan business analysis approach	Business Analysis Planning and Monitoring
Business analysis performance assessment	Manage business analysis performance	Business Analysis Planning and Monitoring
Stakeholder list, roles, and responsibilities	Conduct stakeholder analysis	Business Analysis Planning and Monitoring
Organizational Process Assets (OPAs)	—	—

Business analysts planning business analysis work for the overall project or a specific project phase need to put on their project manager hat for a little while. Planning business analysis activities includes four detailed elements:

- Consider geographic distribution of stakeholders.
- Look at impacts of project type.
- Decide on business analysis deliverables.
- Determine business analysis activities.

Let's take a look at each element in greater detail.

Consider Geographic Distribution of Stakeholders

The location of key business analysis stakeholders can have a significant impact on business analysis efforts. The easiest efforts typically take place when everyone is located in the same physical location or geographic area. The more geographically dispersed your key business analysis stakeholders are, the harder it is going to be to effectively perform business analysis work. This can impact work estimates for tasks and even the sequencing of activities in the schedule. It also adds risk to the overall business analysis effort, as many stakeholders will never meet the business analysis team face-to-face.

Exam Spotlight

If you are faced with an outsourced project with the development team many time zones away, make sure that you plan for more detailed requirements documentation and acceptance criteria. You should also have more frequent review sessions to keep everyone on the same page with the business analysis efforts and building the resulting solution.

Look at Impacts of Project Type

The type of project on which the business analysis team is working can significantly impact business analysis planning. The business analysis activities performed for developing an online order entry system in-house are quite different from the business analysis work that is planned for building a new interstate highway. The business analysis activities for an iterative website development project are very different from building a software system to track military satellites in orbit.

Exam Spotlight

The *BABOK® Guide* lists seven examples of project types that trigger different approaches to planning the business analysis work. These examples are prime candidates for scenarios on your exam, so take a moment to review them:

- Feasibility studies

- Process improvement

- Organizational change

- New in-house software development

- New outsourced software development

- Software maintenance or enhancement

- Software package selection

Decide on Business Analysis Deliverables

Many organizations have defined sets of project deliverables, including deliverables that are traditionally created as a result of business analysis work. The business analysis team needs to decide where in the project lifecycle the business analysis deliverables are created, agreed-upon, and updated. The full list of the recommended *BABOK® Guide* deliverables along with a brief description can be found in Appendix E, "Quick Summary of Business Analysis Deliverables," of this book.

Business Requirements Document

The business analysis team may decide to have separate documents for business, user, system, and transition requirements. For example, an organization's Business Requirements Document may contain several *BABOK® Guide* deliverables, such as the Business Need, Business Case, Required Capabilities, Solution Scope, and Solution Approach.

In addition to deliverables, the *BABOK® Guide* also contains *records*, which are more dynamic deliverables maintaining information regarding progress and performance relative to the business analysis efforts that are underway. *Reports* provide snapshots of certain aspects of the project's business analysis efforts at certain points in time. Records and reports should be placed under configuration management but are not typically subject to change control.

Determine Business Analysis Activities   The *BABOK® Guide* recommends using the project management best practices of a work breakdown structure (WBS) and an *activity list* to define and decompose the scope of business analysis work into smaller pieces. When creating a work breakdown structure, the business analyst decomposes project scope into smaller and smaller pieces to create a hierarchy of work. A WBS may be used to break a project into iterations, releases, or phases to break deliverables into work packages or to break activities into smaller tasks.

The decomposition of activities and tasks creates an activity list for the business analysis effort. Each task in the list should be identified with a unique number, and stated as a verb-noun phrase such as: *Elicit user requirements information*. It is a best practice to include *assumptions*, *dependencies*, and *milestones* for the tasks as well. Assumptions are defined as factors or conditions that are considered to be true. Dependencies document the logical relationships between the tasks. Milestones are significant events that allow you to measure a project's progress.

Exam Spotlight

According to the *BABOK® Guide*, there are three ways to build an activity list from your WBS:

- Start with the deliverables, assign the activities required to complete the deliverables, and then break each activity into its more detailed tasks.

- Divide the project into phases, then deliverables, and then activities and tasks.

- Expand a previous similar project with unique tasks.

There are a number of techniques you can use when you are applying your project management skills and planning the business analysis activities. The key technique with which business analysts must be competent is estimation. Let's look at that technique in greater detail.

Recommended Technique: Estimation

There are many ways for the business analysis team to estimate the range of cost and effort associated with the business analysis work on a project. These estimates are typically developed in conjunction with the project manager and other team members using the project-level estimating tools and techniques. Effective business analysts use estimates to promote better stakeholder decision-making and understanding of the project. Table 2.9 summarizes of the types of estimates commonly used for estimating business analysis efforts.

TABLE 2.9   Common Estimating Techniques

Technique	Description
Analogous estimation	Uses similar projects as the basis for top-down estimates
Parametric estimation	Uses parameters and historical data
Bottom-up estimation	Estimates smaller items first and aggregates upward
Rolling wave	Refines detailed estimates for increments of work over time
Three-point estimation	Estimates optimistic, pessimistic, and most likely cases
Historic analysis	Uses history as basis for bottom-up and top-down estimates
Expert judgment	Relies on those who performed similar work in the past
Delphi estimation	Combines expert judgment and history

Additional Techniques to Consider

Estimation is not the only technique you can use when building the business analysis plan. The *BABOK® Guide* lists additional techniques that may be used when planning business analysis activities for your project. They are summarized for you here.

Functional Decomposition   As part of business analysis planning, decomposing and understanding the business analysis tasks and deliverables sufficiently enables effective estimating. Decomposition can be done in two ways: task-focused using a WBS or product-focused using a solution breakdown structure.

Risk Analysis   Planning and risk analysis should always go hand-in-hand on a project. When the business analyst creates or updates a business analysis plan, they should always be looking for new business analysis-related risks.

Construct the Business Analysis Plan or Plans

The business analysis work plans should resemble the project plans of which they are a part. The level of detail in these plans depends on several factors, including the business analysis approach for the effort and the overall methodology being used for planning. According to the *BABOK® Guide*, the recommended content of a business analysis plan includes:

Description of the scope of work to be done

A deliverable Work Breakdown Structure (WBS)

The activity list associated with the WBS

Estimates for each activity and task

How to address changes to the plan

 Because the business analysis plans determine when and how any business analysis task is performed on a project, they are used to define and manage all business analysis tasks from the other five *BABOK® Guide* knowledge areas.

Once the business analysis plans are complete, they are used as input by a number of other business analysis tasks summarized in Table 2.10. They are picked up and applied by several Business Analysis Planning and Monitoring knowledge area tasks.

TABLE 2.10   Output: Plan Business Analysis Activities

Output	Output Destinations	Destination Knowledge Area
Business analysis plan or plans	Plan requirements management process	Business Analysis Planning and Monitoring
	Plan business analysis communication	Business Analysis Planning and Monitoring
	Manage business analysis performance	Business Analysis Planning and Monitoring

Any business analysis stakeholder can be involved with planning the business analysis activities for a project. Of particular interest is the verification and validation of key business analysis deliverables across the project life cycle. It is essential that the project manager participate in this effort because the business analysis plans are part of the higher-level project plan.

Key business analysis stakeholders may provide information or use the business analysis plans for their own planning efforts. Stakeholders involved with planning activities may include:

- Customers

- Domain SMEs

- End users

- Suppliers

- Operational support

- Testers

- The sponsor

- Implementation SMEs

The business analysis plan addresses the activities, sequence of work, assigned resources, and key deliverables that will be done or produced by the business analysis team. The team also needs to take a closer look at how they plan to communicate with key stakeholders about these business analysis activities during the project. That is defined in the business analysis communication plan. Let's step through how business analysis communication approaches and activities should be planned for a project.

Plan Business Analysis Communication

Effective business analysts recognize that planning for effective stakeholder communications is a key to project success. The business analysis team must determine the stakeholder requirements for communicating about both business analysis activities and the related deliverables. The team must decide what, who, how, and when—what business analysis information needs to be communicated, who needs to receive that information, how the information will be delivered, and when the information will be required.

The business analysis communication plan schedules and structures business analysis work, meetings, and walkthroughs. These events range from very informal conversations to quite formal affairs. The focus is on receiving, accessing, updating, and escalating information to and from the business analysis stakeholders. The initial business analysis communication will require revision based on discovering new stakeholders, addressing major changes, or before each new project phase begins. Experienced business analysts make sure that methods exist to update and refine the communications approach across the project life cycle.

The business analysis communication plan is often a subset of the overall project communication plan. The business analysis team must ensure that their approach to business analysis communications integrates with the project manager's approach to communication at the project level. When building the plan, ask yourself *"What is the urgency of information need and the availability of technology on this project?"* Then, factor the answers into your business analysis communication planning efforts for your project environment.

 The most important aspect of business analysis communication is communicating requirements information across the project life cycle. It is essential to elicit the right information from key stakeholders about the capabilities of the desired solution and to validate that the analyzed requirements information is correct and complete.

Figure 2.5 provides a summary of the tasks required for Plan Business Analysis Communication.

FIGURE 2.5   Task summary: Plan business analysis communication.

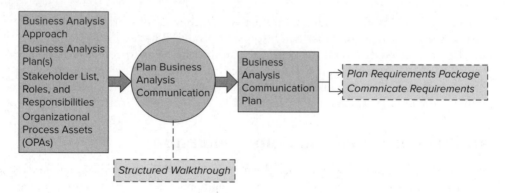

Several key inputs are used in plan business analysis communication information for the project stakeholders. The majority of these inputs are produced by other business analysis planning tasks, including the business analysis approach, the business analysis plan or plans, and the stakeholder list, roles, and responsibilities. The four task inputs used for planning business analysis communication are

Business Analysis Approach   The business analysis approach defines any standards and templates to be used for business analysis communication activities.

Business Analysis Plan or Plans   The deliverables and activities found in the plans may drive the contents of the communication plan if the results need to be communicated. In addition, any significant business analysis communication activities should become part of the business analysis plans.

Stakeholder List, Roles, and Responsibilities   Understanding the communication preferences of key business analysis stakeholders assists the business analysis in communication planning. The list of stakeholders can be used to plan the what, who, how, and when for the stakeholder communication efforts.

Organizational Process Assets   Organizational process assets are an organization's policies, guidelines, procedures, plans, approaches, and standards for conducting work. A subset of these assets may directly define or indirectly govern business analysis work on a project. The business analyst should seek out and use any existing templates for business analysis communications, such as presentation formats, sample meeting agendas, and requirements documents outlines or templates.

Table 2.11 summarizes the inputs to this task and lists the source of the input (if applicable).

TABLE 2.11   Inputs: Plan Business Analysis Communication

Task Input	Input Source	Source Knowledge Area
Business analysis approach	Plan business analysis approach	Business Analysis Planning and Monitoring
Business analysis plan or plans	Plan business analysis activities	Business Analysis Planning and Monitoring
Stakeholder list, roles, and responsibilities	Conduct stakeholder analysis	Business Analysis Planning and Monitoring
Organizational Process Assets (OPAs)	—	—

When planning for business analysis communication, business analysts need to focus on the right communication approach for their key business analysis stakeholders. Planning business analysis communication requires the business analysis team to consider the five detailed elements:

- Look at stakeholder geography
- Factor in cultural diversity
- Consider project type
- Determine communication frequency
- Decide on the level of formality

Let's take a look at each of these communication elements in greater detail.

Look at Stakeholder Geography

The location of business analysis stakeholders links directly to the complexity of the business analysis communication plan. Colocated stakeholders might easily attend a face-to-face meeting with the business analysis team. A more geographically dispersed set of stakeholders could find a team conference call more challenging due to time zone and technology concerns. The business analyst is going to have to design a business analysis communication approach that accommodates the range of stakeholder locations and time zones.

Factor in Cultural Diversity

Cultural considerations play a part in planning business analysis communications, regardless of where the business analysis stakeholders are located. There might be language issues and different views of time, task completion, contracts, and levels of authority. All of these factors must be considered in the business analysis communication plan, as they can have a negative impact on overall project success. Your goal is to plan for them so that they produce a positive impact on your business analysis efforts.

Consider Project Type

The number and formality of project deliverables depends on the type of project being done. Remember the discussion of plan-driven versus change-driven business analysis approaches earlier in this chapter? More traditional, complex projects typically require more formal requirements documentation, while agile development efforts tend to be quite informal in their documentation. Plus, your communication plan needs to be aligned with your project size and complexity. A simple, straightforward project should have a simple, straightforward communication plan.

Determine Communication Frequency

Different business analysis stakeholders may want to hear from the business analysis team at differing time intervals. The business analysis communication plan should define how often business analysis information is shared with the stakeholders. The business analysis team should spend some time defining the communication type and frequency requirements for their key stakeholders. The executive stakeholders may just want a weekly status summary via email while your end users may want to attend a weekly status meeting to discuss the details of this week's efforts.

Decide on Level of Formality

The level of formality required for business analysis communications varies across stakeholders and project phases. The communication plan needs to take this into account instead of using a "one size fits all" approach to communicating business analysis information. The degree of formality is tightly linked to the communication medium and the frequency of sharing information. All three factors should be thoroughly addressed as part of the business analysis communication plan. Be aware that the formality of business analysis communications may vary widely across the stakeholders, project phases, or even for pieces of work contained within a project phase.

The *BABOK® Guide* lists several techniques that may be used when planning for business analysis communication for your project. They are summarized for you here.

Techniques to Consider

Effective communication is a key element of a successful project. These techniques should help you build a thorough and consistent approach to your business analysis communication efforts.

Communication Techniques   While planning for business analysis communications is critical, the ability of the business analyst to use effective communication skills to execute the planned activities is equally important. Remember that the *BABOK® Guide* considers communication skills one of the underlying competencies of an effective business analyst. We will step through this and other underlying competencies in detail in Chapter 8, "Underlying Competencies," of this book.

Structured Walkthrough   A structured walkthrough or requirements review is one of the most common ways to communicate requirements. This will be a common part of the business analysis communication plan. Be sure to allocate enough time to prepare for, conduct, and address any action items or issues arising from the walkthrough in the plan.

Construct the Business Analysis Communication Plan

The business analysis communication plan describes how, when, and why the business analyst will work directly with project stakeholders. The *BABOK® Guide* recommends that the plan contain the following contents:

- Stakeholder communication requirements for business analysis activities on the project

- A description of the format, content, medium, and level of detail for each of these business analysis deliverables

- Business analysis team responsibilities for collecting, distributing, accessing, and updating business analysis information

Once the business analysis communication plan is complete, it is used as an input by a number of other business analysis tasks summarized in Table 2.12.

TABLE 2.12   Output: Plan Business Analysis Communication

Output	Output Destinations	Destination Knowledge Area
Business analysis communication plan	Prepare requirements package	Requirements Management and Communication
	Communicate requirements	Requirements Management and Communication

This plan drives two tasks found in the Requirements Management and Communication knowledge area.

Business Analysis Communication Plan Outline

We always use document templates and checklists to help us get our business analysis work completed. Here is an outline of a business analysis communication plan to give you an idea of what we look for in our projects.

1.0   Communication plan overview

    1.1   Goals and objectives of the plan

    1.2   Intended audience for the plan

2.0   Project overview

    2.1   Business need problem or opportunity

    2.2   Solution scope summary

3.0   Business analysis communications standards

    3.1   Instant Messaging (IM) use and response

    3.2   Cell phone use and response

    3.3   Voicemail response

    3.4   Email response

    3.5   Other

4.0 Key business analysis stakeholder contact list

    4.1 Name and title

    4.2 Role and responsibilities

    4.3 Organization and location

    4.4 Telephone number(s)

    4.5 Email address

5.0 Business analysis team member contact list

    5.1 Name and title

    5.2 Role and responsibilities

    5.3 Associated team manager or leader

    5.4 Location

    5.5 Telephone number(s)

6.0 Business analysis team status and reporting standards

7.0 Key business analysis stakeholder reports

    7.1 Name and purpose

    7.2 Layout and format

    7.3 Sources of report information

    7.4 Report recipients

8.0 Key business analysis stakeholder meetings

    8.1 Meeting type and purpose

    8.2 Required meeting attendees

    8.3 Meeting frequency and schedule

    8.4 Standard meeting agenda

9.0 Standard business analysis team meetings

    9.1 Meeting type and purpose

    9.2 Required meeting attendees

    9.3 Meeting frequency and schedule

    9.4 Standard meeting agenda

    9.5 Attendance and decision-making policies

10.0 Ad hoc meetings

    10.1 When and why they will be called

    10.2 How communicated

    10.3 Attendance and decision-making policies

11.0 Standard business analysis reports

    11.1 Name and purpose

    11.2 Layout and format

    11.3 Sources of report information

    11.4 Report recipients

12.0 Business analysis communications tools

    12.1 Email (what, why, when?)

    12.2 Teleconferences (what, why, when?)

    12.3 Face-to-face meetings (what, why, when?)

    12.4 Others (what, why, when?)

13.0 Business analysis information storage and retrieval

    13.1 Network location and address

    13.2 Levels of access and authorization

    13.3 Update frequency

    13.4 Document control policies

Any business analysis stakeholder can be involved with planning the business analysis communication activities for a project. Stakeholders most likely to be involved are those who play a key role in requirements development efforts. It is essential that the project manager participate in this effort as the business analysis communication plan is part of the higher-level project communication plan.

A number of business analysis stakeholders may provide information to or use the business analysis communication plan. They include:

- Customers
- Suppliers
- Domain SMEs
- End users
- Operational support
- Testers

- Regulators
- The sponsor
- Implementation SMEs

Plan Requirements Management Process

When you ask people what business analysts do, the first answer you usually hear is that business analysts write requirements. That's true. However, developing and managing requirements on a project entails significantly more than just writing requirements. The business analysis team must define their process for developing project requirements. They also must consider how they will approach requirements traceability, requirements prioritization, and changing requirements. This information is formally documented in the requirements management plan.

Once the business analysis team establishes the requirements management process for a project, it is not expected to change significantly across the project life cycle. However, it should be revisited at each phase of the project to ensure that it is being followed and that no changes are required for the work that will be started or based on business analysis performance to date.

In order to plan for requirements development and management, the business analyst must understand the organizational process needs and objectives that apply to the project. These needs and objectives may include compatibility with other organizational processes, constraints on time-to-market, regulatory and governance framework compliance, a desire to evaluate new approaches to solution development, or other business objectives.

In some organizations, a requirements development and management process is already in place. If that is the case, the business analysis team needs to review the existing process and tailor it to fit their current project and environment. Remember that project requirements need to be developed before they can be managed across the project life cycle.

Figure 2.6 summarizes the tasks required for the plan requirements management process.

FIGURE 2.6   Task summary: Plan requirements management process.

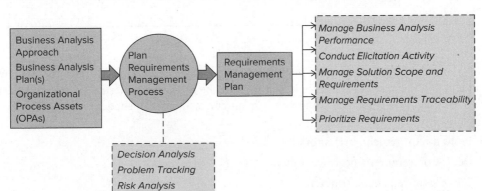

Several key inputs are necessary when planning for requirements development and management on a project. Most of the key inputs are produced by other business analysis planning tasks, including the business analysis approach, the business analysis plan or plans, and the stakeholder list, roles, and responsibilities. The task inputs used when planning the requirements management process include:

Business Analysis Approach   The business analyst should reference the business analysis approach to see if there are any suggested or approved requirements management processes within that document.

Business Analysis Plan or Plans   The requirements management plan addresses the requirements deliverables that are produced for the project. The business analyst should reference these requirements deliverables in the business analysis plan. This is where the deliverables are defined and scheduled.

Organizational Process Assets   The business analyst should seek out and use any existing templates for requirements development and management. If there is an existing requirements development process for the organization, the business analyst should use that process versus reinventing the wheel.

Table 2.13 summarizes the inputs to this task and lists the source of the input (if applicable).

TABLE 2.13   Inputs: Plan Requirements Management Process

Task Input	Input Source	Source Knowledge Area
Business analysis approach	Plan business analysis approach	Business Analysis Planning and Monitoring
Business analysis plan or plans	Plan business analysis activities	Business Analysis Planning and Monitoring
Organizational Process Assets (OPAs)	—	—

Planning the requirements management process for a project requires the business analyst to understand the business and technical drivers for the project. The business analyst addresses several detailed elements when planning for requirements management activities across the project life cycle:

- Build a requirements repository.
- Decide on requirements traceability.
- Select requirements attributes.

- Define the requirements prioritization scheme.
- Plan to deal with changing requirements.
- Tailor the requirements process to fit the project.

Let's take a look at each of these elements in greater detail.

Build a Requirements Repository

It is essential that the business analysis team create a requirements repository for storing requirements. Use of the requirements repository should be linked to the process defined in the requirements management plan. Requirements documentation created during the project life-cycle should be saved in a secured area.

 Practically speaking, all business analysis documents, including the project requirements, should be saved in a business analysis document repository. If the same requirements document is required to be stored both in the project document repository and in the business analysis storage area, the project document repository should contain the unofficial copy.

The storage location for requirements work-in-progress documentation is at the discretion of the project manager or lead business analyst. Documents and copies (electronic or paper) that exist outside the project or requirements document repositories should be made the responsibility of the document originator.

Decide on Requirements Traceability

The requirements management plan is where the business analysis team determines and documents whether and how to trace project requirements. These decisions are based on project type and complexity. Creating and maintaining requirements traceability adds to the business analyst's workload on a project, so it should be reflected in the business analysis plans. We will take a closer look at implementing traceability for our requirements in Chapter 4, "Overarching Tasks: Requirements Management and Communication," when we dig into the Requirements Management and Communication knowledge area.

Select Requirements Attributes

Selecting requirements attributes for a project is an important step. Attributes are intended to be of assistance in the ongoing management of requirements across the project life cycle. Experienced business analysts know how to select the requirements attributes that add value to the requirements information for their project. Attributes allow the team to associate information and add context to individual requirements or groups of requirements.

Be careful when selecting your requirements attributes. Too many attributes can overwhelm business analysts with too much information. Too few attributes will cause the business analysis team to miss critical requirements information later in the project life cycle.

The *BABOK® Guide* recommends that the business analysis team consider using one or more of the common requirements attributes listed in Table 2.14. Business analysts can also select from additional requirements attributes that are less frequently used, such as cost, resource assignment, revision number, traced-from, and traced-to.

TABLE 2.14   Common Requirements Attributes

Attribute	Description
Absolute reference	Unique numeric or text identifier for each requirement
Author of the requirement	Who wrote the requirement if you have any questions later
Complexity	Difficulty in implementing the requirement
Ownership	Individual or group that needs the requirement
Priority	Indicates which requirements should be implemented first
Risks	Associated with meeting or not meeting the requirements
Source of the requirement	Originator of the requirement if you need more information later
Stability	Indicates requirements maturity and if you can start work on it
Status	Proposed, accepted, verified, postponed, cancelled, or implemented
Urgency	How soon the requirement is needed

Define the Requirements Prioritization Scheme

All requirements are not created equal, nor do they deliver equal value to the business and the stakeholders. Business analysts are responsible for establishing the requirements prioritization process technique and level of formality for their projects. The requirements prioritization scheme and process should be defined as early in the project as possible. This enables the project stakeholders to understand and buy into the way the business analysis team will prioritize the project requirements at all levels of detail and focus, including the business, stakeholder, solution, and transition requirements found in the *BABOK® Guide*.

Plan to Deal with Changing Requirements

The business analysis team must decide how to handle changing requirements across the project life cycle. They should address not just baselined requirements but also changes to requirements that are being developed. If the organization has a robust change management process, it can be applied to the requirements work on the project. If not, the requirements management plan needs to address how changing requirements are to be handed. This includes determining the process for requesting requirements changes, authorizing requirements changes, performing impact analysis for significant change requests, and how change requests are worded.

Exam Spotlight

The *BABOK® Guide* recommends that the requirements management process spell out the components found in a request for change. At a minimum, a change request should include cost and time estimates, an assessment of benefits and risks associated with the change, and a recommended course of action.

Tailor the Requirements Process to Fit

When an organization already has an existing requirements management process, the business analysis team might need to tailor that process to fit their current project. Tailoring ensures that planning, control, and governance of requirements-related activities and deliverables are done correctly on the project. Tailoring is typically done by the business analysis team, and the results should be shared with the project manager. Let's briefly step through the factors that should be considered when tailoring an existing requirements management process.

Organizational Culture   Many organizations would prefer a "document light" approach to requirements development and management. Many failed projects relate to poorly documented and poorly understood project requirements. The business analyst should work with key stakeholders to determine a requirements process that maximizes project success.

Stakeholder Preferences   Some stakeholders may not want the requirements development and management process to be formally documented. This adds risk to the project because too much informality can result in problems downstream. The business analyst should recommend a process approach that works for everyone and focuses on "just enough documentation" to get the job done.

Project or Product Complexity   More complex projects and solutions require more formality than simple, straightforward efforts. Formal processes for change control and configuration management at the organizational level assist the business analysis team in determining the degree of rigor for the requirements.

Organizational Maturity   Immature organizations typically do not have a documented requirements development and management process, and often don't want one. A simple requirements process is a powerful tool and should always be considered, even in less mature organizations. These are the folks who need it most.

Resource Availability   A requirements process adds overhead because someone must provide the process with the appropriate maintenance, care, and feeding. The Project Management Office (PMO) or external consultants are often used for this ongoing support.

Techniques to Consider

The *BABOK® Guide* recommends considering the use of one more additional technique when you are defining the requirements management process for your project. These techniques are summarized for you here.

Decision Analysis   When performing an impact analysis on a change request that impacts the requirements, business analysts may use decision analysis to assess the value and the risk of the proposed change.

Problem Tracking   Business analysts and project managers apply this technique to track possible changes and make sure they are addressed.

Risk Analysis   Change brings potential risk along with it for the ride. This business analysis technique identifies and assesses the risks associated with a change request.

Define the Requirements Management Plan

The requirements management plan describes the project's approach and process for developing and managing requirements. The *BABOK® Guide* recommends that the plan contain the following contents:

- Traceability approach for the requirements
- Selection of requirements attributes
- Definition of the requirements prioritization process
- Management of changing requirements, including how to request, analyze, approve, and implement those changes

Once the requirements management plan is complete, it is used as an input by a number of other business analysis tasks summarized in Table 2.15. The requirements management plan provides information to tasks from several knowledge areas that focus on eliciting, analyzing, and communicating project requirements.

TABLE 2.15 Output: Plan Requirements Management Process

Output	Output Destinations	Destination Knowledge Area
Requirements management plan	Conduct elicitation activity	Elicitation
	Manage solution scope and requirements	Requirements Management and Communication
	Manage business analysis performance	Business Analysis Planning and Monitoring
	Manage requirements traceability	Requirements Management and Communication
	Prioritize requirements	Requirements Analysis

The business analyst has the primary responsibility for creating or tailoring the requirements management plan for their project. The project manager also participates in this effort as they have responsibility for managing changes to the project scope and are accountable for delivering the resulting solution. Ideally, the change management approach for the project should also govern any requirements changes.

Several business analysis stakeholders are impacted by the contents of the requirements management plan. They include:

- Domain SMEs
- End users
- Operational support
- Testers
- The sponsor
- Implementation SMEs

Manage Business Analysis Performance

There is no reason to do business analysis planning if the team isn't going to use those plans to measure and control performance. The primary reason for building the business analysis plan is to monitor and report on the business analysis work that is being done. This occurs at two levels: for the overall project and for each project phase. Monitoring and measuring business analysis performance against the business analysis plans ensures that the project's business analysis effort produces the desired outcomes and that the business analysis work is performed efficiently.

Monitoring consists of continuous data collection to ultimately determine if the solution you have delivered is working as it should. Evaluation assesses a deployed solution to make sure it meets its operational objectives over time and looks for ways to improve that solution.

The business analysis team is responsible for determining the *metrics* used to measure business analysis work on the project. *Indicators* are specific numerical measurements that represent a measure for a specific set of business analysis activities or deliverables.

 Real World Scenario

Implementing the Two-Faced Project

Remember the two-faced project we looked at as part of the earlier discussions on plan-driven versus change-driven project approaches? Well, you are a team lead on this online payment-processing system project. The system itself has been defined, designed, and developed. Your job is managing one or more of the change-driven "on-boarding" of new customer implementations. One goal is to complete a successful customer implementation of this system in less than 30 days. A large part of this work is jointly defining customer requirements and working together with the customers to get the payment link on their websites up and running with the customer's look and feel.

Ginger calls you into a meeting to review the current status of your first implementation effort. Not only are you expected to complete the work in less than 30 days, there is also a budget indicator attached to these efforts. Your planned budget for your "on-boarding" effort is $20,000 across the planned 30 days of work. Currently, you are one week into the effort and have spent $9,000 of this planned budget. This budget measurement one week into your efforts is a metric, and it will be compared to the indicator and analyzed to see if all is well at this point in time.

Ginger asks about this status and why almost half of your budget has been spent when you are only a quarter of a way through this project. Lucky for you, this is not a negative thing. You and your team have been defining the customer requirements for the interface and expected to front-load the schedule and budget to get the definition as accurate as possible. Of course, that leaves you $11,000 for the next three weeks of work, so you will watch it closely to make sure both the work and the spending stay on track.

Monitoring and controlling the progress and performance of business analysis work is not simply an objective task. You don't just look at a metric at a point in time and say that things are good or bad. Many additional factors can come into play. Business analysts almost always do some sort of analysis when looking at the current state of things and what is in the business analysis plan. This is how you determine if a particular situation is acceptable at a point in time, or if there are issues to be addressed.

The business analyst must also focus on managing and updating the business analysis-related Organizational Process Assets (OPAs). These are commonly known as the Business Analysis (BA) Process Assets, a subset of the OPAs. Figure 2.7 summarizes the task.

FIGURE 2.7   Task summary: Manage business analysis performance.

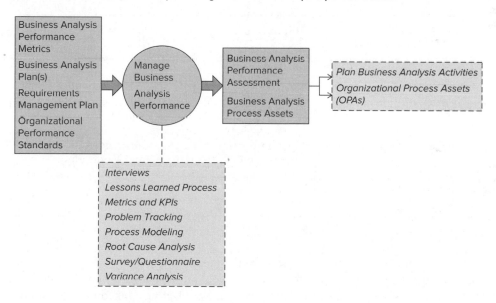

Several key inputs are used in managing business analysis performance for a project. Interestingly enough, many of these inputs are either metrics standards or expectations for performing business analysis work on a project. The task inputs used when managing business analysis performance on a project include:

Business Analysis Performance Metrics   Metrics are collected and analyzed for the business analysis activities on the project. They should be collected and analyzed by the lead business analyst or by the project manager. These metrics become the basis for taking corrective or preventive actions downstream.

Business Analysis Plan or Plans Business analysis performance is traditionally measured in the same way you look at project performance. The business analysis plans are used to measure actual progress against the planned deliverables, activities, tasks, and estimates.

Requirements Management Plan Business analysts should always take a look at the requirements management plan to see if it sets expectations for requirements-related activities, particularly those dealing with managing changing requirements.

Organizational Performance Standards Many organizations have mandated performance standards or expectations for business analysis work. If this is the case, the business analysis team must factor these into the business analysis performance metrics for their project.

Table 2.16 summarizes the inputs to this task and lists the source of the input (if applicable).

TABLE 2.16 Inputs: Manage Business Analysis Performance

Task Input	Input Source	Source Knowledge Area
Business analysis performance metrics	—	—
Business analysis plan or plans	Plan business analysis activities	Business Analysis Planning and Monitoring
Requirements management plan	Plan requirements management process	Business Analysis Planning and Monitoring
Organizational performance standards	—	—

Metrics can be tricky. A metric is a standard of measurement defined for some aspect of business analysis performance. Metrics define a quantifiable level for an indicator that the business analysis team wants to accomplish, such as meeting a schedule date for an activity or staying on budget for a particular phase of project work. Indicators identify specific numeric measurements indicating progress toward achieving something, such as scheduled work estimated to complete an activity or a particular budget number.

If the business analysis team does not select and define relevant metrics, it will be difficult to measure and assess how well business analysis work is done during the project. Effectively managing business analysis performance requires the business analysis team to address three detailed elements:

- Define performance measures.
- Decide on performance reporting.
- Take corrective and preventive actions.

Let's take a closer look at each of these elements.

Define Performance Measures

Business analysts don't always find it easy to define what it is that effective business analysis work consists. It is necessary to determine the appropriate performance measures for effective business analysis work on a specific project. There are the traditional measures such as meeting schedule dates for activities and deliverables that can be applied. There are also more requirements-focused metrics, such as the frequency of requirements changes or the number of review cycles needed. Be sure to consult with the project manager for any required performance metrics that need to apply for business analysis work and deliverables.

Decide on Performance Reporting

The business analysis team must also decide on the methods to be used for reporting tracking and archiving business analysis performance data. These reports can range from formal, written documents and presentations to informal conversations by the water cooler. If the reports are to be archived, then they must be written down. Again many of these requirements may be set at the project level by the project manager, so keep the lines of communication open with that individual on your projects.

Take Corrective and Preventive Actions

After business analysts have the business analysis performance measures in hand for a particular period of time, they can assess those measures and determine if any problems or improvement opportunities exist. Experienced business analysts know they must engage key stakeholders to assist the business analysis team in identifying any *corrective actions* or *preventive actions* that might be required.

Recommended Technique: Variance Analysis

Applying *variance analysis* to compare actual versus planned is a task-specific technique in the *BABOK® Guide*. This technique allows the business analyst to look at the differences between planned and actual performance of business analysis work. Variance analysis is frequently used by project managers to determine the magnitude of discrepancies for work that has been done compared to what has actually taken place during a particular time period.

Variance can be measured for a number of project variables, including the estimated work, costs, or scope of the project. Any variables that need to be measured need to be defined during the planning process in order to measure and track performance against them. Once variances are detected, it is important to understand what caused them and to decide if any corrective or preventive actions are needed to get things back on track.

Exam Spotlight

Corrective and preventive actions are not the same thing. Corrective actions are steps taken to remove the causes of existing nonconformities or errors after they occur. Preventive actions try to stop events from happening in the first place.

Recommended Technique: Metrics and Key Performance Indicators

According to the *BABOK® Guide*, defining and using metrics and *Key Performance Indicators* (KPIs) is one of the 16 required techniques in the fundamental knowledge base of an effective business analyst. Metrics and KPIs are the basis for the monitoring, evaluation, and reporting system that addresses business analysis work, the overall project, and the resulting solution. KPIs are indicators that allow the business analyst or business analysis team to measure performance or progress of solutions and solution components toward strategic goals or objectives. Metrics facilitate the more basic monitoring and evaluation of business analysis work activities and deliverables in your quest to meet the overall solution goals.

Metrics and KPIs are essential for the ongoing *monitoring* and *evaluation* of business analysis activities on any project. Effective monitoring, evaluation, and reporting must address several elements: indicators, metrics, structure, and reporting. In order to measure a particular aspect of a project or solution, you must have at least one indicator. The business analyst needs to know the source of each defined indicator, how to collect the measurement, the person or system doing the collecting, and how often it will be done. Good indicators meet five quality characteristics: they are clear, relevant, economical, adequate, and quantifiable. If indicators can't be quantified and measured when we need them, they are not of much use.

Exam Spotlight

Metrics can be a specific point, a threshold, or a range of values based on what is being measured. They allow the business analysis team or the project manager to track, assess, and report on the quality of business analysis work that is being done.

Other Techniques to Consider

Managing and controlling the business analysis work on your projects must be planned for and monitored consistently throughout the project life cycle. These techniques should help you build a thorough and consistent approach to managing the business analysis work on your projects.

Interviews   Another source of business analysis performance data is to interview key business analysis stakeholders and ask them for their assessment of the business analysis work on the project.

Lessons Learned Process   A lesson learned process allows the business analyst to compile and document successes, failures, and recommendations for improving performance of business analysis activities on future projects. A process focused primarily on a project's business analysis work performance could easily be rolled up into the overall project-level lessons learned process. Lessons learned can be recorded and discussed for each project phase as well as at the end of the project.

Problem Tracking   Issues may be opened for the project that relates to business analysis activities. These issues should be addressed and resolved by the business analysis team.

Process Modeling   Business analysis processes can be modeled and improved using this technique. The business analysis team may find it very helpful to graphically depict the flow of business analysis work in order to improve performance.

Root Cause Analysis   Asking "why?" can help the business analysis team identify the actual cause of problems encountered when performing business analysis work.

Survey/Questionnaire   If you can't speak directly with your key stakeholders, consider sending them a survey or questionnaire to ask them for their assessment of the business analysis work on the project.

Experienced business analysts apply one or more of these business analysis techniques to manage, monitor, and control the performance of a project's business analysis work. On many projects, the project manager steps into this role, looking at business analysis work as a subset of their overall project. At other times, the lead business analyst watches what is going on, decides if all is well, and takes action when needed. Regardless of who is monitoring the business analysis work, the business analysis performance assessment should be created and used by the project team. Let's have a closer look at this key business analysis deliverable.

Produce the Business Analysis Performance Assessment

The business analysis performance assessment helps the business analysis team understand the level of effort to perform business analysis work for a project. It compares the planned versus actual performance of business analysis work activities. If there are significant variances from the plan, this assessment should also address the root cause of these variances.

The business analysis performance assessment provides ongoing performance information to assist the team in planning future project work based on what has happened to date.

Create and Update Business Analysis Process Assets

As a result of assessing business analysis performance, the business analysis team may need to revise the business analysis processes, results, and templates that are being used. The revisions could be adding in new approaches that increase efficiency, or they could be correcting things that are not working well. In either case, these results should be treated as lessons learned and incorporated into the process assets of the organization.

Once the business analysis performance assessment is complete, it is used as an input by a number of other business analysis tasks summarized in Table 2.17.

TABLE 2.17   Outputs: Manage Business Analysis Performance

Outputs	Output Destinations	Destination Knowledge Area
Business analysis performance assessment	Plan business analysis activities	Business Analysis Planning and Monitoring
Business analysis process assets	Organizational Process Assets (OPAs)	—

The business analyst has the primary responsibility for creating the business analysis performance assessment for their project and updating the BA process assets. The project manager also participates in these efforts as they have responsibility for monitoring performance and updating process assets for the project. Ideally, the monitoring, evaluation, and reporting approach for business analysis work should align with the project approach to handling this data.

Several business analysis stakeholders are interested in the contents of the business analysis performance assessment and the business analysis process assets. They include domain SMEs, end users, operational support, testers, the sponsor, and implementation SMEs.

How This Applies to Your Projects

In this chapter, you stepped through planning a serious set of business analysis activities for a project or a project phase. Performing business analysis work is much more straightforward if the team takes the time to plan what they are going to do before they start doing it. Working on projects where the value of business analysis work is discounted can result in little to no planning for the business analysis activities and deliverables for the project. You will have to scramble and rely on your business analysis experience to get the work done if you are not prepared for everything that is needed. This is not the way to do good work. Planning business analysis activities is an important piece of the overall project planning and it should be done for every business analysis effort.

The Shewhart "plan–do–check–act" cycle (Figure 2.8) is a four-step model that forms the basis for all of the tasks and elements found in the *BABOK® Guide*. The concept that "we plan prior to doing the work and measure what has been done" applies throughout the activities in the Business Analysis Planning and Monitoring knowledge area. The business analysis team plans project or project phase activities, deliverables, and approaches prior to actually doing the work. After the work is done, the business analysis team looks at the results to see what was learned and how well the work was performed. Anything that requires improvement is addressed prior to the next round. Things that worked well are repeated and used in subsequent efforts.

FIGURE 2.8 The Shewhart cycle

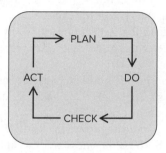

A core set of business analysis planning and documentation should be required for all projects regardless of project size or type. For complex projects, business analysts may choose to use the full set of *BABOK® Guide* deliverables across the six knowledge areas plus any project or technical documents that are required. In some cases, the business analysis deliverables may be combined and simplified for change-driven or straightforward project efforts. Business analysis documents should always be consolidated where feasible.

Some documents might not be required if the information is entered directly into other project documentation. If you choose to use other documents to record business analysis specific data, make a note of this new information location in your business analysis communication plan. When work is being performed at a client site, additional business analysis documentation is often required for a particular project by either the Project Management Office (PMO), project governance, corporate quality management, or the technical management disciplines. This additional documentation is worth discovering early on so you plan your approach and process for producing it.

Another area that requires business analyst's attention is the process for endorsing and approving business analysis documents. We recommend allowing endorsement of business analysis documents for storage in the project document repository one of the following two ways (as long as you are not in a regulated environment):

On Paper   Sign a paper rendition of the document, scan the signature page, and send the scanned image along with the electronic copy of the document to the PMO.

Electronic Sign Off   Ask the signatory to send an email stating that the document has been reviewed and/or accepted, enter the words "email signature" in the signature block of the document, and send a copy of the email along with the electronic copy of the document to the PMO.

Summary

The six tasks of the Business Analysis Planning and Monitoring knowledge area do a nice job of producing a core set of planning and process-focused deliverables that can be referenced and applied across the project life cycle. The focus of these plans is twofold: the overall project and its more detailed project phases. Many planning techniques focused on defining and scheduling activities and deliverables come straight from the project management playbook.

The *BABOK® Guide* recommends business analysts begin their planning efforts by building their business analysis approach. This basically defines the business analysis methodology to be used across the project life cycle. Concurrently, the business analysis team also identifies, analyzes, and categorizes the business analysis stakeholders with which they will be working. Both the business analysis approach and the stakeholder list, roles, and responsibilities are communicated, aligned, and shared with the project manager who is responsible for overall project success.

The business analysis deliverables and activities also need to be planned. Business analysts put on their project management hats for a while and plan this work using a common set of tools and techniques. The *BABOK® Guide* recommends decomposing the scope of work to be done in a Work Breakdown Structure, building an activity list, and linking the business analysis work activities in a logical sequence in order to get them done. Work and costs are then estimated resources are assigned and optimized, and the business analysis team iterates until they have a plan that is good to go. The resulting business analysis plan or plans should easily integrate with the project plans that contain their specific slice of business analysis work.

One of the primary roles of the business analyst is developing and managing requirements across the project life cycle. The business analysis team has to decide on the process they will follow to perform that work, and they document it in the requirements management plan. Business analysis-related communications activities are also defined and planned as part of this knowledge area.

Once these key planning deliverables are in place, they are revisited and revised as necessary. The business analyst should look at them whenever they are planning a new project phase, replanning a phase that needs attention, or dealing with significant changes or issues that impact solution scope or project requirements. The plans and approaches are used as the basis for the ongoing and iterative monitoring, evaluating, and reporting on the performance of business analysis work in the business analysis performance assessment. This allows the business analysis team to see how things are going and take corrective or preventive actions as needed along the way.

Exam Essentials

Be able to list the tasks found in the Business Analysis Planning and Monitoring knowledge area. You will see questions about the tasks, their associated techniques, their more detailed elements, and the key outputs that they produce on your exam. You should memorize the six tasks of this knowledge area and any key outputs or techniques associated with them. The tasks are

Plan the business analysis approach.

Conduct stakeholder analysis.

Plan business analysis activities.

Plan business analysis communication.

Plan the requirements management process.

Manage business analysis performance.

Be able to state the purpose of key deliverables. The good news is that the key deliverables produced by the tasks in this knowledge area are easy to remember because they align nicely with the task names. Here's the list:

Business analysis approach

Stakeholder list, roles, and responsibilities

Business analysis plan or plans

Business analysis communication plan

Requirements management plan

Business analysis performance assessment

Business analysis process assets

Be able to distinguish between plan-driven and change-driven approaches. Plan-driven approaches focus on ensuring that the solution is fully defined before its implementation begins. Change-driven approaches are indicative of a more agile and iterative effort to define and implement the resulting solution.

Be able to define metrics, indicators, and Key Performance Indicators (KPIs). A metric is a standard of measurement that is defined relative to business analysis performance defining a quantifiable level of an indicator that the business analysis team wants to accomplish. Indicators identify specific numeric measurements indicating progress toward achieving something, such as an activity or deliverable. KPIs are indicators that allow the business analyst or business analysis team to measure performance or progress of solutions and solution components toward strategic goals or objectives.

Be able to explain the knowledge area-specific techniques used to analyze business analysis stakeholders. Conducting stakeholder analysis uses many knowledge area specific and general business analysis techniques. The knowledge area–specific techniques are a RACI matrix and stakeholder maps.

Key Terms

This chapter stepped through the contents of the first knowledge area from the *BABOK® Guide*: Business Analysis Planning and Monitoring. Most of this knowledge area focuses on planning for the business analysis deliverables, approaches, activities, and processes that the business analysis team will use throughout the project life cycle.

You should understand how to apply the techniques and tasks in this knowledge area in order to be an effective business analyst. Additionally, you will need to know the six tasks and their associated elements and techniques from this knowledge area in order to be successful on the CBAP® or CCBA™ exams. The tasks include:

Plan business analysis approach.	Plan business analysis communication.
Conduct stakeholder analysis.	Plan requirements management process.
Plan business analysis activities.	Manage business analysis performance.

A number of new key words in Chapter 2 relate to planning and monitoring the business analysis work on a project. Here is a list of some of the key terms that you encountered in this chapter:

activity list	milestones
assumptions	monitoring
business analysis approach	onion diagram
business analysis communication plan	plan-driven approaches
business analysis plan	preventive actions
business case	records
change-driven approaches	reports
corrective actions	requirements management plan
dependencies	rolling wave planning
evaluation	solution scope
expected monetary value indicator	stakeholder list, roles, and responsibilities
Key Performance Indicators (KPI)	stakeholder matrix
metrics	variance analysis
	Work Breakdown Structure

Review Questions

1. You are a business analyst addressing who will receive weekly business analysis status reports for your current project. You are performing tasks from which knowledge area?

   A. Requirements Analysis

   B. Business Analysis Planning and Monitoring

   C. Requirements Management and Communication

   D. Solution Assessment and Validation

2. You are a business analyst working on a project where the timing of the business analysis work is early in the project life cycle. What type of business analysis approach best fits this project?

   A. Plan-driven

   B. Task-driven

   C. Change-driven

   D. Phase-driven

3. What technique might be used when determining the business analysis approach on a project?

   A. Decision analysis

   B. Expert judgment

   C. Stakeholder map

   D. Scope modeling

4. Who is responsible for ensuring that the business analysis plan is compatible with the project plan?

   A. Business analyst

   B. Project manager

   C. Implementation SME

   D. Project sponsor

5. What key input is used to plan the business analysis approach for a project?

   A. Business need

   B. Business case

   C. Business goals

   D. Strategic plan

6. A RACI matrix describes the roles of stakeholders involved in business analysis activities. RACI stands for:

   A. Responsible, Accessible, Contacted, Informed

   B. Responsible, Accountable, Consulted, Involved

   C. Responsible, Accountable, Consulted, Informed

   D. Responsible, Accountable, Coordinated, Involved

7. What technique is recommended for analyzing discrepancies between planned and actual business analysis performance?

   A. Root cause analysis

   B. Business analysis

   C. Variance analysis

   D. Earned value analysis

8. Which statement about conducting stakeholder analysis for the business analysis activities on a project is FALSE?

   A. Done as long as business analysis work continues

   B. Conducted during the project phase to which it applies

   C. Performed as soon as the business need is identified

   D. Determines stakeholder influence and levels of authority

9. All of the following tasks are performed when planning and monitoring business analysis activities except:

   A. Plan business analysis activities.

   B. Conduct stakeholder analysis.

   C. Plan business analysis approach.

   D. Determine solution approach.

10. Which business analysis stakeholder role is involved with all business analysis activities on a project?

    A. Domain SME

    B. Implementation SME

    C. Business analyst

    D. Project manager

11. When planning for business analysis activities, what two planning tools are commonly used?

    A. Milestones and activities

    B. Schedule and activity list

    C. Resources and estimates

    D. Activity list and a WBS

12. The business analyst has defined how, when, and why the business analysis team will work directly with project stakeholders to develop requirements. What deliverable contains this information?

   A. Requirements management plan

   B. Business analysis communication plan

   C. Requirements development plan

   D. Business analysis approach

13. What type of models can be used to define and document the business analysis approach?

   A. Data

   B. Process

   C. Usage

   D. Object

14. What measures will the business analyst define for the business analysis activities and deliverables on a project?

   A. Variables

   B. Metrics

   C. Measures

   D. Forecasts

15. What business analysis artifact is an implied input to tasks in all other knowledge areas after Business Analysis Planning and Monitoring activities are completed?

   A. Business analysis approach

   B. Business goals and objectives

   C. Business analysis plan

   D. Business analysis process assets

16. When planning business analysis activities, the business analyst may break down the project tasks and then estimate the amount of work each task will require. What technique are they using?

   A. Decision analysis

   B. Functional decomposition

   C. Process modeling

   D. Risk analysis

17. The business analyst team creates a high-level plan for the long term project and detailed plans addressing near-term activities. What approach to planning are they taking?

   A. Roadmap

   B. Parametric

   C. Progressive

   D. Rolling wave

18. What knowledge area allows the business analyst to define their approach for tracing project requirements?

    A. Requirements Analysis

    B. Business Analysis Planning and Monitoring

    C. Enterprise Analysis

    D. Requirements Management and Communication

19. You are a business analyst setting expectations for project requirements meetings, work activities, and walkthroughs with your stakeholders. On which elements of communication are you focusing?

    A. Project type, formality, frequency, expectations, and criteria

    B. Deliverables, stakeholders, project type, culture, and metrics

    C. Geography, culture, project type, formality, and frequency

    D. Metrics, criteria, estimates, project type, and stakeholders

20. When planning how the requirements management process will address requests for change, the business analyst should consider the cost and time estimates of the requested change, its associated benefits and risks, and the:

    A. Wording of the change request

    B. Assumptions and constraints

    C. Recommended course of action

    D. Prioritization of the change

Answers to Review Questions

1. B. The Business Analysis Planning and Monitoring knowledge area contains tasks for planning and monitoring of business analysis activities throughout the project.

2. A. Plan-driven business analysis approaches are used when most of the business analysis work occurs at the beginning of the project or during one single project phase.

3. A. The three techniques used when determining the business analysis approach are decision analysis, process modeling, and structured walkthroughs.

4. B. The project manager is responsible for ensuring that the business analysis plan is compatible with the project plan.

5. A. The business need is the key input used when planning the business analysis approach for a project. The business need defines the problem or opportunity faced by the organization. Organizational Process Assets and expert judgment are the other inputs to this task.

6. C. The acronym RACI stands for Responsible, Accountable, Consulted, and Informed. This is a technique used when conducting stakeholder analysis.

7. C. Variance analysis is used to analyze discrepancies between planned and actual performance, determine the magnitude of those discrepancies, and recommend corrective or preventive actions as required.

8. B. Stakeholder analysis is performed as soon as a business need is identified and is an ongoing activity as long as business analysis work is being done on a project. It is typically conducted prior to (not during) the project phase it applies to because the business analysis team needs to know the key stakeholders in order to plan effectively for that phase.

9. D. The tasks in the Business Analysis Planning and Monitoring knowledge area are planning the business analysis approach, conducting stakeholder analysis, planning business analysis activities, planning business analysis communication, planning the requirements management process, and managing business analysis performance.

10. C. The business analyst is a key stakeholder for all business analysis tasks on a project.

11. D. An activity list and a Work Breakdown Structure (WBS) are the planning tools recommended as part of business analysis planning.

12. B. The Business Analysis Communication plan describes how, when, and why the business analyst will work directly with stakeholders relative to any business analysis task.

13. B. Process models built using the process modeling technique can be used to define and document the business analysis approach.

14. B. A metric is a quantitative measure of a process or product describing what is to be measured.

15. C. The business analysis plan or plans are implicit inputs to all tasks in all other knowledge areas. These plans determine when and how all business analysis tasks are performed.

16. B. The functional decomposition technique is used when planning business analysis activities to decompose the products of your project (a solution breakdown structure) or to decompose project tasks (a work breakdown structure).

17. D. Rolling wave planning is when activities are planned for a larger, longer-term initiative by creating a high-level plan for the long term and detailed plans addressing near-term activities. The long-term plan will change as more information becomes available over time.

18. B. The Requirements Management plan that is built as part of the Business Analysis Planning and Monitoring knowledge area defines the project's approach to traceability.

19. C. The five elements of the *Plan business analysis communication* task are geography, culture, project type, formality, and frequency.

20. C. The requirements management process defines the components of a request for change, including the cost and time estimates of the requested change, its associated benefits and risks, and the recommended course of action for the change.

Chapter

3

Controlled Start: Enterprise Analysis

CBAP®/CCBA™ EXAM TOPICS COVERED IN THIS CHAPTER

- ✓ Describe and understand the business need.
- ✓ Assess capability gaps in the organization.
- ✓ Determine the most feasible business solution approach.
- ✓ Define the resulting solution scope.
- ✓ Build a business case for the proposed solution.

In order to achieve a controlled start to a project or project phase, you must be methodical and consistent in its planning and definition. The Enterprise Analysis knowledge area focuses on definition. One essential skill that the business analyst brings to the big picture work is knowledge of the internal and external business environment surrounding the project. This is where experienced business analysts begin to translate an organization's business strategy into a proposed new business solution.

Enterprise Analysis

Now it is time to add some very important context to the business analysis planning tasks discussed in Chapter 2, "Controlled Start: Business Analysis Planning and Monitoring." Planning and managing to a plan isn't going to do the team much good if you don't know what you are supposed to be doing. A controlled project start requires a plan, but it also requires a defined target.

In order to define, design, and deliver a solution that addresses a business need, the team needs to define and agree on the big picture of what needs to be done. This high-level definition of the business requirements for a project is the essential first step in producing a successful project outcome. The *BABOK® Guide* addresses defining the project's big picture in the Enterprise Analysis knowledge area.

The Enterprise Analysis knowledge area focuses on defining and documenting the business requirements for a project. The business requirements justify why a particular project should be initiated to address a particular business need. Business requirements provide much-needed context for detailed requirements activities that take place. The business analyst takes a close look at the organization's current capabilities relative to a business need, problem, or opportunity. They then define a feasible solution scope and approach for addressing that situation.

The tasks in this business-focused knowledge area generate several key business analysis deliverables. These significant deliverables are the four building blocks of the project's business requirements. They include the:

Business need

Required capabilities

Solution scope

Business case

We will cover each item in more detail in this chapter.

The Enterprise Analysis knowledge area is addressed in Chapter 5 of the *BABOK® Guide*. The knowledge areas in this book are sequenced within the framework of a simple life cycle—controlled start, controlled middle, and controlled end. The Enterprise Analysis knowledge area is addressed early in this book because big-picture tasks and business-requirements-focused deliverables of Enterprise Analysis are key components of the controlled start to most projects.

Some folks view business analysis as a strategic discipline where business analysts define marketing strategies, build pricing models, and assess the financial position of a company. This strategic view of business analysis is often held by people who do not have an information technology background. This differs from the more traditional take on business analysis similar to the set of knowledge, tasks, and skills we are talking about in this book. A Master's in Business Administration (MBA) degree is typically a prerequisite for the strategic view of the business analyst role.

The *BABOK® Guide*'s more traditional view of business analysis requires the business analyst to have an associates or undergraduate degree in almost any subject. Augmenting this education with a business analysis certificate, some form of training, or the CBAP/CCBA designation is highly recommended. However, there is a strategic element as part of the traditional view of business analysis. We are going to have a look at it right now because these big-picture activities are found in the Enterprise Analysis knowledge area.

The Business Analyst's Task List

The business analyst has five tasks to perform in the Enterprise Analysis knowledge area. We will look at each of these tasks in greater detail later in this chapter. The task list from the *BABOK® Guide* includes:

- Describing and understanding the business need
- Assessing capability gaps in the organization
- Determining the most feasible business solution approach
- Defining the resulting solution scope
- Defining a business case for the proposed solution

Tasks from the Enterprise Analysis knowledge area focus on defining the business requirements and justifying delivery of the solution scope for the project. The business analyst is responsible for developing, defining, and managing the roles and tasks associated with this work. Tasks performed as part of this knowledge area are governed by the business analysis plan or plans. Business analysis performance metrics for the tasks and deliverables are also defined and tracked. We will step through each of these tasks in greater detail later in this chapter.

When Does Enterprise Analysis Take Place?

> The trick to forgetting the big picture is to look at everything close up.
>
> — *Chuck Palahniuk*

The tasks in the Enterprise Analysis knowledge area take place primarily at the beginning of a project. Many of these tasks are done as a part of pre-project activities or the basis of a project's controlled start. The business requirements created for a project are like the frame on a painting: they frame and control the desired solution scope and the work efforts required to build the solution. The business case, solution scope, and required capabilities may require changes, need updates, or be enhanced with additional details as each subsequent phase of the project life cycle is performed.

As previously discussed, the controlled start of a project includes pre-project activities to determine if it is a viable and worthwhile project for the business. At the end of controlled start, the business analysis team should have the solution scope finalized and a compelling business case built and approved by the senior management team.

 Remember that not all business analysis work is done as part of a project. Enterprise Analysis activities may be performed as pre-project work, part of a business initiative, or during a project's initiation or feasibility phase.

Define the Business Need

The first task found in the Enterprise Analysis knowledge area is defining the business need. According to the *BABOK® Guide*, the business need *"defines the problem that the business analyst is trying to find a solution for."* Not every project gets started because an organization is having a problem. Organizations often consider adding new or changing existing capabilities based on new market opportunities, customer feedback, newly available technologies, or to meet changing legal and regulatory requirements.

In order to complete this task, the business analyst must look at the business drivers and issues to determine if a change is really necessary. The business analyst becomes the master investigator, questioning the business need and any assumptions to make sure that the underlying problem or opportunity is being properly addressed.

Defining the business need starts key stakeholders down the path of fully understanding a business problem or opportunity. Organizations need to stay targeted on the business needs versus reacting too quickly to problems, issues, or perceived inefficiencies. The business need sets the stage for what comes next in the early part of a project, including deciding:

- The range of solution options to consider
- The set of stakeholders to involve
- The appropriate solution approaches to evaluate

After the business need is articulated for a project or initiative, it is not expected to change significantly through that project's life cycle. If the business need for a project does change during that project's life cycle, the business analyst will have to go back to validate all of the high-level planning and definition work to make sure everything is still okay.

Exam Spotlight

According to the *BABOK® Guide,* new business needs are typically triggered by four sources:

- To achieve a strategic goal (top down)
- To address a current process function or system (bottom up)
- To make better decisions or meet business objectives (middle management)
- To meet customer demand or market competition (external drivers)

Figure 3.1 summarizes the inputs, outputs, techniques, and associated tasks for defining the business need for a possible project.

FIGURE 3.1 Task summary: Identify business need.

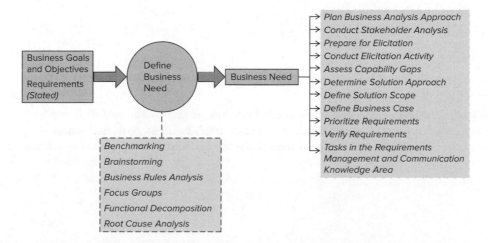

Let's take a look at the task inputs used to assist the business analyst in identifying the business need:

Business Goals and Objectives   Organizations usually have a set of *business goals* and *business objectives* that they are trying to achieve. Some of them are found in the statements of mission, vision, and values outlining what the organization wants to achieve and how they see themselves doing it. Business needs should fit within this more strategic framework of an organization and contribute to the bottom line. When we look at the detailed elements of defining a business need, we will discuss business goals and objectives in greater detail.

Requirements (Stated)   Identifying the business need is the first step in defining a project's business requirements. As part of their identification efforts, business analysts must elicit information from key stakeholders about their high-level needs.

Table 3.1 summarizes the inputs to this task and also lists the particular task that was the source of the input (if applicable).

TABLE 3.1   Inputs: Define Business Need

Task Input	Input Source	Source Knowledge Area
Business goals and objectives	—	—
Requirements (stated)	—	—

Business analysts need to step through three essential elements to identify, analyze, and document a business need triggering a potential project. These detailed elements necessary to identify the business need are

- Aligning to business goals and objectives
- Stating the business problem or opportunity
- Describing the *desired outcome*

Let's step through each of the elements involved in identifying the business need triggering a project.

Align with Business Goals and Objectives   Early in a project or before a project even begins, business analysts are asked to analyze the organization's business goals and objectives as part of defining a particular business need. This strategic information is usually located in the organization's strategic plan, starting with the organization's *mission*, *vision*, and *values*.

Many people mistake the vision statement for the mission statement.

Vision   The vision describes a future identity.

Mission   The mission describes why that future identity will be achieved.

Values   Values provide boundaries for how an organization defines its mission in order to achieve its vision.

Figure 3.2 depicts the levels of detail and the relationships ranging from an organization's vision, mission, and strategic plan to the projects being done in order to achieve those strategic goals.

FIGURE 3.2   Relating strategy and implementation

Business goals are strategic statements describing changes that the organization seeks to establish or current conditions that the organization wants to maintain. A single business goal may be subdivided into one or more *focus areas*, such as customer satisfaction, operational excellence, or business growth.

Business goals must be decomposed into a set of more quantitative business objectives. Business objectives state the predetermined results toward which effort is directed, such as a strategic position to be attained or a purpose to be achieved. Experienced business analysts make sure that their business objectives are SMART (**Specific, Measurable, Achievable, Relevant, and Time-Bound**).

Exam Spotlight

Let's have a closer look at each of these SMART criteria for business objectives. Make sure you are comfortable with these definitions as part of your exam preparation.

Specific   A business objective is specific if it has an observable outcome. This is how the organization ascertains that a particular business objective has actually been met.

Measurable   Quantifiable business objectives have measures that are used to track and measure their observable outcomes. Remember if you can't measure something, you can't prove it is as it should be.

Achievable   Business objectives must also be feasible. This is true relative to its cost, complexity, implementation, and ongoing support.

Relevant   All business goals and objectives must align to the organization's mission, vision, and values. Otherwise, there is no need to pursue them.

Time-Bound   Each business objective should have a defined timeframe for achieving that objective. Business analysts should ensure that the timeframe is also consistent with the business need.

State the Business Problem or Opportunity   The business analyst must investigate the business problem or opportunity to ensure that there is a good reason to move forward and address the problem or opportunity. You are looking for a way to improve the business and add value. The business analyst should consider several factors when performing this work:

- Quantify any adverse impacts.
- Define any increased benefits from the proposed solution.
- Estimate a timeframe for addressing the problem or opportunity.
- Look at the "Do Nothing" option as an alternative approach.
- Identify the underlying cause of the problem.

Describe the Desired Outcome   The business analyst must also describe the desired outcome, which is the business benefits resulting from meeting the business need. Do not confuse the desired outcome with a solution; they are not the same thing. However, solution options will be evaluated relative to the desired outcome to make sure they can deliver the business benefits that are expected.

There are a number of techniques that you may choose to apply when defining the business need for your project. To make sure you consider a range of business needs and desired outcomes before settling on what is driving your potential project, you should use the benchmarking and root cause analysis techniques. Let's take a look at these two techniques in greater detail.

Recommended Technique: Benchmarking

Benchmark studies target using new and different methods, ideas, and tools to improve organizational performance. When conducting such a study, the business analyst compares their organization's strategies, operations, and processes against the best-in-class strategies, operations, and processes of their competitors and peers. After determining how other companies achieve superior performance, the organization can then propose projects to reproduce solutions that work elsewhere.

Recommended Technique: Root Cause Analysis

Business analysts perform *root case analysis* to determine the underlying source of a problem. This structured technique is used to examine a situation in order to establish the root causes and resulting effects of a particular problem. The *BABOK® Guide* recommends two common methods for root cause analysis: the *fishbone diagram* and the *five whys*.

Fishbone Diagram   A fishbone diagram allows the business analyst to show the causes of a problem or an effect. Fishbone diagrams are also called Ishikawa or cause-and-effect diagrams. This diagram allows the business analyst to see all possible causes of a result in a structured way and to make sure that everyone understands the problem or cause that is being addressed.

The business analyst and key stakeholders will brainstorm the categories and the possible causes in each category. Typical categories include things like people, methods, machines, materials, measurements, and environment. After the diagram is built, the business analyst will analyze the results and (hopefully) determine the actual cause of what is taking place.

This fishbone example looks at the possible causes for a specific effect: decreased wine sales revenue. The possible causes are diagrammed and broken down across four areas: people and skills, systems, distributors, and surroundings. A fishbone diagram, like the one shown in Figure 3.3, offers the team the opportunity to analyze and discuss what they think is leading to this decrease in revenue.

FIGURE 3.3   A fishbone diagram offers the opportunity to analyze and discuss.

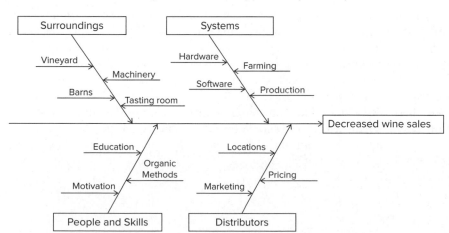

Increased Wine Sales Five Whys   The five whys is a questioning technique that asks, "Why?" repeatedly in order to get to the root cause of a problem. This technique can be used alone or used with the fishbone diagram technique. This is a very simple and effective facilitation tool. Many business analysts customize their use of this tool by asking, "How?" instead of "Why?" or by alternating between the two terms. Often the root cause is identified before the five questions are asked.

Be careful when you use this technique. We were in a meeting once where the facilitator really annoyed the senior user by repeatedly asking, "Why?" in order to determine if automating an existing process would improve customer service. The senior user ended up throwing a powdered sugar doughnut at the facilitator, making a big white spot right on the front of the facilitator's black suit jacket.

Additional Techniques to Consider

The *BABOK® Guide* lists some additional techniques that may be used when defining the business need for your project. They are summarized for you here.

Brainstorming   This technique is frequently used by the business analyst to generate insights and options during root cause analysis. Brainstorming complements root cause analysis efforts, allowing the group to consider a full set of possibilities.

Business Rules Analysis   Business rules analysis allows the business analyst to identify any changes in organizational policies targeting business goals and objectives. This is important because the business need and business goals and objectives are closely linked.

Focus Groups   This group technique allows the business analyst to bring together a selected group of key stakeholders to identify and discuss problems and opportunities as part of identifying the business need for a proposed project.

Functional Decomposition   Functional decomposition allows the business analyst to break down the business goals into the more detailed and measurable business objectives.

Document the Business Need

The business need describes the problem or opportunity that an organization is facing. This problem or opportunity exists within the framework of that organization's business goals and objectives. The business need and the desired outcome from addressing that need guide the identification, definition, and selection of possible solutions and solution approaches for that situation. The business need is the first building block that you need to define the business requirements for your project.

The business need is not typically a standalone deliverable or document. It is a very high-level business requirement and should be included in the business requirements document or business case for a project. You can think of it as an overarching business objective that drives the start of your project. Table 3.2 summarizes the output from the Define Business Need task.

TABLE 3.2   Output: Define Business Need

Task Output	Output Destinations	Source Knowledge Area
Business need	Plan business analysis approach	Business Analysis Planning and Monitoring
	Conduct stakeholder analysis	Business Analysis Planning and Monitoring
	Prepare for elicitation	Elicitation
	Conduct elicitation activity	Elicitation
	Assess capability gaps	Enterprise Analysis
	Determine solution approach	Enterprise Analysis
	Define solution scope	Enterprise Analysis
	Define business case	Enterprise Analysis
	Prioritize requirements	Requirements Analysis
	Verify requirements	Requirements Analysis

 Real World Scenario

Case Study: Palmer Divide Vineyards—Business Goals, Objectives, and Need

As you become more involved with your Palmer Divide Vineyards work, you decide that you need to take a quick look at the organization's business goals, objectives, and needs. As discussed in a recent team meeting, you would like to make sure you have it right. The team is curious about how the green initiative and your IT requirements development part of it fit into the organization's strategic plan. The team likes the idea of becoming a certified Green Business. However, they would like to validate how this business goal fits with the organization's long-term strategy and make sure that the project is really worth doing.

There are many aspects to attaining green certification, and the winery has initiated this current project to help achieve this strategic goal. A business objective for this effort is to conserve 20 percent of the current energy and water resource consumption within the next 18 months. The business need triggering the project came from combining the owner's strategic plans, a desire to operate an organic winery, and a perceived market advantage from selling green-labeled organic wines to the public.

Once the business need is identified, understood, and documented, it is used as an input by many other business analysis tasks. They include conducting stakeholder analysis, eliciting information, and analyzing project requirements at many levels of detail. Additionally, the remaining four Enterprise Analysis tasks require the business need as a key input for performing their "big picture" activities and completing the business requirements definition for a project.

A number of stakeholders are involved with identifying and analyzing business needs within an organization. Typically, the business analyst is responsible for identifying and investigating the need. It is a best practice to appoint a sponsor who owns the business need and authorizes the actions to make sure that need is met. Often this is done by the project that was triggered as a result of the business need being identified and addressed.

Domain SMEs and end users can provide the business analyst with an excellent source of existing problems or limitations with systems and processes. Other key stakeholders involved with identifying the business need include:

- Customer
- Implementation SME
- Regulator
- Supplier

The business need and the desired outcome from addressing that need guide the identification, definition, and selection of new capabilities, possible solutions, and solution approaches. Remember that the business need is the first building block that you need to define the business requirements for your project. We will now take a look at the second building block of a project's business requirements. Using the business need and desired outcome, you will define the required capabilities that the organization must have to meet that business need.

Assess Capability Gaps

After the business analyst identifies the business need, the next step is to identify the new capabilities required in order to meet that business need and deliver the desired outcomes or business benefits. You must determine if the organization's existing capabilities can meet the business need or if additional capabilities are necessary. Typically, projects begin when organizations have to add new capabilities to the mix in order to meet a business need. The required capabilities are the second building block that you need to define the business requirements for your project. Figure 3.4 summarizes the inputs, outputs, techniques, and associated tasks for assessing capability gaps relative to the business need within an organization.

FIGURE 3.4   Task summary: Assess capability gaps.

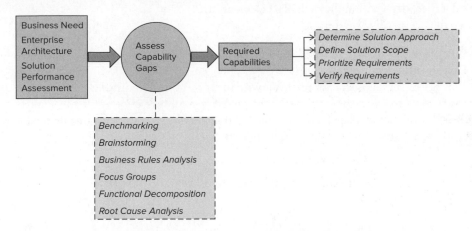

Let's take a look at the task inputs used to assist the business analyst in assessing capability gaps in the organization relative to meeting a business need:

Business Need   The business need is the basis for assessing capability gaps within the organization. The business analyst is focused on what it will take to meet the business need, either using existing capabilities or creating new capabilities.

Enterprise Architecture   The enterprise architecture defines the current capabilities of an organization. It consists of and relates the organization's business processes, software, hardware, people, operations, and current projects. This is the first place you look to gather information about an organization's current capabilities in the areas that are of interest to us.

Solution Performance Assessment   Every existing solution in the organization should have its own solution performance assessment that looks at how it is doing and what it can do. This information may be helpful to you when you need to define and understand the organization's current capabilities relative to meeting a business need.

Table 3.3 summarizes the inputs to this task and also lists the particular task that was the source of the input (if applicable).

TABLE 3.3   Inputs: Assess Capability Gaps

Task Input	Input Source	Source Knowledge Area
Business need	Identify business need	Enterprise Analysis
Enterprise architecture	—	—
Solution performance assessment	Evaluate solution performance	Solution Assessment and Validation

In order to assess existing capabilities relative to desired outcomes, you need to perform three detailed steps within the task. The elements are

- Analyzing current capabilities
- Assessing new capability requirements
- Documenting your assumptions

Capabilities are functions that help the organization achieve its business goals or objectives. Capabilities can be many things:

- Business processes
- Software application features
- End user tasks
- Responses to events
- Products
- Services
- Stakeholder goals

Let's step through each of these elements involved in assessing an organization's existing capabilities relative to a specific business need.

Analyze Current Capabilities   The question you must answer is, "Does the organization have the current business and technology capabilities to meet the business need?" You will look at specific parts of the enterprise architecture that relate to the business need. Hopefully, you will have up-to-date enterprise architecture information. If not, your view of the organization's current capabilities may be incorrect and incomplete. That will require you to spend extra time doing the research to discover what you need to know.

Assess New Capability Requirements   Once you have a handle on the current capabilities, it's time to consider the new capabilities that may be needed to meet the business need. The business analyst is responsible for modeling and describing these new capabilities. One common way to do this is called *gap analysis*: defining what it will take to eliminate or minimize the gap between the current capabilities and the desired future state. Remember, the desired future state equals meeting the business need.

Document Your Assumptions   You will have to make assumptions to define new capabilities. Assumptions are things that are believed to be true regarding meeting the business need. Make sure that you clearly understand any assumptions associated with the new capabilities. Be sure to identify and document each assumption, just in case you discover later on that one or more of them are actually false.

There are a number of techniques that you can use when assessing your organization's current capabilities relative to a new business need. You can almost always use document analysis to help you understand the current state of things. Let's have a look at that technique now.

Recommended Technique: Document Analysis

According to the *BABOK® Guide*, performing document analysis is one of the 16 required techniques in the fundamental knowledge base of an effective business analyst. Document analysis allows the business analyst to elicit, confirm, or cross-check project requirements information by studying existing documentation and other relevant information. These secondary sources of information allow the business analyst to gather details of existing solutions (the "as is" situation) to see if they have components that can be used or should be changed for the new solution that is being proposed (the "to be" situation).

Document analysis assumes that the existing documentation is easily available and up-to-date. If the information is not up-to-date and valid, it will be of little help to the business analyst in eliciting or confirming the requirements. The "existing stuff" is information prepared for another project or purpose but relevant to your requirements development efforts. This type of secondary data can be quite helpful during requirements elicitation.

To conduct document analysis, the business analyst steps through three stages: preparation, the actual document review, and wrap-up. Preparation involves locating and evaluating the relevant system and business documentation. During document review, you study the material, identify the relevant details (technical and business), and document them along with any questions you might have to follow up on with the SMEs. Wrap-up is the "get answers review and confirm" step.

Secondary Information Sources Checklist

We have our own checklist of secondary information sources that we use as a reminder when performing document analysis work or even just basic research about something. This existing stuff may include:

Project and system documentation

Corporate-level documents

Annual reports, strategic plans

Books and other publications

Information out on the company intranet

The company website

Websites of competitors

Organization charts, seating diagrams, phone lists

White papers

Technical standards and guidelines

Informal and casual sources

Internet research

Competitor demos and evaluations

Benchmarking studies

Trade journals

Issue registers

Quality registers

Demographic surveys

User guides

Market research information

Change requests

Problem reports

Help desk reports

Help desk logs

Newsletters

Meeting minutes

Information about related projects

Another Technique to Consider

The *BABOK*® *Guide* provides you with another technique that may be used when assessing capability gaps in the organization relative to a business need.

Strengths, Weaknesses, Opportunities, and Threats (SWOT) analysis lets you look at the organization's current capabilities relative to meeting a new business need. There are two dimensions to this analysis: the internal strengths and weaknesses of the organization and the external opportunities and negative threats that are in play. SWOT analysis is done using a matrix or a grid. Stakeholders brainstorm and complete each quadrant of the grid, and then analyze the resulting data to make sure that the business need and its environment are well understood. Solutions for meeting the business need may then be proposed and considered.

Define the Required Capabilities

The required capabilities define the new capabilities that may be required to meet a business need. These capabilities may be multifaceted, addressing processes, staff, and application features.

Once the required capabilities are identified, understood, and documented, they are used as input by several other business analysis tasks. These tasks are listed in Table 3.4. They have a strong solution focus, and they are integral pieces for defining the solution approach and scope.

TABLE 3.4   Output: Assess Capability Gaps

Task Output	Output Destinations	Source Knowledge Area
Required capabilities	Determine solution approach	Enterprise Analysis
	Define solution scope	Enterprise Analysis
	Prioritize requirements	Requirements Analysis
	Verify requirements	Requirements Analysis

The required capabilities, like the business need, are not usually a standalone deliverable or document. They become part of the project's business requirements and are typically included in a more comprehensive business requirements document or as part of the project's business case.

A number of stakeholders are involved with assessing the capability gaps relative to a particular business need. Business analysts usually drive this work. It is a best practice to appoint a sponsor who owns the business need and authorizes the actions to make sure that need is met. Often this is done by the project that was triggered as a result of the business need being identified and addressed.

Customers and suppliers may be significantly impacted when new capabilities are changed to meet a business need. Sometimes, organizations choose to outsource the new capabilities or to ask customers to provide them for themselves versus undertaking their own project. Other key stakeholders who provide information about the strengths and weaknesses of the current capabilities include:

- Domain SME
- End user
- Implementation SME
- Sponsor

These required capabilities are the second building block of your project's business requirements. Remember, the first building block is the business need. Now you can use these two building blocks to identify, prioritize, and select the solution approach for implementing or obtaining the required capabilities.

🌐 Real World Scenario

Case Study: The Boulder Barn Project

Here is an example of analyzing and documenting current and future capabilities for acquiring property and building a new barn for an equine-assisted learning facility in Colorado.

Overview

Equine-assisted learning is a rapidly growing field. Melisa Pearce, a lifelong horsewoman, psychotherapist, and entrepreneur, focuses on providing experiential horse interaction, coaching, and guidance to a wide variety of private and business clients. Melisa works with clients and horses at her ranch in an integrative approach consisting of ground-based horse interaction combined with positive coaching and guidance.

Melisa's leadership training curriculum is a unique, experiential program where participants work with horse partners. Horses possess their own personalities, behaviors, and attitudes and can therefore provide participants with immediate feedback on their ability to affect actions or change. By creating a partnering relationship with these animals to complete specific tasks, participants learn about compromising, goal setting, overcoming fears, effective communication, in-process adjustments, effective teamwork, and how to act synergistically in order to create mutually beneficial, outcome-based relationships. The significant learning moments are applicable and transferable to both professional and personal life.

Existing Situation and Desired Future State

Five years ago, Melisa and her family moved to her current location in Boulder County, Colorado. She scaled down her property from a 50-acre ranch to 5 acres of property with an existing home. At the new location, Melisa built a covered arena, attached barn, and retail store space to meet her business needs and the needs of her horses and other ranch animals.

While her current location is adequate, Melisa would like to expand. She would like a larger barn with more arena space. Ideally, Melisa would like to sell her current ranch and purchase property in the same general area with approximately 35 acres of land. Most properties of this type would already have an existing home in place. Melisa would then build:

- Office space
- Barn with attached covered arena (35 feet longer and 70 feet wider than the current facility)
- Retail space with an upstairs observation and training room

Since Melisa has designed and built several ranch facilities in the past, this project will apply the plan-driven approach. She is very clear about the elements and materials intended for the new property, and the solution will be fully defined before implementation begins.

Determine Solution Approach

The solution approach describes how you will create or acquire the required capabilities (the solution) in order to meet the business need. This general definition identifies the solution approach and the means of delivering the solution, such as a particular methodology or life cycle model. This information allows you to assess whether or not the organization is capable of implementing that solution. The solution approach can be thought of as the third building block of the project's business requirements. The solution approach accompanies the required capabilities and the business need as you continue to build the necessary business requirements contents (Figure 3.5).

Exam Spotlight

The *BABOK® Guide* recommends a number of practical solution approaches to consider, such as:

- Adding business resources

- Making organizational changes

- Changing business processes

- Partnering or outsourcing

- Using existing software and/or hardware capabilities

- Purchasing or leasing software and/or hardware

- Building your own custom software

Figure 3.5 summarizes the tasks involved in the determine solution approach.

FIGURE 3.5   Task summary: Determine solution approach.

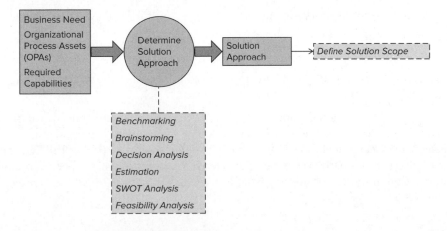

Table 3.5 summarizes the inputs to this task and also lists the particular task that was the source of the input (if applicable). Let's take a look at the task inputs used to determine the solution approach for meeting a business need and deliver the required new capabilities:

TABLE 3.5   Inputs: Determine Solution Approach

Task Input	Input Source	Source Knowledge Area
Business need	Identify business need	Enterprise Analysis
Organizational Process Assets (OPAs)	—	—
Required capabilities	Assess capability gaps	Enterprise Analysis

Business Need   The business need is the basis both for ensuring that the need can be met by the solution approach and for evaluating potential solutions. The business analyst is focused on what it will take to meet the business need by creating or acquiring the required capabilities.

Organizational Process Assets (OPAs)   Organizational Process Assets are an organization's policies, guidelines, procedures, plans, approaches, and standards for conducting work. A subset of these assets may require you to take specific approaches for certain types of solutions.

Required Capabilities   The required capabilities are the new capabilities that the solution must support in order to meet the business need. They bridge the gap between the current situation and the desired future state defined by the business need.

In order to determine the solution approach, you will perform three detailed steps or elements within the task. The elements are

- Identifying alternative solution options
- Generating assumptions and constraints
- Ranking and selecting the solution approach

Let's step through each of these elements involved in assessing the organization's existing capabilities relative to a specific business need.

Identify Alternative Solution Options   The *BABOK® Guide* recommends identifying as many potential solution approach options that deliver the required capabilities and meet the business need as possible. The "Do Nothing" option should be part of this set. It would be wise to also list alternatives that may not meet 100 percent of what is needed but allow the organization more time to address what is needed.

Building a set of solution options falls under the law of diminishing returns. After the first few passes, each iteration of information-gathering results in less new stuff. Be sure to stop your alternatives generation before you discover that the time spent isn't worth the effort.

Generate Assumptions and Constraints   Assumptions and constraints should be recorded for every solution approach option that is being considered. Remember, assumptions are factors that you believe to be true but you have not yet confirmed them to be true. Constraints are boundary conditions or limits that might impact an organization's ability to select certain solution approach options.

Rank and Select the Solution Approach   You should consistently capture the same information for each possible solution approach to have an easier basis of comparison. This facilitates assessing and ranking the solution approaches relative to one another. Once the top-ranking approaches are identified, they can be investigated in greater detail. Don't forget to include the "Do Nothing" option in your choices.

Exam Spotlight

When assessing possible solution approaches, be sure to consider their feasibility in the following areas when they are applicable:

- Operational

- Economic

- Technical

- Schedule-based

- Organizational

- Cultural

- Legal

- Marketing

There are a number of techniques that you may choose to apply when selecting the solution approach for your project. Consider performing a feasibility analysis to ensure that you have the full range of possible solution approaches to consider. Let's take a closer look at how to do a feasibility analysis.

Recommended Technique: Feasibility Analysis

This study-focused technique is used only when conducting stakeholder analysis, and it is defined as part of this specific task in the *BABOK® Guide*. Feasibility analysis activities range from very informal sessions for smaller efforts to formal feasibility studies looking at solution options. In all cases, feasibility analysis focuses on identifying and analyzing potential solution options to determine the most viable solution.

A feasibility study may be produced from your feasibility analysis work. This study presents a preliminary analysis of solution alternatives, evaluating how each option will deliver the desired outcome (business benefits) and meet the business need. It is important to evaluate the technical, economic, and operational feasibility of each solution option including the "Do Nothing" option. Feasibility studies address a business problem to resolve or an opportunity to exploit.

Other Techniques to Consider

The *BABOK® Guide* lists several other techniques that may be used when determining the solution approach for your project. They are summarized for you here.

Benchmarking   Benchmarking studies compare your organization's strategies, operations, and processes against the best-in-class strategies, operations, and processes of their competitors and peers. These studies can help you identify solution approaches that have worked well in other organizations.

Brainstorming   Brainstorming is a very effective way to generate a list of solution approach options to meet a particular business need. The brainstorming approach complements the determining the solution approach by enriching the list of possibilities.

Decision Analysis   This technique allows you to examine and model the consequences of different decisions before actually making or recommending a particular decision. It is possible to use graphical decision trees and financial valuation techniques as part of identifying solution approaches for your specific situation.

Estimation   You can estimate and compare the range of cost and effort associated with each solution approach you are considering. Remember that your estimates should be developed in conjunction with the project manager using the project-level estimating tools and techniques.

SWOT Analysis   SWOT analysis lets you compare possible solution approaches relative to meeting a new business need. As previously discussed, there are two dimensions to this analysis: the internal strengths and weaknesses of the organization and the external opportunities and negative impacts that are in play.

Exam Spotlight

Close your eyes and see how many of the six techniques you can remember for determining the solution approach. The more details you can memorize about each task in each knowledge area, the better. Details include inputs, elements, techniques, and outputs.

Select the Solution Approach

The solution approach describes the approach taken to implement a new set of capabilities and the types of *solution components* that will be delivered. Solution components span the enterprise architecture of the organization and may include things such as new business processes, new software applications, or new hardware. The solution approach should also state the methodology or development life cycle that will be used to deliver the solution components.

Once the solution approach is identified, defined, and selected, it is used as an input to define the solution scope (Table 3.6). This is the only task in the *BABOK® Guide* that uses this deliverable as an input. Selecting the solution approach and defining the solution scope are tightly coupled tasks.

TABLE 3.6 Output: Determine Solution Approach

Task Output	Output Destinations	Source Knowledge Area
Solution approach	Define solution scope	Enterprise Analysis

The business analyst is responsible for getting this work done. The implementation SME is responsible for assessing the feasibility of the possible solution approaches. The sponsor approves the selected solution approach. There are a number of stakeholders that should be involved with solution approach identification activities, including:

- Customers
- Domain SMEs
- End users
- Suppliers

The solution approach needs to be decided upon before you can define what the solution is all about. You can't effectively define the solution scope if you don't know how you plan to go about acquiring or creating the new capabilities to meet the business need. You will use the solution approach, the business need, and the required capabilities as the basis of your solution scope. Let's move on and have a look at this essential Enterprise Analysis task.

Define the Solution Scope

According to the *BABOK® Guide*, the solution scope defines "the set of capabilities a solution must deliver in order to meet the business need." It is derived from the business need, the desired outcome (business benefits), and the required capabilities. The solution scope is impacted by the solution approach that was selected. The solution scope is the third building block of a project's business requirements.

Solution scope focuses on the key business stakeholders of a project. This is where the business analyst defines a recommended solution in enough detail for these stakeholders to understand the new business capabilities the solution will provide. This definition includes all major features, functions, and external interactions of the solution.

Exam Spotlight

Be sure you can distinguish between product, project, and solution scope.

Project Scope   Project scope defines the work needed to deliver a product, service, or result with the specified features and functions.

Product Scope   Product scope describes the features and functions characterizing the product, service, or result.

Solution Scope   Solution scope is the set of capabilities a solution must deliver in order to meet the business need.

Figure 3.6 summarizes the inputs, outputs, techniques, and associated tasks for defining the solution scope.

FIGURE 3.6   Task summary: Define solution scope.

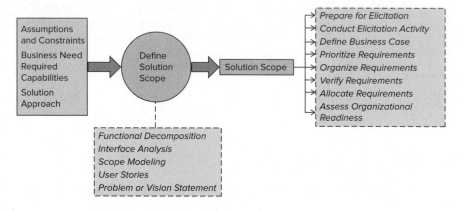

Table 3.7 summarizes the inputs to this task and also lists the particular task that was the source of the input (if applicable). Let's take a look at the task inputs used to assist the business analyst in defining solution scope:

TABLE 3.7   Inputs: Define Solution Scope

Task Input	Input Source	Source Knowledge Area
Assumptions and constraints	Verify requirements	Requirements Analysis
Business need	Identify business need	Enterprise Analysis
Required capabilities	Assess capability gaps	Enterprise Analysis
Solution approach	Determine solution scope	Enterprise Analysis

Assumptions and Constraints   Assumptions and constraints surrounding the solution scope should be identified and documented as part of the business requirements. Assumptions may include things like key stakeholder attitudes or technology availability. Constraints are limits or boundary conditions for the solution, such as schedule or funding limitations or standards to be followed.

Business Need   The business need is driving the solution scope with its definition of the goals, objectives and desired outcomes of the organization.

Required Capabilities   These new, required capabilities are the basis for the solution scope. They will be expanded upon in greater detail and shared with key stakeholders.

Solution Approach   You previously selected the solution approach to deliver the solution capabilities. The selected solution approach impacts the solution scope. It will be used when the business analysts assess options for implementing the more detailed solution components, such as business processes, organizational units, and software applications.

When defining the solution scope, business analysts are expected to address three essential elements when completing the task. The elements are

- Defining the actual solution scope
- Determining the implementation approach
- Capturing solution dependencies

Let's take some time and step through each of these elements involved in thoroughly defining the solution scope for a project:

Define the Solution Scope   Solution scope must describe the major features, functions, and interactions of the proposed solution. You need to be sure to state both the in-scope and out-of-scope solution components across the full enterprise architecture.

Determine the Implementation Approach   The solution scope also contains the implementation approach describing how the chosen solution approach will deliver the solution scope. The implementation approach may involve *release planning* for certain solution components or outsourcing of key processes.

Capture Solution Dependencies   You must capture the internal and external solution scope dependencies, assumptions, and constraints when defining the solution scope. The primary focus is on what it will take to deploy the solution. Remember to look at both business and technical aspects of the solution scope.

There are a number of techniques that you can use to define your project's solution scope. A great way to begin this task is by documenting the problem or vision statement. Let's take a look at this recommended technique in greater detail.

Recommended Technique: Problem or Vision Statement

This scope-focused technique is used only when defining the solution scope. It is defined as part of this specific task in the *BABOK® Guide*. A *problem statement* or *vision statement* describes the positive impact that meeting a business need will have on key project stakeholders. The recommended contents for a problem or vision statement include:

- A description of the problem or vision
- List of affected stakeholders
- Impacts the problem or vision will have on each listed stakeholder
- Key benefits of a successful solution

A problem statement describes a business need that the organization should address in some way. A vision statement defines a desired future state that the organization would like to achieve.

Other Techniques to Consider

The *BABOK® Guide* lists some additional techniques that may be used when defining the solution scope for a project. They are summarized for you here.

Functional Decomposition   Functional decomposition allows you to systematically break down the solution scope components into smaller pieces. This assists you in adding additional details (*work products* or deliverables) as part of the solution scope definition.

Interface Analysis   Interface analysis is a key part of solution scope that focuses on interactions that the solution will have with people and systems outside of its scope. This technique allows you to identify and analyze these external interfaces.

Scope Modeling   Scope modeling assists the business analyst in determining what is in-scope and what is out-of-scope for the solution.

User Stories   User stories describe stakeholders and the goals they have for the proposed solution. This can add additional details to the solution scope.

Building the Solution Scope

The solution scope describes what must be delivered to meet a business need. This includes any effects the solution might have on the business and technology operations and infrastructure of the organization. Solution scope can change throughout the project, based on changes to the business environment or project scope over time.

Once the solution scope is defined and selected, it is used as an input to numerous business analysis tasks (Table 3.8). Solution scope provides the basis for eliciting and analyzing the more detailed solution requirements. Because the solution scope can also include release planning for solution components, it feeds directly into the Solution Assessment and Validation activity, addressing requirements allocation across the solution components.

TABLE 3.8   Output: Define Solution Scope

Task Output	Output Destinations	Source Knowledge Area
Solution scope	Prepare for elicitation	Elicitation
	Conduct elicitation activity	Elicitation
	Define business case	Enterprise Analysis
	Prioritize requirements	Requirements Analysis
	Organize requirements	Requirements Analysis
	Verify requirements	Requirements Analysis
	Allocate requirements	Solution Assessment and Validation
	Assess organizational readiness	Solution Assessment and Validation

The business analyst and project manager are jointly responsible for defining solution scope. The project manager owns the project scope, which is the work necessary to deliver the solution scope. Detailed release planning and component allocation activities must integrate into the project plan that drives getting the solution defined in more detail, designed, and deployed. The implementation SME may also be of assistance in allocating capabilities to solution components. After the task is complete, the sponsor will approve the solution scope.

The solution scope feeds directly into the final Enterprise Analysis deliverable, the business case. This definition of what must be delivered to meet the business need and how its implementation affects the organization are used as input to justify why a solution should be done. So, let's dig into what it takes for us to define a project's business case.

 Real World Scenario

Business Case: Hiking Your Way

Early in her career as a management consultant, Ginger discovered that not all business case development efforts run smoothly. She was sent on an assignment to a major company to help the CIO define the business requirements for a new claims processing system. Her business requirements and business case would be presented to the CEO for approval. Then, a very challenging (and costly) development effort would begin.

What Ginger didn't know was the current state of affairs within the executive management team regarding this proposed solution. She got an idea that things weren't quite right when the business analysis team drew straws for who got to interview the CEO about this proposed new system. Ginger got the short straw and scheduled her interview for later that afternoon.

When she walked into the CEO's office, he was very pleasant. After offering her a cup of tea, he told her to go ahead and ask her questions. His response to the first question about the strategic business priorities of the organization was right on target. However, it was when she asked her second question that things got truly entertaining.

"How will the organization measure the success of this project?"

The CEO told Ginger not to concern herself with the success of the project because it was never going to get off the ground. He then went on to talk about the very limited career that the CIO, who was also the project sponsor, would be having with this company. Before Ginger could make any reply to this outburst, the CEO asked her to leave because the interview was over. When she got up to walk out of his office, he motioned with his hand toward the far corner of the room.

"Go out that way," he said.

So she did. As she put her hand on the door handle, Ginger found herself wondering what was on the other side of the unknown door. Shark tank? Broom closet? Bottomless pit? She opened the door and stepped out into the executive parking lot at the back of the building. Unfortunately, getting back to the front door of the building required a long hike through the cactus and scrub. When Ginger arrived at the front desk, the security guard looked at her and her tattered stockings and smiled sweetly.

"Lucky you," he said. "I see he threw you out of his office. You know, you're the first one today. But I bet you won't be the last."

The guard then presented her with a piece of candy.

Needless to say, the business requirements and the business case were not approved for this particular project. For her next business requirements assignment, Ginger decided to wear trousers on the first day—just in case.

Define Business Case

The final task found in the Enterprise Analysis knowledge area is building the business case. Basically, the business case is used to justify the costs of doing a project in terms of the value the project adds to the business and the associated business benefits. A business case must look at both sides of the equation, comparing both the costs and benefits of a proposed solution. The expected business benefits of the solution should be evaluated relative to achieving business objectives and meeting the business need.

Defining the business case is the business analyst's fourth and final building block in creating the business requirements for the project. Many templates and documents are used for a business case. The template you use for your business case is up to you. Just be sure that the information in your business case is adequate to support a go/no go decision about the project that implements the proposed solution defined in the business requirements.

After the business case is completed and approved for a project, it is time for the detailed requirements development and other project work activities to begin. Many times, the project manager will use the business case as an input for the *project charter*. Figure 3.7 summarizes the inputs, outputs, techniques, and associated tasks for building a business case.

FIGURE 3.7   Task summary: Define business case.

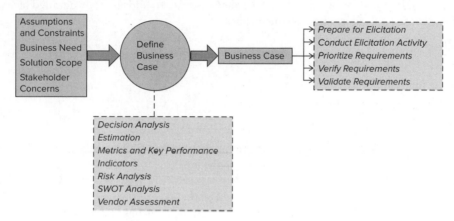

Let's take a look at the task inputs used to help the business analyst build a business case for a project.

Assumptions and Constraints   Assumptions and constraints associated with the costs and benefits of a proposed solution should both be identified and documented in the business case. Many assumptions and constraints will be financial in nature and may be the basis for your revenue or operating cost estimates for the solution.

Business Need   The benefits noted and quantified in the project's business case should still be aligned with the business need that triggered the need for a solution in the first place. The business need is aligned with one or more business goals and objectives.

Solution Scope   The solution scope provides the business case with the new capabilities to be implemented, the methods to deliver those capabilities, and the part of the organization that will be impacted by the new capabilities.

Stakeholder Concerns   The business case isn't just about costs versus benefits. It also addresses any stakeholder concerns about the proposed solution and its impacts on the organization. These concerns may generate risks and issues in the business case that will need to be documented and addressed.

Table 3.9 summarizes the inputs to the Define Business Case task.

TABLE 3.9   Inputs: Define Business Case

Task Input	Input Source	Source Knowledge Area
Business goals and objectives	—	—
Requirements (stated)	—	—

When building a business case, business analysts need to address four detailed elements for the proposed solution. These elements are

- Quantifying the benefits
- Estimating the costs
- Assessing initial risks
- Measuring expected results

Let's step through each of the elements contained in the business case.

Quantify the Benefits   Business benefits are interesting things. This is where the business analyst answers the question, "What's in it for the business if we do this project?" Quantifying the business benefits tells your key stakeholders what implementing a recommended solution will provide to them and to the overall business. This is also where you relate the quantitative and qualitative gains of implementing and operating a solution to the organization's strategic business goals and objectives.

Benefits can be tangible (quantitative) or nontangible (qualitative). Tangible benefits are easy to measure and report after a solution has been implemented. They tend to be financial or numeric values such as improving revenues or reducing the number of trouble reports for an operational system. Nontangible benefits are equally as important; however, they can be difficult to assess. Qualitative measures include things like improved customer satisfaction or employee morale. Sometimes you are aware that these benefits are being achieved, but you can't quite prove it.

Estimate the Costs   Estimating the total net cost of the solution involves many pieces and parts. The business analyst must estimate costs in a number of areas, such as capital expenditures, development costs, and implementation costs. You will need to look at the total costs associated with operating and supporting the solution after it has been deployed. It is also wise to consider the opportunity costs of not selecting other solution options or approaches that may have been cheaper or easier to do.

Assess Initial Risks   Risk management will be performed throughout the project with new risks being identified across the project life cycle and old risks being retired or actually taking place. Performing an initial risk assessment in your business case answers the question: "Does the project carry more risk than the organization is willing to bear?" Sometimes the answer is, "Yes," and a project is not approved. When the business analyst looks at risks for the first time, the focus is on solution feasibility.

Measure Expected Results   The business case should always address how to measure, assess, and evaluate the projected costs and benefits that it contains. The business analyst must define the use for this quantitative evaluation in order to be able to plan for, measure, and report on solution performance and achievements. Good metrics address both *precision* and *accuracy*. Precision focuses on the consistency of measurements, targeting repeated measurements that yield the same value. Accuracy looks at how close the true value is to the measured value. Closer values indicate higher reliability and less uncertainty.

Exam Spotlight

When assessing solution feasibility in the initial risk assessment found in the business case, be sure that you address the technical, financial, and business risks of the proposed solution.

Technical Risks   Will the new technology be able to scale up to the performance requirements of our large organization?

Financial Risks   Will estimated costs be exceeded? Might potential benefits disappear?

Business Risks   Can the organization change in order to realize the solution benefits?

Let's take a look at several strategies that can facilitate your analysis.

Recommended Technique: Risk Analysis

Risk analysis is used when developing a business case to identify areas of uncertainty about the technical, financial, and business feasibility of a proposed solution. Risk analysis is ongoing throughout a project. This initial risk assessment contained in a project's business case is the first step of many in the land of "things will not go as planned." Risks can be positive (opportunities) or negative (threats) events.

One key component of risk analysis is to understand your organization's *risk tolerance*. Organizations may be risk-averse, risk-neutral, or risk-seeking. Interestingly enough, an organization's approach to risk may change over time. Risk-averse organizations want to reduce risks and are willing to receive fewer benefits in return for a more certain outcome. Risk-neutral organizations are squarely in the middle. They typically need to see that the expected benefits equal or outweigh the costs of the proposed solution in order to continue on with things. Risk-seeking organizations will accept high risks if they come with high rewards for success.

To analyze the initial risks related to proposed solution feasibility, the business analyst needs to determine probability and impact of each identified risk. This is usually done with a common scale, such as the numbers from 1 to 5 with a 1 being low and a 5 being high. You can rank order your list of identified risks by multiplying the probability and the impact of each risk in the list. This gives you the magnitude of how likely a risk is to take place and how painful a risk will be if it does occur.

The business analyst and key stakeholders then need to determine the response strategy used to deal with significant risks (positive or negative). Seven risk response strategies are listed in the *BABOK® Guide*; these strategies are summarized in Table 3.10.

TABLE 3.10   Summary of Risk Response Strategies

Strategy	Description	Risk Type
Accept	Accept that the identified risk may occur and choose to do nothing about it	Positive or negative
Transfer	Transfer the responsibility for dealing with a risk to a third party	Negative
Share	Work with a third party to increase the probability an identified risk will occur and share the benefits	Positive
Avoid	Take measures to ensure the identified risk does not occur	Negative
Mitigate	Reduce the probability and/or the impact of an identified risk occurring	Negative
Enhance	Take steps to increase the probability and the benefits for an identified risk	Positive
Exploit	Work to ensure that the identified risk does occur	Positive

Other Techniques to Consider

Depending on your project, you might also find the following techniques useful.

Decision Analysis   This technique allows the business analyst to examine and model the costs and benefits of a proposed solution and its implementation. You can use graphical decision trees and financial valuation techniques to compare and contrast possible outcomes.

Estimation   You can forecast the investment required to deploy and operate the proposed solution found in the business case. The estimates are done in conjunction with the project manager using the project estimating tools and techniques.

Metrics and Key Performance Indicators (KPIs)   Metrics and KPIs are used to measure, manage, and report on the expected benefits of implementing a proposed solution. The business analyst must make sure that the benefits being sought can be proven to exist after the solution is deployed.

 Remember, KPIs are indicators allowing the business analyst to measure performance or progress of solutions and solution components toward strategic goals or objectives. Metrics are quantifiable levels of an indicator measured at a particular point in time.

SWOT Analysis   SWOT analysis lets you compare the costs and benefits of implementing a potential solution. As previously discussed, there are two dimensions to this analysis: the internal strengths and weaknesses of the organization and the external opportunities and negative impacts that are in play. The business analyst is seeking to maximize strengths and minimize weaknesses.

Vendor Assessment   When goods or services may be purchased from a third party as all or part of a proposed solution, an assessment of that vendor should be included as part of the business case. This decision to purchase or outsource is made in the solution approach.

Producing the Project's Business Case

The business case presents the information necessary to support a go/no go decision to invest and move forward with a proposed project. The sponsor typically approves a project's business case and authorizes funding the resulting project effort. Once the business is approved, it is used as an input to numerous business analysis tasks that occur later in the project life cycle (Table 3.11). The business requirements developed in Enterprise Analysis form the basis for detailed solution requirements development as the business analysis team defines the "nuts and bolts" of what needs to be done.

TABLE 3.11   Output: Define Business Case

Task Output	Output Destinations	Source Knowledge Area
Business case	Prepare for elicitation	Elicitation
	Conduct elicitation activity	Elicitation
	Prioritize requirements	Requirements Analysis
	Verify requirements	Requirements Analysis
	Validate requirements	Requirements Analysis

The business analyst and project manager work together to build the business case and its contents. The project manager may provide their expertise in developing times and cost estimates for implementing the proposed solution. The domain and implementation SMEs may assist in estimating business benefits and costs for the proposed solution. The business case, business need, solution scope, and required capabilities create the business requirements for the project. These high-level requirements feed directly into the project's requirements elicitation and analysis activities, which will be discussed in subsequent chapters of this book.

How This Applies to Your Projects

In this chapter, you stepped through defining the business requirements for a project and using a business case to seek the sponsor's approval to get that project underway. Performing business analysis usually starts up at 30,000 feet on most projects. Working on complex projects in which the initial feasibility studies and business case development work are a project themselves that can be enjoyable. It is always fun to figure out the scope of what needs to be done and to justify why an organization needs to do it. Understanding and defining the "big picture" is an important piece of a project's controlled start, and every business analyst should be able to perform this work well.

It should be no surprise that projects are successful when what is to be accomplished is clearly stated and agreed on. Scope definition activities set the framework for the subsequent requirements development activities. The solution scope is defined by negotiation between key business and management level stakeholders. Solution scope definition restricts the detailed requirements development downstream and allows for informed decision-making and prioritization throughout the project life cycle.

Many different project documents can be used to define the scope of a business problem or need and justify why an organization should do something about it. Here is a short list of possible candidates:

- Business Case
- Business Requirements Document (BRD)
- Project Brief
- Feasibility Study
- Opportunity Assessment
- Project Charter
- Operational Concept Description (OCD)
- Scope Definition Document (SDD)

No matter which document template you use or what name you give that document, it should contain most, if not all, of the information that the business analyst builds and collects as part of their Enterprise Analysis tasks. This includes the business need, the justification and rationale for proceeding with the effort, key stakeholders involved with these business-focused efforts, any business constraints, and an initial risk assessment.

Business Requirements Document Outline

Here is a business requirements document template we frequently use. Typically, we modify it for each organization where it is being applied, based on their preferences. It is adapted from the IEEE's Concept of Operations (ConOps) document that is part of their software engineering standards.

Executive Summary

1.0   Introduction and Overview

    1.1   Background

    1.2   Description of Current Situation

    1.3   Concepts for Proposed System

2.0   Scope of Proposed Efforts

    2.1   Statement of Problem or Need

    2.2   Business Areas and Goals

    2.3   Business Requirements

    2.4   Involved Stakeholder Organizations

    2.5   Constraints

3.0   Analysis and Recommendations

    3.1   Justification and Rationale

    3.2   Summary of Improvements

    3.3   Disadvantages and Limitations

    3.4   Impacts and Risks

4.0   Referenced Documents

5.0   Signature Page

Appendix: Glossary of Terms

Appendix: Acronyms

Most organizations have their own templates, examples, and specific requirements for writing a business case, scope definition, and/or business requirements document. Be sure to check with your project manager to see what is commonly used or required for your projects when you are defining the "big picture." Often, document templates provide a valuable road map for what information you will need to gather and analyze during your Enterprise Analysis work.

Summary

The five tasks of the Enterprise Analysis knowledge area focus on defining the business requirements for the project and justifying why that project should be performed. The business requirements are the framework for what capabilities a solution will deliver in order to meet a business need. The resulting business benefits from implementing a particular solution will be defined and the means to measure them will be established. These two items—the business requirements and the expected business benefits—will be referenced throughout the project life cycle.

In the *BABOK® Guide*, the business requirements are considered to be the set of Enterprise Analysis task deliverables: business need, required capabilities, solution scope, and the business case. The tasks in this knowledge area are focused on defining and getting approval for the "big picture" of what capabilities and benefits a proposed new solution will provide to the organization.

The Enterprise Analysis tasks address the most strategic part of business analysis work. Often, these tasks take place before an actual project is planned or even approved. Many organizations assess and evaluate the feasibility and value of possible solutions to their problems and then select the most important projects to be done. The remaining projects get to sit on the back burner and wait for an opportunity to be initiated and done.

Business analysts focus on the strategic priorities business goals and business objectives of their organizations when developing the business requirements. They have to define and understand the business need and determine the desired outcomes the organization would like to see to meet that need. This work requires interacting with senior management to determine what the problem is and what they think might be done to correct it. The underlying competencies of effective communication and interaction are essential for success at this early point in or before the more detailed project work begins.

Once the business need is understood, the business analyst must assess the organization's current capabilities relative to that need. That means looking at the enterprise architecture. As previously discussed in this chapter, the enterprise architecture defines the current capabilities of an organization. It consists of and relates the organization's business processes, software, hardware, people, operations, and current projects.

Next, the business analyst looks at ways to go about implementing a solution that solves the problem and meets the identified business need. This is called the solution approach. The selected solution approach depends a great deal on the nature of the problem and the preferences of the organization. Some organizations might decide to outsource services to implement a solution. Other organizations may prefer to build their own software applications and to provide those services themselves.

Once the solution approach is selected, the solution scope can be defined. The business analyst may find themselves working closely with the project manager in order to get the solution scope definition in place. While the business analyst is focusing on defining the solution scope, the project manager is working in tandem with them, focused on the project scope. Remember the project scope defines the work needed to deliver a product, service, or result, with the specified features and functions. By comparison, the solution scope defines the set of capabilities a solution must deliver in order to meet a business need.

Risk management kicks in as part of the Enterprise Analysis tasks when you build the project's business case. The business case requires the business analyst to identify and analyze the technical, financial, and business risks related to the overall solution feasibility. The business case is really the "authorization to proceed" document. It justifies why the organization should invest in the implementation of a solution. Once the business case is approved, the project itself can get merrily underway.

Exam Essentials

Be able to list the tasks found in the Enterprise Analysis knowledge area.   On your exam, you will see questions about the tasks, their associated techniques, their more detailed elements, and the key outputs that they produce. You should memorize the five tasks of this knowledge area and any key outputs or techniques associated with them. The tasks are

Define business need.

Assess capability gaps.

Determine solution approach.

Define solution scope.

Define business case.

Be able to state the purpose of key deliverables.   The good news is that the key deliverables produced by the tasks in this knowledge area are easy to remember because they align nicely with the task names. Here's the list:

Business need

Required capabilities

Solution approach

Solution scope

Business case

Be able to define what's in the business requirements.   Business requirements are made up of four of the five Enterprise Analysis task deliverables: the business need, the required capabilities, the solution scope, and the business case.

Be able to list the risk responses for positive and negative risks.   The risk responses for positive risks (opportunities) are share, accept, enhance, and exploit. Risk responses for negative risks (threats) are accept, mitigate, avoid, and transfer. Remember that the acceptance risk response is the only response that is used for both positive and negative risks.

Be able to distinguish between project, product, and solution scope.   Project scope defines the work needed to deliver a product, service, or result with the specified features and functions. Product scope includes the features and functions characterizing the product, service, or result. Solution scope is the set of capabilities a solution must deliver in order to meet the business need.

Be able to explain the knowledge area-specific techniques used to build the business requirements.   Performing the Enterprise Analysis tasks to ultimately build the business requirements uses many knowledge area-specific and general business analysis techniques. The knowledge area-specific techniques are feasibility analysis (used when determining solution approach) and problem or vision statement (used when defining solution scope).

Key Terms

This chapter stepped through the contents of the second knowledge area from the *BABOK® Guide*: Enterprise Analysis. Most of this knowledge area focuses on defining the "big picture" business requirements that the business analysis team will use to frame subsequent work activities across the project life cycle.

You should understand how to apply the techniques and tasks in this knowledge area in order to be an effective business analyst. Additionally, you will need to know the five tasks and their associated elements and techniques from this knowledge area in order to be successful on the CBAP® or CCBA™ exams. The tasks include:

Define business need.

Assess capability gaps.

Determine solution approach.

Define solution scope.

Define business case.

A number of new key words in Chapter 3 relate to defining the business requirements for a project using the business need, the required capabilities, the solution scope, and the business case. Here is a list of some of the key terms that you encountered in this chapter:

accuracy	problem statement
business case	project charter
business goals	release planning
business need	required capabilities
business objectives	risk tolerance
desired outcome	root cause analysis
fishbone diagram	solution components
five whys	values
focus areas	vision
gap analysis	vision statement
mission	work products
precision	

Review Questions

1. What governs the performance of all Enterprise Analysis tasks?
    - **A.** Enterprise analysis plan
    - **B.** Business analysis plan
    - **C.** Project management plan
    - **D.** Requirements management plan

2. Which Enterprise Analysis task requires the solution approach as an input?
    - **A.** Define solution scope.
    - **B.** Define business need.
    - **C.** Assess capability gaps.
    - **D.** Define business case.

3. Enterprise Analysis tasks focus on documenting what type of requirement?
    - **A.** Stakeholder
    - **B.** Solution
    - **C.** Transition
    - **D.** Business

4. Where would the sponsor go to find the information necessary to make a go/no go decision for a proposed project?
    - **A.** Business case
    - **B.** Solution scope
    - **C.** Business need
    - **D.** Solution approach

5. What defines the business problem for which the business analyst is seeking a solution?
    - **A.** Business case
    - **B.** Business objectives
    - **C.** Business goals
    - **D.** Business need

6. What term describes the business benefits resulting from meeting the business need?
    - **A.** Solution scope
    - **B.** Performance indicator
    - **C.** Strategic objective
    - **D.** Desired outcome

7. What output is produced when the business analyst assesses the capability gaps between existing and new capabilities of the organization?

    A. Business objectives

    B. Required capabilities

    C. Solution approach

    D. Business need

8. When determining a solution approach, the business analyst identifies the means to deliver the proposed solution. What aspect of solution delivery is the business analyst defining?

    A. Feasibility and alternatives

    B. Life-cycle and initial risks

    C. Initial risks and methodology

    D. Methodology and life cycle

9. What four elements should be addressed in a business case for a proposed project?

    A. Benefits, costs, plans, scope

    B. Costs, benefits, risks, results

    C. Benefits, costs, goals, objectives

    D. Costs, benefits, risks, issues

10. When building a business case, decision analysis can be used to compare the _____ of implementing a proposed solution against the _____ to be gained.

    A. Benefits; costs

    B. Risks; benefits

    C. Costs; benefits

    D. Risks; costs

11. When assessing capability gaps, the business analyst's first step is to analyze current capabilities. To do this, they gather information about the current state of the enterprise. Once this work is done, what is their most likely next step?

    A. Assess current capabilities against objectives.

    B. Compare solution options against objectives.

    C. Identify and analyze all solution options.

    D. Assess future capabilities against objectives.

12. Who typically approves the business case and authorizes funding for the resulting project?

    A. End user

    B. Sponsor

    C. Domain SME

    D. Customer

13. Which business analysis technique allows the business analyst to leverage existing materials to discover and confirm business requirements?

   A. Process modeling

   B. Document analysis

   C. State diagrams

   D. SWOT analysis

14. The business analysis team has determined the solution approach and defined the solution scope. What is the team's most likely next step?

   A. Performing a feasibility study

   B. Assessing capability gaps

   C. Defining the business need

   D. Building the business case

15. What deliverable contains the preliminary analysis of solution alternatives or options to determine how and whether each option can provide an expected business benefit?

   A. Required capabilities

   B. Business case

   C. Strategic analysis

   D. Feasibility study

16. What describes the specific end results an organization is seeking to achieve and the measures to objectively assess if these end results have been achieved?

   A. Business case

   B. Business objectives

   C. Business goals

   D. Business need

17. The way a business need is defined does NOT determine which:

   A. Stakeholders are consulted.

   B. Capability gaps are assessed.

   C. Alternative solutions are considered.

   D. Solution approaches are evaluated.

18. When defining solution scope, which stakeholder role participates in allocating new capabilities to solution components and determining the time and effort required to deliver those capabilities?

   A. Business analyst

   B. Domain SME

   C. Project manager

   D. Implementation SME

19. During Enterprise Analysis, which technique allows the business analyst to break down business goals into achievable objectives and measures?

A. Root cause analysis

B. Business rules analysis

C. Functional decomposition

D. Organization modeling

20. What has been defined when all of the Enterprise Analysis knowledge area tasks are complete?

A. Solution scope and solution approach

B. Business requirements and solution approach

C. Business goals and business objectives

D. Business case and required capabilities

Answers to Review Questions

1. B. All of the enterprise analysis tasks are governed by the business analysis plan created as part of the Business Analysis Planning and Monitoring knowledge area.

2. A. The Enterprise Analysis task Define solution scope is the only task in this knowledge area that uses the solution approach as an input.

3. D. Enterprise Analysis tasks develop the business requirements for the project by defining the business need, business case, solution scope, and required capabilities.

4. A. The business case provides the project sponsor the information that is necessary to make a go/no go decision to approve and begin a proposed project.

5. D. The business need defines the problem for which the business analyst is trying to find a solution.

6. D. The desired outcome describes the business benefits that will result from meeting the business need. Don't forget that the desired outcome is not a solution.

7. B. The required capabilities are produced by the Assess Capability Gaps task found in the Enterprise Analysis knowledge area.

8. D. When determining the solution approach, the task elements (or steps) include identifying the possible approaches, identifying the means by which the solution may be delivered (methodology and life cycle), and assessing the organizational capabilities needed to implement and use the solution.

9. B. The four elements of a business case are benefits, costs, initial risks, and results measurement.

10. C. When building a business case, decision analysis can be used to compare the **costs** of implementing a proposed solution against the **benefits** to be gained.

11. A. Analyzing current capabilities as the first step in assessing capability gaps has three pieces: gather enterprise architecture information about the current state; describe the current capabilities of the organization; and assess the current capabilities against the desired objectives.

12. B. The sponsor typically approves the business case and authorizes funding for the resulting project.

13. B. The document analysis technique allows the business analyst to leverage existing materials to discover and confirm business requirements during Enterprise Analysis.

14. D. During Enterprise Analysis, four tasks (defining the business need, assessing capability gaps, determining the solution approach, and defining the solution scope) are usually completed before the business analyst builds the business case for the proposed project.

15. D. A feasibility study is a preliminary analysis of solution alternatives or options to determine how and whether each option can provide an expected business benefit. The feasibility analysis is contained within the feasibility study.

16. B. Business objectives describe the specific and measurable ends that an organization is seeking to achieve.

17. B. The way the business need is defined determines which alternative solutions are considered, which stakeholders are consulted, and which solution approaches are evaluated. It does NOT determine the capability gaps to be assessed.

18. D. When defining solution scope, the implementation SME participates in allocating capabilities to solution components and determining the time and effort required to deliver these new capabilities.

19. C. During Enterprise Analysis, functional decomposition is used by the business analyst to break down business goals into achievable objectives and measures.

20. B. The business requirements and the solution approach have been defined when the Enterprise Analysis knowledge area activities are complete. The business requirements consist of the business need, required capabilities, solution scope, and business case. The solution approach (used as an input to defining the solution scope) was also created.

Chapter

4

Overarching Tasks: Requirements Management and Communication

CBAP®/CCBA™ EXAM TOPICS COVERED IN THIS CHAPTER

- ✓ Manage solution scope and requirements.

- ✓ Manage requirements traceability.

- ✓ Maintain requirements for reuse after implementation.

- ✓ Prepare requirements packages using the appropriate format.

- ✓ Communicate the requirements.

It isn't enough to just plan the business analysis activities and get the work done. Communicating information about the requirements being developed across the project life cycle is the responsibility of the business analyst (that means you). The overarching set of requirements communication and management tasks is found in the Requirements Management and Communication knowledge area. The tasks in this knowledge area focus on ensuring that the right people are involved with developing, understanding, and approving the project requirements. In addition, the requirements themselves must be accessible and managed during the requirements development work and throughout the project life cycle.

The most important aspect of effective business analysis communication is communicating requirements information across the project life cycle. Consider yourself the master communicator of requirements for the life of your project, starting with requirements elicitation. It is essential for business analysts to elicit the right information from key stakeholders about the capabilities of the desired solution and to validate that the analyzed requirements information is correct and complete. These requirements-related communications can be formal or informal, written or verbal.

Requirements Management and Communication

The Requirements Management and Communication knowledge area targets managing and sharing the solution scope and the project requirements with the project stakeholders. This is where the business analysis team implements and refines the business analysis communication plan. On complex projects, your stakeholder audience can be quite broad and diverse. The key deliverable from this knowledge area is the requirements package. This is the vehicle to accumulate and share all or part of the project requirements with stakeholders. A requirements package can range from a small set of requirements to one or more graphical models to an entire requirements document.

The Requirements Management and Communication knowledge area is also where the business analysis team deals with the challenges of managing changing requirements across the project life cycle. Requirements can change while they are being developed and after they have been approved and baselined.

Change is an interesting beast. Remember when your mother told you that hindsight is always 20/20? Well, your mother was right. Business analysts are experts at recognizing changing circumstances as the project life cycle moves forward. They recognize that their level of knowledge about the solution and its implementation improves over time. However, their ability to respond quickly and easily to requirements changes decreases as the project's delivery date draws near. Managing changing requirements is an integral part of what business analysts do. Figure 4.1 illustrates this strange and wonderful relationship between what they know about projects and how quickly and easily they can respond to changes over time.

FIGURE 4.1   Responding to changing requirements

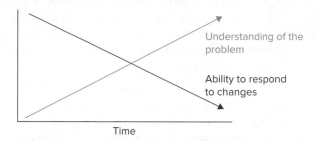

Understanding of the problem

Ability to respond to changes

Time

The tasks in this communication-focused knowledge area consist primarily of actions taken for a project's stakeholder, solution, or transition requirements. They provide the business analysis team and the project with requirements-related outputs that are then used in various ways downstream. We will cover the contents and definition of a requirements package and look at the different requirements states as task outputs in more detail in this chapter. The Requirements Management and Communication knowledge area is addressed in Chapter 4 of the *BABOK® Guide*.

Exam Spotlight

Communicating and managing requirements using the tasks in this knowledge area results in requirements that are:

- Approved and agreed to by project stakeholders

- Communicated to stakeholders in parts or when complete

- Formatted as maintained and reusable requirements for future use

- Traced to other requirements that are part of the solution scope

Requirements Management and Communication typically deals with the detailed requirements development work that occurs after the big picture of the project and its solution has been painted as part of Enterprise Analysis. That said, the tasks in this knowledge area focus on three specific types of requirements:

- Stakeholder requirements

- Solution requirements

- Transition requirements

Stakeholder, Solution, and Transition Requirements

Let's remind ourselves what these three types of requirements are and how they relate to one another as part of your detailed requirements development efforts.

Stakeholder Requirements   Stakeholder requirements bridge between the business requirements and the more detailed solution requirements to define the needs of stakeholders and how they will interact with a solution. They are developed and defined as part of the Requirements Analysis knowledge area. Like the business requirements that preceded them, the stakeholder requirements will be progressively elaborated into the more detailed solution requirements.

Solution Requirements   Solution requirements are the most detailed type of requirements that describe the solution characteristics needed to meet the higher-level business and stakeholder requirements. Typically, solution requirements are subdivided into two specific types: functional requirements and nonfunctional requirements. Solution requirements are developed and defined as part of the tasks found in the Requirements Analysis knowledge area.

Transition Requirements   Transition requirements define the solution capabilities required to transition from the current to the future state and are no longer needed once the transition is complete. Typically, transition requirements are created later in the project life cycle after both the current and new solutions have been defined. They are developed and defined as part of the tasks found in the Solution Assessment and Validation knowledge area.

The Requirements Management and Communication knowledge area also addresses monitoring and reporting on the effects of changing project requirements across the project life cycle. The business analysis team also assesses the effectiveness of the actual solution relative to the organization's business goals and objectives. This ensures that the project's business analysis tracks its organizational alignment and understanding, making it available for use on future projects. How is this accomplished? Let's take a look at the tasks involved.

The Business Analyst's Task List

The business analyst has five tasks to perform in the Requirements Management and Communication knowledge area. We will look at each of these tasks in greater detail later in this chapter. The task list from the *BABOK® Guide* includes:

Managing the solution scope and requirements

Managing requirements traceability

Maintaining requirements for reuse

Preparing *requirements packages*

Communicating the requirements

These tasks focus on making sure that the project stakeholders have a common and consistent understanding of the requirements and the solution that the requirements are defining. The business analyst is responsible for packaging and presenting a set of requirements to the appropriate stakeholder group. (We will step through each of these tasks in greater detail later in this chapter.) The business analyst is also responsible for managing the requirements as they change across the project life cycle.

When Does Requirements Management and Communication Take Place?

> To effectively communicate, we must realize that we are all different in the way we perceive the world and use this understanding as a guide to our communication with others.
>
> —*Anthony Robbins*

The tasks in the Requirements Management and Communication knowledge area begin as soon as requirements development work begins for a project. They accompany the work being done in any knowledge area that develops requirement, including Enterprise Analysis, Requirements Analysis, and Solution Assessment and Validation. Effective business analysts make sure that their requirements-related communication activities take place across the project life cycle.

The solution scope and its requirements can change at any point in the project life cycle. It is critical that the business analyst and the project manager control and manage these changes whenever they occur. They may take place:

- As you develop the solution scope or project requirements for the first time

- After you agree on the solution scope or requirements with the stakeholders

- After you formally baseline the solution scope and its requirements

- After the project is done and the solution is deployed

Several key business analysis deliverables influence and guide managing and communicating about the requirements under development on a project. These plans were created as part of the Business Analysis Planning and Monitoring knowledge area. They include the:

- Business analysis communication plan
- Business analysis approach
- Requirements management plan

The tasks in the Requirements Management and Communication knowledge area rely heavily on the contents of these plans and approaches that define how you will communicate and manage change as you develop your project requirements. With that in mind, let's step through the first task in the Requirements Management and Communication knowledge area: managing the solution scope and requirements.

Exam Spotlight

Approximately 24 of your 150 exam questions focus specifically on Requirements Management and Communication. The questions target specific aspects of the five tasks found in this knowledge area. Be sure you know them well.

Manage Solution Scope and Requirements

The first task in the Requirements Management and Communication knowledge area is managing the solution scope and requirements. The solution scope defines the set of capabilities a solution must deliver to meet a defined business need. The requirements take the solution scope and define it in greater detail, describing the more detailed conditions and capabilities that must be met by the solution or solutions. The requirements define the details that enable the project stakeholders to solve their problems or achieve their objectives.

Managing the solution scope and its more detailed requirements focuses on getting and maintaining stakeholder approval and buy-in for those requirements. This includes any changes that take place after the requirements have been developed. This can be done at almost any point in the project life cycle, although typically the task is performed at the end of a project phase or at key points when developing a requirements document.

Figure 4.2 summarizes the inputs, outputs, techniques, and associated tasks for managing the solution scope and requirements for a project.

FIGURE 4.2 Task summary: Manage solution scope and requirements.

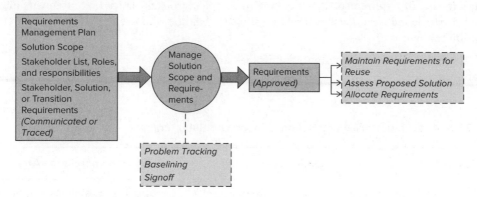

Several key inputs are needed to manage the solution scope and requirements for a project. These key inputs are produced by other business analysis tasks, and include:

- The requirements management plan
- The solution scope
- The requirements themselves
- The stakeholder list, roles, and responsibilities

Let's have a look at each of these task inputs in greater detail.

Requirements Management Plan   The business analysis team defines their process for developing project requirements in the requirement management plan. This plan describes how the team will approach *requirements traceability*, requirements prioritization, and managing changing requirements. In the requirements management plan, the methods for saving and storing the project requirements in a repository are defined.

Solution Scope   The solution scope provides the business case with the new capabilities to be implemented and the methods to deliver those capabilities, and it identifies the part(s) of the organization that will be impacted by the new capabilities.

Stakeholder List, Roles, and Responsibilities   Understanding the preferences of key business analysis stakeholders shapes the resulting business analysis plans to some degree. Stakeholder roles and levels of involvement need to be understood, especially for requirements development activities.

Stakeholder, Solution, or Transition Requirements (Communicated)   Communicated requirements have been shared with and understood by the relevant stakeholders at a particular point in time. The current state of communicated requirements may change over time as they are revised or rewritten. In that case, they will need to be shared with stakeholders again.

Stakeholder, Solution, or Transition Requirements (Traced)   Traceability is an important characteristic of requirements, particularly in complex projects. Traced requirements must have clearly defined and identified relationships to the other requirements found within the solution scope.

Table 4.1 summarizes the inputs to this task and lists the source of the input (if applicable).

TABLE 4.1   Inputs: Manage Solution Scope and Requirements

Task Input	Input Source	Source Knowledge Area
Requirements management plan	Plan requirements management process	Business Analysis Planning and Monitoring
Stakeholder list, roles, and responsibilities	Conduct stakeholder analysis	Business Analysis Planning and Monitoring
Solution scope	Define solution scope	Enterprise Analysis
Stakeholder, solution, or transition requirements (communicated)	Communicate requirements	Requirements Management and Communication
Stakeholder, solution, or transition requirements (traced)	Manage requirements traceability	Requirements Management and Communication

Managing the solution scope and requirements for a project requires the business analyst to be right in the middle of the requirements development efforts for a project. The business analyst will address several detailed elements when performing this task across the project life cycle, such as:

- Managing the solution scope
- Addressing any conflicts and issues
- Presenting the requirements for review
- Obtaining approval for the requirements

Let's take a look at each of these elements in greater detail.

Managing Solution Scope   Stakeholder and solution requirements must fall within the defined solution scope and business requirements for a project. When performing detailed requirements development, the business analysis team must clearly understand the solution scope and business requirements in order to evaluate what they are hearing from the stakeholders.

During stakeholder and solution requirements development, it is not unusual to have stakeholders identify particular requirements that are out of scope for the solution as currently defined. There are two decisions that the business analyst can make in this situation. If the requirements are not necessary to achieve the solution scope, then the business analyst must reach agreement with the stakeholder that they are out of scope and will not be included in the project. If the requirements are determined to be necessary to achieve the solution scope, the existing business requirements and solution scope should be revised to include them.

Addressing Conflicts and Issues Requirements development activities are known for generating conflicts and issues along the way. Conflicts are inevitable when you have multiple stakeholders with multiple (and often differing) points of view. Requirements that are in conflict or that are inconsistent must be resolved before formal approval is given to those requirements. Effective communication between all involved parties gets the issues and conflicts on the table and ready for discussion and resolution.

The *BABOK® Guide* recommends that conflicting requirements be resolved in a number of ways, including:

- Formal meetings among affected stakeholders
- Research into what is actually required
- Third-party arbitration and resolution

 Real World Scenario

How Hard Can This Be?

Peggy was tasked with leading the effort to prioritize the high-level requirements for automating a paper-based inventory management system at her organization. This seemed like it would be a simple enough activity. The paper-based system was cumbersome and inefficient. Developing an automated system offered the opportunity to streamline the paper-based process and take advantage of technology to assist in inventory management and tracking activities.

"How hard can this be?" Peggy thought to herself. She invited key stakeholders to a requirements workshop and provided them with a list of the newly automated capabilities for the system ahead of time. The group set forth to figure out which requirements were the most important and what others were less so. Unfortunately, this requirements prioritization workshop did not go as planned.

The meeting started off smoothly and all participants agreed that the list of new capabilities for the automated inventory system was right on target. However, when the group was asked to prioritize the capabilities, they were unable to do so. Peggy asked the group to use a forced ranking system, where each attendee was asked to rank the new capabilities from first to last in order. She took the lists and the group built a combined list of capabilities, starting with the highest ranked (must do) and ending with the lower-ranked capabilities (could do or do later).

When the group reviewed the ranked list of capabilities, no one would agree that their capabilities should be at the bottom of the list. Even the capabilities that were optional or trivial were fought for by their end users and other constituents. The meeting became less of a requirements workshop and more of a political brawl between departments and individuals. Peggy closed the workshop after its allotted two hours although no agreement had been reached. She rescheduled it for two days in the future and sat down to think about what she might do to facilitate a successful prioritization and agreement on the new capabilities.

When the group returned for the prioritization workshop Round 2, they were met with a much different scenario. There were two predefined prioritization schemes displayed on the wall for the workshop. The new capabilities would be prioritized based on (1) necessity or the core functionality needed and relevant to the primary users in order to do their jobs, and (2) the level of risk associated with automating these capabilities using new and unfamiliar technology.

The prioritization method everyone was asked to use in Round 2 was dot sticking. Each workshop attendee received stickers in three colors: red, green, and blue. Peggy was strategic in supplying the stickers, and she made sure that each attendee received half of their capability stickers in red, and a quarter each in green and blue. Basically, a single person could not rank all capabilities as the most important capabilities for the system.

Each sticker color had a specific assigned meaning. Red stickers were for must-have capabilities, green stickers were for would-like-to-have capabilities, and blue indicated optional or future capabilities. Each attendee put their stickers on the flipchart and ranked the capabilities in this way. The more stickers a particular capability received of a particular color, the more likely it was to be prioritized in that category. Capabilities marked by a rainbow of colors were discussed in detail by the group before assigning them a priority.

The end result of Round 2 was a set of prioritized and agreed-upon new capabilities with two capabilities marked as uncertain, requiring additional discussion before the group could make a decision on their priority. Peggy learned the value of creating an explicit and well-understood requirements negotiation and prioritization process. This is a key component to minimizing the number and the severity of the inevitable conflicts and issues that can and often do arise during requirements development.

Presenting Requirements for Review   When you present requirements for stakeholder review, you must be aware of the level of formality and the detail that your audience requires. Not all requirements reviews need to be a formal meeting with an agenda. Sometimes an informal meeting will suffice. Many times, the level of required presentation formality has already been defined for you in your project's business analysis communication plan. Formal presentations are often done using a structured walkthrough meeting with all of the requirements documentation and supporting information on hand for the attendees. Informal requirements presentations may be done in a conversation, an email message, or a note. Remember that formal requirements presentations typically take more time to prepare and more time to complete. Informal presentations can be done much more quickly, but offer more opportunities for stakeholders to miss or misinterpret the requirements information being presented.

Obtaining Approval for the Requirements   Requirements approval can be obtained for a single requirements statement, a set of related requirements, or an entire requirements document. In all cases, the business analyst is responsible for ensuring that the stakeholder or stakeholders responsible for approving the requirements clearly understand and accept them. The business analyst and the project manager decide if a formal record of the approval is kept and what that record will contain.

There are a number of techniques that you can use to manage the solution scope and requirements for your project. However, using *baselining* and *sign-off* will ensure that your requirements are formally approved and that the approval is duly noted. Let's look at those two techniques in greater detail right now.

Recommended Technique: Baselining

The baselining technique is used only when managing solution scope and requirements, and it is defined as part of this specific task in the *BABOK® Guide*. Baselining requires the business analyst and the business analysis team to follow the project or the organization's change control process when making any changes to the requirements.

A *baseline* is a view of the reviewed and agreed-upon requirements at a specific point in time. A baseline is like a snapshot of the status and state of a project deliverable, such as a requirements document, at a specific point in time. Baselined requirements are considered to be the basis for future project work. Once the business analyst has a baseline state for the project requirements, future changes to those requirements can be recorded and tracked. Any changes to the baselined requirements must go through a formal change control process versus just being added in. The specifics about the change control process relative to project requirements can be found in the requirements management plan for the project.

Maintaining the baselined requirements assigns the business analyst the responsibility to maintain:

- Description of the requirements change
- Name of the person making the change
- Reason why the change was made

Recommended Technique: Sign-Off

Sign-off is used only when managing solution scope and requirements, and is defined as part of this specific task in the *BABOK® Guide*. Requirements sign-off represents formal agreement from the stakeholders that the content and presentation of the requirements was accurate and complete. Most organizations require formal sign-off on their requirements documents.

The sign-off technique typically involves a face-to-face final review of either all of the requirements or a subset of the requirements with the approving stakeholders. At the end of the review, the approving stakeholders are asked to formally approve the requirements that were presented, either verbally or in writing.

Another Technique to Consider

The *BABOK® Guide* contains one additional technique that may be used when managing the solution scope and requirements for your project: *problem tracking*. This technique is summarized for you here.

Problem Tracking   Problem tracking is synonymous with issue management. This technique allows the business analyst to communicate, review, and maintain focus on business analysis-related problems and issues across the project life cycle. The business analyst is responsible for tracking, managing, and resolving defects, issues, problems, and risks that take place during business analysis activities.

There are three key pieces to the problem-tracking technique. The business analyst may set this process up for their project or use the existing project-level approach to managing issues. In either case, the business analyst needs to:

- Create a problem-tracking system containing problem records.

- Decide on a set of problem metrics and Key Performance Indicators to measure and report.

- Manage the recorded problems until they are fixed or it is decided that no action will be taken.

Once you have chosen one or more techniques, you are ready to manage the solution scope and produce the *approved requirements* on your projects. Let's discuss that next.

Produce the Approved Requirements

Requirements are considered to be approved when they have been agreed to by relevant project stakeholders. The approved requirements are complete and ready for use in subsequent business analysis or implementation efforts on the project.

Approved requirements are used as an input by a number of other business analysis tasks summarized in Table 4.2. The approved requirements may be a subset of a particular requirements document, one or more graphical models, or a completed requirements document.

TABLE 4.2   Output: Manage Solution Scope and Requirements

Output	Output Destinations	Destination Knowledge Area
Requirements (approved)	Maintain requirements for reuse	Requirements Management and Communication
	Assess proposed solution	Solution Assessment and Validation
	Allocate requirements	Solution Assessment and Validation

The business analyst has the primary responsibility for managing the solution scope and the associated requirements being developed for their project. Project managers are also part of this effort, as they are responsible and accountable for delivering the project scope and managing project risks. Ideally, the change management approach for the project should also govern any requirements changes.

 Real World Scenario

Version Control Meets the Local Copy of the Requirements Document

Russ, a project manager, was working in an organization that had an excellent documentation management system. Everyone in the company was required to use this system, putting their project documents—large and small—into the same repository. Once the data was stored and placed under version control, everyone could access the information to read it but only the approved folks could check out files, edit or change them, and then put them back in the system. Version control was strictly enforced. Or was it?

Russ attended a meeting where the group was reviewing an approved solution requirements document that had been revised to incorporate three major change requests from the users. This meeting was a formal review and sign-off of the changes with the senior users and the project sponsor at the table.

Unfortunately, the updated solution requirements document was not based on the most current version of the approved solution requirements. The business analyst making the changes had used a local copy of the document that was already on his computer. He didn't look in the system to see if that version was out of date—a very bad decision.

The group didn't notice the discrepancies right away. However, as the meeting progressed it became painfully obvious that something was badly out of sync. The meeting was adjourned and the project team set off to begin again and do some much-needed damage control with their users and the sponsor. Russ learned the value of doing an internal peer review before sending an important document out to key project stakeholders, a process he still follows to this day.

Using a document management or configuration management tool can be a great and wonderful thing on a project. However, it is correctly applying the process for using the tool that makes a world of difference. A peer review for your draft requirements before they get passed up the chain of command should be one practical step in that process.

Several business analysis stakeholders are impacted by and involved with the approved requirements. They include:

- Domain SMEs
- Implementation SMEs
- Sponsor

Producing the approved requirements framed by the solution scope and managing any changes to those requirements is an important step in the requirements development process. Let's take a look at another important step in producing the project requirements—creating and maintaining traceability between the requirements that are being developed.

Manage Requirements Traceability

Requirements traceability provides the business analyst with the ability to identify and document the lineage of each requirement. A requirement's lineage includes its relationship to other project requirements, to work products, and to the solution components. When business analysts say that they can trace a requirement, they are telling you that they can look at that specific requirement and all other requirements to which it is related. Traceability is usually achieved by putting the requirements in a table, spreadsheet, or tool to manage the tracing activities.

Traceability begins with each project's business objectives. The business objectives are used to determine the business requirements. In turn, the business requirements are decomposed into the more detailed stakeholder-requirements level. Stakeholder requirements get broken down once more into the detailed solution requirements that transition the project team from requirements definition to solution design and development. All of the requirements that make up a project's solution scope should trace back to one or more business objectives for that project.

Exam Spotlight

Remember the three aspects of requirements traceability when taking your certification exam:

Derivation: backward traceability of a requirement to its higher-level parent

Allocation: forward traceability of a requirement to its more detailed children

Relationship: dependency and interrelationship of a requirement to other project requirements

Traceability can be built and maintained at many levels within a given set of project requirements. Traceability usually begins with tracing the current requirements under development to the higher-level requirements from which they are being derived. For example, when business analysts build the solution requirements for a project, the first aspect of traceability that they address is derivation from the stakeholder requirements that preceded the solution requirements.

Exam Spotlight

The *BABOK® Guide* recommends that you trace your requirements at one or more levels, as appropriate. The four suggested levels are

- Individual requirements

- Models

- Requirements packages

- Features

You need to decide your approach to traceability as part of the requirements management plan. This should be done before the requirements development work actually begins. Tracing can be performed for:

- Individual requirements
- Graphical models of the requirements
- Requirements packages
- Requirements documents
- Higher-level capabilities or features

It is important to decide the level of traceability and the types of relationships to be traced ahead of time. That allows the business analysis team to do this work concurrently with developing the requirements themselves.

Is It Real or Gold Plating?

Remember that all project requirements must be linked back to a business objective. Otherwise, a requirement is not necessary to meet the business need and deliver the solution scope. Extra requirements that are not necessary to deliver the solution scope are often referred to as gold plating.

Implementing traceability for project requirements demands work from the business analysis team, but it's worth the effort. Traceability is used for many things on a project. Let's run through a few of those important areas right now.

Impact Analysis   Traceability allows the business analyst to thoroughly evaluate the impacts of a change request to both the requirements and the solution components.

Requirements Coverage   Tracing requirements back to the business objectives shows the business analyst how those objectives will be accomplished. This also allows the business analyst to confirm that all of the business objectives are included in the solution scope and the solution components.

Requirements Allocation   Traceability allows the business analyst to trace the subset of requirements that are allocated to each of the solution components.

Requirements Are Considered Traceable If...

We use a simple checklist to implement traceability on our projects. It is important that all stakeholders understand what is needed on a project from a traceability perspective. Traceability begins in earnest with the requirements development activities on your projects. We believe project requirements are traceable if:

- The source of the requirement is documented. Common sources include people, other documents, or if a requirement has been derived from other requirements.

- Each requirement has a unique identifier so we can reference and locate it whenever necessary.

- The rationale for the requirement is available, telling us why that requirement exists.

- All requirements related to a specific requirement are documented, from parent to child and vice versa. This shows the derivation, allocation, and relationships between requirements.

- How the requirement is met later in the project life cycle is documented, showing us how it was achieved or completed. On IT projects, this traces a requirement from design to implementation and into any user documentation.

- The requirements can be tracked through development and on to test for verification purposes.

You should always be able to prove you delivered the capabilities that you said you were going to deliver.

Figure 4.3 summarizes the inputs, outputs, techniques, and associated tasks for managing requirements traceability on a project.

FIGURE 4.3 Task summary: Manage requirements traceability.

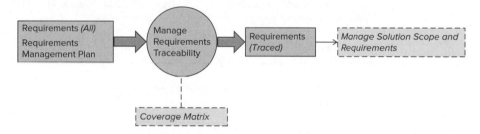

Several key inputs are needed to create and manage requirements traceability for a project. These key inputs are produced by other business analysis tasks, and they include the requirements management plan and the requirements themselves. Let's take a closer look at these inputs.

Requirements (All)   Any and all requirements may be traced to other requirements on a project. According to the *BABOK® Guide*, all solution and stakeholder requirements must be traceable to a business requirement.

Requirements Management Plan   The requirement management plan defines how the team will approach traceability. The business analysis team should use this plan to guide their traceability activities during requirements development and after the requirements have been completed.

Table 4.3 summarizes the inputs to this task and lists the source of the input (if applicable).

TABLE 4.3   Inputs: Manage Requirements Traceability

Task Input	Input Source	Source Knowledge Area
Requirements (all)	—	Produced by multiple tasks in multiple knowledge areas
	(Allocated) Allocate requirements	Solution Assessment and Validation
	(Analyzed) Specify and model requirements	Requirements Analysis
	(Approved) Manage solution scope and requirements	Requirements Management and Communication
	(Communicated) Communicate requirements	Requirements Management and Communication
	(Maintained and reusable) Maintain requirements for reuse	Requirements Management and Communication
	(Prioritized) Prioritize requirements	Requirements Analysis
	(Stated, Unconfirmed) Document elicitation results	Elicitation
	(Stated, Unconfirmed) Confirm elicitation results	Elicitation
	(Traced) Manage requirements traceability	Requirements Management and Communication
	(Validated) Validate requirements	Requirements Analysis
	(Verified) Verify requirements	Requirements Analysis
Requirements management plan	Plan requirements management process	Business Analysis Planning and Monitoring

Business analysts need to step through three essential elements to create and manage requirements traceability for their projects. These elements are

- Recording dependencies and relationships
- Performing impact analysis for change requests
- Using a Configuration Management System

Let's step through each of these elements now.

Recording Dependencies and Relationships   Key dependencies and relationships between requirements should be recorded so they can be traced across the project life cycle. Creating and maintaining this information assists the business analyst in sequencing project work activities to design and deploy the capabilities found in the requirements. It also assists the business analyst in correctly allocating requirements to solution components.

There are five common relationships between requirements that may be tracked and recorded during and after requirement development. They are listed in Table 4.4.

TABLE 4.4   Common Relationships Between Requirements

Relationship	Description
Necessity	A requirement and another related requirement must be implemented at the same time for a specific reason.
Effort	A requirement is easier to implement if a related requirement is implemented at the same time.
Subset	A requirement is a decomposed outcome (one of the children) of another requirement.
Cover	A higher-level requirement is the sum of its subrequirements. In this case, all of the subrequirements must be implemented in order for this higher-level requirement to be met.
Value	Including a particular requirement increases or decreases the desirability of implementing a related requirement.

Performing Impact Analysis for Change Requests   Traceability facilitates better decision making when it comes to assessing the impact of change requests on a project. For example, if an approved requirement changes on a project, the business analyst can use the traceability to review the impact of that change on other requirements or solution components.

Using a Configuration Management System   Although traceability can be done manually using a spreadsheet, complex projects often require a more streamlined approach. Many business analysts prefer to use a requirement management tool or a configuration management system to trace large numbers of requirements.

The *BABOK® Guide* recommends that you use a coverage matrix to create and maintain traceable requirements. Let's have a look at this technique in greater detail.

Recommended Technique: Coverage Matrix

The *coverage matrix* technique is specific to the Manage Requirements Traceability task in the *BABOK® Guide*. Basically, a coverage matrix is a table or spreadsheet used to manage and facilitate tracing of requirements. This simple approach is used on simple projects where there are only a few requirements or on projects where traceability is very limited and not too detailed.

 Real World Scenario

Palmer Divide Vineyards: Concerns Over Elapsed Study Time

You are a team member at Palmer Divide Vineyards, currently defining the IT requirements for their new green initiative. You have been assigned the task of tracing the requirements in a particular requirements package. During your review of the set forward and backward traceability matrices, you notice the following stakeholder requirements.

> SH1: Users shall perform research studies.

> SH2: Users shall customize the contents of their research studies.

The children of these stakeholder requirements are the more detailed solution requirements, which are traced back to their parents.

> SH1 traces forward to one solution requirement:

>> S1: The system shall calculate elapsed study time.

> SH2 traces forward to two solution requirements:

>> S2: The system shall allow creation of custom data queries.

>> S3: The system shall accept customized user study data.

While you are looking at requirement S1, you find yourself wondering if the elapsed study time will be calculated for all studies, both standard and customized. The traceability matrix led you to this question, and you make a note to clarify it with the involved stakeholders at your earliest opportunity. Clarifying this concern during requirements development could save the project team the rework costs downstream if this requirement is interpreted incorrectly in the solution design and implementation.

Once you have decided if you will apply the coverage matrix technique or use a tool to implement traceability on a more complex project, you are ready to produce the traced requirements for your project. Remember that this decision should be documented as part of business analysis planning in the requirements management plan. Let's discuss the traced requirements one more time.

Produce the Traced Requirements

Traced requirements have clearly defined relationships to the other requirements within the solution scope. Traceable requirements are used by the business analyst to identify the effects on other requirements of a requirements change or planned implementation.

Factors to Consider When Documenting Traceability

How do you decide if a spreadsheet is good enough for tracking requirements traceability? It really depends on how complicated you think your requirements traceability will be. You should think about the following factors as part of your decision-making process.

Number of Requirements   Generally, complex projects have more requirements which generate a greater need for a traceability tool. In complex systems, business analysts must strive to limit the traceability information that is maintained to a usable and reasonable set of data. The more requirements you have, the more relationships there tend to be between those requirements. This may make maintaining traceability in a spreadsheet difficult, and point you toward a more sophisticated requirements management tool that uses a database to relate the requirements to one another.

Estimated System Lifetime   The longer a system or solution will be used within an organization, the greater the need for traceability using either a tool or a spreadsheet. This will assist the team in evaluating the impacts of changes to the operational solution. You also need to consider whether the system is critical or noncritical to daily operations.

Level of Organizational Maturity   Traceability tools are easier to acquire and use when your requirements development and project management processes are mature. Acquiring a new requirements management tool at the beginning of a major requirements development effort is bad timing. It will be difficult for the business analysis team to learn to use the new tool and to do their requirements development work simultaneously.

Once the requirements are approved by the relevant stakeholders at a specific point in time, they are used as an input to another task in the Requirements Management and Communication knowledge area, managing the solution scope and requirements. This task is summarized in Table 4.5.

TABLE 4.5   Output: Manage Requirements Traceability

Output	Output Destinations	Destination Knowledge Area
Requirements (traced)	Manage solution scope and requirements	Requirements Management and Communication

Business analysts have the primary responsibility for creating and managing requirements traceability for their projects, particularly during requirements development activities. The project managers are also part of this effort, as they use traceable requirements to support the project-level change management activities. Several business analysis stakeholders also have a need for traceable requirements, including:

- Implementation SMEs
- Testers

Producing the traced requirements is an interim and necessary step in creating the approved requirements for a project. Traced requirements are strongly recommended as an accompaniment to the approved requirements for your project. Let's take a look at another aspect of producing project requirements: maintaining requirements for reuse on your future projects and initiatives.

Maintain Requirements for Reuse

Some requirements developed for a particular project might also be candidates for long-term use or reuse by the organization. The requirements that you choose to maintain might relate to infrastructure, hardware, software, or operational capabilities that the organization must meet on an ongoing basis versus just for your particular project.

The *BABOK® Guide* contains a typographical error. It spells "reuse" as "re-use" throughout its pages. Please be aware that you will see this spelling on your certification exam.

Requirements that may be reused on other projects must be named, defined, and easily available to other business analysts in the organization. These requirements often become part of the organization's Organizational Process Assets (OPAs) and are stored and managed in a requirements repository. Some organizations save and maintain all ongoing, operational requirements to assist support and maintenance teams in evaluating possible impacts of changes to the deployed solutions and systems.

Figure 4.4 summarizes the inputs, outputs, techniques, and associated tasks for managing requirements traceability on a project.

FIGURE 4.4 Task summary: Maintain requirements for reuse.

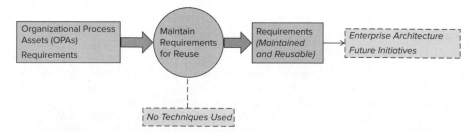

Several inputs are needed to maintain reusable requirements after a project is complete. These key inputs are produced by other business analysis tasks and include the requirements management plan and the requirements themselves. Let's take a closer look at these inputs.

Organizational Process Assets (OPAs)   Any standards for how and when requirements should be maintained for reuse can be found in the OPAs.

Requirements   Requirements that are maintained for reuse typically describe the current state of an organization and the systems and solutions that are being used.

Table 4.6 summarizes the inputs to this task and lists the source of the input (if applicable).

TABLE 4.6   Inputs: Maintain Requirements for Reuse

Task Input	Input Source	Source Knowledge Area
Organizational Process Assets (OPAs)	—	—
Requirements (all)	(Allocated) Allocate requirements	Solution Assessment and Validation
	(Analyzed) Specify and model requirements	Requirements Analysis
	(Approved) Manage solution scope and requirements	Requirements Management and Communication
	(Communicated) Communicate requirements	Requirements Management and Communication
	(Maintained and reusable) Maintain requirements for reuse	Requirements Management and Communication
	(Prioritized) Prioritize requirements	Requirements Analysis
	(Stated, Unconfirmed) Document elicitation results	Elicitation
	(Stated, Unconfirmed) Confirm elicitation results	Elicitation
	(Traced) Manage requirements traceability	Requirements Management and Communication
	(Validated) Validate requirements	Requirements Analysis
	(Verified) Verify requirements	Requirements Analysis

Effective business analysts should consider saving and maintaining two different types of requirements for reuse on their future projects. They include:

- *Ongoing requirements*
- *Satisfied requirements*

Let's step through each of these types of reusable and *maintained requirements* now.

Ongoing Requirements   Ongoing requirements are those requirements that the organization must meet on a continuous basis, such as contractual obligations, quality standards, business processes, or Service Level Agreements (SLAs). The organization may have to prove that the ongoing, operational requirements are met by the deployed solution.

Satisfied Requirements   Requirements that are met or satisfied by a deployed solution should be maintained as long as they are needed by the business stakeholders. This can be a great help in getting future product enhancements and system changes done and done well.

Exam Spotlight

Unapproved or unimplemented requirements might also be maintained for later use on future projects or initiatives.

The *BABOK® Guide* does not recommend using a specific technique to maintaining reusable requirements after a project is complete.

Produce Maintained and Reusable Requirements

Maintained and reusable requirements often become part of the Organizational Process Assets (OPAs) and the Enterprise Architecture of an organization. These requirements should be formatted and suitable for long-term or future use by the organization. The output from this task and its destinations are summarized for you in Table 4.7.

TABLE 4.7 Output: Maintain Requirements for Reuse

Output	Output Destinations	Destination Knowledge Area
Requirements (maintained and reusable)	—	Enterprise Architecture Future Initiatives

As a business analyst, you have the primary responsibility for formatting and storing maintained and reusable requirements after your project is complete. It is likely that these requirements will be used by a different business analyst at a future date, so you should make sure that the requirements are accessible and easily understood. Several other business analysis stakeholders also have a need for reusable and maintained requirements, including:

- Domain SMEs

- Implementation SMEs

Reusable and maintained requirements are not always produced on every project. The only requirements that you will consider for this task are those that the organization must meet on a continuous basis (ongoing requirements) or those that are needed by business stakeholders (satisfied requirements). Let's look at another essential task in producing project requirements: preparing requirements packages for communication with your key project stakeholders.

Prepare a Requirements Package

Think of a requirements package as a set of requirements that you are getting ready for an important project stakeholder to review. You get everything that they need all together in one place, make it look nice and neat, and then you wrap it up in a nice presentation or document with a big red bow. Thus, a requirements package is created and made into a friendly communication vehicle between you, the business analyst, and your very important stakeholder.

Business analysts use requirements packages for selecting and structuring a set of requirements to present to stakeholders. This information should be communicated clearly and unambiguously. A requirements package may be a requirements document, a presentation, or a package of requirements that is ready for stakeholder review. Requirements packages may contain all or some of the project requirements. They may contain a table of contents for ease of navigation.

Exam Spotlight

Requirements packages can be prepared for a number of reasons, including:

- Early assessment of quality and planning

- Evaluation of possible alternatives

- Formal presentation of requirements for reviews and approvals

- Preparation of inputs for solution design

- Proof of conformance with contractual and regulatory obligations

- Maintenance of requirements for reuse

Figure 4.5 summarizes the inputs, outputs, techniques, and associated tasks for preparing requirements package on a project.

FIGURE 4.5   Task summary: Prepare requirements package.

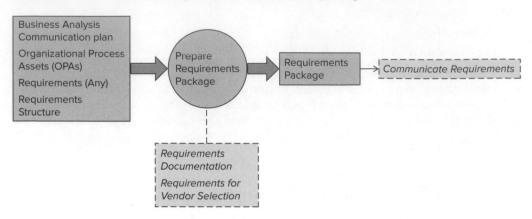

Several key inputs are used to prepare a requirements package during a project. These inputs are produced by other business analysis tasks. Let's take a closer look at these inputs.

Business Analysis Communication Plan   The business analysis communication plan defines how communication about business analysis activities and deliverables is conducted with stakeholders. The focus is on the requirements development tasks and the resulting deliverables. The business analysis communication plan is usually a subset of the project communication plan.

Organizational Process Assets (OPAs)   The OPAs may include templates that the business analyst can use to package requirements. These packages may be an entire requirements document, a set of graphical models of the requirements or a subset of requirements being addressed.

Requirements   Business analysts are responsible for deciding on the requirements in a specific requirement package. Requirements can be packaged and communicated to stakeholders at any point in the requirements development process.

Requirements Structure   The *requirements structure* defines how a requirements package should be put together. The requirements package should contain a consistent, cohesive, and coherent set of requirements for stakeholder review, understanding, and approval.

Table 4.8 summarizes the inputs to this task and lists the source of the input (if applicable).

TABLE 4.8 Inputs: Prepare Requirements Package

Task Input	Input Source	Source Knowledge Area
Business analysis communication plan	Plan Business Analysis Communication	Business Analysis Planning and Monitoring
Organizational Process Assets (OPAs)	—	—
Requirements (all)	(Allocated) Allocate requirements	Solution Assessment and Validation
	(Analyzed) Specify and model requirements	Requirements Analysis
	(Approved) Manage solution scope and requirements	Requirements Management and Communication
	(Communicated) Communicate requirements	Requirements Management and Communication
	(Maintained and reusable) Maintain requirements for reuse	Requirements Management and Communication
	(Prioritized) Prioritize requirements	Requirements Analysis
	(Stated, Unconfirmed) Document elicitation results	Elicitation
	(Stated, Unconfirmed) Confirm elicitation results	Elicitation
	(Traced) Manage requirements traceability	Requirements Management and Communication
	(Validated) Validate requirements	Requirements Analysis
	(Verified) Verify requirements	Requirements Analysis
	(Allocated) Allocate requirements	Solution Assessment and Validation
Requirements structure	Organize requirements	Requirements Analysis

Business analysts step through two essential elements as they build a requirements package. These two elements are

- Producing work products or *deliverables*

- Deciding the requirements package format

Let's step through each of these elements in more detail.

Producing Work Products and Deliverables   Requirements packages may contain work products, deliverables, or a combination of the two. Work products are documents, notes, or diagrams used by the business analyst during requirements development. Examples of work products include meeting minutes and status reports. Work products may or may not become business analysis deliverables. Deliverables are specific business analysis process outputs that the team plans to deliver, such as the formal requirements documents themselves.

Deciding the Requirements Package Format   The business analysis communication plan guides the presentation of requirements packages. One requirements package may use more than one presentation format in order to ensure that stakeholders understand the requirements that are being reviewed.

When designing or choosing a requirements document template, make sure you know the audience (who), scenario (how it will be used), and purpose (why it was written).

The *BABOK® Guide* recommends that you consider using two techniques when building a requirements package: requirements documentation and requirements for vendor selection. Frequently, detailed requirements documents are developed when the requirements for procuring goods or services are being planned. Let's step through these recommended techniques now, since you should make yourself familiar with both of them.

Recommended Technique: Requirements Documentation

Requirements are often specified in a formal document or set of documents, particularly for plan-driven projects where defining what is to be done takes place before the design and development work gets started. On complex projects, the requirements documents can be complex and interrelated. However, as individual documents they should be made simple and understandable.

Using more formal requirements documentation on complex projects is the preferred approach. Regardless of project size and type, documenting requirements allows the stakeholders and the business analysis team to:

- Understand and agree on what has to be accomplished

- Target consistent documentation of project requirements

- Manage the solution scope of the resulting efforts

- Show the relationship between what is required and how the requirement will be met in the solution

- Facilitate evaluating and managing the inevitable changes

Requirements documents or document sets can have many names and structures. They can be based on the level of detail for the requirements that they contain, such as one document each for a project's business, stakeholder, solution, and transition requirements. Sometimes the structure and content of a requirements document or document set is based on the organization's process and templates or specific industry guidance.

Exam Spotlight

The *BABOK® Guide* lists several common types of requirements documents available to you for formally documenting your requirements, including:

- Business requirements document

- Product roadmap

- Software or system requirements specification

- Supplementary requirements specification

- Vision document

Documenting requirements for in-house projects can be more straightforward than documenting requirements used when selecting vendors to provide you with required goods and services. Let's step through a second requirements documentation technique that is more externally focused.

 Real World Scenario

The Requirements Package as Luggage

Ginger, a management consultant, was involved in an interesting IT systems project focusing on providing physicians with the ability to order patient blood tests and access the results online. She participated in the detailed requirements development effort at the customer site and soon discovered that they had one of the most unique requirements packages she had ever seen.

The project manager always attended the regularly scheduled review meetings for the solution requirements. Interestingly enough, she also brought a friend along to those meetings—an enormous stack of documents strapped to a metal luggage cart. As the project progressed, the stack of documents on the project manager's luggage cart grew and grew.

At the first preapproval meeting for the solution requirements, the project manager and the luggage cart showed up on time along with the rest of the meeting attendees. This meeting was the internal requirements team's first look at the completed draft document. Their goal was to scrub the document in order to get it ready for presentation to senior management team for approval and sign-off.

Unfortunately, not all of the sections in the solution requirements document contained the same level of detail. The team came to a particular requirement stating that all assay tests must be included in the list displayed on the user's screen. Everyone attending had comments on that particular requirement, finding it ambiguous and in need of additional detail. When I go to test this requirement, how will the assay tests look on the user's screen? How are they accessed from the database? When should the data actually appear on the screen? How should the screen look? What operations can be performed on the data once it is on the screen? The questions went on and on.

As the meeting facilitator scribbled the questions down for further review, the project manager piped up. She pointed to the luggage cart full of documentation and asked everyone to look at all of the project documentation she brought to the meeting. "There is no need for these questions or for additional details," she stated with authority. "How can you say we don't have enough information? Everything we need to know is in these documents somewhere." A new requirements package was born—one with wheels and bright blue elastic straps. Luckily, this requirement package had a short life and did not survive the meeting.

A requirements package has to be appropriate to the audience and to the information you are trying to communicate. The luggage cart approach to requirements packages conveys a little too much information for an executive audience to review and sign off on a requirements document. You can load up with as much documentation as you want, but it has to be the right documentation. Otherwise, things will not work out very well.

Recommended Technique: Requirements for Vendor Selection

You might find yourself working on a project where a vendor or a set of vendors will be chosen to do the actual work. In this situation, you might be asked to develop solution requirements to be used during the vendor selection process to procure the solution from external vendors. In this situation, you will also build the vendor evaluation criteria and process used to consider and choose from the possible vendors. Requirements for vendor selection are typically captured and documented in one of three ways. The approaches differ in the degree of formality present in the associated vendor selection process. Let's quickly step through the three approaches.

Request for Information (RFI)   RFIs are usually short documents asking specific questions about the services that a particular vendor provides. RFIs tend to be used to prequalify potential solution vendors and to look for more solution-specific information from external vendors. This approach is used when input about solution options or approaches is needed.

Request for Quote (RFQ) An RFQ is a request for solution pricing based on the contents of an RFI or the more detailed and specific RFP. This allows vendors to provide a solution cost or total cost of ownership. An RFQ is used to get an idea of the costs to procure specific vendor goods or services.

Request for Proposal (RFP) RFPs provide potential vendors with detailed information, such as the solution requirements. Vendors answer specific, solution-focused questions about how their solution will meet the organization's needs and goals. RFPs are used when you know what you want and are making a detailed vendor selection in order to get it.

Create a Requirements Package

Requirements packages are used as inputs to another task in the Requirements Management and Communication knowledge area, communicating the requirements that are contained in that package to your project stakeholders. This output trail is summarized in Table 4.9.

TABLE 4.9 Output: Prepare Requirements Package

Output	Output Destinations	Destination Knowledge Area
Requirements package	Communicate requirements	Requirements Management and Communication

You have the primary responsibility for preparing requirements packages as part of your requirements development duties on a project. This means that you need a solid understanding of what the different stakeholders need to see in their requirements packages. Table 4.10 summarizes these requirements package needs for each business analysis stakeholder role.

TABLE 4.10 Focusing Requirements Packages by Stakeholder

Stakeholder Role	Needs a Requirements Package That . . .
Domain SMEs and End Users	Assists them in understanding every requirement in the solution scope from an operational point of view
Implementation SMEs	Provides an overall understanding of the requirements for the project, focused on the requirements that will be used in solution design
Project Manager	Focuses on the deliverables that need to be part of the project plan so they can be tracked as milestones

TABLE 4.10   Focusing Requirements Packages by Stakeholder *(continued)*

Stakeholder Role	Needs a Requirements Package That . . .
Regulators	Supports the legal, contractual, or governance standards guiding the requirements document content
Sponsors	Summarizes the high-level requirements at an executive level, such as the solution scope, Return on Investment (ROI), business benefits, costs, and schedule
Testers	Targets the critical success factors of the project for the business users so that an effective testing strategy can be built

Producing requirements packages occurs throughout the project life cycle, although the majority of requirements packages are produced as part of requirements development activities. Let's take a look at another aspect of producing project requirements: communicating the requirements to your project stakeholders.

Communicate Requirements

Much of the work that you perform as part of the Requirements Management and Communication knowledge area gets your project requirements organized and structured appropriately. After they are in good shape, you can share them with key stakeholders for their review, understanding, and approval. This final task holds you responsible for effectively communicating requirements to ensure stakeholder understanding.

 Real World Scenario

A Cat in the Hat Moment: Phase 1 and Phase 2

Phil, a business analyst, had a lot of fun with a recent project in his organization. The sales department decided one day that the company was lagging hopelessly behind other retail establishments because they forced their customers to physically sign a paper contract when purchasing services.

"After all," they protested, "even Walmart lets you sign on an electronic pad." "We must have electronic contracts!" said the business side of the house.

And the eContract project was born.

Phil and his team started working to determine the project requirements defining just what should, could, and must be delivered. It was an entertaining project. Operational questions were ignored. Legal constraints were ignored. All attempts to define eContracts in detail turned to dust. Group-focused meeting invitations went unanswered. Private meetings yielded conflicting and contradictory requirements.

However, at every executive management review or chance encounter in the hallways, Phil was asked, "Why is IT late on eContracts?"

In a last ditch effort to deliver, Phil divided the project into Phase I and Phase II. Phase I included building the storage and retrieval backbone for contract images along with a method to scan the backlog of all existing paper contracts into a new database. The requirements were developed, communicated, and approved with executive management and the project work began.

Right about the time that Phase I was developed and ready for beta testing, Phil was told that none of the business sponsors would accept the project in phases. They needed to get the entire thing, Phase I and Phase 2 (kind of like Thing 1 and Thing 2 from *The Cat in the Hat*). On the heels of this revelation, Phil heard in passing that another department had taken the same challenge and had fully developed eContracts using a PDF form methodology. Never mind that it didn't offer any storage, retrieval, or integration with the sales tools. It was complete and it was ready to rock and roll.

Of course, the next question for Phil was how to integrate this new eContracts PDF form methodology with the existing systems? Effective requirements communication with your stakeholders is certainly an art form.

Requirements communication tends to be iterative and ongoing in nature. It is usually done in parallel with most of the other business analysis tasks found in the *BABOK® Guide*. Requirements communication can be formal or informal in nature and includes conversations, notes, documents, presentations, and discussions with your stakeholders.

Figure 4.6 summarizes the inputs, outputs, techniques, and associated tasks for effectively communicating your project requirements.

FIGURE 4.6   Task summary: Communicate requirements.

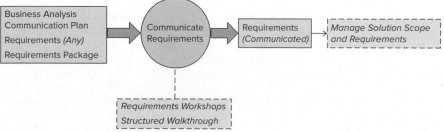

Several key inputs are used when communicating requirements during a project. These inputs are produced by other business analysis tasks. Let's take a closer look at these inputs.

Business Analysis Communication Plan   The business analysis communication plan defines how to communicate about business analysis activities and deliverables with your stakeholders. Your focus is on the requirements development tasks and the resulting deliverables. The business analysis communication plan is usually a subset of the project communication plan.

Requirements   You are responsible for determining which requirements should be contained in a specific requirement package. Requirements can be packaged and communicated to stakeholders at any point in the requirements development process.

Requirements Package   This set of requirements is grouped together as the primary vehicle for communicating about requirements with the business analysis stakeholders. Typically, a requirements packet is a requirements document, part of a requirements document, or a presentation by the business analyst.

Table 4.11 summarizes the inputs to the business analysis task of communicating requirements and lists the source of the input (if applicable).

TABLE 4.11   Inputs: Communicate Requirements

Task Input	Input Source	Source Knowledge Area
Business analysis communication plan	Plan business analysis Communication	Business Analysis Planning and Monitoring
Requirements (all)	—	
	(Allocated) Allocate requirements	Solution Assessment and Validation
	(Analyzed) Specify and model requirements	Requirements Analysis
	(Approved) Manage solution scope and requirements	Requirements Management and Communication
	(Communicated) Communicate requirements	Requirements Management and Communication
	(Maintained and reusable) Maintain requirements for reuse	Requirements Management and Communication
	(Prioritized) Prioritize requirements	Requirements Analysis

Task Input	Input Source	Source Knowledge Area
	(Stated, Unconfirmed) Document elicitation results	Elicitation
	(Stated, Unconfirmed) Confirm elicitation results	Elicitation
	(Traced) Manage requirements traceability	Requirements Management and Communication
	(Validated) Validate requirements	Requirements Analysis
	(Verified) Verify requirements	Requirements Analysis
	(Allocated) Allocate requirements	Solution Assessment and Validation
Requirements package	Prepare requirements package	Requirements Management and Communication

You need to perform the elements that are part of this task in order to effectively communicate their project requirements to the stakeholders. The two elements are

- General communication
- Making presentations

Let's step through each of these elements now.

General Communication   Formal requirements communication follows the contents of the business analysis communication plan. Informal communication takes place whenever it is needed. Business analysts are expected to effectively communicate about tasks being performed in four other knowledge areas:

- Enterprise Analysis
- Elicitation
- Requirements Analysis
- Solution Assessment and Validation

Let's look at these four knowledge areas in greater detail and see what the communication should focus on for each of them.

About Enterprise Analysis   You should communicate about the business case for the proposed project and the solution scope as it is being defined and agreed upon with the key project stakeholders.

About Elicitation   Communication during elicitation is critical to developing requirements. The communication skills and techniques required depend on the elicitation techniques being used to gather information.

About Requirements Analysis   Requirements analysis is where you take the elicited information and makes sense out of it. As the real requirements are being refined, modified, and clarified, they must be shared often with the stakeholders until finalized.

About Solution Assessment and Validation   Later in the project life cycle, assessments of the solution, solution components, organizational readiness, and the transition requirements must be communicated with stakeholders and the organization.

Exam Spotlight

According to the *BABOK® Guide*, requirements presentations are used for many reasons, including:

- Ensuring adherence to internal project quality standards

- Ensuring a cross-functional fit with other business process areas

- Obtaining business, delivery team, or testing team acceptance and sign-off of requirements

- Examining solution options with the delivery team

- Prioritizing a set of requirements before moving to the next project stage

- Making decisions regarding solution scope and requirements

Making Presentations   Business analysts are expected to have good presentation skills. These skills include creating the presentations, as well as delivering them to the stakeholders. Requirements presentations may be formal or informal, and they should fit both the audience and the situation.

Formal presentations are well-organized and structured events. Often, the participants have received the materials being discussed ahead of time, and they are expected to be ready to ask any questions they might have about the presentation's content. Formal presentations are used when the business analyst needs to obtain acceptance and sign-off for requirements.

Informal presentations are less structured and more impromptu in nature. They are typically used when the business analyst is communicating requirements to other project team members or informally walking through a requirements document.

Techniques to Consider

The *BABOK® Guide* recommends two techniques for communicating requirements with your stakeholders: *requirements workshops* and *structured walkthroughs*. Let's summarize each of those techniques.

Requirements Workshop   Requirements workshops are structured meetings where a selected group of stakeholders works together to define or refine a set of project requirements. During a requirements workshop, specific requirements may be presented to make everyone familiar with the existing solution scope and current requirements.

Structured Walkthrough   Structured walkthroughs are organized peer-level or team reviews of project deliverables, such as requirements. Attendees are looking for errors or omissions in the requirements. These sessions typically begin by presenting the requirements that will be stepped through and scrubbed.

Once you have applied one or more of the recommended techniques to communicate your requirements, you can say that those requirements have been communicated. Remember that communicating requirements ensures that the stakeholders understand what they have been told. Let's review the concept of communicating requirements one more time.

Communicating Requirements to your Stakeholders

Once you have decided how to approach formally or informally documenting your requirements, you are ready to communicate those requirements with your stakeholders. Remember that the communicated requirements are not just transmitted from the business analyst to the stakeholders. They must be received, understood, and acknowledged by those stakeholders in order for effective requirements communication to have taken place. This straightforward output trail is summarized in Table 4.12.

TABLE 4.12   Output: Communicate Requirements

Output	Output Destinations	Destination Knowledge Area
Requirements (communicated)	Manage solution scope and requirements	Requirements Management and Communication

You have the primary responsibility for communicating requirements during the requirements development activities on a project. However, all business analysis stakeholders may have a role in this task and could be involved with requirements communication activities across the project life cycle. They may be a sender or a receiver of the communicated requirements information.

How This Applies to Your Projects

In this chapter, you stepped through tasks that help you to manage and communicate project requirements with your stakeholders. One of the biggest challenges that you encounter on your projects is managing changing requirements. Sometimes it takes no more than five minutes after requirements sign-off to start hearing the inevitable changes creeping back into what was just approved. This can be caused by a number of factors, among them:

- Increased level of interaction and information sharing both within and between systems

- Lack of requirements traceability yielding poor understanding of requirements dependencies

- Changes in business plans and objectives that create a high-level focus shift impacting your existing requirements

- Changes in technology, law, policies, regulations, or directives

- Boundary conditions and constraints that move, causing your requirements to change as well

- Customers and users who change their minds about what they need

- Developers who add their own special twists, creating undocumented features that come back to haunt us

Configuration management (CM) is the key to managing changing requirements. Effective issue and change management is possible only if it is supported by CM. Configuration management is a technical and administrative activity focusing on creating, maintaining, and controlling change to the solution and its components (a configuration) throughout that solution's life cycle.

All organizations should have a Configuration Management Strategy for their projects. The strategy can be developed on a project-by-project basis or be applied to all projects that the organization undertakes. The Configuration Management Strategy identifies how, and by whom, the project's products will be controlled and protected. It answers the questions:

- How and where will the project's products be stored?

- What storage and retrieval security will be put in place?

- How will the products and the various versions and variants of these products be identified?

- How will changes to products be controlled?

- Where does responsibility for configuration management lie?

A Configuration Management Strategy is typically derived from a number of information sources, including any corporate configuration management, quality management or information management systems and strategies. Typically, the strategy is based on either the user's or the supplier's quality management systems and is targeted to support meeting the customer's quality expectations. The specific needs of the solution and the environment where it is being developed also plays a part in this strategy, as does the project management team structure with its identified configuration management roles and responsibilities.

To control and protect your solution and its assets, use a Configuration Management Strategy focusing on the solution and the solution components of your project. This is the best way to provide a framework ensuring that your solution deliverables are identified, tracked, and protected. The five generic steps are illustrated in Figure 4.7: Plan—Identify—Control—Account—Verify. Let's take a quick look at each step.

FIGURE 4.7   A framework for configuration management

Plan   Configuration management planning defines how you will address storage, retrieval, security, version control, and change control for the solution deliverables. Timing for these activities should also be defined.

Identify   Identification encompasses specifying and identifying all components of the final product. This is where you would create unique identifiers and records for each solution component.

Control   Configuration control invokes the ability to approve and baseline deliverables. Changes to approved products can only be made by following the formal change procedure for the solution.

Account   Status accounting is the recording and reporting of all current and historical data concerning each deliverable or configuration.

Verify   The project's Configuration Management System should provide you with the ability to audit actual deliverables against information recorded about those deliverables in the system, such as current status.

Summary

The five tasks of the Requirements Management and Communication knowledge area guide the business analyst in effectively managing requirements changes and communicating requirements to stakeholders across the project life cycle. One of the primary roles of the business analyst is developing and managing requirements across the project life cycle. Effective communication skills are an underlying competency enabling the business analyst to do this work. Successful projects start with defining and agreeing to what is needed. Without the ability to make these requirements understood, you will find it difficult to perform your job well.

The *BABOK® Guide* recommends business analysts plan for managing changing requirements before the real project work gets started. This information can be found in the requirements management plan, which was built as part of the Business Analysis Planning and Monitoring knowledge area. The same holds true for effectively communicating project requirements to the stakeholders. This information was also planned for and is located in the business analysis communication plan.

Most of the deliverables produced in the Requirements Management and Communication knowledge area focus on adding details to the stakeholder, solution, and transition requirements as specific actions are taken by the business analysis team. In addition to the requirements themselves, you must be able to build requirements packages to communicate those requirements with stakeholders.

Exam Essentials

Be able to list the tasks found in the Requirements Management and Communication knowledge area.   On your exam, you will see questions about the tasks, their associated techniques, their more detailed elements, and the key outputs they produce. You should memorize the five tasks of this knowledge area and any key outputs or techniques associated with them. The tasks are

Manage the solution scope and requirements.

Manage requirements traceability.

Maintain requirements for reuse.

Prepare requirements packages.

Communicate the requirements.

Be able to discuss how requirements are transformed by the tasks in this knowledge area.   The key deliverables produced by the tasks in this knowledge area focus on actions being taken to communicate project requirements to your stakeholders and manage any changes to those requirements. Luckily, the task name gives away the state of the requirements after the task is successfully performed. Here's a quick summary:

Manage solution scope and requirements yields the approved requirements.

Manage requirements traceability yields the traced requirements.

Maintain requirements for reuse yields the maintained and reusable requirements

Communicate requirements yields the communicated requirements.

Be able to explain the difference between formal and informal presentations. Formal presentations are well-organized and structured events, used when the business analyst needs to obtain acceptance and sign-off for requirements. Informal presentations are less structured and more impromptu in nature.

Be able to list and describe the five common traceability relationships between requirements. These relationships may be tracked and recorded during and after requirements development. They are

Necessity

Effort

Subset

Cover

Value

Be able to explain the knowledge area-specific techniques used to manage and communicate requirements. Managing and communicating requirements uses many knowledge area specific and general business analysis techniques. The knowledge area-specific techniques are baselining, sign-off, coverage matrix, requirements documentation, and requirements for vendor selection.

Be able to explain what "all requirements" means when it is used as a task input. When you see "Requirements [all] or [any] of *" used as a task input, that reference is telling you that any requirement may be an input to that particular task. Here is a short list of key things for you to remember about the tasks in the Requirements Management and Communication knowledge area:

All requirements may be traced to other requirements.

All stakeholder and solution requirements must be traceable to a business requirement.

Requirements may be maintained for reuse as long as they describe information of use to the organization beyond the lifetime of an initiative.

All or some part of the requirements may be included in a requirements package at the business analyst's discretion.

Any requirements may be communicated to stakeholders (within or without a requirements package).

Key Terms

This chapter stepped through the contents of the third knowledge area from the *BABOK® Guide*: Requirements Management and Communication. Most of this knowledge area focuses on effectively managing changes and communicating about requirements during the requirements development phase of a project.

You should understand how to apply the techniques and tasks in this knowledge area in order to be an effective business analyst. Additionally, you will need to know the five tasks and their associated elements and techniques from this knowledge area in order to be successful on the CBAP® or CCBA™ exams. The tasks include:

Manage the solution scope and requirements.

Manage requirements traceability.

Maintain requirements for reuse.

Prepare requirements packages.

Communicate the requirements.

A number of new key words in Chapter 4 related to managing and communicating requirements on a project. Here is a list of some of the key terms that you encountered in this chapter:

approved requirements	requirements allocation
baseline	requirements coverage
baselining	requirements package
configuration management (CM)	requirements structure
coverage matrix	requirements workshop
deliverable	satisfied requirements
maintained requirements	sign-off
ongoing requirements	structured walkthrough
problem tracking	traced requirements

Review Questions

1. Which Requirements Management and Communication task may seek approval and sign-off on the communicated requirements?

    A. Obtain requirements sign-off

    B. Communicate requirements

    C. Conduct requirements review

    D. Create requirements package

2. Which document determines how the business analyst shares requirements information with their stakeholders?

    A. Requirements management plan

    B. Project management plan

    C. Requirements package

    D. Business analysis communication plan

3. What stakeholder is responsible and accountable for the project scope?

    A. Project sponsor

    B. Business analyst

    C. Project manager

    D. Process owner

4. The performance of the Requirements Management and Communication tasks is governed by which plan?

    A. Requirements management plan

    B. Project management plan

    C. Business analysis plan

    D. Configuration management plan

5. What technique is recommended for tracing requirements when there are relatively few requirements?

    A. Coverage matrix

    B. RACI matrix

    C. Onion diagram

    D. Process model

6. Which statement is TRUE about communicating requirements?

A. Requirements must be verified and validated in order to be communicated.

B. Requirements must be formally distributed, reviewed, and agreed upon.

C. Requirements must be traced and reusable prior to being communicated.

D. Requirements may be communicated without using a requirements package.

7. An email message is sent to project stakeholders with a graphical model subset of the solution requirements attached to the message. This is an example of what type of requirements presentation format?

A. Informal

B. Targeted

C. Formal

D. Virtual

8. You are a business analyst tasked with ensuring that stakeholders with approval authority agree about the requirements that the solution should meet. You are most likely performing tasks from which knowledge area?

A. Business Analysis Planning and Monitoring

B. Enterprise Analysis

C. Requirements Management and Communication

D. Solution Assessment and Validation

9. The two techniques used to communicate requirements are

A. Requirements workshops and requirements packages

B. Structured walkthroughs and requirements workshops

C. Informal presentations and formal presentations

D. Requirements baselining and requirements workshops

10. What states of requirements outputs are contained in the Requirements Management and Communication knowledge area tasks?

A. Analyzed, allocated, and confirmed

B. Prioritized, approved, and validated

C. Stated, unconfirmed, and verified

D. Approved, communicated, and traced

11. What is another name for an organized peer-level review of a requirements document?

A. Structured walkthrough

B. Brainstorming session

C. Focus group

D. Requirements workshop

12. Approved requirements must support the:

    A. Solution scope

    B. Stakeholder needs

    C. Solution approach

    D. Business objectives

13. What is a specific output of the business analysis process that the business analyst or business analysis team has agreed to produce?

    A. Work product

    B. Requirements package

    C. Deliverable

    D. Traceability matrix

14. What provides the business analyst with a view of the reviewed and agreed-upon requirements at a specific point in time?

    A. Requirements package

    B. Requirements document

    C. Requirements review

    D. Requirements baseline

15. What should a business analyst use to formally present the solution requirements to their stakeholders for review, approval, and sign-off?

    A. Requirements checklist

    B. Requirements package

    C. Traceability matrices

    D. Graphical models

16. When defining your approach to requirements traceability on your project, what levels will you choose from when deciding how to trace the requirements?

    A. Business, stakeholder, or solution

    B. Capability, conditions, or constraints

    C. Individual, model, package, or feature

    D. Requirements, components, or artifacts

17. You are defining stakeholder requirements for a mission-critical software system using a new technology. What is the BEST recommendation for you to make to the project manager regarding the format options for the requirements?

    A. Stakeholder requirements documentation must be informal.

    B. Stakeholder requirements documentation must be formal.

    C. Stakeholder requirements documentation may be formal.

    D. Stakeholder requirements documentation may be informal.

18. Which traceability relationship addresses when one top-level requirement fully includes another requirement?

    A. Subset

    B. Effort

    C. Cover

    D. Value

19. What is the basis for requirements management during a project, ensuring that proposed requirements support business goals and objectives?

    A. Business case

    B. Business need

    C. Solution scope

    D. Desired outcome

20. You have just developed and distributed your requirements workshop meeting agenda to the participants. What have you just created?

    A. Work product

    B. Work artifact

    C. Deliverable

    D. Work package

Answers to Review Questions

1. B. The communicate requirements task may result in approval and sign-off on the requirements that have been communicated.

2. D. The business analysis communication plan determines how to communicate with stakeholders and provides a basis for meeting and communication expectations.

3. C. The project manager is responsible and accountable for the project scope, assessing the solution scope in order to define the project scope as part of the Requirements Management and Communication knowledge area.

4. C. Performance tasks found in the Requirements Management and Communication knowledge area are governed by the business analysis plan or plans for the project.

5. A. A coverage matrix is a table or spreadsheet used to trace requirements when there are relatively few requirements or when tracing is limited to the high-level requirements only.

6. D. Requirements communication can be formal or informal. You do not have to use a requirements package or a formal document to communicate requirements to your stakeholders. Requirements can be communicated at any point in time and in any way you choose.

7. A. Requirements may be presented informally using an email message, note, or verbally.

8. C. The tasks in the Requirements Management and Communication knowledge area are performed to ensure that all stakeholders have a shared understanding of the nature of a solution and to ensure that those stakeholders with approval authority are in agreement as to the requirements that the solution shall meet.

9. B. The two recommended techniques for communicating requirements are structured walkthroughs and requirements workshops.

10. D. The requirements output from the Requirements Management and Communication knowledge area include approved, communicated, maintained/reusable, and traced.

11. A. Structured walkthroughs are organized peer-level or team reviews of project deliverables, such as requirements. Attendees are looking for errors or omissions in the requirements.

12. A. Approved requirements must support the solution scope.

13. C. A deliverable is a specific output of the business analysis process that the business analyst or the business analysis team has agreed to produce.

14. D. A baseline is a view of the reviewed and agreed-upon requirements at a specific point in time.

15. B. Solution requirements should be packaged into a comprehensive requirements document for stakeholder review, approval, and sign-off.

16. C. Requirements tracing may be done at the individual requirement level, at the model level, the package level, or the feature level.

17. B. The stakeholder requirements documentation will be more formal under certain circumstances, such as when you are dealing with large projects to be delivered in phases, complex business areas, using new technology, or documenting requirements that are subject to regulatory review.

18. C. Cover is the traceability relationship where one requirement fully includes another requirement.

19. C. The solution scope is the basis for requirements management during a project, ensuring that proposed requirements support business goals and objectives.

20. A. A work product is a document or collection of notes or diagrams used by the business analyst to organize and analyze the requirements. A work product may or may not be a deliverable. Examples of work products include meeting agendas/minutes, interview questions/notes, facilitation session agendas, notes, the issues log, work plans, status reports, presentation slides, and traceability matrices.

Chapter

5

Controlled Middle: Elicitation

CBAP/CCBA EXAM TOPICS COVERED IN THIS CHAPTER

- ✓ Prepare for elicitation.
- ✓ Conduct elicitation activity.
- ✓ Document elicitation results.
- ✓ Confirm elicitation results.

Business analysts elicit the necessary information to develop their business, stakeholder, solution, and transition requirements for their projects. The four tasks in the Elicitation knowledge area guide you in gathering and understanding what your project stakeholders need from a new solution. Remember that effective elicitation is not just asking questions. It is a human-based activity in which you determine the right sources for your requirements and decide how to gather the right information from those sources.

Elicitation is very much like a scientific investigation. You will find yourself actively engaged in research, reading, talking, and observing what is going on in the organization as it relates to your project requirements. Elicitation includes organizing and evaluating the results to make sure you have well-organized information, the right level of knowledge, and a good handle on the scope and status of your elicitation efforts.

Requirements Elicitation

The Elicitation knowledge area focuses on gathering the right information to develop project requirements. The requirements for your project are the foundation for a solution that will be designed and deployed by the project and its efforts. Elicitation is defined as "to draw forth or bring out something latent or potential" or to "call forth or draw out information or a response." The *BABOK® Guide* states that when eliciting requirements, you should be able to:

- Understand the commonly used requirements elicitation techniques
- Select the appropriate technique or set of techniques to be used
- Prepare, execute, and complete each requirements elicitation technique

Requirements elicitation can be very challenging. When working with your stakeholders to define requirements, you are often faced with stakeholders who express those requirements in their own terms. You must learn to speak the stakeholders' language in order to understand the capabilities that are being described. Stakeholders don't always tell you everything that you need to know, at least not the first time around. Elicitation techniques must be selected to gather as much relevant information as quickly as possible.

Requirements elicitation is performed for all types of requirements found in the *BABOK® Guide*: business, stakeholder, solution, and transition. Elicitation is performed for your project's high-level business requirements as well as your more-detailed solution requirements. The tasks in the Elicitation knowledge area are performed in parallel with other requirements development tasks from the following knowledge areas:

- Enterprise Analysis (business requirements)
- Requirements Analysis (stakeholder and solution requirements)
- Solution Assessment and Validation (transition requirements)

Enterprise Analysis, Requirements Analysis, and Solution Assessment and Validation

Be sure you know which of the three knowledge areas are involved directly with requirements development work and how they relate to the elicitation efforts that we discuss in this chapter.

Enterprise Analysis   Enterprise Analysis focuses on identifying the business needs that drive a project and defining a feasible solution scope that can be implemented by the business. This knowledge area includes developing the business requirements for a project that define the high-level goals, objectives, and needs of the organization, and the high level business functionality needed in the resulting solution.

Requirements Analysis   Requirements Analysis steps you progressively through elaborating and prioritizing the stakeholder and solution requirements for a project. Stakeholder requirements define the needs of stakeholders and how they will interact with a solution. They act as a bridge between high-level business requirements and more-detailed solution requirements. In turn, the solution requirements describe the solution characteristics that are needed to meet the higher-level business and stakeholder requirements.

Solution Assessment and Validation   Solution Assessment and Validation assesses and validates the proposed, in progress, and implemented solutions before, during, and after the project life cycle. This is also where the project's transition requirements are defined. Transition requirements define the solution capabilities required to transition from the current to a future state and are no longer needed once the transition is complete.

The Elicitation knowledge area also addresses monitoring and reporting on the performance of the elicitation activities throughout the project. The business analysis team is responsible for assessing the effectiveness of the techniques being used to elicit requirements. The Elicitation knowledge area is addressed in Chapter 3 of the *BABOK® Guide*.

We will step through 10 commonly used requirements elicitation techniques in detail when we discuss the conducting elicitation activity later in this chapter. The techniques are

- *Brainstorming*
- Data Dictionary and Glossary
- Document Analysis
- Focus Groups
- Interface Analysis
- Interviews
- Observation
- Prototyping
- Requirements Workshops
- Survey/Questionnaire

You must learn to judge when you have elicited and acquired enough requirements information to start documenting and analyzing what you have learned. Experienced business analysts find themselves moving between requirements elicitation, requirements analysis, and requirements documentation activities many times on their projects. This is very much like the wand on a metronome, moving left to right to left again in order to keep the beat for the music being played.

The Business Analyst's Task List

You have four tasks to perform in the Elicitation knowledge area. (We will cover each one of these tasks in detail later in this chapter.) The task list from the *BABOK® Guide* includes:

- Preparing for requirements elicitation
- Conducting the elicitation activity
- Documenting the elicitation results
- Confirming the elicitation results

These tasks focus on obtaining the right information from the right sources in order to develop the right requirements for your project. Remember, effective requirements elicitation in your projects is multifaceted and requires:

- The right sources
- The right information
- The right technique
- Clear organization
- Evaluation and understanding
- Accurate reporting

If requirements elicitation is done correctly, the dividends that get paid downstream in the project life cycle can be tremendous. It is like a series of interlocking puzzle pieces. The correct project requirements lead to an appropriate solution design. When the solution design is implemented and deployed, the requirements are still framing the work effort, keeping the team on track to meet the project stakeholder's needs and expectations.

When Does Elicitation Take Place?

> Data is like garbage. You'd better know what you are going to do with it before you collect it.
>
> —*Attributed to Mark Twain*

The tasks in the Elicitation knowledge area begin early in the project life cycle and typically peak during the more detailed requirements development phase of the project. Requirements can be elicited at any point in the project life cycle. Typically, you elicit information for the first time early in the project life cycle. You will also find yourself eliciting information to clarify things you have missed or misinterpreted along the way. Changing requirements also trigger additional elicitation efforts later in the project life cycle.

Don't underestimate the importance of the work that gets done by these four tasks on your projects. Without the right requirements information from the right people, your project will probably not succeed. Let's step through the first task in the Elicitation knowledge area: preparing for a particular elicitation effort or activity.

Exam Spotlight

Approximately 14 percent (21 questions) of the 150 question-CBAP exam questions focus specifically on Elicitation. Although the numbers are not published for the CCBA exam, our experience has been that a similar focus is placed on Elicitation there. The exam questions target specific and detailed aspects of the four tasks found in this knowledge area.

Prepare for Elicitation

The first task in the Elicitation knowledge area is where you prepare a detailed schedule of your elicitation activities. Your elicitation activities can include interviewing an individual face-to-face, creating a survey to send out to a thousand worldwide end users, or facilitating a group workshop of 15 people. Your preparation work should include:

- Building a detailed schedule for the elicitation activity
- Defining the more detailed tasks that need to be done
- Scheduling those detailed tasks

This preparation step ensures that the necessary stakeholder resources are organized and scheduled in advance. This step also allows you to get all of your ducks in a row—from meeting room logistics, to required materials, to attendance and attention from the right people. Figure 5.1 summarizes the inputs, outputs, techniques, and associated tasks used to prepare for requirements elicitation.

FIGURE 5.1   Task summary: Prepare for elicitation.

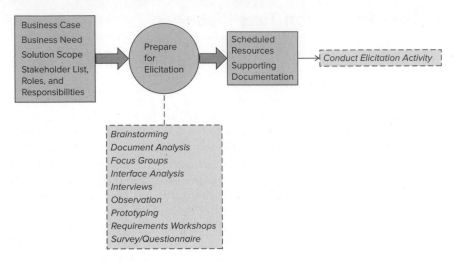

Several key inputs are needed to adequately prepare to elicit requirements information on your project. These key inputs are produced by a number of other business analysis tasks, and they include the business case, business need, and solution scope. Let's have a look at each of these task inputs in greater detail.

Business Case   The business case assesses the costs and benefits of a proposed project. This business framework is used along with the solution scope to determine the information to be elicited when developing stakeholder, solution, and transition requirements.

Business Need   The business need defines the problem or opportunity being faced by the business. This information is used to determine the information to be elicited when developing business requirements early in the project life cycle.

Solution Scope   The solution scope provides the business analyst with the set of capabilities a solution must deliver to meet a defined business need. This solution definition is used along with the business case to determine the information to be elicited when developing stakeholder, solution, and transition requirements.

Stakeholder List, Roles, and Responsibilities   This list of business analysis stakeholders is used to identify the stakeholders who should participate in the requirements elicitation activities for developing the business, stakeholder, solution, and transition requirements on a project.

Table 5.1 summarizes the inputs to this task and lists the source of each input (if applicable).

TABLE 5.1   Inputs

Task Input	Input Source	Source Knowledge Area
Business case	Define business case	Enterprise Analysis
Business need	Define business need	Enterprise Analysis
Solution scope	Define solution scope	Enterprise Analysis
Stakeholder list, roles, and responsibilities	Conduct stakeholder analysis	Business Analysis Planning and Monitoring

When preparing to elicit requirements information across the project life cycle, the business analyst should perform several elements, including:

- Clarifying the scope of the selected elicitation techniques and gathering any supporting materials
- Scheduling the resources (people, facilities, equipment)
- Notifying appropriate parties of the elicitation plan

Exam Spotlight

There are ways to add value when preparing for requirements elicitation on your projects. You should take the time to agree with the involved stakeholders about how you will provide them with feedback, verify the information, and sign off as you agree on your elicitation results. You should also make certain that you establish the ground rules up front for dealing with individuals and groups during the scheduled elicitation activities.

There are several techniques you may use to prepare for eliciting requirements information on your projects. We will list those techniques here. However, we will describe all 10 of the elicitation techniques in detail as part of the conducting elicitation activity task. That is the next task in this chapter.

Techniques to Consider

The *BABOK® Guide* recommends using one or more of the following techniques when you are preparing for the elicitation activities on your project. They are listed for you here:

- Brainstorming
- Document Analysis
- Focus Groups
- Interface Analysis

- Interviews
- Observation
- Prototyping
- Requirements Workshops
- Survey/Questionnaire

Once you have selected and applied one or more techniques as part of your preparation efforts, you are ready to conduct the elicitation activity itself. We will discuss that next.

Produce Scheduled Resources and Supporting Materials

Preparing for elicitation yields two distinct deliverables: the *scheduled resources* and the *supporting materials*. The scheduled resources are exactly what they sound like—the people, facilities, and equipment that you need for requirements elicitation. The resource schedule should include the resource name or names, the location of the elicitation activity, and anything else that might be needed.

Supporting materials are anything that you need in order to perform the elicitation activity. These materials could be required for a particular elicitation technique, such as having a whiteboard available for a requirements workshop.

 Real World Scenario

Palmer Divide Vineyards Elicitation Worksheet

The IT staff at the vineyard has a long history of projects that don't go according to plan. Almost every effort is over budget and behind schedule. The team has been assessing their current project practices in order to achieve more successful results. Taylor, the head of IT, has decided that this has gone on for long enough. She is determined to put project management processes in place that enable better project outcomes and less rework.

One area of weakness is the team's approach to requirements development. In the past, senior management has been reluctant to allot much time for defining what needs to be done. They ask, "When will you guys be doing the real work and producing something useful?"

For the research study project, Taylor and the team have defined a simple requirements development process that they plan to follow. Senior management has agreed to allot them the extra time to define requirements before the design and coding efforts begin.

One step in Taylor's process is requirements elicitation. She believes that gathering the right information from the right folks makes all the difference. Even though the vineyard is a small company, there are many opinions on what needs to be done and what is most

---

important. Taylor hopes to harness that information and target defining high-quality requirements for this and every subsequent project.

Taylor and the team have decided to plan their elicitation efforts thoroughly. They are using an information-gathering worksheet to document the questions they want to ask and the methods they want to use to gather that information. The team plans to ask the same question more than once and to organize the results by question for further analysis and decision making. Taylor is correct in assuming that this will be the first step in a more robust, well-planned requirements elicitation effort at Palmer Divide Vineyards.

Business analysts often like to use a worksheet to plan their elicitation efforts and get a handle on the questions they will be asking. Table 5.2 provides an example of a requirements elicitation worksheet populated for a round of solution requirements elicitation at Palmer Divide Vineyards. You can use questions and apply techniques, as shown here, or add additional information to your worksheet based on your organization and the nature of your project.

An elicitation worksheet helps you define your elicitation activity objectives and allows you to prepare your questions ahead of time and review them. By thinking through your questions and documenting them in this way, you are also setting the basis for organizing your elicitation results.

TABLE 5.2 Palmer Divide Vineyards Elicitation Worksheet

Palmer Divide Vineyards Green Project

Objective: Get stated solution requirements from stakeholders about the research study capabilities of the new system.

Approach: We will interview people individually and then follow up with a requirements workshop to discuss the results of this elicitation session.

Elicitation Questions	Whom to Ask	Technique(s) to Apply
1. What current research study activities do you currently perform?	Hector (Marketing director) Sawyer (Vineyard manager) Dan (Winemaker, SME) Ginger (Product manager) Taylor (IT manager)	Interviews (individual) Requirements Workshop (entire group) Document Analysis of existing capabilities Observation
2. What does your job consist of?	Hector, Sawyer, Dan, Ginger, Taylor	Interviews (individual) Requirements Workshop (entire group)

TABLE 5.2   Palmer Divide Vineyards Elicitation Worksheet *(continued)*

Elicitation Questions	Whom to Ask	Technique(s) to Apply
3. What are the most important activities the new research study capabilities should address?	Hector, Sawyer, Dan, Ginger, Taylor	Interviews (individual) Requirements Workshop (entire group)
4. Which of your needs is most important? Which need should be met first?	Hector, Sawyer, Dan, Ginger, Taylor	Interviews (individual) Requirements Workshop (entire group)
5. If you could change two or three things about your existing research study activities, what would you change?	Hector, Sawyer, Dan, Ginger, Taylor	Interviews (individual) Requirements Workshop (entire group)
6. What better, new, or different information do you need to perform research studies for the vineyard?	Hector, Sawyer, Dan, Ginger, Taylor	Interviews (individual) Requirements Workshop (entire group)
7. What system functionality do you use? Not use?	Hector, Sawyer, Dan, Ginger, Taylor	Interviews (individual) Requirements Workshop (entire group)
8. What capabilities do you think the new solution should provide for others? Why?	Hector, Sawyer, Dan, Ginger, Taylor	Interviews (individual) Requirements Workshop (entire group)
9. What activities will you perform using the new solution?	Hector, Sawyer, Dan, Ginger, Taylor	Interviews (individual) Requirements Workshop (entire group)
10. From your point of view, what are the key new requirements for the research study aspects of the solution? Why?	Hector, Sawyer, Dan, Ginger, Taylor	Interviews (individual) Requirements Workshop (entire group)

Once you have completed your elicitation preparation, it is time to go get the information that you need from your stakeholders. Scheduled resources and supporting materials (summarized in Table 5.3) are used as an input to conducting elicitation.

TABLE 5.3   Outputs: Prepare for Elicitation

Output	Output Destinations	Destination Knowledge Area
Scheduled resources	Conduct elicitation activity	Elicitation
Supporting materials		

As a business analyst, you are responsible for adequate requirements elicitation preparation. On large projects, this responsibility often falls to the collective members of the business analysis team, who will be simultaneously eliciting requirements information from different stakeholders. Be sure to coordinate who is doing what when, and make sure you plan to sit down and accumulate what everyone has learned. Any business analysis stakeholder can be involved in requirements elicitation. The project manager may also be involved in scheduling resources. Let's take a look at the next step in effective requirements elicitation—successfully conducting the elicitation activity.

Conduct Elicitation Activity

There are a number of ways to elicit requirements for your projects. The most common elicitation technique is a face-to-face meeting with one or more of your project stakeholders to gather information regarding their needs. However, elicited information doesn't have to come directly from people. It can also come to you indirectly, based on your research and review of existing documents and other data.

Exam Spotlight

The *BABOK® Guide* lists three types of elicitation techniques: events, performed work, and collected work. Make sure that you can recognize each individual elicitation technique and that you remember which type
of technique it is.

- Elicitation events take place using one of six techniques: brainstorming, focus groups, interviews, observation, prototyping, and requirements workshops.

- Elicitation work is performed by the business analyst using the document analysis or interface analysis technique.

- Elicitation work is distributed and collected using surveys/questionnaires that are sent out to the stakeholders.

That takes care of nine elicitation techniques. There is also a tenth technique that is used to conduct requirements elicitation. That technique is building a business glossary of key terms and definitions as part of your elicitation efforts.

Figure 5.2 summarizes the inputs, outputs, techniques, and associated tasks used to conduct requirements elicitation.

FIGURE 5.2   Task summary: Conduct elicitation activity

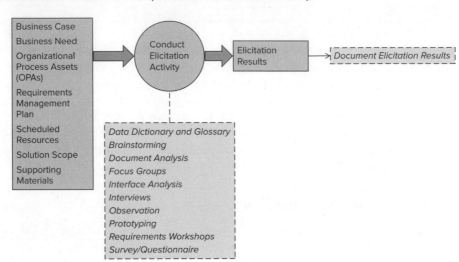

Several key inputs are needed when eliciting requirements information. These key inputs are produced by a number of other business analysis tasks. They include outputs from the elicitation preparation work you already performed: the scheduled resources and the supporting materials. Let's look at each of these task inputs in greater detail.

Business Case   The business case assesses the costs and benefits of a proposed project. This business framework is used along with the solution scope to determine the information to be elicited when developing stakeholder, solution, and transition requirements.

Business Need   The business need defines the problem or opportunity being faced by the business. This information is used to determine the information to be elicited when developing business requirements early in the project life cycle.

Organizational Process Assets (OPAs)   Organizations often have templates and processes to assist the business analyst in eliciting requirements. If they are available to you, make use of them.

Requirements Management Plan   The requirements management plan defines the process for developing project requirements. This is where you and the business analysis team describe the requirements attributes to be associated with the project requirements as they are developed. This information must be noted, gathered, and tracked as part of the project's requirements elicitation and analysis efforts.

Scheduled Resources   Scheduled resources include the people, facilities, and equipment that must be available for the elicitation activity that is taking place.

Solution Scope   The solution scope provides you with the set of capabilities a solution must deliver to meet a defined business need. This solution definition is used along with the business case to determine the information to be elicited when developing stakeholder, solution, and transition requirements.

Supporting Materials   Supporting materials such as flipcharts or existing documents must be made available as part of the requirements elicitation activity.

Table 5.4 summarizes the inputs to this elicitation task and lists the source of each input (if applicable).

TABLE 5.4   Inputs

Task Input	Input Source	Source Knowledge Area
Business case	Define business case	Enterprise Analysis
Business need	Define business need	Enterprise Analysis
Organizational Process Assets (OPAs)	—	—
Requirements management plan	Plan requirements management process	Business Analysis Planning and Monitoring
Scheduled resources	Prepare for elicitation	Elicitation
Solution scope	Define solution scope	Enterprise Analysis
Supporting materials	Prepare for elicitation	Elicitation

There are several elements that you should perform when eliciting project requirements information across the project life cycle, including:

- Tracing requirements
- Capturing requirements attributes
- Collecting elicitation metrics

Let's look at each element in greater detail.

Tracing Requirements   You should be tracing requirements as part of your elicitation efforts. At a minimum, tracing the requirements back to the business goals and objectives can keep the new capabilities within the defined solution. Remember, the traceability approach is defined in the project's requirements management plan.

Capturing Requirements Attributes   Experienced business analysts proactively capture requirements attributes as part of the elicitation process. This is much easier than having to go back to the stakeholders and ask additional questions about requirements prioritization and ownership later. The requirements attributes to be captured for the project are defined in the project's requirements management plan.

Collecting Elicitation Metrics   Tracking the time it took to complete an elicitation activity time and comparing it to what was originally planned is very helpful for planning future requirements elicitation work. This information allows you to refine your time and effort estimates for eliciting requirements in the future.

The *BABOK® Guide* contains 10 recommended elicitation techniques that you should be able to use as needed. Each technique is an excellent way to elicit requirements. The technique you choose should be the best fit for the situation that you find yourself in. For instance, scheduling telephone interviews with 100 individual users is not time effective. Building a survey/questionnaire to send to them combined with a requirements workshop for a selected subset of senior or key users may be a better approach to gathering information. The 10 techniques are listed for you here:

- Brainstorming
- Data Dictionary and Glossary
- Document Analysis
- Focus Groups
- Interface Analysis
- Interviews
- Observation
- Prototyping
- Requirements Workshops
- Survey/Questionnaire

Exam Spotlight

A great many questions for the Elicitation knowledge area will focus on the details of how you apply the 10 elicitation techniques. Make sure that you are very familiar with the details of these techniques.

The techniques found in the *BABOK® Guide* are applicable to many situations. Nine of these 10 techniques are not used exclusively by the Elicitation knowledge area. Building a data dictionary and glossary is exclusively used when conducting requirements elicitation. The other nine elicitation techniques may be used by tasks in other knowledge areas as well.

Think of each recommended elicitation technique as a three-step process: prepare, conduct, and wrap-up. Figure 5.3 illustrates the sequence of the steps for you. First, you prepare to use the technique you have chosen for eliciting requirements. The preparation activities will be driven by the technique you have selected. Then, you conduct the elicitation activity and use the selected technique in the appropriate way. After the elicitation activity is done, you then are responsible for wrapping things up by reviewing, reporting, and, as needed, further investigating what you have learned.

FIGURE 5.3   Applying the elicitation techniques

Let's take the time now to step through each of the 10 business analysis techniques. These techniques are commonly used during requirements elicitation on your projects.

Recommended Elicitation Technique: Brainstorming

According to the *BABOK® Guide*, brainstorming is one of the 16 required techniques in the fundamental knowledge base of an effective business analyst. This elicitation technique fosters creative thinking about the capabilities of a new solution. Brainstorming enables out-of-the-box thinking in a nonjudgmental environment. Out-of-the-box thinking is also called lateral thinking.

Using brainstorming as an elicitation technique produces numerous new ideas from the people involved. If you haven't used brainstorming as part of your requirements elicitation efforts, you should try it on for size. You can draw on the experience and creativity of the participants in your brainstorming session, yielding a plethora of interesting and relevant results that require further analysis.

A productive brainstorming session has two parts: *idea generation* and *idea reduction*. Idea generation is the creative part where people share their ideas with one another, no matter how off the wall those ideas might be. Idea reduction is where the group takes the generated ideas and cleans them up a bit to make the information useful for the situation at hand.

Preparing for a brainstorming session involves defining the session itself, including the particular area of interest for the session and the amount of time that will be spent by the participants. A longer brainstorming session is needed for larger groups of people. The ideal brainstorming session contains six to eight people.

Other logistics need to be determined prior to the session start. The session's facilitator and participants need to be selected. Expectations for the session should also be defined, focusing on the area of interest. The evaluation and rating criteria for the idea reduction step should also be set and agreed to in advance.

Over the years, we have found that the success of a brainstorming session depends on the willingness of the participants to actually participate and contribute. It is essential that ideas not be debated during idea generation in order to maximize contributions from the group. Personal feelings and organizational politics need to be set aside during the session in order to achieve the best results.

Once the ideas are generated and recorded, they need to be analyzed and reduced to something useful. Wrapping up is where the idea reduction part of a brainstorming session takes place. The group discusses and evaluates ideas using the evaluation and rating criteria that were previously defined and agreed upon by the group as part of the meeting. A condensed list will be built by combining some ideas, deleting some ideas, and eliminating any duplicate ideas. The resulting list will then be distributed to the appropriate parties for review.

Recommended Technique: Data Dictionary and Glossary

You should take the time to identify and define all of the terminology that is being used as part of your project. If you are lucky, you work in an organization that already maintains a business glossary of terms that apply to your project efforts. If not, you need to build one. This work should start when you define the business need and business requirements, and continue across the project life cycle. The two recommended ways to define and track important terminology across your project life cycle are with a glossary and a data dictionary.

Glossaries allow you to document any key business terms along with their definitions. It is a best practice to start your business glossary immediately during that project's controlled start and to keep it updated throughout the project life cycle. Much of the information that goes into the glossary will be a result of your business, stakeholder, solution, and transition requirements development efforts.

Data dictionaries are a bit more technical in nature. A data dictionary is used to define data elements, their meanings, and their allowable values. Building a data dictionary for your project should begin when your project requirements are being developed. Two types of data elements are found in a data dictionary: *primitive data elements* and *composite data elements*. Let's take a closer look at each type.

Primitive Data Elements   Primitive data elements contain basic information about data elements. Each data element has a unique name. The data element may also have aliases in addition to its unique name. You will see this when different stakeholder groups call the same data element something different. Every data element needs to state the acceptable values for that data element. This could be a range of numbers or limits to the number of characters allowed in a name. Primitive data elements must also be defined in the data dictionary. For example, a primitive data element might be defined as customer name, customer title, customer age, or a customer phone number. The data values become the basis for your data base technical design by defining the contents, relationships, and format of solution data that will be needed.

Composite Data Elements Composite data elements are assembled from primitive data elements. Composite data elements allow you to manage multiple pieces of related data as a single, composite data element. This can be done in three ways: sequences, repetitions, and optional elements. Sequencing primitive data elements specifies that they must always occur in the same order. Repeating primitive data elements has them occurring more than one time in the composite element. Optional elements are primitive data elements that may or may not occur as part of a composite data element. A composite data element might consist of an array of values for a unique customer containing the four primitive data elements previously listed: customer name, customer title, customer age, and customer phone number.

Recommended Elicitation Technique: Document Analysis

According to the *BABOK® Guide*, document analysis is another of the 16 required techniques in the fundamental knowledge base of an effective business analyst. Document analysis allows you to elicit, confirm, or cross-check project requirements information by studying existing documentation and other relevant information. These secondary sources of information allow the business analyst to gather details of existing solutions.

Document analysis assumes that the existing documentation is easily available and up-to-date. If the information is not up-to-date and valid, it will be of little help in eliciting requirements. Experienced business analysts also look for related information that may have been prepared for another project or purpose (also known as secondary data) but is relevant to their requirements elicitation efforts.

To conduct document analysis, you step through three stages: preparation, review, and wrap-up. Preparation involves locating and evaluating the documents that are relevant to your planned elicitation activity. Document review has you studying those materials, identifying any relevant details, and documenting those details along with any questions you might have. Wrap-up allows you to get the answers to any questions you might have and confirm what you have discovered with your stakeholders.

Recommended Elicitation Technique: Focus Groups

Focus groups provide you with an interactive group environment to elicit ideas and attitudes from selected stakeholders about a product, service, or opportunity. The work done in a focus group may be similar to a brainstorming session, but a focus group is a more structured event. Focus groups are a form of qualitative research in which your participants are prequalified to address a set of questions about a particular topic.

Real World Scenario

Getting Things in Focus

Ginger was assigned the task of eliciting business requirements for the senior management team of an overseas bank. She enjoyed her trip across the ocean and really looked forward to facilitating several focus group sessions that targeted the definition of and the agreement to the business requirements for developing a new IT system. Ginger believed this was going to be an interesting and rewarding consulting assignment. She was right.

The initial focus group session kicked off mid-morning on Tuesday. Ginger, in her role as moderator, arrived early to make sure the room was arranged correctly and that all required materials were available to share with the attendees. She made certain that the room was arranged in the traditional U-shape that many facilitators prefer. This arrangement would allow Ginger to facilitate effectively by walking the inside of the tables to make points, clarify issues, and minimize any conflicts.

This particular group was a heterogeneous set of vice presidents from the numerous operating units at the bank. The discussion guide for this session focused on the high-level business drivers justifying the project and the big-picture capabilities that would be required. Everyone arrived pretty much on time, and dressed for success. The coffee was poured into lovely ceramic mugs with the bank logo on them, breakfast treats were selected, introductions were made, and the focus group was off and running.

About an hour into the session, it became apparent to Ginger (and everyone else in the room) that two of the vice presidents had conflicting opinions about the definition of the new system capabilities. They were sitting right across the tables from one another. Voices were rising and the conflict began to escalate. Ever the well-trained facilitator, Ginger walked briskly down the tables in order to physically stand between them and shut down their conflict.

Just as Ginger stepped between them, one of the angry vice presidents threw his coffee cup across the table right at the other fellow. Alas, that coffee cup never got to the other fellow—it hit Ginger in the face. The room went very still as the cup fell to the floor. Ginger knelt down, picked up the cup, and stood back up.

"Well," she said, "Let's get on with things, shall we?"

She then moved on to the next topic in her discussion guide.

Funny thing, there were no more conflicts in that particular focus group. Even funnier, there were no conflicts in the sessions that followed. The business requirements for the project were defined and agreed upon, and the project was off and running. After she got back home, Ginger found herself wondering if it was her strong facilitation skills that made those focus groups go so very well, or if it was her black eye that got everyone's undivided attention during the rest of the week.

Focus group preparation requires you to select and recruit the right participants for the session. The *BABOK® Guide* recommends a focus group size of 6 to 12 attendees. A moderator and a recorder for the session should also be assigned ahead of time. It is essential that your focus group be guided by a trained moderator. In many organizations, the trained moderator is the business analyst. The moderator creates a discussion guide defining the goals and objectives of the session and five or six questions to be discussed. The focus group location and any necessary technical services also need to be set up in advance.

The focus group should be conducted in a one-to-two-hour session. The moderator is responsible for guiding the discussion using the discussion guide as a road map. The recorder is responsible for capturing the group's comments. It is not advisable for the moderator to be the recorder—it is quite difficult to facilitate a focus group and take notes at the same time.

Focus groups may contain homogeneous or heterogeneous participants. Homogeneous participants all have similar characteristics; heterogeneous participants have diverse backgrounds. For example, a homogeneous focus group may consist of key end users who deal with the order entry aspect of the business, discussing the order entry capabilities for a new solution. A heterogeneous focus group would be one with a cross section of end users from all aspects of the business being present to discuss those very same order entry capabilities from multiple perspectives.

After the session is complete, the moderator is responsible for analyzing and documenting the session results as group themes and perspectives. This captures agreements, as well as disagreements, in the areas being discussed. The moderator produces the report and sends that report to key stakeholders, business analysts, or marketing staff

Recommended Elicitation Technique: Interface Analysis

Interface analysis identifies and defines the requirements for how a new solution and its components will interact with everything else that is already out there. Everything else usually includes existing solutions and their components. An *interface* is a connection between two components of a system. All external interfaces should be considered stakeholders on your projects.

Exam Spotlight

For your exam, be sure to remember the three common interface types that are typically defined by the business analyst:

- User interfaces with the solution

- Interfaces to and from external applications

- Interfaces to and from external hardware devices

Interface analysis establishes a basis for interoperability by recognizing inputs, outputs, and key data elements. This allows you to clarify the solution boundaries and reach agreement on any required interfaces. Preparing for interface analysis work involves reviewing current documentation and looking for any interface requirements. You should visualize the interfaces to and from your solution and any external parties, applications, or devices. Your goal is to identify interfaces early in the project. Remember, if you miss one, it can come back to haunt you later.

Each identified interface is analyzed and evaluated. You will identify which interfaces are needed for each stakeholder or system interacting with the solution and the solution components. Be sure to describe the purpose, type, and the high-level details of each identified interface. Interface identification creates the need for collaboration with other systems or projects with which the new solution interfaces, and it impacts integration and implementation at the end of the development life cycle.

When wrapping up interface analysis work, specify the interface requirements. Describe the inputs, outputs, associated validation rules, and any event triggers. Early interface identification is helpful in addressing the interoperability of a new solution. Interoperability issues can impact the planned solution delivery date due to additional work and testing of the interfaces and data, so the sooner the interfaces are identified, the better.

Recommended Elicitation Technique: Interviews

According to the *BABOK® Guide*, interviews are yet another required technique in the fundamental knowledge base of an effective business analyst. Effective business analysts possess very good interviewing skills. A good interviewer comes to the table with a high level of domain understanding, experience in conducting elicitation interviews, and the skills to ask relevant questions and document the interview results.

Your interviewing abilities are balanced out by the interviewee's willingness to provide you with relevant information. You need to clearly understand and communicate what the new system will provide to the stakeholder and the business while establishing rapport with your interviewee. These interpersonal aspects of requirements elicitation can be very challenging for some folks.

Requirements elicitation interviews may be structured or unstructured. Structured interviews are driven by a predefined set of questions. Unstructured interviews are more of an informal, open-ended conversation with someone.

While most people think of interviewing as an individual activity, interviews may also be done with groups of people. If you are using interviews to elicit requirements from a group of people, be sure that each member of the group answers each question.

Exam Spotlight

The *BABOK® Guide* recommends that you organize your interview questions using either priority or logical order. When questions are organized by priority, the business analyst asks the most important questions first. Of course, you will have to determine the priority relative to something relevant, such as meeting the business objectives or delivering the solution scope. Questions organized logically may follow several schemes, including from general questions to more specific questions or by stepping through a process from start to finish.

Effective interviewing follows a systematic process from preparation to the interview itself to follow-up. Preparing for a requirements elicitation interview starts with defining the goal of the interview and identifying the interviewee. You will need to design the interview (structured versus unstructured). You also need to create and organize your interview questions. The location, mode (face-to-face or electronic), and time for the interview should be decided and agreed upon.

It is considered a best practice to open an interview by introducing yourself and stating the purpose of the interview. You should stay focused on your interview goal and try to ask the predefined questions that you prepared. Any concerns raised by the interviewee should be addressed during the interview, if possible. Good interviewers are active listeners, confirming that they understand what has been said.

After an interview has been completed, organize the information from the interview as soon as possible. Send the notes of the session to the interviewee for their review and comments. This ensures that both your notes and resulting stated requirements are correct and complete.

We have found it extremely effective to close down our requirements elicitation interviews by asking some version of the following four questions:

- Is there anyone else we should speak to?

- Have we missed anything?

- Do you have any questions for us?

- Can we contact you directly if we have any additional questions or require any additional clarification?

Recommended Elicitation Technique: Observation

Observation is a great way to study people while they are performing their jobs. During requirements elicitation, understanding what folks are doing now sets the basis for the new capabilities they will need in the future. Those new capabilities are what you are defining in your project requirements. Observation is also called job shadowing or simply following people around. There are variations on observation, such as the business analyst:

- Participates in the actual work as an end user

- Becomes a temporary apprentice for someone

- Watches a demonstration of what should be done.

The observation technique provides you with a hands-on feel for how people get their work done. If you observe more than one person, you should try to identify the commonalities and differences across multiple users doing the same job or using the same system. Be careful though; when someone is watching, people sometimes behave differently than they normally do.

To prepare for observation, you need to determine who and what you want to observe and what questions you would like to answer. You also need to select your observation approach: *passive observation* or *active observation*.

Passive (Invisible) Observation   During passive observation, you watch the user doing their work; you do not ask questions during that work. Instead, you record what you see, write down any questions, and stay out of the way. Once the user is finished, you can ask questions about what you witnessed.

Active (Visible) Observation   Active observation is interactive; you observe and talk with the user. You can ask questions right away, even if they interrupt the user.

When conducting your observation, don't forget to introduce yourself to the user. You might want to suggest that they think aloud while they do their job, so you can hear what they are thinking. Be sure to take detailed notes. Remember, your goal is to put yourself in the user's shoes.

Recommended Elicitation Technique: Prototyping

Prototyping is a great way to add detail to your solution interface requirements and integrate those requirements with the other requirements defining the new solution. Essentially, a prototype is an initial or preliminary version of a solution or system.

Prototypes are extremely valuable for identifying, describing, and validating your solution and user interface needs during requirements development. There is tremendous value in allowing early user interaction and feedback with a new solution. For software projects, mock up screens, or report layouts, allow users to interact with and comment on the solution.

Two high-level categories of prototypes are defined in the *BABOK® Guide*: *functional scope* prototypes and usage throughout the *System Development Life Cycle (SDLC)* prototypes. Let's take a closer look at each category.

Functional Scope Prototypes   Functional scope prototypes model the functionality or capabilities of the solution or system. Basically, they show the end users what the system can do for them and how it gets done. Functional scope prototypes come in two flavors: horizontal or vertical. Let's take a look at each flavor.

Horizontal   Horizontal functional scope prototypes (or horizontal prototypes) model a shallow and wide view of the solution functionality. Typically, no business logic is running under the covers of the mocked-up user interface. One example of a horizontal prototype might be representing the full set of high-level online ordering capabilities for call center representatives. However, no capability would contain much detail about how things were done.

Vertical   Vertical functional scope prototypes (or vertical prototypes) focus on a deep and narrow slice of solution functionality. Using the previous call center example, a vertical prototype might be a detailed, multilevel mock-up of the online circuit provisioning capabilities for call center representatives. These would be one key aspect of the full set of online ordering capabilities available to the end users.

SDLC Prototypes   SDLC prototypes are built to be used cross the Systems Development Life Cycle of the project. They will be used to elicit requirements and reused across the life cycle. For example, SDLC prototypes might be revisited during design activities to make sure that requirements are still being met in a designed solution. SDLC prototypes come in two varieties: throw-away and evolutionary. Let's have a look at each variety.

Throw-Away   *Throw-away prototypes* are built to uncover and identify user interface requirements using simple tools. These tools can be paper based or computer based. A throw-away prototype is intended to be discarded after the final system is complete. These prototypes don't have anything much under the covers that would be of operational use. Throw-away prototypes are used to gather requirements information.

Evolutionary   *Evolutionary prototypes* are built to be the basis for the new fully functioning system. In order to use them in this way, the prototypes must be built using a specialized prototyping tool or language. They ultimately become the working software application that is part of the solution. Evolutionary prototypes are also called functional prototypes.

Exam Spotlight

There are two significant decisions for you to make when using prototyping as a requirements elicitation vehicle:

- Use a throw-away prototype (discard after system developed) or an evolutionary/functional prototype (becomes all or part of the system)?

- Use a vertical perspective (narrow detailed area) versus a horizontal point of view (broad brush of all capabilities at a very high level)?

To prepare for prototyping, you must clearly identify the functionality that will be modeled and select your prototyping approach. Then, build the prototype in an iterative fashion, adding details as appropriate. It is important to make sure that the interface elements of the prototype can be traced back to the solution requirements, such as processes, data rules, and business rules. Prototypes are intended for end users, so make sure that the prototype actually meets their needs for the new solution.

 ### Real World Scenario

Throw-Away Does Not Mean Keep

Phil, the business analyst, frequently uses throw-away prototypes for his user-facing software systems. He believes (and rightfully so) that prototyping the user interface is a great way to get input before spending enormous amounts of time and effort in the actual system development and implementation. As Phil is fond of saying to his team, end users sure seem to know what they don't like when they see it. By using a throw-away prototype or storefront, Phil is frequently able to get a handle on the user's interaction with the new system and discover their likes and dislikes.

While working on developing a software system for a large telecommunications firm, Phil determined that prototyping was the best approach to use. The development team knocked a storefront together and scheduled meetings with people who were to use the eventual system and those who received the outputs from the proposed new application.

Phil's experience was interesting to say the least. The users spent hours making suggestions on layout, color, and error messages. They concentrated on the human interface pieces of the system. They didn't say a word to Phil or to the team about the functionality behind the user screens. The higher-level managers didn't say too much about the storefront's functionality either. They took one look at the screens and beamed, "Nice work, you finished the application ahead of schedule!"

As Phil and his team learned, it is easy to get burned in your throw-away prototyping efforts. Remember to make sure that the folks interacting with the prototype are consistently made aware that this particular prototype is just a shell, not the actual process or system. That way, they won't be surprised to learn that the throw-away prototype will be discarded (hence the name throw-away), and the system will be designed and developed using enhanced requirements based on the prototyping efforts. Keep reminding everyone that throw-away prototypes typically don't have much substance hidden under the mocked-up user interface covers.

Prototypes are often used to model an interface that appears to an end user on a computer screen. You can build a screen interface prototype in several ways: as an abstract storyboard, a more detailed screen prototype, or a realistic screen layout. Table 5.5 describes each method for you.

TABLE 5.5 Methods for Prototyping a Screen Interface

Method	Description
Storyboard	Provides abstractions of each screen along with directional arrows indicating the navigational flows between the screens
Screen prototype	Provides additional screen details for the users such as data attributes, selection criteria, and supporting business rules
Screen layout or mock-up	Graphically and realistically represents the elements on the screen including any organizational standards or style guides

Your goal when building a screen interface prototype is developing an end-to-end understanding with your end users (and for yourself) of how that screen interface actually works.

Recommended Elicitation Technique: Requirements Workshops

According to the *BABOK® Guide*, requirements workshops are another of the 16 required techniques in the fundamental knowledge base of an effective business analyst. Requirements workshops are structured meetings where a selected group of stakeholders works together to define or refine a set of project requirements. During a requirements workshop, specific requirements may also be presented to make everyone familiar with the solution scope and current requirements.

Requirements workshops have some very specific goals. They include scoping, discovering, defining, prioritizing, and reaching closure on the requirements that are being defined for the new solution. Requirements workshops also seek to promote understanding, trust, and communication among the project stakeholders. Successful requirements workshops require you to carefully select the stakeholders and SMEs to attend this short, intensive meeting.

A requirements workshop works best when it is led by a trained facilitator and supported by a scribe. That may be you, the business analyst, or it may be someone else on the project team. Some organizations bring in external facilitators for meetings of this type to reduce any perceived or actual bias. The *BABOK® Guide* makes the facilitator responsible for:

- Establishing a professional, objective tone for the meeting
- Introducing the meeting goals and agenda
- Enforcing discipline, structure, and ground rules during the meeting
- Managing the meeting and keeping the team on track
- Facilitating decision making and building consensus
- Ensuring that all stakeholders participate
- Asking the right questions

Effective requirements workshop wrap-up includes following up on any action items and making sure that workshop attendees and the sponsor receive copies of the completed meeting documentation.

Recommended Elicitation Technique: Survey/Questionnaire

Most business analysts use surveys or questionnaires to elicit requirements information from many stakeholders in a short time period. Typically, those stakeholders are located far away from where the business analyst has their nameplate on the wall. This technique allows you to collect requirements-related information from your stakeholders about many things: customers, products, work practices, and attitudes. You do this by administering a set of written questions to your project stakeholders and SMEs. You should choose whether or not to have your survey responses returned to you anonymously.

Exam Spotlight

In the *BABOK® Guide*, the terms survey and questionnaire are synonymous. Feel free to use the term that you prefer back at work, although be aware of both terms for examination purposes.

One key step in preparing a survey is creating your questions. Survey questions are typically one of two types: *open-ended questions* or *closed-ended questions*. Let's take a closer look at these two question types.

Open-Ended Questions   Open-ended questions allow stakeholders to determine how they will answer. They invite stakeholder involvement in requirements elicitation activities and draw on their expertise. However, these questions can be very time-consuming because the length and value of the answer is unpredictable. Open-ended questions are often used when the business analyst is not familiar with the area being discussed. Open-ended questions can be thought of as a fishing expedition and used when you are fishing for information. One example of an open-ended question is, "What concerns do you have about the proposed new system features?"

Closed-Ended Questions   This type of question ask the stakeholder to select from a predetermined set of answers to an elicitation question, such as "yes" or "no," multiple choice, or ratings scales. You see these all the time in your everyday life when you fill out warranty information for appliances and answer questions asking you to define the demographic you fit into as a customer—income, education, lease or own. Closed-ended questions are difficult to design and should be used when you want to compare a specific set of predetermined responses from many stakeholders for a specific reason.

A second key step is selecting your survey respondents. This is driven by the purpose of your survey and the contents of your questions. You will need to decide how to distribute the survey and collect the results from everyone. You are using this survey to elicit project requirements, so stay focused on that objective.

Exam Spotlight

When preparing your elicitation survey, try to get the information that you need but minimize the amount of time (no more than 10 minutes) the respondent must take to complete the survey.

When wrapping up your survey activity, be sure to collate, analyze, and summarize your responses. Typically, you will report your findings to the project sponsor, your project manager, or the business analysis team.

Now that you've finished looking at the final elicitation technique for this chapter, let's get back to the task at hand, conducting the elicitation activity. Once you have conducted that activity, you are ready to produce the elicitation results that document what your stakeholders have told you. We will discuss that task output next.

Produce the Elicitation Results

The *elicitation results* are just what their name says: the informally documented results of your requirements elicitation efforts. These might be your informal notes, scribbles, and pictures representing what you have been told. Your informal elicitation results are then used as input to the document elicitation results task, where they will be formally documented. This transaction is summarized in Table 5.6.

TABLE 5.6   Outputs: Conduct Elicitation Activity

Output	Output Destinations	Destination Knowledge Area
Elicitation results	Document elicitation results	Elicitation

As the project business analyst, you have the primary responsibility for informally documenting your elicited project requirements information. The format that you select depends on the information that you are documenting. You may use text, graphical models, or a combination of the two. The technique or techniques you selected to elicit requirements may also play a role in how the elicitation results are informally collected. Other business analysis stakeholders might be involved with providing the business analyst with the requirements information that they are seeking.

Let's take a look at the next step in effective requirements elicitation—more formally documenting your elicitation results.

Document Elicitation Results

The third task in the Elicitation knowledge area is where you document the results of your elicitation activity. Most business analysts take notes as they go along. It is essential to record the information provided by the stakeholders for the subsequent requirements analysis efforts. Figure 5.4 summarizes the inputs, outputs, techniques, and associated tasks used to document the requirements elicitation results.

FIGURE 5.4   Task summary: Document the elicitation results

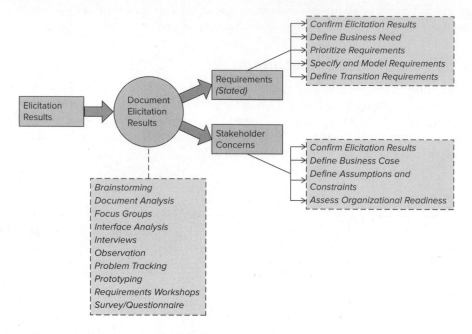

A single input is required to document your elicitation results—the elicitation results themselves.

Elicitation Results   This is the information that you have elicited from your stakeholders using one or more of the 10 common elicitation techniques. The expectation is that a more formal summary of the elicitation event will be produced, including the stated requirements and any stakeholder issues or concerns.

Table 5.7 summarizes the single input and its source knowledge area.

TABLE 5.7   Inputs

Task Input	Input Source	Source Knowledge Area
Elicitation results	Conduct elicitation activity	Elicitation

Summarizing a particular elicitation event is typically done using:

- Written documents (such as meeting minutes)
- Visual or audio recordings
- Whiteboards for note taking during the elicitation activity

You may not have a lot of success recording interview sessions with stakeholders. Many people are uncomfortable with this approach to noting what was said, so it is best to ask permission to record an elicitation interview or session as part of your elicitation preparation activities. You should also have an alternative plan if your request to record an elicitation session is not approved by the involved parties or not allowed by the organization.

Techniques to Consider

The *BABOK® Guide* recommends that you plan to document the stated requirements and stakeholder concerns resulting from your elicitation efforts for eight of the 10 common elicitation techniques, including:

- Brainstorming
- Document Analysis
- Focus Groups
- Interface Analysis
- Interviews
- Observation
- Prototyping
- Requirements Workshops

Additionally, the problem-tracking technique is used to document any stakeholder concerns. Once you have documented the elicitation results of one or more of the previous techniques, you are ready to validate those elicitation results with your relevant stakeholders. We will discuss that in the next (and final) task of this knowledge area, validating elicitation results.

Document the Elicitation Results

The documented results of your elicitation efforts are found in two deliverables: the stated requirements and the stakeholder concerns. The stated requirements are the requirements documented that provide the stakeholder's point of view of what is needed. Think of this as raw stakeholder information; your stakeholders tell you what they think is needed. Stakeholder concerns are any stakeholder issues that arise from your elicitation activities. They can be many things, such as risks, assumptions, and constraints that accompany the requirements information you are gathering. Once these concerns are captured and documented, they will need to be addressed by the business analysis team.

Once you have documented the elicitation results, it is time to make sure you got it right. Your next step will be confirming the elicitation results with the stakeholders. The full set of tasks that utilize these outputs is summarized for you in Table 5.8.

TABLE 5.8   Outputs: Document Elicitation Results

Output	Output Destinations	Destination Knowledge Area
Requirements (stated)	Confirm elicitation results	Elicitation
	Define business need	Enterprise Analysis
	Prioritize requirements	Requirements Analysis
	Specify and model requirements	Requirements Analysis
	Define transition requirements	Solution Assessment and Validation
Stakeholder concerns	Confirm elicitation results	Elicitation
	Define business case	Enterprise Analysis
	Define assumptions and constraints	Requirements Analysis
	Assess organizational readiness	Solution Assessment and Validation

As the business analyst, you are responsible for documenting the stated requirements from their elicitation efforts. You are also the point person for documenting any associated stakeholder concerns. No other stakeholders should participate in this task; it belongs solely to you. Now let's take a look at the final step in effective requirements elicitation—confirming the stated requirements and stakeholder concerns that were just elicited and documented.

Confirm Elicitation Results

During the final task of the Elicitation knowledge area, you confirm the stated requirements and stakeholder concerns with your stakeholders. This important step ensures that you clearly understand the stakeholder intentions and any related issues that might impact your requirements and your project. You must make sure that you involve all stakeholders who participated in the elicitation event in this confirmation step. Figure 5.5 summarizes the inputs, outputs, techniques, and associated tasks used to confirm the stated requirements and any associated stakeholder concerns.

FIGURE 5.5 Task summary: Confirm the elicitation results

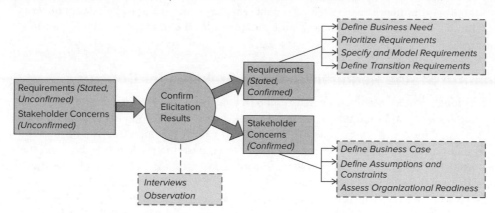

Two inputs are involved when confirming the elicitation results: the stated, unconfirmed requirements and any associated stakeholder concerns. These key inputs are produced by another Elicitation task, documenting the elicitation results. Let's take a look at each of these task inputs in greater detail.

Stated, Unconfirmed Requirements   The stated and unconfirmed requirements represent the business analyst's documented understanding of the stakeholder's intentions. They were obtained using one or more elicitation techniques. They have yet to be reviewed with the involved stakeholders to make sure everything is correct and complete.

Unconfirmed Stakeholder Concerns   The unconfirmed stakeholder concerns are stakeholder issues that were brought up during requirements elicitation. They often include risks, assumptions, and constraints about the stated requirements or the solution scope. This information should be confirmed and addressed by the business analyst.

Table 5.9 summarizes the two task inputs and their destination task and knowledge area.

TABLE 5.9 Inputs

Task Input	Input Source	Source Knowledge Area
Requirements (stated, unconfirmed)	Document elicitation results	Elicitation
Stakeholder concerns (unconfirmed)	Document elicitation results	Elicitation

The *BABOK® Guide* recommends that you use interviews or observation to confirm the stated requirements and stakeholder concerns. Let's revisit the stakeholder concerns and stated requirements once more before moving on to the next task in the Elicitation knowledge area.

Confirm Stated Requirements and Stakeholder Concerns

As previously stated, the documented results of your elicitation efforts are found in two deliverables: the stated requirements and the stakeholder concerns. This information needs to be documented and confirmed with the involved parties to make sure the business analyst got it right. The stated requirements are the requirements documented from the stakeholder's point of view. Stakeholder concerns consist of a list of stakeholder issues that arose during your elicitation activities.

Once you have confirmed the stated requirements and stakeholder concerns, you may find yourself transitioning to one of many requirements development tasks. The possible business analysis tasks that use one or both of the two confirmed outputs are summarized for you in Table 5.10.

TABLE 5.10   Outputs: Confirm Elicitation Results

Output	Output Destinations	Destination Knowledge Area
Requirements (stated, confirmed)	Define business need	Enterprise Analysis
	Prioritize requirements	Requirements Analysis
	Specify and model requirements	Requirements Analysis
	Define transition requirements	Solution Assessment and Validation
Stakeholder concerns (confirmed)	Define business case	Enterprise Analysis
	Define assumptions and constraints	Requirements Analysis
	Assess organizational readiness	Solution Assessment and Validation

The business analyst is responsible for confirming the stated, unconfirmed requirements and their associated stakeholder concerns. Any business analysis stakeholder involved with requirements elicitation activities may also find themselves involved with this particular task.

How This Applies to Your Projects

In this chapter, you stepped through tasks guiding you in eliciting information for your project's business, stakeholder, solution, and transition requirements. Remember that requirements elicitation work is iterative and incremental in nature. One of the biggest challenges that you will encounter in your projects is making sure that you ask the stakeholders all of the right questions. After all, the goal is to get the right information so you can develop correct and complete requirements defining what capabilities the new solution has to offer.

Many types of questions are used in gathering requirements information. Using all types of questions as part of your requirements elicitation activities allows you to organize and discover what the stakeholders need and want within the scope of the proposed solution. Remember, skilled requirements analysts are experts at asking questions, especially when they don't know the answers. The types of questions a skilled business analyst should be proficient with include:

- Research questions
- Detailed questions
- Directive questions
- Meta questions
- Open-ended questions
- Closed-ended questions

We'll take a quick look at each of these question types, but first let's see how one seasoned business analyst uses them in interviews.

 Real World Scenario

What Is the Real Problem?

We have found that asking different types of elicitation questions with a plan in mind really helps us find out what the stakeholders need from our project. Design your elicitation questionnaire like a funnel, with the top of the funnel representing high-level, scoping questions. As you progress down the funnel toward the ground, your questions become more and more detailed based on what you have learned. At the bottom of the funnel, ask very specific and detailed questions about what your stakeholders do and what they need from your project.

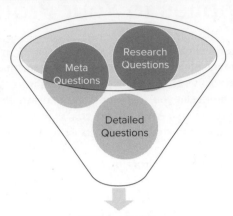

Elicitation Results

The shipping team at Palmer Divide Vineyards expressed concern about the reliability of current inventory data at the winery. Recently, several cases of a particular wine were sold to a distributor when they were not currently in stock. Taylor, the IT director, sat down with Bob, the shipping team lead, to figure out what was going on.

Taylor started her information gathering at the top of the funnel with a research question.

"What is the problem that we need to address?"

Bob responded, "Well, we have a serious issue with inventory."

Taylor used a meta question to clarify the response.

"What makes you say that there is an inventory issue?" she asked.

Bob replied, "This organization has no idea of how many items we have in the warehouse at any given time."

Taylor used a detailed question to ask for more information.

"Is the issue with keeping track of incoming quantities of wine, outgoing quantities of wine, or both?"

Bob responded, "I think it is both, but I believe that we should focus on keeping track of incoming quantity and our current stock of each wine first."

Taylor dug deeper for more details to provide direction for subsequent elicitation interviews and involvement with this pending effort.

"Who should keep track of incoming quantity? What should they keep track of? How often should they keep track of it? Where should they do it?"

Bob pointed to Warren, the warehouse manager, as the person having primary responsibility for the current wine inventory. From a data perspective, Bob listed the item number, item quantity, and weekly shipments as the key data values currently being tracked. He explained that the vineyard has a simple, spreadsheet-driven inventory system that might require an update or replacement.

Taylor made good use of the funnel approach in her first round of elicitation questions. She asked a high-level research question about the inventory problem and then focused the conversation using a meta question to narrow the discussion. She then asked several detailed questions about the current situation. Taylor was not in a situation to use directive questions to seek agreement or consensus during this elicitation interview. Remember, you can mix your research, meta, detailed, and directive questions with open- and close-ended questions to collect the right information from your stakeholders.

Research Questions   These are general questions inviting your stakeholders to provide you with information about their concerns, interests, and needs relative to the solution scope. Research questions allow a skilled business analyst to scope out the stakeholder needs. People are comfortable answering research questions when the questions are not limited or specific and the answers are not controlled in any way. An example of a research question might be, What constitutes success for this project?

Detailed Questions   Detailed questions focus on gathering specific information within the predefined solution scope. These questions are typically the step after research questions and help the business analyst focus on more specific information that is needed. To be thorough, detailed questions should be framed around the five Ws: who, what, where, when, and why. As your questions become more specific, it is very important to discourage one-word answers, such as yes and no. This can often be achieved in the phrasing of each question. An example of a detailed question is, Who provides you with this information?

Directive Questions   Directive questions are used primarily by business analysts in group settings where there are contradictions in what the business analyst has been told. Directive questions direct the other parties to an area where agreement needs to be reached and sometimes away from an area that is contentious. For project requirements information, these questions can be used to get consensus on specific features and functionality and to encourage stakeholder decision making. One example of a directive question might be, What is the relative priority of this key feature?

Meta Questions   Meta questions are powerful tools. They allow you to clarify and enhance what has just been said. Basically, meta questions are questions about questions. This communications strategy allows the business analyst to promote open communication in a nonthreatening way. Meta questions clarify and summarize what the business analyst has been told. They are an active listening technique that proves that the business analyst has really been listening to what a particular stakeholder is saying during requirements elicitation. An example of a meta question is, "Do you mind if I ask you about . . . ?"

Both research and detailed questions can be open-ended or closed-ended questions. Be sure you can distinguish between the two types of questions, as this is a topic that could appear on your certification exam.

Using a good blend of question types at all levels of detail allows you to elicit more complete and correct requirements information for your projects. Saving your questions and reusing them is another best practice that you should apply on all of our projects. Once you have well-written, general questions, it is easy to use them on another project. Building requirements elicitation questionnaires or surveys based on your proven questions often raises the quality and quantity of information received. It also saves you from reinventing the wheel.

Summary

The four tasks in the Elicitation knowledge area guide a business analyst in effectively gathering and organizing requirements information at any level of detail. It is difficult to develop complete and correct requirements for your project if you do not elicit complete and correct information from your stakeholders. Remember, elicitation is not just asking questions.

Effective communication skills are an underlying competency enabling a business analyst to do this work. Successful projects start with defining and agreeing to what is needed. Without the ability to elicit high-quality requirements information, business analysts will find it difficult to perform their jobs well.

The *BABOK® Guide* recommends that business analysts apply one or more of 10 elicitation techniques to elicit requirements information for their projects. You don't need to be an expert in every technique, but most experienced business analysts are comfortable using a representative subset of those techniques. Each elicitation technique should be approached and applied using the same marching orders: prepare, conduct, and wrap up.

Your elicitation results must be documented and confirmed in order to be used in subsequent requirements development activities such as analysis and specification. The stated, confirmed requirements and any stakeholder concerns are the building blocks from which the real requirements for our projects will be derived.

Exam Essentials

Be able to list the tasks found in the Elicitation knowledge area.   You will see questions about the tasks, their associated techniques, their more detailed elements, and the key outputs that they produce on your exam. You should memorize the four tasks of this knowledge area and the key outputs associated with them. The tasks are

Prepare for elicitation.

Conduct elicitation activity.

Document elicitation results.

Confirm elicitation results.

Be able to list, describe, and apply the 10 elicitation techniques.   Understanding and applying the 10 elicitation techniques will be a key focus for your Elicitation knowledge area exam questions. Be sure that you can list and describe how to use the 10 requirements elicitation techniques. Here's the list:

Brainstorming

Data dictionary and glossary

Document analysis

Focus groups

Interface analysis

Interviews

Observation

Prototyping

Requirements workshops

Survey/questionnaire

Be able to explain the different types of elicitation prototypes and when they might be used.   Functional scope prototypes are either horizontal or vertical; horizontal prototypes present a shallow, wide view of the functionality, while vertical prototypes highlight a deep, narrow slice of the functionality. SDLC prototypes can be throw-away or evolutionary. Throw-away prototypes allow you to quickly uncover and clarify interface requirements and then discard the prototype when the system is done. Evolutionary or functional prototypes extend your initial requirements into the fully functional system.

Be able to distinguish between structured and unstructured elicitation interviews. Structured interviews are driven by a predefined set of questions. Unstructured interviews are more of an informal, open-ended conversation.

Be able to compare passive and active observation.   In passive (invisible) observation, you observe work being performed, but you do not ask questions during that work. You record what you see, write down any questions that arise, and stay out of the way. Once the work is finished, you can ask questions about what you just witnessed. In contrast, active (visible) observation allows you to observe and to talk with the user at the same time as the work is being performed. You can ask questions, even if they interrupt what the user is doing.

Key Terms

This chapter stepped through the contents of the fourth knowledge area from the *BABOK® Guide*: Elicitation. Most of this knowledge area focuses on gathering the requirements information you need to define the solution capabilities being built by your project.

You should understand how to apply the techniques and tasks in this knowledge area in order to be an effective business analyst. Additionally, you will need to know the four tasks and their associated elements and techniques from this knowledge area in order to be successful on the CBAP® or CCBA™ exams. The tasks include:

Prepare for elicitation.

Conduct elicitation activity.

Document elicitation results.

Confirm elicitation results.

Chapter 5 introduced a number of new key words related to eliciting requirements on a project. Here is a list of some of the key terms that you encountered in this chapter:

active observation	interface
brainstorming	open-ended questions
closed-ended questions	passive observation
composite data elements	primitive data elements
elicitation results	prototypes
evolutionary prototypes	scheduled resources
functional scope	SDLC prototypes
idea generation	supporting materials
idea reduction	throw-away prototypes

Review Questions

1. All of the following tasks are performed during elicitation except:
    A. Select elicitation techniques
    B. Confirm elicitation results
    C. Prepare for elicitation
    D. Conduct elicitation activity

2. You are reviewing documents for the current system in order to confirm the existing requirements. Document analysis is an effective technique for doing this work as long as the documents being reviewed are
    A. Not current and invalid
    B. Not current, but valid
    C. Current, but not valid
    D. Both current and valid

3. What is the proper sequence for conducting a brainstorming session?
    A. Reduce, reuse, and recycle
    B. Prepare, conduct, and wrap up
    C. Prepare, analyze, and reduce
    D. Generate, reduce, and assess

4. During an active observation session, the business analyst watches the user carefully, asks them probing questions, and:
    A. Acts as an apprentice
    B. Reviews the findings
    C. Takes detailed notes
    D. Studies the process

5. What prototype allows you to learn about user interface needs and then to evolve the requirements into a fully functioning system?
    A. Throw-away
    B. Horizontal
    C. Evolutionary
    D. Vertical

6. Who may participate in requirements elicitation activities?
    A. Any stakeholder
    B. Stakeholder list
    C. Subject matter experts
    D. Project team

7. "Does the existing functionality currently meet your needs?" is an example of what type of structured interview question?

   A. Closed-ended

   B. Open-ended

   C. Research

   D. Meta question

8. The recommended time that your recipients must spend responding to a requirements elicitation survey is

   A. Less than 5 minutes to complete

   B. Less than 10 minutes to complete

   C. Less than 15 minutes to complete

   D. Less than 20 minutes to complete

9. What elicitation technique might best assist you in understanding the existing processes that are being used in an online order entry system?

   A. Interviewing

   B. Observation

   C. Focus group

   D. Prototyping

10. When preparing for observation, you plan to ask questions while the work is being done. You are preparing to do _____ observation.

   A. Visible

   B. Passive

   C. Invisible

   D. Proactive

11. The Elicitation knowledge area focuses on eliciting business, stakeholder, solution, and _____ requirements.

   A. Implementation

   B. Functional

   C. Transition

   D. Nonfunctional

12. You are working with a group trying to build a list of possible approaches as to how the team might solve a specific business problem. What technique should the group consider applying?

   A. Observation

   B. JAD session

   C. Focus group

   D. Brainstorming

13. You have just discovered that the business process expert for the existing system currently being upgraded is no longer employed by the company. Which elicitation technique might you apply in this situation?

   A. Document analysis

   B. Reverse engineering

   C. Interface analysis

   D. Elicitation workshop

14. You are planning a focus group to elicit requirements for a new online order-entry system, addressing a wide variety of end users interacting with the system in different ways. What type of users should you include in your focus group?

   A. Miscellaneous

   B. Heterogeneous

   C. Homogeneous

   D. Collaborative

15. What are the three types of interfaces typically looked at during interface analysis?

   A. People, process, and project

   B. User, application, and device

   C. Input, output, and process

   D. User, system, and software

16. The requirements elicitation technique that uncovers and visualizes the interface requirements before an application is designed or developed is called:

   A. Prototyping

   B. Interface analysis

   C. Observation

   D. Reverse engineering

17. What technique provides an effective method for eliciting requirements information from many people in a short period of time?

   A. Workshop

   B. Interview

   C. Survey

   D. Review

18. Eliciting requirements using a brainstorming session enables the participants to exercise _____ thinking.

   A. Creative

   B. Parallel

   C. Focused

   D. Critical

19. You and the project sponsor are discussing what the business expects from a proposed new system. What type of elicitation interview are you conducting?

A. Structured

B. Functional

C. Unstructured

D. Discussion

20. The functional scope of a prototype can be categorized in which of the following ways?

A. Visible or invisible

B. Horizontal or vertical

C. Active or passive

D. Structured or unstructured

Answers to Review Questions

1. A. Elicitation knowledge area tasks include prepare for elicitation, conduct elicitation activity, document elicitation results, and confirm elicitation results.

2. D. Document analysis results in improved requirements coverage as long as the documents being reviewed are up to date (current) and valid.

3. B. Brainstorming involves preparing, conducting, and wrapping up. This is true for all 10 techniques used to elicit requirements.

4. C. When conducting an active observation, the business analyst or observer should take detailed notes and ask probing questions about why certain tasks are being done.

5. C. Evolutionary prototypes allow designers and developers to learn about user interface needs and evolve the system requirements.

6. A. Any stakeholder can participate in requirements elicitation activities.

7. A. Closed-ended questions elicit a single response, such as yes or no.

8. B. The recommended parameter for efficient and effective elicitation surveys is that it takes no longer than 10 minutes for the recipient to complete.

9. B. Observation assesses the individual's work environment to document details about current processes.

10. A. Active, or visible, observation is when the business analyst observes the individual performing their job and asks questions and talks with the worker while they are performing the work.

11. C. The Elicitation knowledge area focuses on eliciting business, stakeholder, solution, and transition requirements.

12. D. Brainstorming promotes creative thinking, producing a broad or diverse set of options for a specific topic or problem.

13. A. Document analysis elicits requirements of existing systems by reviewing available documentation and leveraging existing materials to discover or confirm requirements. It is also used when SMEs for existing systems are no longer available.

14. B. Heterogeneous individuals have diverse backgrounds and offer different perspectives during a focus group.

15. B. Interface types include user interfaces, external application interfaces, and interfaces with external hardware devices.

16. A. Prototyping for requirements elicitation targets uncovering and visualizing the interface needs before an application is designed or developed.

17. C. A survey or questionnaire provides an effective method for eliciting requirements information from many people in a short period of time.

18. A. The nonjudgmental environment of a brainstorming session for requirements elicitation enables creative thinking.

19. C. Unstructured interviews are where the business analyst has no predefined questions, but sits with the interviewee to discuss what the business expects from the target system.

20. B. The functional scope of a prototype can be either horizontal or vertical. Horizontal prototypes model a shallow, wide view of the system's functionality, while vertical prototypes model a deep, narrow slice of system functionality.

Chapter

6

Controlled Middle: Requirements Analysis

CBAP®/CCBA™ EXAM TOPICS COVERED IN THIS CHAPTER

✓ Prioritize requirements.

✓ Organize requirements.

✓ Specify and model requirements.

✓ Define assumptions and constraints.

✓ Verify requirements.

✓ Validate requirements.

Requirements analysis takes elicited information and makes sense of it. The tasks found in the Requirements Analysis knowledge area focus on analyzing the stated requirements from your elicitation efforts and building the real stakeholder or solution requirements for your project. The stated requirements were provided to you by your project stakeholders during requirements elicitation. The real requirements define the derived needs of your stakeholders after your structured and collaborative requirements analysis efforts are complete.

Deriving and refining requirements for a project is repetitive and systematic in nature. Experienced business analysts find themselves moving between requirements elicitation, requirements analysis, and requirements documentation or specification activities many times throughout their projects. There can be a significant difference between the stated requirements elicited from stakeholders and the real requirements that define the resulting solution.

Requirements Analysis

The Requirements Analysis knowledge area focuses on analyzing what your stakeholders have told you and defining which capabilities need to be part of the resulting solution. According to the *BABOK® Guide,* the Requirements Analysis knowledge area is where you develop your stakeholder and solution requirements for your project. Business requirements are developed by tasks in the Enterprise Analysis knowledge area, and transition requirements are built by the Solution Assessment and Validation tasks.

The tasks in this knowledge area take the elicited information (the stated requirements) and make sense of it. The stated requirements reflect what the stakeholders have told you about what they need. The stated requirements become analyzed requirements after they are acted upon by the tasks in this knowledge area. *Analyzed requirements* are defined as requirements that have been specified and modeled.

This requirements development-focused knowledge area generates several key business analysis deliverables. They include the:

- *Assumptions and constraints*
- *Requirements structure*
- Prioritized stakeholder and solution requirements
- Validated stakeholder and solution requirements
- Verified stakeholder and solution requirements

We will cover each deliverable in more detail later in the chapter.

The exercises will step through each of the commonly used requirements analysis techniques in detail as you work through each task contained in this knowledge area. Requirements analysis work is multifaceted and applies a wide range of techniques for categorizing project requirements and making good decisions about their priorities, their structure, and their quality.

The analysis techniques that are of primary interest right now focus on ways to specify and model requirements. A number of general techniques are also used by tasks in other knowledge areas. The 17 general techniques used to specify and model requirements are:

- Acceptance and Evaluation Criteria Definition
- Business Rules Analysis
- Data Dictionary and Glossary
- Data Flow Diagrams
- Data Modeling
- Functional Decomposition
- Interface Analysis
- Metrics and Key Performance Indicators (KPIs)
- Nonfunctional Requirements Analysis
- Organization Modeling
- Process Modeling
- Prototyping
- Scenarios and Use Cases
- Sequence Diagrams
- State Diagrams
- User Stories

We will explore these techniques in greater detail throughout this chapter.

Exam Spotlight

The tasks in the Requirements Analysis knowledge area apply to the stakeholder and solution requirements for your project. The Requirements Analysis knowledge area also addresses monitoring and reporting on the performance of the analysis activities throughout the project. The business analysis team is responsible for assessing the effectiveness of the techniques being used to analyze and specify the stakeholder and solution requirements for their project. The Requirements Analysis knowledge area is addressed in Chapter 6 of the *BABOK® Guide*.

The Business Analyst's Task List

The business analyst has six tasks to perform in the Requirements Analysis knowledge area. We will look at each one of these tasks in detail later in this chapter. The task list from the *BABOK® Guide* includes:

- Prioritizing requirements
- Organizing requirements
- Specifying and modeling requirements
- Defining assumptions and constraints
- Verifying requirements
- Validating requirements

These tasks focus on making sure that the stakeholder and solution requirements for your projects are thoroughly analyzed and documented for you, your team, and your stakeholders. The goal is to use the capabilities defined in these requirements as the basis for designing and constructing the solution.

When Does Requirements Analysis Take Place?

> Everything should be made as simple as possible, but not simpler.
>
> —*Albert Einstein*

The tasks in the Requirements Analysis knowledge area begin by developing the project's stakeholder requirements and continue until the more detailed solution requirements are completed. Typically, defining the stakeholder and solution requirements on your projects takes place in the controlled middle of the project life cycle as part of the project's requirements development or definition phase.

The controlled middle of a project is where the actual work gets done—one stage or phase at a time. Business analysis tasks typically include those from the Elicitation, Requirements Analysis, and Solution Assessment and Validation knowledge areas, with a little Requirements Management and Communication thrown in for good measure.

Let's step through the first task in the Requirements Analysis knowledge area: prioritizing the stakeholder or solution requirements for your project.

Prioritize Requirements

The first task in the Requirements Analysis knowledge area is prioritizing the project's stakeholder or solution requirements. Requirements prioritization allows you to determine the relative importance of requirements. There are many ways to prioritize requirements. At this point in your project, your requirements prioritization scheme has already been planned and defined for you and your team in the requirements management plan. This plan was built by the Define Requirements Management Process task in the Business Analysis Planning and Monitoring knowledge area.

 Real World Scenario

A Must-Do Requirements Stew

Phil was asked to finish up the requirements for a project that had languished in the requirements development stage for years. The project approach was to procure a commercial product to provide the required capabilities and customize that product as needed. Contributing departments had gold plated the project requirements to such an extent that there were no commercial products that came close to meeting the defined needs of the business. The solution scope had expanded from meeting a single unit's business need to addressing multiple business processes across departments and organizations.

All efforts to focus on the set of core functionality required to meet the original business need came to naught. Phil got the key users together and attempted to prioritize the existing requirements set. No one would back down from ranking their requirements at the highest priority, regardless of the prioritization method Phil invoked. They tried forced ranking with no success. They tried voting with even less success. They stuck dots on the wall, they used sticky notes, they timeboxed, and they budgeted. To add to the confusion, the marketing department (a key player) consistently refused to state any clear requirements other than needing total flexibility to react to changes in the marketplace.

Phil discovered that sometimes the people creating the requirements are incapable of objectively prioritizing the features they have spent time dreaming up. He also found that his key stakeholders had difficulty distinguishing between the core functionality and the optional features of a solution. As Phil discovered, working on projects where the key stakeholders have identified more requirements than can be economically implemented is a serious challenge, indeed.

How did Phil solve this conundrum? He couldn't solve it this time around. It was impossible for any single software product on the market to meet this diverse set of requirements stew. The project issues were escalated to senior management and eventually the project was scrapped. However, Phil learned many lessons on prioritizing requirements and dealing with stakeholders; he applied these successfully to future projects. Sometimes the best business analysis lessons are the painful and unsuccessful ones. Just try to keep those lessons to a minimum.

Figure 6.1 summarizes the inputs, outputs, techniques, and associated tasks used to prioritize stakeholder or solution requirements. Remember, requirements prioritization is a consultative process. Your stakeholders play a key role in prioritizing the project requirements and should make the final decision on which new solution capabilities are most important to them as well as which capabilities are absolutely required to get the job done.

FIGURE 6.1   Task summary: Prioritize the requirements.

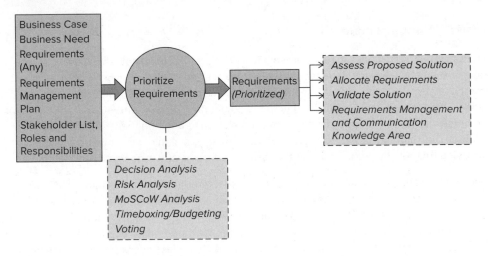

Several key inputs are needed to adequately prioritize stakeholder or solution requirements. These key inputs are produced by a number of other business analysis tasks, and they include the business case, business need, and the requirements management plan. Let's look at each of these task inputs in greater detail.

Business Case   Requirements priorities should align with the goals, objectives, and success measures that are defined in the project's business case.

Business Need   If there is no business case for a project, the business need serves the same purpose and requires the same degree of alignment to its goals and objectives.

Requirements (Any)   Any requirement may be prioritized at any point in its life cycle. The only prerequisite is that the requirement being prioritized must be a stated requirement from the project stakeholders.

Requirements Management Plan   The requirements management plan, built during Business Analysis Planning and Monitoring, defines the approach for the business analyst to take on the project when prioritizing the project requirements.

Stakeholder List, Roles, and Responsibilities   The stakeholder list provides the business analyst with the stakeholder information necessary to determine which stakeholders need to be involved in the requirements prioritization efforts on a project. The roles and responsibilities of each stakeholder give you the information that you need to decide who should be involved in each aspect of your requirements prioritization efforts. After all, you want to involve the right stakeholders in order to get your requirements priorities as they should be.

Table 6.1 summarizes the inputs to this task and lists the task and knowledge area sources for each input used to prioritize requirements.

TABLE 6.1   Inputs: Prioritize Requirements

Task Input	Input Source	Source Knowledge Area
Business case	Define business case	Enterprise Analysis
Business need	Define business need	Enterprise Analysis
Requirements (any)	(Allocated) Allocate requirements	Solution Assessment and Validation
	(Analyzed) Specify and model requirements	Requirements Analysis
	(Approved) Manage solution scope and requirements	Requirements Management and Communication
	(Communicated) Communicate requirements	Requirements Management and Communication
	(Maintained and reusable) Maintain requirements for reuse	Requirements Management and Communication
	(Prioritized) Prioritize requirements	Requirements Analysis
	(Stated, Unconfirmed) Document elicitation results	Elicitation

TABLE 6.1   Inputs: Prioritize Requirements (*continued*)

Task Input	Input Source	Source Knowledge Area
	(Stated, Unconfirmed) Confirm elicitation results	Elicitation
	(Traced) Manage requirements traceability	Requirements Management and Communication
	(Validated) Validate requirements	Requirements Analysis
	(Verified) Verify requirements	Requirements Analysis
Requirements management plan	Plan requirements management process	Business Analysis Planning and Monitoring
Stakeholder list, roles, and responsibilities	Conduct stakeholder analysis	Business Analysis Planning and Monitoring

When prioritizing the stakeholder or solution requirements on your projects, you should perform several tasks, such as:

- Defining the basis or criteria for prioritizing the requirements
- Considering challenges present when facilitating prioritization

Let's look at each of these tasks in greater detail.

Defining the Basis for Requirements Prioritization   A number of prioritization schemes and approaches can be used, such as prioritization based on looking at which requirements should be implemented first in a solution. The *BABOK® Guide* provides you with eight possible criteria to choose from, either standalone or in combination with one another. These eight criteria for prioritizing requirements are summarized in Table 6.2.

TABLE 6.2   Requirements Prioritization Criteria

Prioritization Criteria	Requirements Are Implemented First That . . .
Business Value	Provide the most business value
Business or Technical Risk	Pose the highest risk to project success
Implementation Difficulty	Are easiest for the team to implement
Likelihood of Success	Yield quick or certain successes
Regulatory or Policy Compliance	Address regulatory or policy requirements

Prioritization Criteria	Requirements Are Implemented First That . . .
Relationship to Other Requirements	Support other high business value requirements
Stakeholder Agreement	Receive stakeholder consensus on their use and value
Urgency	Have a degree of time sensitivity

Considering Prioritization Challenges   Facilitating a session to prioritize requirements can be quite challenging. There is a tendency for stakeholders to issue nonnegotiable demands relative to the importance of their requirements, such as ranking all of their requirements as the most important requirements of the bunch (whether they really are or not). The problems aren't confined to the stakeholders, though. It is not unusual to find the solution development team trying to influence the prioritization results, perhaps because they have some interesting technology they would like to implement. The facilitator must recognize and focus on the need for trade-off decision making and compromise in a session that takes on these characteristics.

There are several techniques that you may choose to apply when prioritizing your project requirements. You should consider adding MoSCoW analysis, timeboxing/budgeting, and voting to your list of possibilities. Let's take a look at these three recommended techniques in greater detail.

Recommended Technique: MoSCoW Analysis

This categorization technique is used specifically for prioritizing requirements and is defined as part of this specific task and knowledge area in the *BABOK® Guide*. *MoSCoW analysis* helps you to reach a common understanding with your stakeholders on the importance they place on the delivery of each requirement. You use this technique to divide the requirements into four categories: must, should, could, and won't. There are very specific definitions for each of these four categories.

Must   These requirements are must haves. Think of them as very high-priority requirements for your project. They must be part of the final solution in order for that solution to be considered successful.

Should   These requirements are also high-priority requirements, and they are every bit as important as the requirements in the must category. However, there might be workarounds that satisfy these requirements or they may not be as time critical.

Could   These desirable requirements are of lesser priority and are nice-to-have capabilities in the resulting solution. They really don't affect anything else in the solution one way or the other and will be included if time and resources permit.

Won't   These requirements will not be implemented in a given solution release. They may be considered for inclusion in a future release (future requirements that stakeholders would like to have) or be omitted from the solution altogether. When using MoSCoW analysis to prioritize a set of requirements:

- One or more requirements might be redefined, deleted, or added to the set.

- The prioritized list of requirements might change based on new information and insight.

- Requirements might move up or down the prioritization list as you iteratively apply the technique and discuss your options.

MoSCoW analysis works best as a group technique. The group needs to recognize up front that due to project constraints not everything can be in the must category. A simple way of using MoSCoW analysis is to list the requirements being prioritized on a flipchart, and then write M, S, C, or W next to each requirement. You can also write the ideas on sticky notes and move them between flipchart pages taped to the wall for each of the four categories. Another good recommendation is to rank your requirements so that 25 percent of those requirements are must, 25 percent of the requirements are should, 25 percent are could, and the remaining 25 percent are won't. If these percentages don't work for you, you can select numbers that fit your project and your set of requirements to prioritize.

Recommended Technique: Timeboxing/Budgeting

This technique is used specifically for prioritizing requirements and is defined as part of this specific task and knowledge area in the *BABOK® Guide*. Timeboxing and budgeting prioritizes requirements for implementation based on the allocation of a fixed resource, usually either time (timeboxing) or money (budgeting). This technique is most effective when it is framed by the defined solution scope for the project.

The *BABOK® Guide* contains three approaches that you can use to decide which requirements should be included in a timeboxed or budgeted iteration or implementation. Let's step through them quickly right now.

All In   Assign duration (time) or cost to implement each requirement that is being prioritized. Start with all eligible requirements in the hypothetical box (project) and then remove them one-by-one, based on how you plan to meet the schedule dates or budget limit.

All Out   Assign duration (time) or cost to implement each requirement that is being prioritized. Start with all eligible requirements out of the box and then add them to the box one-by-one until you meet the schedule dates or budget limit.

Selective   Identify high priority requirements that have been added to the calendar or budget. Add or remove them one by one in order to meet the schedule dates or budget limit.

Recommended Technique: Voting

This business analysis technique is used specifically for prioritizing requirements and is defined as part of this specific task in the *BABOK® Guide*. Voting is exactly what it sounds like—using voting methods to facilitate requirement prioritization by a group of project stakeholders. Voting is pretty straightforward, allowing votes to be distributed across a set of proposed features or requirements in order to prioritize them and get everyone to agree to their prioritization. Be sure to decide up front whether your voting decisions will be based on a plurality or a majority. If you are using a plurality vote, the largest number of votes drives the requirements prioritization decision. That means that if one requirement receives 10 votes and another requirements receives 9 votes, then the requirement with 10 votes is a higher priority. In contrast, a majority vote requires that a majority of votes (typically 50 percent or 67 percent) need to be cast for a particular requirement in order for requirements prioritization decisions to be made.

Additional Techniques to Consider

The *BABOK® Guide* recommends using one or more of the following additional techniques when you are prioritizing requirements for your project. They are summarized for you here.

Decision Analysis   You can use this technique to examine and model the consequences of different decisions before actually making a well-informed decision. When prioritizing project requirements, business analysts may use decision analysis to identify and assess high-value requirements.

Risk Analysis   Risky requirements often need to be investigated further to determine what should be done with them. Some organizations prefer to implement risky requirements early on to minimize the costs of failure, while others prefer to defer risky requirements until later in the life cycle in order to decide what to do with them.

Once you have selected and applied one or more techniques as part of your requirements prioritization efforts, you are ready to continue with some of the other analysis tasks at hand. We will discuss those tasks shortly.

Produce the Prioritized Requirements

Prioritized requirements are stated requirements that have been assigned a priority attribute indicating their relative importance to the stakeholders and to the organization. Sometimes you will find yourself assigning a priority value to a group of related requirements as opposed to a single, standalone requirement. Once you have prioritized your requirements, it is time to perform any number of follow-on tasks. The prioritized stakeholder and solution requirements are used as an input to several solution-related tasks. They are summarized in Table 6.3.

TABLE 6.3   Outputs: Prioritize Requirements

Output	Output Destinations	Destination Knowledge Area
Requirements (prioritized)	Assess proposed solution	Solution Assessment and Validation
	Allocate requirements	Solution Assessment and Validation
	Validate solution	Solution Assessment and Validation
	—	Requirements Management and Communication knowledge area

A number of stakeholders are involved with prioritizing stakeholder and solution requirements. Remember that the primary responsibility for prioritizing requirements is shared between the business analyst and the key stakeholders who are involved as part of the requirements prioritization process.

Several key business analysis stakeholders should also be involved in prioritizing requirements. The project manager uses your prioritized requirements during the implementation planning efforts. Other stakeholders participating in requirements prioritization include the:

- Domain SME
- Implementation SME
- Sponsor

Let's take a look at the next task found in the Requirements Analysis knowledge area—deciding how to organize your stakeholder and solution requirements to facilitate stakeholder understanding and agreement.

Organize Requirements

Project requirements should not be a jumble of information. Your requirements need to be structured and organized into a set of information that is complete, comprehensive, consistent, and understandable to your stakeholders. You are responsible for deciding how to structure your individual requirements, group those requirements, and show the relationships between them. A good requirements structure targets consistency, repeatability, and a high level of requirements quality.

Figure 6.2 summarizes the inputs, outputs, techniques, and associated tasks used to structure and organize project requirements.

FIGURE 6.2   Task summary: Organize the requirements.

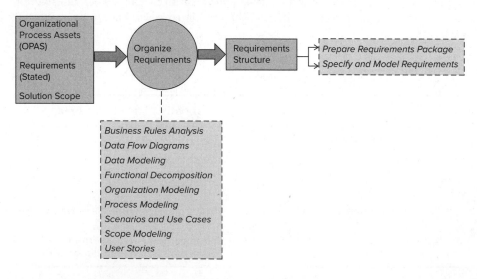

Several key inputs are needed to assist you define your requirements structure during requirements analysis. These key inputs are produced by a number of other business analysis tasks, and include the stated requirements and the solution scope. Let's have a look at each of these task inputs in greater detail.

Organizational Process Assets (OPAs)   You need to look to the OPAs to see if the preferred requirements structure for your stakeholders has been previously created and is saved there for your use.

Stated Requirements   The focus of requirements analysis takes the stated requirements provided during elicitation and derives the real requirements for your project. The stated requirements are analyzed, documented, and modeled based on the requirements structure you create with this task.

Solution Scope   The selected requirements structure must describe the solution scope fully and from all stakeholder perspectives. Think of the solution scope as the frame for the more detailed picture you are painting with your project requirements.

There are several elements that business analysts should address when deciding how to structure and organize requirements on their projects, such as:

- Defining the level of abstraction or detail for your requirements
- Selecting appropriate requirements modeling techniques

Let's look at each of these elements in greater detail.

Defining the Level of Abstraction or Detail   When the different types of requirements found in the *BABOK® Guide* (business, stakeholder, solution, and transition) are discussed, the names are provided for the different levels of abstraction or detail found in those requirements. For example, business requirements are high level and focus on the big picture of what an organization requires in order to address a business need. Solution requirements are far more detailed, providing a basis to design and develop the capabilities needed in a new solution and its components. It is important for you to understand the levels of abstraction in your project requirements and factor them into your requirements elicitation and analysis activities across the project life cycle.

Selecting Requirements Modeling Techniques   Experienced business analysts are able to determine which types of models to use to describe the solution scope for their stakeholders. Models are abstract and simplified views of the business domain for your project. Five general modeling concepts are relevant to business analysis. Let's look at each one of these concepts in greater detail.

User Classes, Profiles, or Roles   These models categorize and describe the people who directly interact with the solution, grouping them by their needs, expectations, and goals for that solution. Roles often correspond to project stakeholders and are identified during stakeholder analysis. User classes, profiles, and roles are used by a number of common requirements analysis models, including organization models, process models, and use cases.

Concepts and Relationships   Concepts show us something in the real world, such as a person, place, or thing. They define facts relative to that something and its relationships with other concepts. Business analysts can take this approach one step further, using data models as part of requirements analysis modeling to describe the attributes associated with a particular concept or set of related concepts.

Events   Events are triggers that prompt the business or a solution to respond to the event and do something, such as processing a customer order that has just been placed online. Events can be internal or external to the business, and they can occur randomly or at regularly scheduled times. The stimulus-response flow of events is used by a number of common requirements analysis models, including scope models, process models, state diagrams, and use cases.

Processes   Process models are like a series of events without any trigger. Processes are series of repeatable activities performed by an organization involving its people and systems. Processes describe who does something and when that something must be done. Processes are used by a number of common requirements analysis models, including organization models, state diagrams, and use cases.

Rules   Rules guide how people make decisions within an organization. They guide how information about something can change and define the range of valid values for change. Rules often reflect organizational priorities, and they are often embedded in process models, state diagrams, and use cases.

There are several techniques that you may choose to apply when deciding on the requirements structure for your project. You should consider using functional decomposition and organization modeling to assist you in determining what the best requirements structure might be for your project. Let's take a look at these recommended techniques in greater detail right now.

Recommended Technique: Functional Decomposition

Functional decomposition breaks down or decomposes the solution scope into their component parts based on a group of related functionalities. You can then create a model of what needs to be done to deliver all or part of the solution. Functional decomposition is an excellent way to break things into manageable pieces and to understand the relationships between those pieces.

Functional decomposition is typically used during requirements analysis to break an organizational unit or the solution scope into its component parts. Each resulting part may have its own set of requirements. This is very similar to building a Work Breakdown Structure (WBS) for a project where you break down or decompose the project scope into phases, work packages, and deliverables. The *BABOK® Guide* recommends breaking things down until the parts found at the lowest level cannot be broken down further. You should then analyze each part independently.

Recommended Technique: Organization Modeling

According to the *BABOK® Guide*, *organization modeling* is one of the 16 required techniques in the fundamental knowledge base of an effective business analyst.

Organization modeling is used during requirements analysis to describe the organizational units, the stakeholders, and the relationships between them. This allows you the opportunity to structure your project requirements based upon the needs of each stakeholder group.

Most of us have seen an organization chart showing the hierarchy of an organization. This is an example of an organizational model. The model defines the purpose and structure of an organization or an organizational unit. When this technique is used for business analysis, an organization chart that shows the organizational units, lines of reporting, the roles, and the people in those roles is basically built.

Additional Techniques to Consider

The *BABOK® Guide* recommends using one or more of the following additional techniques when you are organizing the requirements for your project by defining the requirements structure. They are summarized for you here.

Business Rules Analysis   Many people recommend that you document the business rules separately from the project requirements in your requirements structure. Business rules typically apply to decision making across the organization, impacting multiple projects and ongoing operations. Business rules should be implemented and managed using a separate business rules engine or tool.

Data Flow Diagrams   Data flow diagrams allow you to organize your requirements based on how information or data flows through the system.

Data Modeling   Data models organize requirements by describing the concepts and relationships between the concepts that are relevant to the defined solution scope.

Process Modeling   Process models organize your requirements using a hierarchy of processes and subprocesses and addressing those processes from start to finish.

Scenarios and Use Cases   Scenarios and use cases organize requirements using events and how the solution will respond to the associated triggers.

Scope Modeling   Scope models organize requirements based on the solution components to which they are related. Solution components are parts of a solution spanning the enterprise architecture of the organization, including business processes, software applications, or hardware.

User Stories   User stories organize requirements by the stakeholder objectives the solution will support.

Once you have selected and applied one or more techniques as part of your requirements organization efforts, you are ready to continue with the other requirements analysis tasks in this knowledge area. We will discuss those tasks later in the chapter. First let's look at the requirements structure that helps you organize the requirements during your analysis work.

Produce the Requirements Structure

The *requirements structure* defines an organized structure for stakeholder and solution requirements and the documented relationships between them. The requirements structure defines the scope of each specific model or set of requirements and provides a location where each specific requirement can be found. The requirements structure is not the same as traceability. Traceability links related requirements. The requirements structure tells you where the specific requirements for a project can be found.

 Real World Scenario

One Size Does Not Fit All

Ginger was helping the IT department structure a set of requirements documents for their IT projects. She was also tasked with building templates for each of those documents so that project teams could use them consistently across the organization. On first glance, this requirements-focused consulting assignment seemed very straightforward. And it was—at least until she started asking questions about the projects and the current process for developing requirements.

The organization had projects in all sizes. They had extra-small maintenance and support efforts lasting a few weeks and medium-size software development projects lasting about six months or so. They were doing agile development of their customer-facing websites and inline capabilities in six-week sprints. They had small projects that were noncritical and focused on a few months of work from a small team and mission-critical complex projects lasting for a year or more and costing millions of dollars.

Ginger quickly decided that this was not a "one size fits all" project environment. The project teams would have to tailor her requirements document set for their project type and scale it for the size of their efforts. That would be the resulting requirements structure that they would use during requirements development.

Using the project taxonomy that was provided, Ginger built a set of requirements documents that could be tailored and scaled to fit the projects. She also built a guidance document providing guidelines for scaling and tailoring the requirements documents based on project type, complexity, cost, and associated risks. This generic document set and guidance document became part of the requirements development process and part of the organizational process assets for the company.

Project teams used Ginger's generic document set as an input to organizing the requirements on their projects. They tailored and scaled the generic documents to fit their projects within the provided framework. The resulting requirements structure was used to document all of their project requirements.

The requirements structure is used as an input to preparing a requirements package for communication with stakeholders and for specifying and modeling requirements. These destination tasks and their knowledge areas are summarized in Table 6.4.

TABLE 6.4 Outputs: Organize Requirements

Output	Output Destinations	Destination Knowledge Area
Requirements structure	Prepare requirements package	Requirements Management and Communication
	Specify and model requirements	Requirements Analysis

A number of stakeholders are involved with defining the requirements structure. Remember that the primary responsibility for deciding how to organize requirements falls to the business analyst. The project manager uses the resulting organized set of requirements to verify solution scope and assess the work that needs to be done. Other business analysis stakeholders participating in requirements organization include the:

- Domain SME
- End user
- Implementation SME
- Sponsor

Let's take a look at the next task found in the Requirements Analysis knowledge area—specifying and modeling your requirements.

Specify and Model Requirements

The next task in the Requirements Analysis knowledge area is specifying and modeling the stakeholder and solution requirements for your project. For most projects, this work is not done all at once. The higher-level stakeholder requirements are typically defined and decomposed into the more detailed solution requirements. Your requirements structure drives how you accomplish this by defining the combination of text, charts, diagrams, and models that you will use.

Figure 6.3 summarizes the inputs, outputs, techniques, and associated tasks used to specify and model your requirements.

FIGURE 6.3 Task summary: Specify and model the requirements.

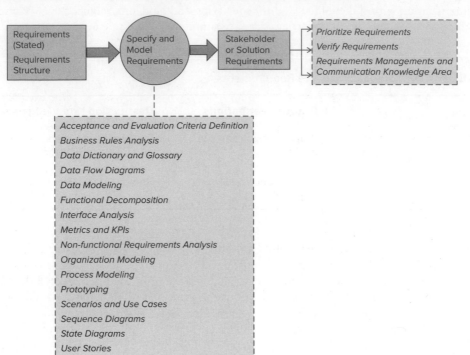

Several key inputs are needed to specify and model the stakeholder and solution requirements for your project. These key inputs are the stated requirements that were elicited from your stakeholders and the requirements structure defining how the stakeholder and solution requirements will be organized. Let's have a look at each of these task inputs in greater detail.

Stated Requirements   Requirements priorities should align with the goals, objectives, and success measures that are defined in the project's business case.

Requirements Structure   The requirements structure tells you how the requirements that you are currently working on fit into the general set of requirements being developed for your project. It also tells you how all of the project requirements will be organized and what requirements will be part of which requirements document.

Table 6.5 summarizes the inputs to this task and lists the task and knowledge area sources for each input used to prioritize requirements.

TABLE 6.5 Inputs: Specify and Model Requirements

Task Input	Input Source	Source Knowledge Area
Requirements (stated)	Document elicitation results (stated, unconfirmed)	Elicitation
	Confirm elicitation results (stated, confirmed)	Elicitation
Requirements structure	Organize requirements	Requirements Analysis

You should apply several elements when specifying and modeling the stakeholder or solution requirements on your projects, such as:

- Writing text requirements
- Using matrix documentation such as tables
- Building textual or graphical models
- Capturing requirements attributes
- Seeking opportunities for improvement

Let's look at each of these elements in greater detail. Working with each of these elements used to the appropriate degree is a skill found in experienced business analysts. You must decide what to model, how to effectively model it, and how much detail is necessary in your models.

Writing Text Requirements   You will find yourself using textual requirements to describe your solution capabilities, conditions, and constraints. Good technical writing skills are essential. Writing text requirements is not an exercise in creative writing. You want your text requirements to be written in simple sentences that are clear, concise, and complete.

Using Matrix Documentation   The most common matrix seen in requirements is a two-dimensional table or spreadsheet. Requirements attributes and data dictionaries lend themselves to being developed in a table format. A table can be much more effective than a bunch of sentences when you are trying to show simple relationships between pieces of your requirements information, such as requirements priorities or traceability relationships.

Building Textual or Graphical Models   Models are a simplified representation of something real. They can be textual, graphical, or a combination of both. The phrase "a picture is worth a thousand words" is certainly true when it comes to analyzing and documenting your requirements. Many analysts find using models—formal or informal— to be helpful during their requirements elicitation efforts, as well as during requirements analysis.

Exam Spotlight

Here are the six reasons you might choose to use text or graphical models during requirements analysis activities. You might see them again on your exam.

- Describe a situation or define a problem.

- Define business domain boundaries.

- Describe processes and the flow of action.

- Categorize and create hierarchies of items.

- Show components and their relationships.

- Show business logic.

Formal textual or graphical models must follow the rules for their model type. Typically, modeling rules are set either by your organization, by your selected modeling tool vendor, or by a set of standards and guidelines for the particular type of modeling technique that you have selected. That means that you are expected to consistently use the correct notation and meaning for every element in your model. Formal models are powerful tools as long as your stakeholder audience understands the language they are speaking. Informal models have no formal definition, connecting elements in ways that have meaning for you and for your stakeholder audience.

Capturing Requirements Attributes   Make sure you capture the requirements attributes associated with each of the requirements that you specify and model. The attributes that you need to capture for each type of requirement are defined for you in the requirements management plan that you produced as part of the Business Analysis Planning and Monitoring knowledge area.

Seeking Opportunities for Improvement   Requirements work is incomplete without looking for opportunities to improve the business where you work and the way you perform business analysis work. The *BABOK® Guide* lists several areas that you should keep in mind:

- Automating or simplifying the work people do

- Improving information access across the organization

- Reducing the complexity of interfaces between systems and people

- Increasing the consistency in how people behave

- Eliminating redundancy across your stakeholders

There are several techniques that you may choose to apply when specifying and modeling stakeholder and solution requirements. Let's take a look at a number of these modeling techniques in greater detail.

Recommended Technique: Business Rules Analysis

According to the *BABOK® Guide*, *business rules* analysis is another of the required techniques in the fundamental knowledge base of an effective business analyst. Business rules analysis allows you to define the business policies and rules that govern business decisions and operations in your organization. Business policies are directives that support business goals. Business rules, by contrast, are actionable and testable directives that support the business policies. Complex business rules are often represented using a decision tree or table.

Business rules require you to create or to use a defined glossary of terms and an understanding of the relationships between them. There are two types of business rules:

- *Operative business rules*
- *Structural business rules*

Operative business rules guide the actions of people who work in your organization, and are typically enforced by organizational policies. Structural business rules determine when something is or is not true. They structure and categorize the knowledge and information found in your organization. When analyzing, stating, and managing business rules, you should:

- State the business rules using the appropriate terminology.
- Keep the business rules independent of their implementation.
- Document business rules separately from how they are enforced.
- State business rules at the atomic level using a declarative format.
- Separate business rules from the processes that the rules support or constrain.
- Maintain the business rules in a way that allows for changes as business policies change.

In order to effectively perform business rules analysis, you need to have a data dictionary and glossary for your specific project or your organization.

Recommended Technique: Data Flow Diagrams

According to the *BABOK® Guide*, building and using *data flow diagrams* is one of the required techniques in the fundamental knowledge base of an effective business analyst. Data flow diagrams (DFDs) model how information flows within a system. They look at:

- External entities that are sources or destinations for data
- Data processes that transform the data in some way
- Data stores that collect the data for some period of time
- Data flows moving data between external entities, processes, and data stores

DFDs help you understand the range of data found within a solution or solution component. They are created after a context diagram has been built that shows you the high-level view of the solution and its associated data flow. However, DFDs do not show you who performs the work nor do they show you any alternative paths through the process.

Real World Scenario

Palmer Divide Vineyards: Selecting a Data Flow Diagram Notation

You are currently modeling the new functionality associated with requesting and performing research studies at Palmer Divide Vineyards. You choose to use data flow to model the basic capabilities that will be found in the solution.

SH1: Users shall perform research studies.

S1: The system shall calculate elapsed study time.

SH2: Users shall customize the contents of their research studies.

S2: The system shall allow creation of custom data queries.

S3: The user shall analyze the customer query results.

You draw two models using both the Gane-Sarson and Yourdon notations just for comparison's sake. You decide to show the models to the project team to see if they have a preference between them.

Because your project is software-development intensive, you and the team decide to use the Gane-Sarson notation for the data models. Everyone has seen models like this before, and they are most comfortable with that notation. You know that either notation would work to model the data flow for customizing research studies at Palmer Divide vineyards, but think it best to go with the one that people find easiest to understand.

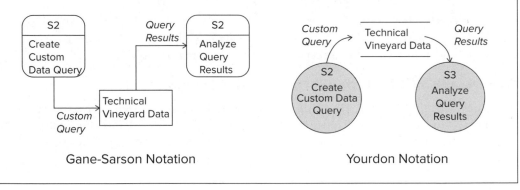

Gane-Sarson Notation   Yourdon Notation

DFDs can be created using a number of notations, including Yourdon or Gane-Sarson. Stakeholders and users usually find either notation style easy to understand and to follow. Table 6.6 compares the features found in these two common DFD notations based on the descriptions in the *BABOK® Guide*.

TABLE 6.6 The Two Common Data Flow Diagram Notations

Elements	Yourdon	Gane-Sarson
External entities	Labeled rectangle	Labeled rectangle
Data stores	Label for the data store name between two parallel lines	Labeled rectangle with the right side open or a labeled rectangle with a square containing the data store name
Data process	Labeled circle with a 'verb-object' structure naming the process	Labeled rectangle with curved corners with a 'verb-object' structure naming the process
Data flow	Single or forked line with an arrow along with a noun-phrase descriptor of the data being moved	Single or forked line with an arrow along with a noun-phrase descriptor of the data being moved

During requirements analysis, you will create additional diagrams, entity-relationship diagrams (ERDs), to represent the user's view of the solution and its capabilities in terms of entities, attributes, and relationships. Often you will refine these models during the design phase of the project, particularly if you are defining capabilities of a software application. During design, the ERDs are refined and the physical data model that becomes the basis for a relational database is ultimately created.

Recommended Technique: *Data Modeling*

Data models visually represent the people, places, things, and concepts that are important to the business. The two most common types of data models are the ERD or the class diagram. ERDs are often used for projects where a relational database is part of the solution, while class diagrams are a better fit for object-oriented software development efforts.

Logical data models look at the concepts, attributes, and relationships for the information relevant to the organization in detail or at a high level. *Physical data models* describe how data is stored and managed by a software application that is part of the solution scope. Concepts are something significant to the organization about which the organization needs data. Attributes are used to define specific pieces of information associated with a concept, such as its name, acceptable values, and a description. Relationships are significant business associations between concepts.

Real World Scenario

Palmer Divide Vineyards: Data Flow Diagrams or Data Models?

You are still in the early stages of modeling the new functionality associated with requesting and performing research studies at Palmer Divide Vineyards. You and the project team choose to use data flow diagrams and Gane-Sarson notation to model the basic capabilities that will be found in the solution. However, one of the technical team members has proposed an alternative to this modeling technique. She believes that using data models would be a better way to describe the people, places, and things involved with this new functionality.

The two of you sit down and look at the requirements you were using for selecting a modeling technique.

SH1: Users shall perform research studies.

S1: The system shall calculate elapsed study time.

SH2: Users shall customize the contents of their research studies.

S2: The system shall allow creation of custom data queries.

S3: The user shall analyze the customer query results.

You consider the advantages and disadvantages of using either class diagrams, or ERDs, as ways to effectively model the solution requirements. The two of you create two simple models using both approaches to help you evaluate the models and see if they fit your project, as shown next.

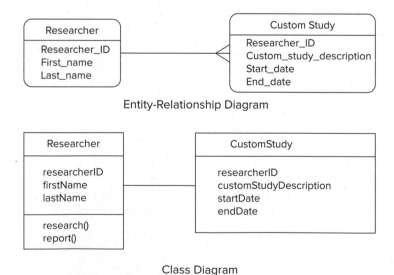

Because your project is a traditional software development effort—workflow-intensive, as opposed to information-intensive—you both agree that neither one of these techniques fits your project as well as the simpler data models. Although the models created using ERDs could become the basis of a relational database for the vineyard's technical data, you decide to pass on these models during requirements analysis. You both agree, though, that ERDs might be useful to the technical team once the project enters its design phase.

In addition to defining the information and its relationships, data models also describe the context, use, and validity of their business information using *metadata*, or data about data. Metadata tells a business analyst when and why information in a system is being changed in some way. Table 6.7 summarizes and distinguishes (as defined by the *BABOK® Guide*) between the two types of data models commonly used by business analysts.

TABLE 6.7   The Data Models

Elements	Entity-Relationship Diagram (ERD)	Class Diagrams
Concept	Uniquely identified entity in a rectangle with the unique identifier shown under the entity name	Uniquely identified class in a rectangle or square with an optional stereotype above it in brackets defining additional properties
Attributes	Listed below the unique identifier for the entity in the rectangle	Listed in a box below the name with operations listed below the attributes
Relationships	Indicated by a line which is annotated to show cardinality, such as any number from zero to many, zero to one, only one or any number from one to many	Indicated by a line which is annotated to show multiplicity, such as zero to many, exactly any number from *x* to *y* or any number from one to many

Data models are strong vehicles for transitioning through the planning, analysis, design, and implementation of projects. They are subject to rigorous rules for correctness and completeness that typically result in more accurate final products. In some cases, your stakeholders can find detailed data models difficult to understand, so you must be prepared to build them to the appropriate level of detail and be able to explain them thoroughly to your audience when required. According to the *BABOK® Guide*, performing data modeling is one of the required techniques in the fundamental knowledge base of an effective business analyst.

Recommended Technique: Nonfunctional Requirements Analysis

Nonfunctional requirements define the overall qualities or attributes of the resulting solution or solution components. Basically, they constrain how the solution requirements are to be met by the solution itself. Nonfunctional requirements state the qualities of behavior or quality attributes that your stakeholders want. Nonfunctional requirements augment the description of solution functionality by stating the solution's characteristics in various dimensions that are important to the users or the developers.

You should consider using a checklist for eliciting and developing your nonfunctional requirements. It is easiest to capture the functional and nonfunctional requirements at the same time. Checklists can help you organize your nonfunctional requirements by category and make sure you are not missing anything. The *BABOK® Guide* recommends using a set of seven categories for your nonfunctional requirements. Let's step through those categories now.

Reliability   Reliability focuses on the solution's availability when the stakeholders need it. You should also look at the solution's ability to recover from errors or failures.

Performance Efficiency   Performance efficiency looks at the time it takes to perform activities and the resource utilization levels for the solution.

Operability   Operability measures the extent to which your stakeholders can recognize whether or not a solution meets their needs. It also evaluates the ease of learning to use the new solution, its capabilities, and how usable the solution actually is.

Security   Security is a very big deal these days, particularly in software systems. This category looks at the solution's ability to store information and protect it from unauthorized use. Authentication of solution users and audit reporting is also considered.

Compatibility   Most solutions today need to operate effectively and either coexist or interact with other solutions in the same environment.

Maintainability   Maintainability focuses on how easy it will be to change one solution component without affecting other components. You also need to consider component reuse, ease of diagnosing problems, and the ability to implement changes without causing unexpected failures.

Transferability   You need to determine whether your solution can be migrated to, installed in, and uninstalled from different environments when needed.

Nonfunctional Requirements Checklist

This nonfunctional requirements checklist allows you to run through a list of typical items and ensure that you haven't missed conditions or constraints that might be important to your project requirements.

- Reliability (mean time between failures [MTBF])
- Availability (expected hours of operation)

- Maintainability (ease with which components can be replaced)

- Performance (must return prompt within two seconds)

- Environmental conditions (such as dirty, dark, or dusty environments)

- Accessibility (different navigation for novice, experienced, and disabled users)

- Ergonomic (use of specific colors to reduce eye strain)

- Safety (signals loud enough to be heard but not to harm hearing)

- Security (physical and system access defining who is authorized to do what?)

- Facility requirements (require special electrical or phone capabilities)

- Transportability (weight limits of handheld units)

- Training (are tutorials or textbooks required?)

- Documentation (online help, reference manuals)

- External interfaces (support industry-standard protocols)

- Testing (support remote diagnostics)

- Quality provisions (minimum required calibration intervals)

- Policy and regulatory (government requirements, constraints)

- Compatibility to existing systems (support analog phone lines)

- Standards and technical policies (conform to electrical codes)

- Conversion (will support data from older versions of system)

- Growth capacity (will support x end users in y years)

- Installation (ability to put the new system into service)

Once you have captured your nonfunctional requirements, you will need to document them. Nonfunctional requirements are typically documented alongside the functional solution requirements that they constrain. That makes sense, because the functional and nonfunctional requirements are both subsets of your solution requirements. It's a good idea to document the nonfunctional requirements that define your global constraints in their own section of your requirements document because they impact all of your solution requirements in some way.

Recommended Technique: Process Modeling

Process models organize your requirements using a hierarchy of processes and subprocesses, and they address those processes from start to finish. You use them to document the steps your stakeholders take to get their work done. Process models are very easy to understand and to work with on your projects. Think of graphically depicting a series of steps to place an online order on a whiteboard with arrows between them to show the sequence of events. That flowchart is a simple process map.

According to the *BABOK® Guide,* process models are visual representations of the sequential flow and control logic of a set of related activities. Process models may consist of manual steps performed by the stakeholders, automated steps taken by a software system, or some combination of the two. Process models may be developed at a high level to get a general understanding of what is going on, or they may be very detailed steps that your stakeholders take to perform their work.

 Real World Scenario

Palmer Divide Vineyards: Are Process Models Even Better?

Your users were not pleased with the Gane-Sarson data model you presented to show the information flow associated with the research study project at the vineyard. They have asked you to model something more from the user's point of view. Several end users chimed in that they would like models that show who needs to do what and in what order it needs to be done. You agree to look at some other modeling techniques that may be more workflow focused.

Once again, you review the requirements you were using for selecting a modeling technique.

SH1: Users shall perform research studies.

S1: The system shall calculate elapsed study time.

SH2: Users shall customize the contents of their research studies.

S2: The system shall allow creation of custom data queries.

S3: The user shall analyze the customer query results.

You think to yourself that perhaps a simple flow chart noting the user at each step might just do the trick. You create one for this small set of requirements and ask the users what they think of this approach. The response is an overwhelming yes, and the final decision is that simple workflow models are the way to go on this project.

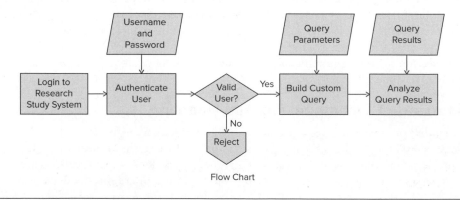

Flow Chart

Numerous notations can be used in your process models. The two most common notations are flowcharts and activity diagrams. Table 6.8 contains a summary of the key elements found in your process models.

TABLE 6.8 Process Model Notation Elements

Element	Description
Activities	Individual steps or pieces of work being performed to execute a business process
Decisions	Forks where workflow takes different directions or merges back together based on a decision being made
Events	External factors such as actions taken or messages received that create, interrupt, or terminate a process
Flow	Indicates direction of the sequence of activities, typically drawn as top to bottom or left to right
Roles	Represent a type of person or a group found in the organization
Swimlanes	Horizontal or vertical sections of a process model showing which activities are performed by and are the responsibility of a particular role
Pools	Organizational boundaries that include a number of swimlanes or roles
Terminal Points	The beginning or end of a process or process flow

Recommended Technique: Scenarios and Use Cases

Scenarios and use cases offer you a way to model how your stakeholders interact with the solution capabilities in order to get their jobs done. The stakeholder roles are called actors. Scenarios and use cases show how actors interact with the solution to accomplish one or more of their goals or in response to a particular event. They are excellent ways to model the solution scope and the behavior and goals of the actors interacting with that solution.

 Real World Scenario

Palmer Divide Vineyards: Addressing Our Visual Learners

William, one of the vineyard's co-owners, prefers to review and approve high-level requirements by walking through graphical models containing as little text as possible. He is a visual learner and one of your visual stakeholders, too. Because William is responsible for providing funding for the research study project, it is important that you meet his needs in your upcoming review meetings with senior management.

On past projects, you have successfully used high-level use-case diagrams to facilitate discussion of functionality and which stakeholders interact with that functionality. Even though many IT project teams only build use case diagrams when they are developing an object-oriented system, you know that is not an absolute requirement for your more traditional development project. The summary diagram will help you explain the high-level use cases or processes, the key stakeholder roles (actors), and the interactions between them (associations). If you discover an actor with no association to any of the use cases in your model, it might be that they are not a direct user of your system. If you have a use case with no actors associated with it, you will question the inclusion of those capabilities in your new system or discover who should interact with that particular capability.

You build a summary-level use-case diagram as part of your modeling efforts to prepare for the upcoming meeting. The diagram models the new functionality associated with requesting and performing research studies at Palmer Divide Vineyards, as shown next.

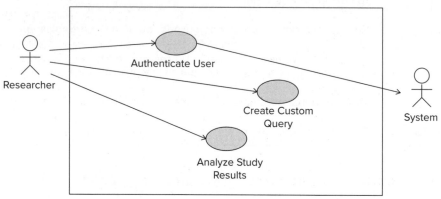

Use Case Diagram

For the last time, you take a look at the requirements you were using for selecting a modeling technique.

SH1: Users shall perform research studies.

S1: The system shall calculate elapsed study time.

SH2: Users shall customize the contents of their research studies.

S2: The system shall allow creation of custom data queries.

S3: The user shall analyze the customer query results.

Scenarios and use cases are very much related. Scenarios are a series of steps performed by a stakeholder in order to document one way in which that person could use a solution capability to achieve a goal. Use cases consist of a set of scenarios describing all ways that stakeholder might achieve (or fail to achieve) a particular goal. Table 6.9 contains a summary of the key elements found in scenarios and use cases.

TABLE 6.9   Scenario and Use Case Elements

Element	Description
Name	Unique name for each scenario or use case within the project, usually a verb-noun phrase such as Process Order.
Actor(s)	Unique name representing the role of each external person, system, or event that interacts with the solution through a use case.
Preconditions	Any fact that the solution can assume to be true when the use case begins.
Flow of Events	Description of what the actor and the solution do during the execution of the scenario, usually consisting of a primary flow and alternate flows.
Post-Conditions	Any fact that must be true when the use case is complete.
Relationships	Associations between actors and use cases indicating that the actor has access to the functionality represented by the use case.
Stereotypes	The name given to relationships between use cases.
	Extend: Inserts additional behavior into a use case that has been captured in a separate use case versus being an alternative flow.
	Include: Allows one use case to use or share some functionality present in another use case.

Recommended Technique: Sequence Diagrams

Sequence diagrams can be thought of as if they were tracking the information flow between two people having a conversation. They show how the information gets passed back and forth between the two people. Sequence diagrams are commonly used during object-oriented analysis to show how classes and objects interact during a scenario. You can also use them to show how the user interface components or software components interact in your solution.

In a nutshell, sequence diagrams shows stimuli flowing between objects. The stimulus is a message, and the arrival of the stimulus at the object is called an event. Each object name is in a rectangle with a single vertical line drawn beneath it called a lifeline. Messages are depicted starting at the top of the lifeline and moving down that lifeline over time.

There are two ways to send messages between objects: asynchronous and procedural. Procedural flow transfers a message to the receiving object and waits for a response or return message before it can do anything else. Asynchronous flow allows the sender to continue with its own processing after sending the message to the receiver.

Recommended Technique: State Diagrams

State diagrams show a sequence of states that an object, entity, or concept goes through during its lifetime. These diagrams also define the events that cause a transition between these states. The functionality and behavior of a particular object will be different based on its current state. For example, a mainframe computer system in batch-processing mode may be unable to process real-time queries from a user during the time it is in that state.

State diagrams are also called state machine diagrams. A state represents a unique condition that an object can be in or a status that the object may have. All states for an object are mutually exclusive, which means that an object can be in only one state at a time. All state machines have an initial state and any number of intermediate or end states. Transitions define the behaviors that move an object from one state to another state. They are often triggered by completed activities or events.

We have defined our own state machine for our requirements development activities using the *BABOK® Guide*. The transitions for the requirements that are under development are the knowledge area tasks that change the state of those requirements as you work on them. For example, during requirements analysis the analyzed solution requirements (that are specified and modeled) go through a quality check using the verify requirements task. When the requirements emerge from this task, they have changed to a new state, becoming the verified solution requirements.

Recommended Technique: User Stories

User stories are commonly used for change-driven requirements development. They briefly describe the functionality your solution provides to its users. You should define acceptance and evaluation criteria for each user story so you can prove that its functionality has been met by the solution. User stories are written from the user's point of view and they contain:

- The actor or stakeholder benefiting from the user story
- A high-level description of the functionality in the story
- The business benefits that the story delivers

User stories create customer ownership of requirements by having your users write stories about what the solution needs to accomplish for them. You can use these stories to support your iterative, incremental development environments. They allow you to define key features of the solution that can be implemented by the project team in one to three weeks.

Additional Techniques to Consider

The *BABOK® Guide* recommends using one or more of the following additional techniques when you are specifying and modeling the requirements for your project. They are summarized for you here.

Data Dictionary and Glossary   Glossaries allow you to document key business terms along with their definitions. Much of the information that goes into the glossary will be a result of your business, stakeholder, solution, and transition requirements development efforts. Data dictionaries are a bit more technical in nature and are used to define data elements, their meanings, and their allowable values. Building a data dictionary for your project might be a necessary step in your requirements specification and modeling activities.

Functional Decomposition   Functional decomposition allows you to systematically break down the solution scope components into smaller pieces and more detailed requirements based on similar or related functionalities or features. This assists you in adding additional details as part of your requirements analysis efforts.

Interface Analysis   Interface analysis establishes a basis for interoperability by recognizing inputs, outputs, and key data elements that enable your solution and its components to interact with everything else that is already out there. During requirements analysis, this allows you to clarify the solution boundaries and reach agreement on any required interfaces. Interfaces are bidirectional, running to and from your solution scope and any external parties, applications, or devices.

Metrics and KPIs   Metrics and KPIs are used to measure, manage, and report on the expected benefits of implementing a proposed solution. Business analysts must make sure that the benefits being sought can be proven to exist after the solution is deployed.

Organization Modeling   Most of us have seen an organization chart showing the hierarchy. This is an example of an organizational model. The model defines the purpose and structure of an organization or an organizational unit. When you use this technique for requirements analysis, you basically build an organization chart that shows the organizational units, lines of reporting, the roles, and the people in those roles.

Prototyping   Prototyping is a great way to add additional details to your solution interface requirements and integrate those requirements with the other requirements defining the new solution. Essentially a prototype is an initial or preliminary version of a solution or system. Prototypes are helpful during requirements analysis. They identify, describe, and validate our solution scope and user interface needs.

Once you have selected and applied one or more techniques as part of your requirements specification and modeling efforts, you are ready to continue with some of the other requirements analysis tasks. We will discuss those tasks right after we review the output of our current task, the analyzed stakeholder, or solution requirements for the project.

Create the Analyzed Requirements

Analyzed requirements are used as an input to several solution-related tasks. Remember the definition for analyzed requirements: the modeled and specified stakeholder and solution requirements for your project. The destination tasks utilizing your analyzed requirements are summarized in Table 6.10.

Exam Spotlight

Remember, the business requirements are analyzed and created by tasks in the Enterprise Analysis knowledge area, and the transition requirements are analyzed and created by tasks in the Solution Assessment and Validation knowledge area. Your stakeholder and solution requirements are created by specifying and modeling requirements in the Requirements Analysis knowledge area.

TABLE 6.10   Outputs: Specify and Model Requirements

Output	Output Destinations	Destination Knowledge Area
Stakeholder or Solution Requirements (analyzed)	Prioritize requirements	Requirements analysis
	Verify requirements	Requirements analysis
	—	Requirements Management and Communication knowledge area

You are responsible for specifying and modeling the stakeholder and solution requirements on your project. You will have to decide if this work is to be done alone or as a team effort. If you perform this task alone, you will specify and model the requirements, create the requirements package, and then communicate those requirements with the stakeholders for their review and/or approval. You can also choose to involve the stakeholders in this task so that the requirements package contents and the requirements themselves are not a surprise to anyone.

Exam Spotlight

Guidelines for writing text requirements include:

- Express one requirement at a time.
- Write in the active voice.
- Use consistent terminology.
- Use a verb or verb phrase.
- Avoid complex conditional clauses.
- Do not assume reader has domain knowledge.
- Use terminology familiar to your stakeholders.

Let's take a look at the next task in the Requirements Analysis knowledge area—defining any assumptions and constraints that should go hand in hand with your stakeholder and solution requirements.

Define Assumptions and Constraints

Assumptions and constraints are factors that impact your requirements and their resulting solution. People make assumptions about things they believe to be true all the time. When was the last time that you left the house headed to work and calculated the time it would take to get there based on your assumptions for what the morning traffic would be like? Of course, there is always the risk that you will arrive at work later than planned if the traffic does not behave as you assume it will. By comparison, constraints are fixed boundary conditions or limits on what you can do. Figure 6.4 summarizes the inputs, outputs, techniques, and associated tasks used to define assumptions and constraints.

FIGURE 6.4   Task summary: Define assumptions and constraints.

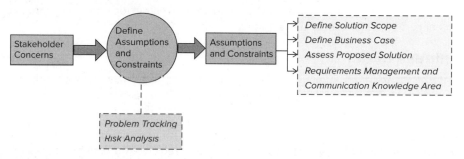

The input to defining assumptions and constraints is the stakeholder concerns that were elicited along with the stated requirements. Let's have a look at each of these input sources in greater detail.

Stakeholder Concerns   Assumptions and constraints come to you through the stakeholder concerns that are raised during requirements elicitation. They are analyzed during requirements analysis and are documented along with the requirements that they affect.

Table 6.11 summarizes the inputs to this task and lists the task and knowledge area sources for each input used define assumptions and constraints.

TABLE 6.11   Inputs: Define Assumptions and Constraints

Task Input	Input Source	Source Knowledge Area
Stakeholder concerns	Document elicitation results	Elicitation
	Confirm elicitation results (confirmed)	Elicitation

As you define, analyze, and document the assumptions and constraints on your project, you should be looking for three elements: assumptions, business constraints, and technical constraints. Let's review the elements to make sure you can distinguish between them.

Assumptions   Assumptions are factors that are believed to be true, although these factors have not been confirmed. Assumptions add risk to a project because it is possible that they will turn out to be false. They can impact any part of the project lifecycle and the resulting solution implementation, and they should be documented and analyzed.

Business Constraints   Business constraints limit the solution or the current organizational state. They tend to be focused on the available time, money, and resources for your project. Common areas for business constraints include budget and time restrictions, resource limitations, and resource skill limitations.

Technical Constraints   Technical constraints focus on architecture decisions that limit the solution design. They tend to be inflexible and unchanging, and they can impact your solution implementation. They include areas such as development languages, hardware, and software that must be used for your project.

There are two techniques that you may choose to apply when prioritizing your project requirements. Let's take a look at them now.

Techniques to Consider

The *BABOK® Guide* recommends using two techniques when you are defining the assumptions and constraints that accompany your requirements. They are summarized for you here.

Problem Tracking   Problem tracking is synonymous with issue management. This technique allows the business analyst to communicate, review, and maintain focus on business analysis-related problems and issues across the project life cycle. The business analyst is responsible for tracking, managing, and resolving defects, issues, problems, and risks that take place during business analysis activities.

Risk Analysis   Assumptions and constraints often add risk to your project. These new risks should be identified and analyzed using the risk analysis technique. This is particularly true if assumptions change from true to false or if known constraints are removed or revised.

Once you have selected and applied one or more techniques as part of your definition efforts, you are ready to continue with the other requirements analysis tasks in this knowledge area. We will discuss those tasks later in the chapter. First let's look at the assumptions and constraints that you have defined.

Assumptions and Constraints

The assumptions and constraints are important aspects of your stakeholder and solution. You need to make sure that you analyze and document them appropriately on your projects. Although they are not requirements, you should document them along with the requirements that they impact. It is a simple step to manage and communicate the requirements assumptions and constraints using the tasks found in the Requirements Management and Communication knowledge area.

Assumptions and constraints are used as input to several business analysis tasks, including defining the solution scope and assessing proposed solutions using this information. These destination tasks and their knowledge areas are summarized for you in Table 6.12.

TABLE 6.12 Outputs: Define Assumptions and Constraints

Output	Output Destinations	Destination Knowledge Area
Assumptions and constraints	Define solution scope	Enterprise Analysis
	Define business case	Enterprise Analysis
	Assess proposed solution	Solution Assessment and Validation
		Requirements Management and Communication knowledge area

Any stakeholder may be involved with defining the assumptions and constraints associated with your stakeholder and solution requirements. The business analyst has the primary responsibility for defining this information. The project manager uses the assumptions and constraints to identify potential risks that may impact project delivery. The Implementation SME will take the assumptions and constraints into account when designing the resulting solution from the solution requirements.

Now let's look at the next task found in the Requirements Analysis knowledge area— verifying requirements.

Verify Requirements

Requirements verification is a quality check of the analyzed requirements. This task involves making sure your requirements are correct and complete, and that they meet the quality standards defined for them. Requirements verification can be thought of as an internal check by the business analysis team and the involved stakeholders to make sure the requirements are ready to be seen out in public. Out-in-public requirements are ready for formal review and approval so they can be used as the basis for subsequent project work, such as design and implementation.

Figure 6.5 summarizes the inputs, outputs, techniques, and associated tasks used to define assumptions and constraints.

FIGURE 6.5   Task summary: Verify the requirements.

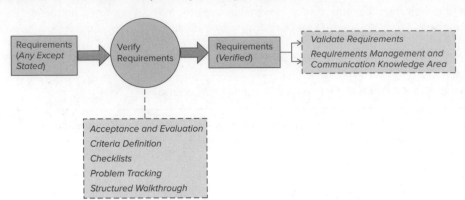

In order to verify the requirements, you need to have those requirements in hand. These requirements can be of many types and in many states, as long as they are not the stated requirements you elicited from your stakeholders.

Table 6.13 summarizes the inputs to this task and lists the task and knowledge area sources for each input used to prioritize requirements.

TABLE 6.13   Inputs: Verify Requirements

Task Input	Input Source	Source Knowledge Area
Requirements (any except stated)	Document elicitation results	Elicitation
	(Allocated) Allocate requirements	Solution Assessment and Validation
	(Analyzed) Specify and model requirements	Requirements Analysis
	(Approved) Manage solution scope and requirements	Requirements Management and Communication
	(Communicated) Communicate requirements	Requirements Management and Communication
	(Maintained and reusable) Maintain requirements for reuse	Requirements Management and Communication
	(Prioritized) Prioritize requirements	Requirements Analysis

Task Input	Input Source	Source Knowledge Area
	(Traced) Manage requirements traceability	Requirements Management and Communication
	(Validated) Validate requirements	Requirements Analysis
	(Verified) Verify requirements	Requirements Analysis

Any type of requirement can be verified, including business, stakeholder, solution, or transition requirements. Because verification is a quality check of the analyzed requirements, the requirements cannot be the stated requirements resulting from your elicitation efforts. They must have been analyzed, specified, and modeled.

Well-written requirements aren't a random event—they are planned for and they are thoroughly reviewed and revised to meet most if not all of the characteristics listed in the *BABOK® Guide*. The elements you focus on during requirements verification include a set of characteristics for well-written requirements and the work activities to make sure these characteristics are properly applied. Let's review the two elements of well-written requirements in more detail.The *BABOK® Guide* provides you with the eight characteristics of well-written, high-quality requirements. Think of this as your well-written requirements quality checklist and make frequent use of it during your requirements development efforts.

Cohesive   Cohesive requirements are a set of requirements relating to one particular thing, such as a business process. Requirements should be organized in your documents as cohesive sets of information rather than random chunks of information. Your approach to requirements organization is addressed in your requirements structure. In order to be cohesive, your requirements organization should provide for reference, navigation, traceability, and completeness.

Complete   Your goal is to produce a complete set of requirements defining what is needed for a solution or a solution component. Your requirements should specify everything that is needed at the appropriate level of detail. While building your requirements document, ask yourself if you have missed anything. If you see unresolved issues or incomplete documentation fix it.

A number of approaches can be used to find incomplete requirements in your document, including:

- Static inspection (reading the document)
- Using the requirements checklist for writing and review
- Applying prototyping as an elicitation/analysis technique
- User review (nothing is better than an extra set of eyes)

Consistent   Consistent requirements do not contradict or conflict with one another. If they do, they should be revised or removed. Consistency should also be applied to the level of detail in your requirements document structure. All requirements at a specific numbering level in your document should be written at the same level of detail. Checking for consistency often requires a manual review and analysis of the complete set of requirements.

Correct   Correctness must be determined and targeted across all steps of the requirements development process. A requirements document is correct if every requirement stated within it is one that will be met by the resulting solution. There is no tool or procedure to ensure correctness of individual requirements or the requirements document. Remember that requirements containing defects introduce those defects into the solution they define.

You should address requirements correctness at two levels of detail: the overall requirements document and the individual requirements that it contains.

> **Requirements Document**   Compare the requirements document with other relevant project documentation and standards to see if it agrees. You should also seek stakeholder review and agreement to the requirements document contents.

> **Individual Requirements**   Show that the individual requirements in your document are correct and relevant by comparing them with their source. You should also select an appropriate requirements verification method to confirm that they are well-written and correct.

Feasible   Feasibility of requirements relates to implementation. The existing infrastructure, budget, timeline, and resources of the organization should be adequate to implement your requirements as defined. If not, your requirements will need to be revised to include any additional capabilities that are needed to implement them.

Modifiable   Requirements should be written and structured to allow easy changes. Modifiable requirements allow you to easily modify your requirements within the existing document structure and style.

Modifiable and well-organized requirements documents contain the following minimum set of components:

- Table of contents for the document
- Index of key terms
- Unique numbering of individual requirements
- Cross references when necessary
- No duplication or redundancy of content

Unambiguous   Can your requirements be interpreted in more than one way? If so, they are ambiguous. Well-written requirements have only one meaning. People should not be able to read your requirements and come up with multiple meanings for what has been stated. When terms have multiple meanings, consider defining those terms in your glossary.

Real World Scenario

Choose the Right Word

Here is an example of why choosing the right word is not always as easy as you might think. Let's take a very simple word: bug. Susan's mother says that a bug is an insect of some sort. Terri's nephew says that a bug is something he needs to fix in his software code. A military customer says a bug is a secret listening device that shouldn't be there. Funny thing is that they are all correct.

Here's why. In the dictionary, a bug is commonly defined in one of two ways: any small insect or a concealed microphone. However, in the software world, a bug is the name given to an error in software application code. Synonyms for the word *bug* include germ, virus, and wiretap.

Watch your word choices. Words can mean many different things when they are used in your requirements document. If you need to, document the word and your selected meaning in your glossary to make sure everyone uses that word the way you intended.

Testable   Can you ensure that a requirement is met by your resulting solution? If not, that requirement should be removed or revised, because all requirements must be measurable and provable in some way. Testing proves that what is needed is indeed present in the solution. That means that each requirement in your document must be provable as a single, standalone statement or within a specific functional scenario. Numerous techniques exist for ensuring that requirements are met (Table 6.14).

TABLE 6.14   Techniques for Ensuring That Requirements Are Met

Technique	Description
Demonstration	Involves running the full system in the normal mode of operation
Inspection	Where you look at (inspect) characteristics of the system or its output
Execution	Uses another system or testing equipment to simulate your data
Analysis	Performs analysis of the system characteristics to prove it works
Prior qualification	A component has already been tested and is being used unmodified

Requirements Verification Activities   You will find yourself verifying requirements many times during the project life cycle. When you are doing this task, remember to look at all of the specified requirements including text, tables, and graphical models.

There are several techniques that you may choose to apply when verifying your requirements. You should consider using checklists, along with structured walkthroughs, as a part of this work. Let's take a closer look at both of these techniques.

Recommended Technique: Checklists

Checklists are used specifically for verifying requirements. The technique is defined as part of this specific task and knowledge area in the *BABOK® Guide*. Checklists are an excellent quality control technique to apply to your requirements documentation. Checklists ensure that important items are included in the final requirements deliverables for your project, such as the eight characteristics of well-written requirements previously discussed. Checklists may also contain process steps to guide you through the requirements verification activities that should be done on your project.

Recommended Technique: Structured Walkthroughs

You should try using structured walkthroughs to verify the quality of your stakeholder and solution requirements with key stakeholders and team members. A structured walkthrough is a meeting with a tour guide. Your destination is the verified requirements, and your meeting agenda will walk you through the possibilities in order for the group to evaluate and revise the requirements. The group's goal is to develop a set of verified and well-written requirements. Another common name for a structured walkthrough is a requirements review.

Structured walkthroughs have a set of prerequisites:

- A complete requirements package for review
- A list of appropriate reviewers
- A meeting vehicle, either face-to-face or remote

Participants are expected to prepare prior to attending the walkthrough. This means that they should have read the requirements document prior to the meeting. It is nice to provide participants with a well-formed requirements checklist for use as they read the document and verify your requirements.

Structured walkthroughs have a set of roles to be played by the appropriate meeting participants. Let's step through these roles now.

Author   You (the business analyst) are usually the author of the requirements document being reviewed. Your role is to answer questions about the document and listen to stakeholder suggestions and comments. These suggestions and comments may be incorporated into the document after the meeting has ended.

Scribe   The scribe takes notes, documenting all comments, suggestions, issues, and concerns arising during the walkthrough. The author may play this role, as long as it doesn't interfere with interacting with the stakeholders.

Moderator   This mandatory role is played by a neutral facilitator. You could choose to play this role; however, it may conflict with your author or scribe role in the review. The moderator facilitates the session and makes sure that everything goes well.

Peer   Peer review of the requirements document is always recommended. There is nothing like another set of business analyst eyes on your requirements document to help make it better.

Reviewer   Reviewers are any of your stakeholders who are involved with the requirements under review. They should come to the meeting prepared to ask questions, offer comments, and make suggestions for changes or improvements to the document.

Additional Techniques to Consider

The *BABOK® Guide* also recommends using one or more of the following techniques when you are verifying project requirements.

Acceptance and Evaluation Criteria Definition   As part of requirements verification, you must determine the quality criteria against which you will evaluate your requirements. This gives the folks verifying your requirements the metrics to use in their evaluation of them.

Problem Tracking   Problem tracking is synonymous with issue management. This technique allows a business analyst to communicate, review, and maintain focus on business-analysis-related problems and issues across the project life cycle. Any problems identified during requirements verification may be tracked using this technique.

Once you have selected and applied one or more techniques as part of your verification efforts, you are ready to continue with the other requirements analysis tasks in this knowledge area. We will discuss those tasks later in the chapter. First, let's have a look at the verified requirements produced by this task.

Produce the Verified Requirements

Verified requirements are well-written requirements that can be used in other project work, such as technical design. Verified requirements must be of reasonable quality so that the team can use them and not worry about having to redo things later. Verified requirements are used as input to several business analysis tasks, including validating requirements and communicating verified requirements with your stakeholders for their review or approval. These destination tasks and their knowledge areas are summarized in Table 6.15.

TABLE 6.15   Outputs: Verify Requirements

Output	Output Destinations	Destination Knowledge Area
Requirements (verified)	Validate requirements	Requirements Analysis
		Requirements Management and Communication

You are responsible for making sure that the quality criteria for your requirements have been met. Any business analysis stakeholder may assist you with this task, including your domain and technical experts.

Let's look at the final task found in the Requirements Analysis knowledge area—validating the requirements.

Validate Requirements

Validating requirements ensures that your requirements align to the business requirements and the business objectives for your project. By definition, valid requirements contribute directly or indirectly to the project's business case. Requirements validation is ongoing across the project life cycle; it ensures that each level of detail you add to your requirements aligns with the big picture. Figure 6.6 summarizes the inputs, outputs, techniques, and associated tasks used to validate requirements.

FIGURE 6.6   Task summary: Validate the requirements.

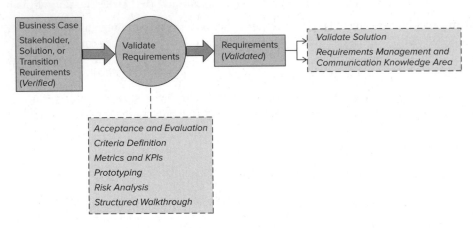

The inputs to validating requirements include the business case with its business requirements and the stakeholder, solution, or transition requirements that you are validating. Let's look at each of these task inputs in greater detail.

Business Case   The business contains the business goals and objectives that valid requirements and their resulting solution will deliver when the project is complete. Additional business requirements can be found in the business need, required capabilities, and solution scope for your project. You will also use these business requirements for requirements validation purposes.

> ## Business Requirements Refresher
>
> What are the business requirements and how do they relate to the requirements validation task and the big picture deliverables? Four Enterprise Analysis knowledge area deliverables become your project's business requirements:
>
> **Business Need**   The business need describes the problem or opportunity that an organization is facing. This problem or opportunity exists within the framework of that organization's business goals and objectives. The business need and the desired outcome from addressing that need guide the identification, definition, and selection of possible solutions and solution approaches for that situation.
>
> **Required Capabilities**   The required capabilities define the new capabilities that may be required to meet a business need. These capabilities may be multifaceted—addressing processes, staff, and application features of the new solution.
>
> **Solution Scope**   Solution scope defines the major features, functions, and interactions of your proposed solution. It describes what must be delivered to meet a business need, including any effects the solution might have on the business and technology operations and infrastructure of the organization.
>
> **Business Case**   A business case justifies the cost of doing a project in terms of the value the resulting solution adds to the business. A business case looks at both sides of the equation, comparing the costs and benefits of a proposed solution. The expected business benefits of the solution are evaluated relative to achieving the business objectives and meeting the business need.
>
> These four deliverables are not always found in a standalone deliverable or document. They are each part of the project's business requirements and are typically included in a more comprehensive business requirements document or as part of the project's business case.

Stakeholder, Solution, or Transition Requirements (Verified)   Requirements must be verified in order for requirements validation to be complete. However, requirements validation activities can begin on partially verified requirements. Unverified requirements cannot be successfully implemented and, therefore, cannot align with the business requirements to meet the defined business need driving your project.

Table 6.16 summarizes the two inputs to this task and lists the task and knowledge area sources for each input used to validate requirements.

TABLE 6.16   Inputs: Validate Requirements

Task Input	Input Source	Source Knowledge Area
Business case	Define business case	Enterprise Analysis
Stakeholder, solution or transition requirements (verified)	Verify requirements	Requirements Analysis

You need to keep a number of elements in your line of sight as you validate your stakeholder, solution, or transition requirements. They include:

- Identifying any assumptions
- Defining measurable evaluation criteria
- Determining the business value of the solution
- Determining requirements dependencies
- Evaluating your alignment with the business case

Let's review each of these elements in more detail. Each of these elements deals with a detailed area of the project's business case, focuses on making sure that the defined business benefits of the project are achievable, and shows how you will prove that those business benefits have been achieved.

Identify Assumptions   Within a project's business case, you might have documented assumptions about realizing the business benefits. Any assumptions about a specific business benefit should be documented and linked to the requirements that deliver those benefits. This might introduce additional risk into the premises contained in the business case, since it is possible that the assumptions might not be true in the end.

Define Measurable Evaluation Criteria   One item of interest found in your business case is the business benefit that the project will provide to the organization once it is complete and the solution is up and running. Business benefits can be measured only if you define the measurement criteria and how you will evaluate whether or not you have achieved them. If you are lucky, they were defined in the business case. If not, you will need to define them now during requirements validation.

Determine Business Value   Your project's business case is the vehicle for determining the business value that the resulting solution provides. You can evaluate this for the full solution scope or for the individual requirements that comprise the solution scope. Requirements that don't deliver any business value (directly or indirectly) are good candidates for elimination or revision during your requirements validation activities. Remember that business value is not just monetary value. Requirements can deliver business value by meeting legal or regulatory standards or by making your end users happy with the resulting solution.

Determine Requirements Dependencies   Another way that individual requirements add business value is by supporting or being linked to other requirements that provide financial value to the organization. Tracing requirements relationships was discussed in Chapter 4, "Overarching Tasks: Requirements Management and Communication," in the Requirements Management and Communication knowledge area. Traceability allows key dependencies and relationships between requirements to be recorded and traced across the project life cycle.

Evaluate Business Case Alignment   Beware of requirements that are beloved by your stakeholder yet add little or no business value to the organization. The best rule to follow is that requirements that do not align with a business case result in either a revised business case or their removal from the solution scope. Watch out for the opportunity cost of implementing such requirements. Sometimes it is best to remove requirements that don't align with the business case versus investing the time and money to make them work. Your time and money might be better spent elsewhere. Every opportunity (or requirement) has an associated cost.

There are two techniques that you may choose to apply when prioritizing your project requirements. You should strongly consider using the problem tracking technique for defining, managing, and communicating the assumptions and constraints found on your projects. Let's take a look at that technique right now.

Techniques to Consider

The *BABOK® Guide* recommends using one or more of the following techniques when you are validating your project's stakeholder, solution, or transition requirements relative to your project's business requirements.

Acceptance and Evaluation Criteria Definition   Acceptance criteria are the quality metrics that must be met by a requirement, a solution component, or the solution itself in order to be accepted by the project stakeholders. Evaluation criteria are used to measure how successful a deployed or operational solution is in providing business benefits.

Metrics and Key Performance Indicators (KPIs)   Metrics and KPIs are used to select and define performance measures for your requirements, solution components, or solutions.

Prototyping   Prototyping may be used to get user agreement on the solution scope from your project stakeholders.

Risk Analysis   Risks are generated when you make assumptions about your requirements, such as achieving the potential business benefits or building a solution that adds value to the organization. Risk analysis might result from the need to evaluate those assumptions and the associated potential risks.

Structured Walkthrough   This technique is used a great deal by business analysts seeking agreement from their stakeholders that the requirements meet their needs and can be considered to be validated.

Let's move on and take a look at the validated stakeholder, solution, or transition requirements that are produced by this task.

Produce the Validated Requirements

Validated requirements are stakeholder, solution, or transition requirements that are aligned with the business goals and objectives found in your project's business requirements or business case. These requirements benefit the organization and will provide value when they are implemented by the resulting solution. Remember that validated requirements fall within the framework of your defined solution scope.

Validated requirements are used as an input to several business analysis tasks, including managing and communicating those requirements using tasks in the Requirements Management and Communication knowledge area. These destination tasks and their knowledge areas are summarized in Table 6.17.

TABLE 6.17   Outputs: Validate Requirements

Output	Output Destinations	Destination Knowledge Area
Stakeholder, solution, or transitions requirements (validated)	Validate solution	Solution Assessment and ValidationRequirements Management and Communication knowledge area

All business analysis stakeholders are impacted by or involved in requirements validation activities during your project. As the business analyst, you are ultimately responsible for ensuring that the solution scope and requirements align with the business requirements and deliver value to the organization.

How This Applies to Your Projects

In this chapter, you stepped through the tasks guiding you in analyzing the stakeholder and solution requirements for your project. One of the biggest challenges that you will encounter on your projects is making sure that the requirements you develop for your projects are testable. As you develop your stakeholder and solution requirements, keep asking yourself for each and every requirement: Can I prove that this requirement has been met in the resulting solution? If the answer is no, then you need to rewrite that requirement to make it measurable and testable. If the answer is yes, you need to figure out how you will acquire that proof. That means you should put on your tester's hat and start thinking about your fit criteria while you are specifying and modeling your requirements. Fit criteria define the measurable goals that determine if the testing of a solution satisfies the original requirements for that solution. This is true for every requirement that you write.

Fit criteria are quantified and testable statements of a requirement that show the requirement has indeed been met. They can be applied to both functional and nonfunctional requirements. Let's take a look at more details about defining the fit criteria for each type of solution requirement you may write, functional and nonfunctional.

Remember, functional requirements are capabilities that the solution or a solution component must have. Your fit criteria are the yardstick that is used to test whether or not those capabilities have been successfully implemented. They are a quantified goal, containing numbers or measurements that your solution has to meet. As you write your functional requirements, you should ask yourself:

- Has the function been successfully implemented?

- Do the results satisfy the originator of the requirement?

- What are the defined user acceptance criteria?

If you have a functional requirement to calculate a certain value, then the fit criteria for that requirement are that the calculation results conform to the intended result. Your fit criteria should satisfy the source of your requirement. Either the source is capable of saying that they are satisfied, or the result of the action taken will be measurable and consistent with a standard set for that kind of action.

Nonfunctional requirements are properties or characteristics that your solution or a solution component must have. The fit criteria quantify the necessary behavior or quality indicated by the nonfunctional requirement. Some nonfunctional requirements might at first seem a little hard to test. Writing fit criteria for nonfunctional requirements is a matter of finding the appropriate quantification. For nonfunctional requirements, you should ask yourself if you can quantify the defined behaviors or properties that the solution must have using these quality characteristics.

Summary

The six tasks in the Requirements Analysis knowledge area guide you as you analyze the stakeholder and solution requirements for your project. Requirements analysis is one of the most challenging activities for business analysts, even experienced ones. There are many ways to organize, document, and model your requirements in order to define what your solution will do for its users. It is up to you to be familiar with all of the options and to make the right decisions on documentation and models based on the nature of your project and the preferences of your organization and your stakeholders.

Effective technical writing and graphical modeling skills are an underlying competency enabling you to do this requirements analysis work. Successful projects start with defining and agreeing to what is needed. Without the ability to analyze your stakeholder's stated requirements and determine the real requirements for your project, you will find it difficult to deliver a successful solution to your stakeholders.

The *BABOK® Guide* recommends that you apply one or more of the 17 recommended modeling techniques to specify and model the stakeholder and solution requirements for your projects. You don't need to be an expert in every modeling technique, but most experienced business analysts are comfortable using a representative subset of those techniques. Each requirements modeling technique should be evaluated to see if it fits the nature of your project and your requirements. Using object-oriented modeling techniques for a traditional, relational database project would be cumbersome at best.

A number of deliverables are produced by the tasks in this knowledge area, including the ultimate deliverable of requirements analysis: your validated stakeholder or solution requirements for your project. These requirements form the basis for your design and development efforts later in the project life cycle.

Exam Essentials

Be able to list the tasks found in the Requirements Analysis knowledge area.   You will see questions about the tasks, their associated techniques, their more detailed elements, and the key outputs that they produce on your exam. You should memorize the tasks of this knowledge area and the key outputs associated with them. The six tasks are:

Prioritize requirements.

Organize requirements.

Specify and model requirements.

Define assumptions and constraints.

Verify requirements.

Validate requirements.

Be able to understand and apply the 17 requirements modeling techniques.   Understanding and applying the techniques to specify and model requirements is a key focus for your Requirements Analysis knowledge area exam questions. Be sure that you can name these 17 techniques and that you know what they are all about. Here's the list:

Acceptance and Evaluation Criteria Definition

Business Rules Analysis

Data Dictionary and Glossary

Data Flow Diagrams

Data Modeling

Functional Decomposition

Interface Analysis

Metrics and KPIs

Nonfunctional Requirements Analysis

Organization Modeling

Process Modeling

Prototyping

Scenarios and Use Cases

Sequence Diagrams

State Diagrams

User Stories

Survey/Questionnaire

Be able to distinguish between validated requirements and verified requirements. Validated requirements are stakeholder, solution, or transition requirements that are aligned with the business goals and objectives found in your project's business requirements or business case. Verified requirements are input to validating requirements. They are requirements of sufficient quality to allow further project work based on those requirements to be done.

Be able to list and explain the eight characteristics of well-written requirements.   The eight characteristics of well-written, high-quality requirements are:

Cohesive

Complete

Consistent

Correct

Feasible

Modifiable

Unambiguous

Testable

Be able to discuss the five general modeling concepts that are relevant to business analysis. The five general modeling techniques used by business analysts include:

User classes, profiles, or roles

Concepts and relationships

Events

Processes

Rules

Be able to define the five roles of a structured walkthrough and describe what they do. The five roles in a structured walkthrough or requirements review meeting are:

Author

Scribe

Moderator

Peer

Reviewer

Key Terms

You have just finished stepping through the contents of the fifth knowledge area from the *BABOK® Guide*: Requirements Analysis. There is one more knowledge area to go after this one, so stay tuned.

You should understand how to apply the techniques and tasks in this knowledge area in order to be an effective business analyst. Additionally, you will need to know the six tasks and their associated elements and techniques from this knowledge area in order to be successful on the CBAP® or CCBA™ exams. The tasks include:

Prioritize requirements.

Organize requirements.

Specify and model requirements.

Define assumptions and constraints.

Verify requirements.

Validate requirements.

Chapter 6 has a number of new key words related to analyzing stakeholder and solution requirements on your projects. Here is a list of some of the key terms you encountered in this chapter:

business rules

data flow diagrams

data models

functional decomposition

logical data models

metadata

MoSCoW Analysis

operative business rules

organization modeling

physical data models

prioritized requirements

process models

requirements structure

sequence diagrams

state diagrams

structural business rules

user stories

validated requirements

verified requirements

Review Questions

1. The tasks and techniques in the Requirements Analysis knowledge area are used to define what types of requirements?

    A. Business and stakeholder

    B. Stakeholder and transition

    C. Solution and stakeholder

    D. Transition and solution

2. What requirements analysis task ensures that solution requirements align to the business requirements?

    A. Validate requirements.

    B. Verify requirements.

    C. Prioritize requirements.

    D. Specify requirements.

3. When reviewing a set of related requirements, you discover that two of the requirements describe the same feature but produce different results. Based on your well-written requirements checklist, you would note that these requirements are not _____.

    A. Complete

    B. Consistent

    C. Cohesive

    D. Correct

4. Data flow diagrams show how _____ flows through a system.

    A. Processes

    B. Requirements

    C. Decisions

    D. Information

5. What is the name for an abstraction representing some or all of a proposed solution?

    A. Diagram

    B. Concept

    C. Matrix

    D. Model

6. What is defined as a sequence of repeatable activities executed in an organization?

    A. Rule

    B. Event

    C. Process

    D. Object

7. To determine which requirements can be delivered by the project team in a fixed amount of time, you begin with all eligible requirements and remove them in order to meet the calendar date. Which timeboxing approach are you applying?

    A. All in

    B. Time-driven

    C. All out

    D. Iterative

8. What component of an entity-relationship diagram is contained in the labeled rectangle and represents a source or destination of data?

    A. Attribute

    B. Relationship

    C. Entity

    D. Constraint

9. Tasks performed as part of requirements analysis include:

    A. Specify and model requirements.

    B. Manage solution scope and approach.

    C. Prepare requirements package.

    D. Manage requirements traceability.

10. Process models show how the system behaves over the course of time through the:

    A. Structures describing what is important to the enterprise

    B. Execution of business processes or a series of events

    C. Set of related set classes and associations between them

    D. Business's policies, guidelines, standards, and regulations

11. When facilitating a requirements prioritization session, you encounter a stakeholder who wants to rank all of their requirements as high-priority requirements for the project. What type of challenge is this?

    A. Nonnegotiable demand

    B. Unrealistic tradeoff

    C. Stakeholder avoidance

    D. Unrealistic expectations

12. What imposes limitations on your solution?

    A. Attributes

    B. Constraints

    C. Assumptions

    D. Priorities

13. Which deliverable defines your process for prioritizing solution requirements?

    A. Solution approach

    B. Business analysis approach

    C. Requirements management plan

    D. Business analysis plan

14. What is the purpose of nonfunctional requirements?

    A. Addressing educational needs of users interacting with the solution

    B. Defining quality attributes and design constraints of the solution

    C. Protecting and preventing access to data that the solution uses or creates

    D. Describing the likely growth of use of the deployed and maintained solution over time

15. You are currently reviewing a specific requirement to see if it is modifiable. What is a modifiable requirement?

    A. Operationally feasible and fits within budget and schedule constraints

    B. Logically structured in a related group and able to be changed

    C. Technically feasible with a wide range of implementation options

    D. Testable and representing all relevant requirements as a set

16. Which technique organizes your requirements based on the solution components to which they are related?

    A. Data dictionary

    B. Business rules

    C. Scope modeling

    D. Class diagram

17. The two inputs to specifying and modeling requirements are:

    A. Business rules and the requirements management plan

    B. Solution scope and stakeholder list, roles, and responsibilities

    C. Stakeholder concerns and a documented business need

    D. Stated requirements and a requirements structure

18. What is the name for the individual pieces of information that describe an entity in an entity relationship diagram?

    A. Identifier

    B. Relationship

    C. Attribute

    D. Cardinality

19. What is another name for the quality check performed following analysis of a requirement?

    A. Verification

    B. Validation

    C. Approval

    D. Clarification

20. Assumptions and constraints are defined and clarified as requirements are understood and documented with their associated:

    A. Limitations

    B. Attributes

    C. Restrictions

    D. Requirements

Answers to Review Questions

1. C. Requirements analysis tools and techniques are used to develop the stakeholder and solution requirements.

2. A. Requirements validation ensures that all requirements support the delivery of value to the business by ensuring that stakeholder, solution, and transition requirements align to the business requirements.

3. B. Consistent requirements do not contradict or conflict with one another.

4. D. Data flow diagrams show how information flows through the system.

5. D. A model serves as an abstraction representing some or all of the proposed solution.

6. C. A process is defined as a sequence of repeatable activities executed in an organization.

7. A. All-in timeboxing determines which requirements can be delivered by the project team in a fixed amount of time by beginning with all eligible requirements and removing them in order to meet the calendar date.

8. C. Entities in an entity-relationship diagram are the things about which data is needed. They are contained in the labeled rectangle of the diagram.

9. A. The six tasks of requirements analysis are prioritize requirements, organize requirements, specify and model requirements, define assumptions and constraints, verify requirements, and validate requirements.

10. B. Process models show how the system behaves over the course of time through executing business processes or resulting from events that occur inside the solution scope.

11. A. Challenges in facilitating requirements prioritization sessions include nonnegotiable demands such as avoiding difficult choices, not making tradeoffs, or ranking all requirements as a high priority.

12. B. Constraints impose limitations imposed on the solution that do not support the business or stakeholder needs.

13. C. The requirements management plan built as part of the Business Analysis Planning and Monitoring knowledge area defines the process used to prioritize requirements during requirements analysis.

14. B. Nonfunctional requirements define quality attributes, design, and implementation constraints and external interfaces the product must have. They are a type of solution requirement.

15. B. Modifiable requirements are logically structured in a related group and able to be changed.

16. C. Scope modeling organizes requirements based on the solution components to which they are related.

17. D. The two inputs to specifying and modeling requirements are the stated requirements and the requirements structure.

18. C. The four main components of an entity relationship diagram are the entities, their attributes, unique identifiers for each occurrence of an entity, and relationships between the entities. Attributes are individual pieces of information that describe an entity.

19. A. Verification is a quality check performed after a requirement is analyzed. Verification activities are typically performed iteratively throughout the requirements analysis process.

20. B. Assumptions and constraints are defined and clarified as requirements are understood and documented with their associated attributes such as date identified, owner, impact, and any associated risks.

Chapter

7

Controlled End: Solution Assessment and Validation

CBAP®/CCBA™ EXAM TOPICS COVERED IN THIS CHAPTER

- ✓ Assess proposed solution.
- ✓ Allocate requirements.
- ✓ Assess organizational readiness.
- ✓ Define transition requirements.
- ✓ Validate solution.
- ✓ Evaluate solution performance.

Solution Assessment and Validation provide care and feeding for your selected solution across the project life cycle. The tasks found in this knowledge area focus on assessing proposed solutions, allocating requirements to solution components, and validating the solution to make sure it will meet the business need and deliver value to the organization and its stakeholders. The transition requirements are also developed as part of this knowledge area. They define how the solution will be implemented after the project work is complete.

Care and feeding of a solution has many facets. One important aspect is the assessment of the organization's readiness to effectively use the solution once it is made available. Training, information sharing, and documentation may be required to overcome any obstacles to changing the way things are done. During the solution's operational life, you will want to measure its performance and quantify the business value it delivers. Keep in mind that there are many ways to implement a solution once it has been selected. Experienced business analysts always make sure that the solution is defined, designed, and implemented well.

Solution Assessment and Validation

The Solution Assessment and Validation knowledge area focuses on ensuring the solution can be successfully implemented within the organization in order to meet the business need driving your project. You must have knowledge of your business environment and be able to assess how each of your project's proposed solutions would affect that environment. Communicating solution requirements and implementation-specific information to your stakeholders is also your responsibility.

According to the *BABOK® Guide,* this knowledge area is where you will develop your project's transition requirements. Remember that the business requirements are developed by tasks in the Enterprise Analysis knowledge area, and your stakeholder and solution requirements are built by tasks found in the Requirements Analysis knowledge area.

Exam Spotlight

Transition requirements describe the solution capabilities required to transition from the current organizational state to the future state. Transition requirements are no longer needed once the transition to the new solution is complete.

The tasks in this knowledge area follow the solution from early in the project life cycle, where the solution begins to take form, to the end of the life cycle, where the project itself ends and the solution is deployed. This solution-focused knowledge area generates several key business analysis deliverables. They include the:

- Proposed solution assessment

- Organizational readiness assessment

- Allocated stakeholder and solution requirements

- Transition requirements

- Solution performance assessment

- Solution validation assessment

- Identified defects and mitigating actions

We will cover each deliverable in more detail later in this chapter.

Many commonly used solution assessment and validation techniques can be applied for each knowledge area task. Solution assessment and validation work is multifaceted and applies a wide range of techniques for validating the solution and its components relative to the business case and allocating the stakeholder and solution requirements to the solution components and releases.

Exam Spotlight

Four different assessments are created by and used in this knowledge area, so make sure you can distinguish between them:

- *Solution Performance Assessment* describes how the operational solution is performing relative to business goals and objectives.

- *Solution Validation Assessment* assesses the solution's ability to meet the business need at an acceptable level of quality.

- *Organizational Readiness Assessment* describes stakeholder readiness to accept the change associated with a solution and their ability to use the solution effectively.

- *Assessment of Proposed Solution or Solutions* assesses the value delivered by each proposed solution and recommends the best solution.

The Solution Assessment and Validation knowledge area also addresses monitoring and reporting on the performance of the assessment and validation activities across the project life cycle. It includes a task specifically focused on assessing the solution performance after the solution is operational and in use. The business analysis team is responsible for assessing the effectiveness of the techniques being used to assess and validate their project's resulting solution. The Solution Assessment and Validation knowledge area is addressed in Chapter 7 of the *BABOK® Guide*.

The Business Analyst's Task List

A business analyst has six tasks to perform in the Solution Assessment and Validation knowledge area. We will look at each one of these tasks in detail later in this chapter. The task list from the *BABOK® Guide* includes:

- Assessing the proposed solution
- Allocating requirements
- Assessing organizational readiness
- Defining transition requirements
- Validating the solution
- Evaluating solution performance

These tasks focus on making sure that you select the best solution to meet your project's business need and that you define, design, and implement that solution well. Your ultimate goal is to deploy the right solution that meets the business need and adds value to the business. You know your business environment and can assess how each proposed solution would affect that environment. You must also ensure that your project stakeholders fully understand the prioritized and approved solution requirements. Any implementation decisions that are being made during solution assessment and validation should align with those requirements.

When Does Solution Assessment and Validation Take Place?

> When the territory and the map disagree, believe the territory.
>
> —*Swiss Army Manual*

The tasks in the Solution Assessment and Validation knowledge area begin early in the project life cycle as the solution to the business problem or need is proposed, evaluated, and agreed upon. The tasks in this knowledge area appear in both the controlled and controlled end of the generic life cycle that is described in Chapter 1, "Foundation Concepts." The controlled middle of a project is where the actual work gets done, one stage or phase at a time. Business analysis tasks during this part of your project are typically from the Elicitation, Requirements Analysis, and Solution Assessment and Validation knowledge areas with a little Requirements Management and Communication thrown in for good measure.

Specific tasks in the Solution Assessment and Validation knowledge area focus on the controlled end to your project. In addition to wrapping things up, you also plan how you will transition the new solution into its operational life and get ready to measure the business benefits of the solution after it is in use. Typically, defining the transition requirements on your projects takes place in the controlled middle or early on in the controlled end of the project life cycle as part of the project's requirements development or definition phase.

Let's step through the first task in the Solution Assessment and Validation knowledge area: assessing your proposed solution or a set of multiple proposed solutions to make sure they will meet your stakeholder's needs and add business value.

Assess Proposed Solution

The first task in the Solution Assessment and Validation knowledge area is assessing your proposed solution or solutions relative to the stakeholder and solution requirements. When you assess one or more solutions, be sure to evaluate the solution or solutions relative to the approved stakeholder and solution requirements for your project. If the requirements are not yet approved, you will not be able to make a final decision on whether or not your solution meets the requirements, addresses the business need, and provides value to the business.

You may find yourself assessing multiple solutions to determine which solution is the best. The solution you choose must meet the stakeholder and solution requirements and address the business need. You will evaluate and compare each solution with the requirements, as well as with one another. You are in search of the solution that delivers the most value to the business, so you will compare the advantages and disadvantages of each proposed solution.

Figure 7.1 summarizes the inputs, outputs, techniques, and associated tasks used to assess a proposed solution or a set of solutions

FIGURE 7.1 Task summary: Assess the proposed solution.

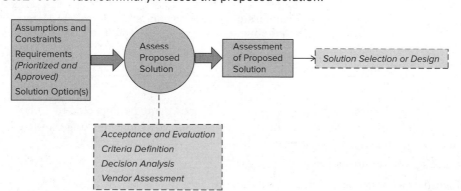

Several key inputs are needed to adequately assess a proposed solution. These key inputs are produced by a number of other business analysis tasks; they include assumptions and constraints, the prioritized and approved requirements, and the solution option or option to be assessed. Let's look at each of these task inputs in greater detail.

Assumptions and Constraints   Assumptions are factors that you believe to be true, but you have not yet confirmed. Assumptions may lead you to favor certain solutions during your solution assessment activities. Constraints are limits or boundary conditions that impact your solution. Constraints might limit the number of solution options that are available for you to assess.

Requirements (Prioritized and Approved)   Prioritized stakeholder and solution requirements allow you to evaluate solutions relative to the most important requirements on your project. Approved stakeholder and solution requirements should be used during solution assessment so you can make a decision based on a baselined set of capabilities.

Solution Option or Options   Each possible solution should be assessed using relevant information about that solution. You and your organization need to decide exactly what solution information should be evaluated. If you are comparing multiple solutions, each solution should be presented with the same information to facilitate a well-informed decision.

Table 7.1 summarizes the inputs to this task and lists the task and knowledge area sources for each input used to assess proposed solution.

TABLE 7.1   Inputs: Assess Proposed Solution

Task Input	Input Source	Source Knowledge Area
Assumptions and constraints	Define assumptions and constraints	Requirements Analysis
Requirements (prioritized and approved)	Prioritize requirements	Requirements Analysis
	Manage solution scope and requirements	Requirements Management and Communication
Solution option(s)	—	—

When you perform the Assess Proposed Solution task, you are expected to address the two detailed elements of that task. These elements guide you in prioritizing the stakeholder or solution requirements on your projects by:

- Ranking the solution options
- Identifying additional solution capabilities

Ranking the Solution Options   If you are evaluating a number of solution options, you should use a set of evaluation criteria to assess them. For simple, straightforward solution options, an assessment of the differences may provide you with enough information to make a decision. For more complex problems, you should consider building a scoring and weighting system to use in your assessment. After scoring the options, you can review the highest scoring options in greater detail before making a decision.

Identifying Additional Solution Capabilities   You might find that your solution options provide capabilities beyond the required capabilities found in your stakeholder or solution requirements. You will need to decide if these additional solution capabilities provide value to the organization, either now or in the future.

Several techniques are available for assessing a solution or a set of multiple solution options. You should consider adding acceptance and evaluation criteria definition and vendor assessment to your list of possibilities. Let's take a look at these two recommended techniques in greater detail right now.

Recommended Technique: Acceptance and Evaluation Criteria Definition

According to the *BABOK® Guide*, defining and applying acceptance and evaluation criteria is one of the required techniques in the fundamental knowledge base of an effective business analyst. Both acceptance and evaluation criteria can be tied to contractual obligations, which can introduce associated legal and political issues and risks into the project.

Acceptance criteria define a minimal set of requirements that must be met in order for a solution or a solution component to be considered acceptable to its key stakeholders. These criteria should be defined early in the project life cycle and must be met in order to say that a solution is complete, correct, and worth implementing. Test cases can and should be written that verify the solution against these defined and agreed-upon acceptance criteria.

Evaluation criteria are a set of requirements used to choose between multiple solutions to a particular problem. They are typically built to allow scoring of the various solutions under consideration. In order to evaluate potential solutions, this set of requirements is prioritized and ranked by order of importance. The solutions will then be scored against the ranked set of requirements using a preestablished evaluation scale. A must-have requirement that is not met by a proposed solution should remove that solution from consideration.

Recommended Technique: Vendor Assessment

Vendor assessments allow you to assess an external vendor's ability to provide all or part of your solution. You look at their technical ability, financial stability, staff skills, and reputation in their work space. External vendors are often involved in the design, construction, implementation, and maintenance activities on our projects.

Here is a quick list of things you may want to consider.

- Knowledge and expertise
- Experience, reputation, and stability
- Licensing and pricing models

- Product reputation and market position
- Contractual terms and conditions

Vendor assessments are used to ensure that your vendors are reliable and that they will be able to meet your expectations.

An Additional Technique to Consider

The *BABOK® Guide* recommends considering the use of one more additional technique when you are assessing one or more proposed solutions for your project. This technique is summarized for you here.

Decision Analysis   According to the *BABOK® Guide*, decision analysis is one of the required techniques in the fundamental knowledge base of an effective business analyst. Decision analysis allows you to examine and model the consequences of different decisions before actually making or recommending a particular decision. After all, your primary goal during solution assessment is to make a well-informed decision. Effective decision analysis requires you to effectively structure the decision problem and process, keeping in mind any relevant values, goals, and objectives.

You need to clearly understand the nature of the decision that must be made. It is essential to identify the areas of uncertainty affecting the decision and the consequences of each possible decision. Decision analysis may also involve trade-off decision making, where your decision involves evaluating and valuing multiple objectives or solutions. Remember that your decisions and their resulting outcomes can be either financial or nonfinancial in nature.

Once you have selected and applied one or more of these techniques as part of your solution assessment efforts, you are ready to continue with the other assessment and validation tasks at hand. We will discuss those tasks shortly.

Assessment of the Proposed Solution

Assessing a proposed solution or set of solution options requires you to assess the value that each proposed solution delivers to the business. Your project's prioritized stakeholder and solution requirements are used as an input to solution selection and design tasks that are out of the scope of the *BABOK® Guide*. This destination for the results of your solution assessment efforts is summarized in Table 7.2.

TABLE 7.2   Outputs: Assess Proposed Solution

Output	Output Destinations	Destination Knowledge Area
Assessment of proposed solution	—	Solution Selection or Design

Remember that this assessment should be based on the prioritized and approved stakeholder and solution requirements for your project. Several key business analysis stakeholders might be involved in the selection process when solution options are being assessed. The project manager will need to plan and manage this solution assessment process as part of the project. Other stakeholders participating in solution assessment include the:

- Domain SME
- Implementation SME
- Operational support
- Suppliers
- Sponsor

Now let's take a look at the next task found in the Solution Assessment and Validation knowledge area—allocating your stakeholder and solution requirements across your solution and its components.

Allocate Requirements

Your next task in the Solution Assessment and Validation knowledge area is allocating your stakeholder and solution requirements to solution components and *releases*. A release is the distribution of all or part of a scheduled operational solution, such as a release consisting of software application code, related documents, and support materials. The business value of a solution changes depending on how its requirements are implemented. Some solution implementation approaches cost more money but take less time to perform, such as purchasing a proven commercial product versus developing your own software application. On the flip side, some solution implementation approaches are low cost but may eliminate capabilities in the initial deployment. These low-cost alternatives fail to provide end users with the complete functionality needed to do their jobs.

While allocating requirements sounds like a technical task, it is actually the business analyst's responsibility to get this work done. You should strive to allocate your requirements in a way that maximizes the value the solution delivers. Some trade-offs will be required to assess your allocation alternatives while striving to maximize business value and benefits and reduce costs.

Solution Components

Let's make sure you remember the definition of *solution components*. They are the pieces and parts of a solution that span the enterprise architecture of the organization including things like:

- Business processes, policies, and rules
- People along with their job functions and responsibilities
- Software applications and application components
- Organizational structure and its internal/external interactions

Allocating requirements begins early in a project, typically right after the solution approach is determined as part of the Enterprise Analysis knowledge area work. Requirements allocation is ongoing and incremental, continuing until all of the solution requirements for your project have been allocated. This effort takes you well into the middle of your project life cycle, often as far as solution design and construction activities. Figure 7.2 summarizes the inputs, outputs, techniques, and associated tasks used to allocate your project's stakeholder and solution requirements to the solution components and releases.

FIGURE 7.2   Task summary: Allocate the requirements.

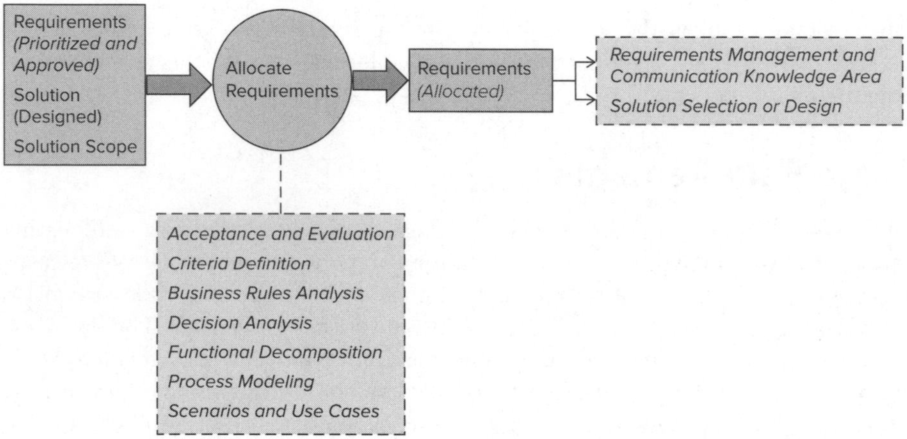

Several key inputs are needed to allocate requirements. These key inputs are produced by a number of other business analysis tasks. They include the prioritized and approved stakeholder or solution requirements, the *designed solution*, and the solution scope. Let's look at each of these task inputs in greater detail.

Requirements (Prioritized and Approved)   Requirements can be allocated for stakeholder and solution requirements in any state, although you have not completed the task until the requirements you are allocating have been formally approved. Requirements in any state include the stated, analyzed, verified, or validated stakeholder and solution requirements.

Solution (Designed)   Designed solutions contain the defined solution components to which you will allocate your requirements and their functionality. The costs and effort to deliver each component will have been estimated by the project manager and the technical team. You will use this information to make decisions about allocating functionality to each component and the cost of developing the component.

Solution Scope   The solution scope defined during Enterprise Analysis allocates your high-level business requirements to solution components and releases. The more detailed stakeholder and solution requirements should match the business requirements allocation. If not, you must revise the solution scope to reflect the current requirements allocation decisions.

Table 7.3 summarizes the inputs to this task and lists the task and knowledge area sources for each input used to assess proposed solutions.

TABLE 7.3   Inputs: Allocate Requirements

Task Input	Input Source	Source Knowledge Area
Requirements (prioritized and approved)	Prioritize requirements	Requirements Analysis
	Manage solution scope and requirements	Requirements Management and Communication
Solution (designed)	—	—
Solution scope	Define solution scope	Enterprise Analysis

The elements to be considered when allocating stakeholder and solution requirements are

- Allocating requirements to solution components
- Performing release planning

Let's look at each of these elements in greater detail.

Allocating Requirements to Solution Components   Most solutions consist of multiple components. Each component implements a subset of the requirements. Your project's business, stakeholder, and solution requirements are then associated with the solution components that will implement them. The business requirements are already associated with solution components as part of the solution scope.

Remember that allocating your stakeholder and solution requirements to solution components, such as business rules, processes, and software applications, drives the costs associated with implementing the solution. You will most likely allocate your requirements several times before achieving a cost-effective implementation of the solution scope. Requirements allocation will involve assessing available resources, solution constraints, and your requirements dependencies.

Performing Release Planning   You also have to decide which requirements will be included in each project release. Deploying solutions with a phased approach reduces the initial cost of implementation and offers you the ability to phase in solution functionality over time. The solution capabilities that deliver the most value should be implemented first, if possible.

There are several techniques that you may choose to apply when allocating requirements. Be sure to add business rules analysis to your list of possibilities. Changes to business policies and procedures must be addressed as part of your requirements allocation work. Let's take a look at this recommended technique.

Recommended Technique: Business Rules Analysis

According to the *BABOK® Guide*, business rules analysis is one of the required techniques in the fundamental knowledge base of an effective business analyst. This technique allows you to identify any business policy or rule changes resulting from your allocated requirements and release schedule. Your organization's business rules may be managed manually or by using a business rules engine that is part of a software tool.

Your organization's *business policies* are directives that support business goals. *Business rules,* by contrast, are actionable and testable directives that support the business policies. Complex business rules are often represented as a decision tree or table. Business rules are independent of their implementation within the organization. Although they constrain and support the processes found in your solution, they are not a part of that solution. In order to effectively perform business rules analysis, you will need a data dictionary and glossary for your project or organization.

Business rules require a defined glossary of terms and an understanding of the relationships between them. There are two types of business rules, operative and structural. Operative business rules guide the actions of people working in the organization and are enforced by the organization as a matter of policy. Structural rules determine when something is or is not true; they structure and categorize the knowledge and information found in the organization.

There are several other techniques you may use to allocate the stakeholder and solution requirements on your projects. Let's have a quick look at them.

Additional Techniques to Consider

The *BABOK® Guide* recommends considering the use of one or more techniques when you are allocating your stakeholder and solution requirements. These techniques are summarized for you here.

Acceptance and Evaluation Criteria Definition   One best practice is defining measurable acceptance criteria for each of your project releases. This set of acceptance criteria defines the set of requirements that must be met in order for your release and its accompanying capabilities to be considered acceptable to its key stakeholders. Test cases will be written to verify the release using your defined acceptance criteria.

Decision Analysis   Decision analysis allows you to examine and model the costs and benefits of different requirements allocation schemes before making or recommending a particular decision.

Functional Decomposition   Functional decomposition is frequently used to break down the solution scope and its allocated business requirements into the more detailed stakeholder and solution requirements for your project.

Process Modeling   Process models can be used to help you allocate your stakeholder and solution requirements by allocating work activities to job roles from those models. Process models can also help you see functionality that may be deferred to a later release.

Scenarios and Use Cases   Scenarios and use cases offer you the ability to take your alternative flows and make them capabilities that will be implemented in a future release. The main flows associated with the primary goals of your users should be implemented sooner rather than later.

Once you have selected and applied one or more of these techniques as part of your requirements allocation efforts, you are ready to continue with the other assessment and validation tasks. First, let's look at the key output from this task, the allocated requirements.

Produce the Allocated Requirements

Allocated stakeholder and solution requirements are associated with the solution component that will implement those requirements. Your *allocated requirements* are used as input to the solution selection and design tasks that are out of the scope of the *BABOK® Guide*. They are also communicated to your key project stakeholders using the tasks in the Requirements Management and Communication knowledge area. These destinations for the results of your requirements allocation efforts are summarized in Table 7.4.

TABLE 7.4   Outputs: Allocate Requirements

Output	Output Destinations	Destination Knowledge Area
Requirements (allocated)	—	Requirements Management and Communication knowledge area
	—	Solution Selection or Design

A number of stakeholders are involved with allocating requirements on your project. You should always involve project managers with requirements allocation; they need to be aware of what is happening in order to manage project scope and project work. End users should also be made aware of your requirements allocation results because they will be impacted by the capabilities that will be present in a given release.

A number of additional business analysis stakeholders may be affected by your requirements allocation work, including:

- Customers
- Domain SME
- Implementation SME
- Operational support
- Suppliers
- Sponsor
- Testers

Let's move on and take a detailed look at the next task found in the Solution Assessment and Validation knowledge area—assessing the organization's level of readiness for a new solution and the changes that that solution will bring.

Assess Organizational Readiness

Another interesting task in the Solution Assessment and Validation knowledge area is assessing the level of organizational readiness for a new solution. As a business analyst, you are an agent of change; you shepherd new solutions from conception to completion. The trick is making sure that folks are ready and willing to use the new solutions to get their job done. Plus, the organization needs to be willing to maintain and support this new way of doing business.

Assessing organizational readiness involves communicating the impacts that a new solution will have on the business. This allows everyone to be prepared for the upcoming changes versus being surprised by them. Training is another aspect of organizational readiness. You might need to train your end users to use the new solution before it is operational. In all situations, existing organizational change management practices should be followed.

Figure 7.3 summarizes the inputs, outputs, techniques, and associated tasks used to assess the readiness of your organization to adopt and use a new solution.

FIGURE 7.3   Task summary: Assess organizational readiness.

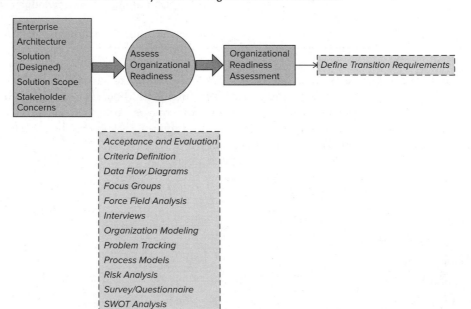

Several key inputs are needed to assess your organization's readiness for a new solution. These key inputs are produced by a number of other business analysis tasks, and they include the designed solution, the solution scope, and any concerns your stakeholders might have about the solution. Let's look at each of these task inputs in greater detail.

Enterprise Architecture   The enterprise architecture tells you the current state of the organization. You can assess the organizational structure existing business processes, existing systems, and information relative to your new solution. Hopefully, you looked at the current state of things during requirements development so you can build from your solution scope instead of starting from scratch.

Solution (Designed)   The designed solution should be used when assessing your organizational readiness. It is the technical design and definition of the solution that will be built and deployed. Use this in tandem with the solution scope.

Solution Scope   The solution scope defines the parts of the business or enterprise architecture that are impacted by this solution. Use this as your starting point for assessing organizational readiness for the new solution.

Stakeholder Concerns   Stakeholder concerns are the documented issues and problems that you discovered while developing your project requirements. You need to check this list, as it may contain solution implementation issues or problems that need to be addressed when assessing organizational readiness for that new solution.

Table 7.5 summarizes the inputs to this task and lists the task and knowledge area sources for each input used to assess organizational readiness.

TABLE 7.5   Inputs: Assess Organizational Readiness

Task Input	Input Source	Source Knowledge Area
Enterprise architecture	Solution (designed)	Solution scope
Solution (designed)	—	—
Solution scope	Define solution scope	Enterprise Analysis
Stakeholder concerns	Document elicitation results	Elicitation

Three key elements are found in a thorough organizational readiness assessment. Together they make up the bulk of your assessment findings. They are

- Cultural assessment
- Operational or technical assessment
- Stakeholder impact analysis

Let's look at each of these three elements in greater detail.

Cultural Assessment   The cultural part of your assessment focuses on the willingness of your key stakeholders to change. You need to put your marketing hat on and sell this solution as part of your business analysis activities. This involves understanding each key stakeholder's willingness to change and getting them on board with the changes that are coming with the new solution. Your stakeholders need to understand and buy into the rationale for the new solution and the benefits it provides.

Operational or Technical Assessment   This part of your assessment focuses on the capabilities that the new solution will provide and how the stakeholders will use those capabilities. You might need to create new policies and procedures governing use of the solution. Training might be needed so folks know how to use the solution correctly. Systems support and maintenance also need to be planned and put in place prior to solution implementation.

Stakeholder Impact Analysis   Your assessment must address how the changes from your new solution will affect your stakeholders. There are a number of things to consider.

Functions   Your impact analysis should look at the solution capabilities that each stakeholder group uses and address the significant work changes. This includes new or modified processes, as well as specific applications that the stakeholders will now be using as part of their jobs.

Location   Stakeholder location also comes into play when assessing the impacts of change. If your stakeholders are all located in one place, it will be easier to train and support their use of the new solution. If your stakeholders are found in multiple locations, you will have to address how they learn to use the new solution and get assistance when they have questions in a virtual environment.

Tasks   If your new solution changes the way tasks are performed, the changes need to be noted and addressed. Training might be necessary to show folks the new way of doing things. They might also need to acquire new skills to do the work.

Concerns   Stakeholder concerns and issues should also be addressed in your analysis. There are several areas to consider, such as solution usability, work demands, potential job loss, or changes in work satisfaction.

There are several techniques that you may use when assessing organizational readiness. Be sure to add business rules analysis to your list of possibilities. Addressing the changes to business policies and procedures as part of requirements allocation is important. Let's take a closer look at this technique.

Recommended Technique: Force Field Analysis

Force field analysis is associated with assessing organizational change readiness relative to deploying a new solution. This technique lets you evaluate the pros and cons of each significant change associated with the solution. Force field analysis graphically depicts the positive and negative forces that either support or oppose a particular change. When using this technique, you are looking for ways to strengthen support, reduce opposition, and generate new forces that view the upcoming change in a positive manner.

Force field analysis has three simple steps:

1. Identify the forces that are for or against the change.

2. Depict those forces on each side of the line.

3. Estimate the strength of each force.

The individual estimates can then be summed up for each type of force to give you an idea of the magnitude of your support and opposition. Figure 7.4 provides an example of how you might draw the graphic and sum up your support and opposition when using the force field analysis technique to evaluate an office-wide change of desktop computers from Mac to PC.

FIGURE 7.4 Force field analysis.

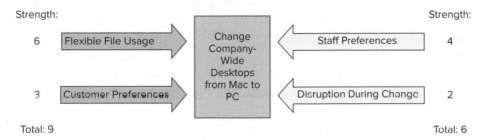

Additional Techniques to Consider

The *BABOK® Guide* recommends using one or more of the following techniques when you are assessing the organization's readiness for change. These techniques are summarized for you here.

Acceptance and Evaluation Criteria Definition Your measurable acceptance criteria define the set of requirements that must be met in order for the solution capabilities to be considered acceptable to the key stakeholders. Be sure to define solution performance levels that the solution can actually meet in order to inspire confidence in your stakeholders.

Data Flow Diagrams Data flow diagrams can be very helpful as you identify activities that will change when the new solution gets implemented. They also tell you which stakeholders perform these activities so you know who is impacted by the change.

Focus Groups Focus groups provide you with a forum for identifying stakeholder concerns or issues with the new solution. They also offer a means to consider how these issues can be addressed in a facilitated group setting.

Interviews Interviews provide a forum for identifying stakeholder concerns or issues with the new solution and discussing possible solutions or workarounds.

Organization Modeling   Organization models offer a view of your stakeholder groups and stakeholders to use while assessing organizational readiness.

Problem Tracking   Problem tracking is the formal vehicle for identifying and tracking stakeholder issues with the new solution and its associated changes. This technique ensures that the issues are addressed and resolved.

Process Models   Process models identify activities that will change when the new solution is implemented and tell you which stakeholders perform these activities. This allows you to focus on who is impacted by the change.

Risk Analysis   Some stakeholder issues or concerns with the new solution might require risk assessment in order to determine what might be done to address them.

Scenarios and Use Cases   Scenarios and use cases provide a forum for identifying stakeholder concerns or issues with the new solution. They allow you to look at primary and alternative workflows. After all, many times there are multiple ways to get the same job done using the solution capabilities that are provided.

Survey/Questionnaire   Surveys and questionnaires are techniques that give you a forum for identifying stakeholder concerns or issues with the new solution.

SWOT Analysis   The strengths, weaknesses, opportunities, and threats (SWOT) analysis technique assesses how you plan to respond to an identified issue by categorizing the strengths, weaknesses, opportunities, and threats associated with your response.

Once you have selected and applied one or more of these techniques as part of your requirements allocation efforts, you are ready to continue with the other assessment and validation tasks. Before moving on, let's look at the key output from this task, the organizational readiness assessment.

Build an Organizational Readiness Assessment

Your organizational readiness assessment describes the level of preparation required to get your stakeholders ready for a new solution. You always need to keep in mind that a solution isn't a success if people are unable to use it effectively. Your organizational readiness assessment identifies stakeholder issues and decides how best to respond to those issues.

The organizational readiness assessment is required in order to develop the transition requirements for your project. This output and the task that picks it up and uses it are summarized in Table 7.6.

TABLE 7.6   Outputs: Assess Organizational Readiness

Output	Output Destinations	Destination Knowledge Area
Organizational readiness assessment	Define transition requirements	Solution Assessment and Validation

A number of stakeholders will be involved with assessing organizational readiness for a new solution. The project manager must be provided with the organizational readiness assessment in order to see if additional project work must be performed based on its contents. Any new tasks should be included in the project implementation plan. A number of Implementation SMEs also should be a part of this effort. Organizational Change Management SMEs can assist you with assessing, communicating, and selling the positive impacts of change to your stakeholders. Usability SMEs can evaluate the impacts of your new solution on the end user. Training SMEs may develop a training plan and the actual training to help folks use the solution more effectively.

Several other business analysis stakeholders might be involved with the organizational readiness assessment, such as:

- Domain SME
- Operational support
- Sponsor

Let's move on and step through the next task found in the Solution Assessment and Validation knowledge area—defining transition requirements.

Define Transition Requirements

Transition requirements define what needs to be done to transition from the existing solution to your new solution. The capabilities defined in the transition requirements target making a smooth transition from the old solution to the new solution. Transitioning to a new solution can be very challenging. In many projects, it may be necessary to have an operational system in place during the solution transition activities. In such instances, be sure to develop comprehensive implementation plans to ensure the job is done right and nothing is forgotten.

 Real World Scenario

The Missing Transition Requirements Strike Back

Russ, a project manager, held a meeting at a biotechnology company to discuss kick-off plans for a new project targeting the upgrade of their existing Laboratory Information Management System (LIMS). This company is a leading human therapeutics company in the biotechnology industry, focused on providing drugs that support cancer treatments.

The current LIMS system was homegrown and had evolved over many years to reach its current state. Although the system supported the integration of the laboratory software, hardware, and instruments, the product quality team felt that a newer system could do a much better job of tracking laboratory-related work, planning samples, and automating workflow.

As part of his introduction to the organization, the plant manager took Russ on a tour of the production facility. Russ was very impressed with the plant and its operations. At one point on his tour, Russ stopped in front of a very large processing vat placed beneath a very large skylight.

"What an interesting piece of equipment." Russ commented. "What is it used for?"

Dan, the plant manager, replied that this particular piece of equipment was used to distill the drug as part of its production.

Russ looked up at the skylight and asked, "Does the process require this much natural light?"

Dan smiled and shook his head. "Oh, no," he replied. "This is my daily reminder of what happens when you don't spend enough time planning for implementation."

Dan went on to explain to Russ that this particular piece of equipment was ordered from Germany and shipped to the plant location in the United States. When it arrived at the new plant building, the installation team was stunned to discover that the vat did not fit in the doors.

In order to get this critical piece of equipment into the new building, Dan had to authorize cutting a skylight in the roof and using a crane to drop the vat into place. As Dan told Russ, the transition requirements that assist you in implementing your project are quite critical. And they are even more critical when you discover after the fact that you missed something.

Transition requirements are elicited, analyzed, managed, and communicated just like the other requirements for your project. However, transition requirements are not just any old requirement. They are very specific to implementing the solution and cannot be defined until after that solution has been designed. Transition requirements are no longer needed after the new solution is operational, because they focus only on what is required to get that solution up and running.

Exam Spotlight

Transition requirements do not need to be analyzed if there is no existing solution that is being replaced. This occurs when your solution adds a new capability or set of capabilities to the business versus changing or improving something that is already in use.

The transition period between solutions requires effective planning, communication, and coordination. A successful transition period may include:

- Operating the old and new solutions in parallel
- Migrating information between the old and new solution

- Conducting stakeholder training on the new solution
- Developing new capabilities to support the transition period

Figure 7.5 summarizes the inputs, outputs, techniques, and associated tasks used to assess the readiness of your organization to adopt and use a new solution.

FIGURE 7.5   Task summary: Define the transition requirements.

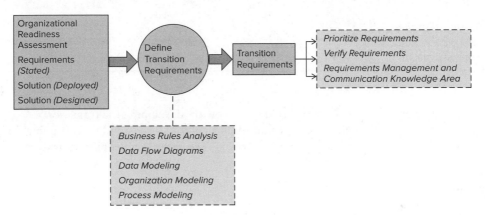

Several key inputs are needed to define transition requirements. These key inputs are produced by a number of other business analysis tasks, as well as tasks external to the scope of the *BABOK® Guide.* They include the designed solution, the deployed solution, stated requirements, and the organizational readiness assessment just discussed. Let's have a look at each of these task inputs in greater detail.

Organizational Readiness Assessment   Your organizational readiness assessment provides you with a good look at the areas in the organization that will be impacted by the new solution. Areas to be addressed include using, operating, and maintaining the new solution.

Requirements (Stated)   Stated requirements come from your stakeholders during requirements elicitation. This is where they tell you what they think is needed in order to transition the new solution into its operational life.

Solution (Deployed)   The deployed solution is another name for the existing or old solution. This is the solution that will be replaced by the new solution created by your project. Analysis is required to make sure you understand the deployed solution's capabilities and what needs to be done to replace it with the new solution.

Solution (Designed)   The designed solution is the new solution being created by your project. It should be used when assessing your organizational readiness. It is the technical design and definition of the solution that will be built and deployed.

Table 7.7 summarizes the inputs to this task and lists the task and knowledge area sources for each input used when developing your transition requirements.

TABLE 7.7 Inputs: Define Transition Requirements

Task Input	Input Source	Source Knowledge Area
Organizational readiness assessment	Assess organizational readiness	Solution Assessment and Validation
Requirements (stated)	Document elicitation results	Elicitation
Solution (deployed)	—	—
Solution (designed)	—	—

Three key elements must be considered when you are developing the transition requirements for your project. It is very important that you understand what is going on with the current, deployed solution. Key sources to consider when defining your transition requirements include:

- Data
- Ongoing work
- Organizational change

Let's look at each of these three elements in greater detail.

Data   Be sure to have a look at the data in and used by the existing solution. Some data might need to be archived, while other data might need to be migrated to the new solution. Migrated data might require conversion or reformatting in order to be used by the new solution. The business rules governing data usage should also be revisited to see if they require revision or replacement.

Ongoing Work   Stakeholders typically need to continue working with the deployed solution while the new solution is being implemented. You will need to decide how to handle this need to get work done and decide what happens when the new solution is up and running.

Organizational Change   Often, you will find yourself creating a process for managing the changes your new solution brings to the people who will use it. Job functions might change as a result of the new solution. New information from the new solution might now be available to stakeholders, and new skills might be required in order to use the new solution effectively.

You can select from five general techniques to develop your transition requirements. Let's take a look at them now.

Techniques to Consider

The *BABOK® Guide* recommends using one or more of the following techniques when you are developing transition requirements for your new solution. They are summarized here.

Business Rules Analysis   Additional business rules might be required in order to transition from the deployed (existing) to the designed (new) solution. You may find yourself maintaining two sets of business rules for a time if you phase in the new solution at the same time you phase out the old solution.

Data Flow Diagrams   Data flow diagrams help you to identify information and activities that will change when the new solution is implemented.

Data Modeling   Physical data models can be used to map information needs from the old solution to the new solution. This will help you decide what data needs to be archived, transferred, or revised in order to get the new solution up and running.

Organization Modeling   Organization models offer a view of your stakeholder groups and stakeholders for use when assessing organizational readiness and developing transition requirements.

Process Modeling   Process models help you to identify who does what and when they do it in both the old and the new solutions.

Once you have selected and applied one or more of these techniques as part of your requirements allocation efforts, you are ready to continue with the other Solution Assessment and Validation tasks that are part of this knowledge area. Before moving on, let's look at the key output from this task—your transition requirements.

Develop the Transition Requirements

Transition requirements define the solution capabilities required to transition from the current to the future state and are no longer needed once the transition is complete. Typically, transition requirements are created later in the project life cycle after both the current and new solutions have been defined. They are developed and defined as part of the tasks found in the Solution Assessment and Validation knowledge area.

Your project's transition requirements must be elicited, analyzed, and verified just like any other requirements developed for your project. These activities are performed by tasks found in the Requirements Analysis knowledge area. Transition requirements will also be communicated to your stakeholders and managed across the project life cycle by one or more of the tasks found in the Requirements Management and Communication knowledge area. This output and the tasks that use it are summarized in Table 7.8.

TABLE 7.8   Outputs: Define Transition Requirements

Output	Output Destinations	Destination Knowledge Area
Transition requirements	Prioritize requirements	Requirements Analysis
	Verify requirements	Requirements Analysis
	—	Requirements Management and Communication Knowledge Area

You are responsible for developing the transition requirements for your project. A number of stakeholders are ready and able to assist you in defining these requirements for transitioning to a new solution. The project manager must be involved with the transition requirements. These requirements might impact the project scope and typically add work activities to the project plan.

Several other business analysis stakeholders may be involved with your transition requirements definition efforts, including the:

- Customer
- Domain SME
- End user
- Implementation SME
- Operational support
- Regulator
- Tester
- Sponsor

Let's move on and have a more detailed look at the next task found in the Solution Assessment and Validation knowledge area—validating the solution against its requirements.

Validate Solution

Solution validation makes certain that your new solution addresses the business and stakeholder needs that triggered your project in the first place. To do this, compare your solution and its capabilities against the project's business, stakeholder, and solution requirements that were created earlier in the project life cycle. Any problems or discrepancies you find during solution validation are recorded, prioritized, and resolved. Figure 7.6 summarizes the inputs, outputs, techniques, and associated tasks used to validate your solution against its requirements.

FIGURE 7.6   Task summary: Validate the solution.

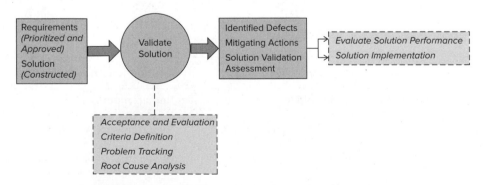

Several key inputs are needed for solution validation. These inputs are produced by a number of other business analysis tasks, as well as tasks external to the scope of the *BABOK® Guide*. They include the prioritized and validated requirements along with the constructed solution. Let's have a look at each of these task inputs in greater detail.

Requirements (Prioritized and Validated)   You will use your project's prioritized and validated requirements to determine whether the outputs of the solution fall within acceptable limits. These requirements should be associated with acceptance criteria that define the acceptable limits or values to measure against.

Solution (Constructed)   A solution must be built in order for you to validate it. The solution you are validating might be in operational use or it might be currently functioning in a test environment. In order to validate a solution, the solution must be constructed and functioning. The technical work activities creating the *constructed solution* are not in the scope of the *BABOK® Guide*.

Table 7.9 summarizes the inputs to this task and lists the task and knowledge area sources for each input used when validating a solution.

TABLE 7.9   Inputs: Validate Solution

Task Input	Input Source	Source Knowledge Area
Requirements (prioritized and validated)	Manage requirements traceability	Requirements Management and Communication
	Validate requirements	Requirements Analysis
Solution (constructed)	—	—

When validating your new solution relative to its requirements, you'll need to:

- Investigate defective solution outputs.
- Assess any defects and issues.

Let's look at each of these two activities in greater detail.

Investigate Defective Solution Outputs   Defective solution outputs occur when the outputs are below the previously defined acceptable level of quality for that output. Defective outputs require investigation and resolution as part of your solution validation activities.

Assess Defects and Issues   Any defects that are identified during solution validation need to be reviewed and assessed. Some defects require immediate resolution, while others may be mitigated using a workaround or accepted for the time being. There are several ways to mitigate the impact of a defect using a workaround, such as:

- Adding quality control checks
- Introducing new manual processes
- Removing support for exceptions and errors

Areas that you need to consider when assessing solution defects include the severity and probability of the defect and analyzing any business impacts.

Exam Spotlight

Make sure you know the difference between a *defect* and an *issue*. Defects are deficiencies in your solution, reducing the quality of that solution. Issues are points or matters in dispute or in question.

The *BABOK® Guide* provides three general techniques for you to select from when validating a solution and addressing any defects or issues that you might find. Let's take a look at them now.

Techniques to Consider

The *BABOK® Guide* recommends using one or more of the following techniques when you are developing the transition requirements for your new solution. They are summarized for you here.

Acceptance and Evaluation Criteria Definition   It is essential that you define the set of requirements that will be used to validate the solution. This set of requirements must have defined, measurable, acceptance criteria for you to use in your validation efforts.

Problem Tracking   Problem tracking is your formal vehicle for identifying and tracking *identified defects*. This technique ensures that the defects found during solution validation are addressed and resolved.

Root Cause Analysis   Root cause analysis allows you to determine the underlying reason for a defect. This allows you to correct the actual cause of the defect versus correcting a symptom of that defect and not the defect itself.

Once you have selected and applied one or more of these techniques as part of your solution validation efforts, you are ready to continue with your other assessment and validation tasks. Before moving on, let's look at the three outputs from this task.

Defects, Mitigating Actions, and the Solution Validation Assessment

Your solution validation efforts produce three distinct and related outputs:

- Identified defects
- *Mitigating actions*
- Solution validation assessment

Let's review each output in greater detail.

Identified Defects   Identified defects are known problems that have been found in a constructed solution. They should be logged, reviewed, and resolved.

Mitigating Actions   Mitigating actions are steps or process that you will take to reduce or eliminate the impacts an identified defect has on a stakeholder or stakeholder group. Think of mitigating actions as workarounds, allowing you to sidestep the impacts of the defect instead of directly addressing and correcting its cause.

Solution Validation Assessment   The solution validation assessment documents whether the constructed solution meets the business need and the project requirements at an acceptable level of quality.

Each output is used by one or more business analysis tasks. Identified defects are used to evaluate the solution performance once the solution is operational. The mitigating actions and solution validation assessment are used by solution implementation tasks that are out of the scope of the *BABOK® Guide*. The outputs and the tasks that use them are summarized in Table 7.10.

TABLE 7.10   Outputs: Validate Solution

Output	Output Destinations	Destination Knowledge Area
Identified defects	Evaluate solution performance	Solution Assessment and Validation
Mitigating actions	—	Solution implementation
Solution validation assessment	—	Solution implementation

You are responsible for performing solution validation on your project. There are a number of stakeholders who should assist you in doing this work. Testers play a primary role in solution verification, where they make certain that the solution behaves as the solution requirements say that it will. Implementation SMEs will be key players in this task, working with you to investigate and correct defects. The project manager must be involved with validating the solution so they can coordinate the resources required to perform the work.

Several other business analysis stakeholders may be involved with your solution validation efforts, including the:

- Domain SME
- End user
- Operational support
- Project manager
- Regulator
- Sponsor

Let's move on and have a more detailed look at the final task of the Solution Assessment and Validation knowledge area—evaluating the solution's performance.

Evaluate Solution Performance

Evaluating solution performance begins once your constructed solution is deployed and in operational use. You will find yourself investigating how the solution is being used and assessing the positive and negative impacts it has on the organization and its stakeholders. Some folks evaluate solution performance in a post-implementation assessment performed shortly after their project is complete.

 Real World Scenario

Do We Have the Right Acceptance Criteria?

In a recent consulting assignment, Ginger discovered first hand that solution performance evaluations can yield some surprising results. She was performing a post-implementation review of a large software systems implementation at a major telecommunications company.

The new system automated the trouble-ticketing and problem-resolution capabilities between the telecommunications company and its business partners. Whenever a circuit problem was reported, the system would initiate and carry on an electronic conversation between the two companies. The conversation stepped through the problem-resolution process from start to finish with the computer systems on each end performing the lion's share of the work.

Rather than talk with one another and do a lot of manual data entry and status updates, the service representatives were able to simply check the status of the trouble tickets and make sure the repairs that needed to be done were actually scheduled and completed. The new system was viewed by senior management as a system that would greatly enhance workplace productivity by minimizing the manual transactions and telephone conversations that took up so much of the service representative's time.

As part of her solution performance evaluation work, Ginger visited a major service center to see how well the new system was being used. She expected to see a very quiet and efficient workspace with a lot of activity going on behind the computer screens. What Ginger expected and what she encountered on her visit were two very different things.

Ginger walked around the service center to see the end users in action. As predicted, once the trouble ticket was opened in the new system, the computer took over the conversation with the company responsible for addressing the problem. However, instead of allowing the electronic conversation to go on unaided, the service reps were on the phones with the counterparts at the other company. As the computer systems exchanged information and updated problem status, they were discussing what they saw on the screens and making sure that all was going as planned. This behavior on the part of the end users was most unexpected.

The project team and the business had failed to take into account how much enjoyment the service representatives took from their interactions and relationships with the folks at the other companies. They wanted to continue those activities and found an easy workaround allowing them to do just that—all they had to do was pick up the phone and dial.

As Ginger briefed the senior management team on the results of the post-implementation assessment, she made the point that your solution's end users can be quite creative when it comes to figuring out new and unintended ways to use the capabilities that a solution provides. Ginger told the senior managers that the project had obviously missed defining the acceptance criteria focusing on job satisfaction and relationship building between the involved companies and personnel. These automated systems are working quite well to this day, and the people-to-people conversations are still going on right along with the electronic ones.

End users are masters of adapting and modifying how a solution gets used. There are several ways to do this, including:

- Using manual workarounds
- Recording additional information
- Adopting informal policies and procedures

If you see new ways of using an operational solution, keep an open mind and analyze why these methods of use are taking place. The unofficial approaches to using the solution might also add benefits to the business and its bottom line.

Figure 7.7 summarizes the inputs, outputs, techniques, and associated tasks used to validate a solution against its business requirements.

FIGURE 7.7   Task summary: Evaluate solution performance.

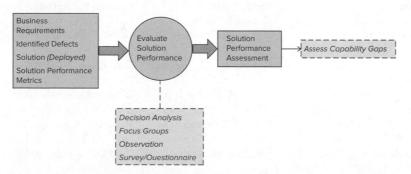

Several key inputs are needed to evaluate how an operational solution is performing. These key inputs are produced by a number of other business analysis tasks, as well as tasks external to the scope of the *BABOK® Guide*. These inputs include the newly deployed solution, any *solution performance metrics*, and the business requirements. Let's look at each input in greater detail.

Business Requirements   The project's business requirements defined during Enterprise Analysis are the basis for evaluating a solution's operational performance. The goals for the project and its resulting solution are documented here.

Exam Spotlight

Remember the four building blocks of a project's business requirements? They are created by the tasks in the Enterprise Analysis knowledge area and include the business need, required capabilities, solution scope, and the business case.

Identified Defects   If identified defects are being tracked but are not yet resolved, they need to be taken into account as you assess the solution's performance.

Solution Performance Metrics   Solution performance metrics define the criteria that are used to measure and assess solution performance. They may be quantitative or qualitative in nature. Examples of quantitative metrics include numerical measures of time, revenue, or transaction volume. Qualitative metrics are softer measures, such as customer satisfaction or recommendations.

Solution (Deployed)   The deployed solution for this task is the fully operational new solution that was implemented as part of your project. It is being used by its end users and should be providing both value and benefits to the business.

Table 7.11 summarizes the inputs to this task and lists the task and knowledge area sources for each input used to evaluate solution performance.

TABLE 7.11   Inputs: Evaluate Solution Performance

Task Input	Input Source	Source Knowledge Area
Business requirements	Define business need	Enterprise Analysis
	Assess capability gaps	Enterprise Analysis
	Define solution cope	Enterprise Analysis
	Define business case	Enterprise Analysis
Identified defects	Validate solution	Solution Assessment and Validation
Solution performance metrics	—	—
Solution (deployed)	—	—

Three elements are involved with evaluating solution performance. The solution being evaluated must be live and in operation. If it isn't being used, there won't be much for you to evaluate. The detailed elements of this task include:

- Understanding the value delivered by the solution
- Validating the solution metrics
- Considering solution replacement or elimination

Let's look at each of these three elements in greater detail.

Understanding the Value Delivered by the Solution   You need to collect the metrics that describe solution performance. Some software applications may provide these metrics to you automatically. Other types of solutions will require manual collection of quantitative and qualitative solution metrics for evaluation.

Validating the Solution Metrics   If you have a solution that is over- or under-performing and not meeting one or more of the business goals and objectives, it may be that your solution metrics associated with those goals and objectives are flawed. The solution metrics should also be validated and defined more appropriately.

Considering Solution Replacement or Elimination   At some future time, it will become necessary for you to evaluate your solution as a candidate for replacement or elimination. This can happen for a number of reasons, including outdated technology or new business goals and objectives. There are four issues that might influence your decision to replace or eliminate a deployed solution.

Ongoing Cost versus Initial Investment   You might discover that the costs to maintain a solution over time have increased. This needs to be balanced by looking at new solutions that may have a high initial investment cost but lower maintenance costs over time. Doing a cost-benefit analysis is always a good idea when evaluating solutions for elimination or replacement.

Opportunity Cost   Opportunity costs are the potential value you are giving up by continuing with an existing solution rather than doing something different. Opportunity cost equals the benefits from doing something different. Be sure that you are not giving up a significant future opportunity by staying with your old solution.

Necessity   Most solutions and solution components have a limited lifespan. After a certain point in time, it may be impossible to maintain them and they will need to be replaced or eliminated. Solutions frequently need to be upgraded or replaced when vendors stop supporting older versions of their products.

Sunk Cost   *Sunk costs* are the money and effort you have already spent for the current solution. Sometimes it is difficult to consider replacing or eliminating a solution when you look at what you have invested in that solution. You need to make sure that you look at future investment and benefits as well.

When evaluating solution performance, you can select from four recommended techniques. You can use one or several of these techniques to produce the solution performance assessment that is generated as an output by this task.

Techniques to Consider

The *BABOK® Guide* recommends using one or more of the following techniques when you are evaluating solution performance. They are summarized for you here.

Decision Analysis   Decision analysis allows you to examine and model the consequences of different decisions when evaluating the financial impacts a solution is having on your business. You must make sure that you look at all solution costs and benefits that are relevant to the organization's values, goals, and objectives.

Focus Groups   Focus groups provide a facilitated group approach to understanding the value the solution provides to its stakeholders. Focus groups can also be used to define or validate the solution performance metrics that are being used.

Observation   Observation allows you to observe the stakeholders using the solution. This technique may reveal problems or issues that have not been noticed or reported.

Survey/Questionnaire   Surveys and questionnaires provide you with a vehicle to gather quantitative and qualitative information from large numbers of stakeholders about how a solution is performing.

Once you have selected and applied one or more of these techniques as part of your solution performance evaluation efforts, you are ready to produce the key business analysis output from this task—the solution performance assessment. Let's review this deliverable.

Build the Solution Performance Assessment

The solution performance assessment describes how the solution is performing relative to the business goals and objectives that led to its creation and implementation. The contents of this assessment may be used to assess capability gaps as part of the tasks found in the Enterprise Analysis knowledge area. This output and the task that uses it are summarized in Table 7.12.

TABLE 7.12   Outputs: Evaluate Solution Performance

Output	Output Destinations	Destination Knowledge Area
Solution performance assessment	Assess capability gaps	Enterprise Analysis

You are responsible for ensuring that the solution evaluation work on your project gets done. If you are unable to follow through due to reassignment to another project, you will need to plan for the work and hand off your plan to another responsible party. There are a number of other business analysis stakeholders who may be involved with this post-implementation assessment, including the:

- Customer
- Domain SME

- End user
- Operational support
- Regulator
- Supplier

The project sponsor is ultimately responsible for solution operations from a business point of view and needs to review the results of your solution performance assessment to see if any improvements or changes to the solution need to be made.

How This Applies to Your Projects

In this chapter, you stepped through tasks focusing on the solution that is being built and deployed by your project. These tasks ensure that the solution defined in your solution requirements can be successfully implemented within the organization. Transition requirements define what needs to take place in order to complete a successful transition from the deployed (existing) solution to the newly constructed solution.

Let's take a closer look at some of the planning that needs to accompany these transition requirements as part of your implementation work. In many organizations, the business analyst is responsible for supporting the business stakeholders as the solution is implemented and facilitating their transition to the new ways of doing things. Part of your responsibility is planning for the actual set of implementation activities down to the right level of detail.

Your solution implementation plan and approved solution design enable you to create data conversion requirements and build any necessary business transition strategies. It is helpful to produce an implementation plan, a data conversion plan, and any high-level requirements for the next solution release as part of our preparations for transitioning from the old solution to the new solution. A conversion plan maps data from the old solution to the new solution. It details the business rules for data conversion and sets the timing of the work.

You might have a small set of transition requirements addressing your implementation plan as part of your transition requirements. For example, they may state:

TR 1.0 Develop implementation plan for constructed solution.

TR 2.0 Plan work activities to support contents of implementation plan.

However, the actual implementation plan may be far more detailed based on the solution that is being implemented. Table 7.13 provides you with a sample implementation plan for a software solution implementation.

TABLE 7.13 Sample Implementation Plan

Date/Time *(All times MST)*	Task Description
	PRE-ROLLOUT STEPS
	Send release notes to sys admin to post. Send support documentation to sys admin.
	Update website with upcoming maintenance message via GUI interface.
	Confirm production environment is ready for release rollout.
7/12/10 12:00 AM	Set up all new policy templates.
7/12/10 12:00 AM	Set up Oracle templates (release data).
7/12/10 12:00 AM	Set up Oracle templates (asset data).
7/15/10 10:30 AM	Shut down Oracle database.
7/15/10 10:45 AM	Drop the replication for groups that have changed.
7/15/10 11:30 AM	Run the Table, Stored Proc, and Data changes.
7/15/10 11:30 AM	Run DB update scripts.
7/15/10 12:00 Noon	Verify the scripts ran successfully.
7/15/10 12:00 Noon	Set the Billing start time to 00:05.
7/15/10 12:30 PM	Rebuild the changed replication groups.
7/15/10 2:00 PM	Restart Oracle.
7/15/10 2:00 PM	Join conference bridge for checkpoint.
7/15/10 2:00 PM	Publish build kit to lab to test rollout procedure.
7/15/10 4:00 PM	Copy latest/final build out to all production servers in two data centers.
	ROLLOUT STEPS
7/15/10 12:00 Midnight	Verify that all participants have joined the Maintenance bridge and that there are no network jeopardies that would cause this maintenance to be rescheduled.

Date/Time *(All times MST)*	Task Description
7/15/10 9:00 AM	Post maintenance message on websites.
7/16/10 12:01 AM	Verify that billing has completed.
7/16/10 12:02 AM	Reset billing to its original start time.
7/16/10 12:03 AM	Stop services and web servers.
7/16/10 12:05 AM	Export a copy of application in case you have to roll back.
7/16/10 12:30 AM	Shut down Oracle database (15 minutes).
7/16/10 12:45 AM	Drop the replication for groups that have changed (45 minutes).
7/16/10 1:30 AM	Run the Table, Stored Proc, and Data changes (1 hour).
7/16/10 1:30 AM	Run DB update scripts.
7/16/10 2:00 AM	Verify the scripts ran successfully (5 minutes, overlapping).
7/16/10 2:00 AM	Rebuild the changed Replication Groups (90 minutes).
7/16/10 3:30 AM	Restart Oracle (5 minutes).
7/16/10 6:00 AM	Copy configuration file in SFTPFileFetcher directory to temp to preserve the data.
7/16/10 6:00 AM	Publish application code to data center production servers.
7/16/10 6:30 AM	Copy config file from temp directory and verify.
7/16/10 6:30 AM	Move `SetDBDefaults.exe` to `c:\netfiles\bin` to run it to avoid errors.
7/16/10 6:30 AM	Run script for web service `DeploymentUtil\UtilityScripts\Rollout 6.0\Run.bat`.
7/16/10 6:30 AM	Ensure all services are running in production.
7/16/10 6:30 AM	Join conference bridge for checkpoint:
7/16/10 6:30 AM	Verify correct application operation over a period of time. (Unit Testing)

TABLE 7.13 Sample Implementation Plan (*continued*)

Date/Time (All times MST)	Task Description
7/16/10 7:00 AM	Join conference bridge for checkpoint and Quality Control Handoff.
7/16/10 8:00 AM	Quality assurance testing period begins.
7/16/10 8:00 AM	1 End-to-end Test of Policy Propagation (Client–Manual/ Auto).*Note: Expect testing to take 10 to 12 hours.*
7/16/10 12:00 Noon	Join conference bridge for checkpoint.
7/16/10 4:00 PM	Join conference bridge for checkpoint.
7/17/10 9:00 AM	Verify billing is back up and running.
7/17/10 9:00 AM	Copy updated software download files to each of the web servers in preparation for the Saturday deployment.
7/17/10 12:00 AM	Set up URL links in export server.
7/17/10 9:00 AM	Copy updated software download files to each of the web servers.
7/17/10 6:30 AM	Correct an issue with the policy feed.
7/18/10 11:00 PM	Request a final security scan of all servers.
7/19/10 12:00 AM	External system production testing.
7/19/10 6:00 AM	Release complete; publish management and customer notifications.

This particular solution implementation plan was built and performed for a software upgrade at a client site in Colorado. As you can see, the two statements—build the plan and schedule the work from that plan—exploded into a very detailed set of steps to support implementation of this software release.

Summary

The six tasks in the Solution Assessment and Validation knowledge area guide you in effectively assessing, selecting, and validating the solution that will be implemented in the organization to meet the business requirements. You will also develop the transition requirements and perform release planning for your project. Transition requirements define the solution capabilities required to transition from the existing solution to the new solution. One interesting fact about these requirements is that they are no longer needed once the transition to the new solution is complete.

Effective problem-solving skills are an underlying competency enabling you to do this solution-focused work. You will be asked to analyze problems with the designed and constructed solution and recommend ways to address any defects and issues that you and your stakeholders find. Applying your structured problem-solving skills results in implementing a solution that meets or exceeds its quality and acceptance criteria.

The *BABOK® Guide* recommends applying a number of techniques as part of your solution validation and assessment efforts. You don't need to be an expert in every technique, but most experienced business analysts are comfortable using a representative subset of those techniques.

No high-profile business analysis deliverables are produced by the Elicitation knowledge area. However, elicitation results must be documented and confirmed in order to be used in subsequent requirements development activities, such as analysis and specification. The stated, confirmed requirements and any stakeholder concerns are the building blocks from which the real requirements for our projects will be derived.

In addition to the transition requirements, a number of key business analysis deliverables are produced by the tasks found in this knowledge area. You will produce several assessments looking at the solution, the organization's readiness to adopt that solution, and its performance once operational. These assessments are a key part of your role in making sure the right solution is implemented in the right way for your business.

Exam Essentials

Be able to list the tasks found in the Solution Assessment and Validation knowledge area. You will see questions about the tasks, their associated techniques, their more detailed elements, and the key outputs that they produce on your exam. You should memorize the tasks of this knowledge area and the key outputs associated with them. The six tasks are

> Assess proposed solution.
>
> Allocate requirements.
>
> Assess organizational readiness.
>
> Define transition requirements.
>
> Validate solution.
>
> Evaluate solution performance.

Be able to understand and apply the techniques found in this knowledge area. Understanding and applying the techniques to assess and validate your solution is a key focus for your Solution Assessment and Validation knowledge area exam questions.

Be sure that you can name the techniques recommended here and associate them with the tasks that use them.

Be able to describe the four types of assessments. Make sure you can define and distinguish between the four assessments that are created and used by the tasks in the Solution Assessment and Validation knowledge area.

> Solution Performance Assessment
>
> Solution Validation Assessment
>
> Organizational Readiness Assessment
>
> Assessment of Proposed Solution or Solutions

Be able to define the different types of solutions. The *BABOK® Guide* uses three modifiers to describe the solution that is being defined, developed, and implemented for a project. Make certain you understand the state of the solution when it is referred to using a particular term: designed solution, deployed solution, and constructed solution.

Be able to discuss the four aspects of stakeholder impact analysis relative to a new solution. Your organizational readiness assessment addresses how the changes from your new solution will affect your stakeholders. The areas to be considered include the stakeholder's job function, location, tasks, and any concerns they might have about the new solution.

Be able to distinguish between the solution, the solution components, and a release. A solution is a set of changes to an organization's current state enabling the organization to meet a business need, solve a problem, or take advantage of an opportunity.

Solutions are made up of solution components, the parts of a solution that span the enterprise architecture of the organization, such as new business processes, new software applications, or new hardware. Each solution component implements a subset of the solution requirements.

Solutions are typically implemented in releases. A release is the distribution of all or part of a scheduled operational solution, such as a release consisting of software application code, related documents, and support materials.

Key Terms

You have just finished stepping through the contents the sixth and final knowledge area from the *BABOK® Guide*: Solution Assessment and Validation. The tasks in this knowledge area focus on making sure that the defined solution can be successfully implemented in the organization and used by its stakeholders.

To be an effective business analyst, you should understand how to apply the techniques and tasks in this knowledge area. Additionally, you will need to know the six tasks and their associated elements and techniques from this knowledge area in order to be successful on the CBAP® or CCBA™ exams. The tasks include:

Assess proposed solution.	Define transition requirements.
Allocate requirements.	Validate solution.
Assess organizational readiness.	Evaluate solution performance.

A number of new key words in Chapter 7 relate to assessing and validating your new solution. Here is a list of some of the key terms that you encountered in this chapter:

allocated requirements	identified defects
assessment of proposed solution(s)	mitigating actions
constructed solution	organizational readiness assessment
designed solution	solution performance assessment
designed solution	solution performance metrics
force field analysis	solution validation assessment

Review Questions

1. You will use testable requirements during solution verification to determine if the solution receives a score of pass or fail. What type of criteria are you developing?

    A. Evaluation

    B. Acceptance

    C. Transition

    D. Performance

2. Which input best provides you with an assessment of a solution's ability to meet the business need at an acceptable level of quality?

    A. Solution performance assessment

    B. Organizational readiness assessment

    C. Solution validation assessment

    D. Proposed solution assessment

3. What technique ensures that issues arising from an organizational readiness assessment are addressed and resolved?

    A. SWOT analysis

    B. Force field analysis

    C. Problem-tracking

    D. Root cause analysis

4. Which statement is FALSE regarding your project's transition requirements?

    A. Created using same tasks as other requirements

    B. Not defined until the solution has been designed

    C. Relevant after the existing solution is eliminated

    D. Used for transition between old and new solutions

5. You are determining the most appropriate response to identified defects in a delivered solution. What activity are you performing?

    A. Validating the solution

    B. Assessing solution options

    C. Verifying the solution

    D. Assessing the solution

6. What outputs are produced from ensuring that a delivered solution meets the business needs on an ongoing basis?

    A. Identified defects and mitigating actions

    B. Mitigating actions and change requests

    C. Accepted solution and identified defects

    D. Mitigating actions and transition plan

7. You used prioritized solution requirements to assess several solution options. In order to make a decision, these prioritized requirements must also be:

  A. Verified

  B. Approved

  C. Allocated

  D. Traced

8. Which stakeholder approves the allocation of requirements to components and releases?

  A. Business analyst

  B. Project sponsor

  C. Domain SME

  D. Project manager

9. Requirements that are associated with the solution component that will implement them are called:

  A. Verified requirements

  B. Solution requirements

  C. Traced requirements

  D. Allocated requirements

10. You are making decisions about what solution requirements to include in your project iterations in order to cause minimal disruption of business activities during solution implementation. What activity are you performing?

  A. Release planning

  B. Change management

  C. Rolling wave planning

  D. Agile project planning

11. What is another name for the existing solution?

  A. Designed solution

  B. Deployed solution

  C. Constructed solution

  D. Allocated solution

12. When should you begin to allocate requirements during a project?

  A. When the real project requirements are derived

  B. When the proposed solution is being assessed

  C. When the solution approach is determined

  D. When solution design and construction starts

13. When should transition requirements be defined?

   A. While the solution is being designed

   B. After the solution has been designed

   C. Before the solution is actually designed

   D. When required capabilities are defined

14. What general technique would you select to discover if a solution defect is a symptom of a deeper, underlying problem?

   A. Root cause analysis

   B. SWOT analysis

   C. Force field analysis

   D. Decision analysis

15. You are investigating how a solution is being used after it has been deployed. What Solution Assessment and Validation task are you performing?

   A. Assessing organizational readiness

   B. Defining transition requirements

   C. Assessing proposed solution

   D. Evaluating solution performance

16. Solution validation can only be performed against a solution that is _____.

   A. Confirmed

   B. Designed

   C. Constructed

   D. Deployed

17. What type of requirements should address employee training, conversion of existing information, and user acceptance testing?

   A. Stakeholder

   B. Transition

   C. Implementation

   D. Functional

18. What source might assist you in defining transition requirements?

   A. Ongoing work using the old solution

   B. Upcoming work using the old data

   C. Ongoing work using the old data

   D. Upcoming work using the old solution

19. Which task has solution performance metrics as an input?

    A. Define Transition Requirements

    B. Evaluate Solution Performance

    C. Assess Proposed Solution

    D. Validate and Verify Solution

20. What is the best reason for involving a business analyst in the Solution Assessment and Validation tasks?

    A. They bring technical skills to the solution assessment process.

    B. They have built relationships with all key project stakeholders.

    C. They are most knowledgeable about the business environment.

    D. They work closest with the project manager and the project team.

Answers to Review Questions

1. B. Acceptance criteria describe the minimal set of requirements that must be met in order for a particular solution to be worth implementing.

2. C. The solution validation assessment provides an assessment of the solution's ability to meet the business need at an acceptable level of quality.

3. C. The problem-tracking technique is used to ensure that issues identified by the organizational readiness assessment are resolved.

4. C. Transition requirements are not relevant after the new solution is implemented and should be discarded. All of the remaining statements are true.

5. A. Solution validation ensures that a delivered solution meets the business needs on an ongoing basis and that any identified defects are reported and prioritized for resolution.

6. A. Outputs from the validate solution task include identified defects, mitigating actions, and the solution validation assessment.

7. B. Requirements must be prioritized and approved in order to allow a decision to be made about possible solution options during solution assessment.

8. B. The project sponsor is responsible for funding the project and required to approve the allocation of requirements to components and releases based on the recommendations of the business analyst and the project team.

9. D. Allocated requirements are associated with a solution component that will implement them.

10. A. You are performing release planning, part of allocating your requirements. Release planning involves making decisions about which requirements are included in each phase or iteration of the project.

11. B. The deployed solution is the existing solution that will be replaced by a new solution.

12. C. Requirements allocation typically begins early in the project life cycle (as soon as the solution approach can be determined) and continues to be performed until all valid requirements are allocated, typically through design and construction of the solution.

13. B. Transition requirements are defined after the solution has been designed.

14. A. During solution validation, the root cause analysis technique can be used to ensure that the underlying reason for a defect is identified, rather than simply correcting the output which may be a symptom of a deeper underlying problem.

15. D. Evaluating solution performance is where you investigate how a solution is actually used after it is deployed and assess its positive and negative effects.

16. C. Solution validation can only be performed against a solution that exists. Although the solution may or may not be in actual use by the enterprise, it must be constructed.

17. B. Transition requirements define capabilities needed to support the transition from the old system to the new solution, including employee training, conversion of existing information, and user acceptance testing.

18. A. Sources of transition requirements include the actual data and metadata managed by the old system, the ongoing work in the old version of the solution, and the process for managing the organizational change resulting from the transition to the new system.

19. B. Inputs for the Evaluate Solution Performance task include the solution performance metrics, the deployed solution, any identified defects, and the business requirements.

20. C. The business analyst knows the business environment and can assess how each proposed solution would affect the environment. Business analysts are also responsible for ensuring that the stakeholders fully understand the solution requirements and that implementation decisions align with those requirements.

Chapter

8

Underlying Competencies

CBAP®/CCBA™ EXAM TOPICS COVERED IN THIS CHAPTER

- ✓ Business analysis underlying competencies

- ✓ Analytical thinking and problem-solving skills

- ✓ Key business-analysis behavioral characteristics

- ✓ Business and software knowledge

- ✓ Communication and interaction skills

Skilled business analysts possess a wide spectrum of skills and knowledge. Being a technical expert in a particular area or possessing subject matter expertise in a particular industry does not guarantee success as a business analyst on a project. Effective business analysts possess a core framework consisting of business, technical, and domain knowledge. This core framework is further enhanced by your management, interpersonal, communication, business, and structured problem-solving skills.

The required knowledge and skills range from applying structured analysis techniques to managing issues to addressing solution usability. You must be able to provide relevant business and domain knowledge for the organization's products, processes, markets, and systems and incorporate specific business and software application knowledge. The knowledge and skills you bring to and acquire for your role as a business analyst are known as the underlying competencies.

Essential Skills of Effective Business Analysts

Underlying competencies are the behaviors, characteristics, knowledge, and personal qualities that make you an effective business analyst on a project. The *BABOK® Guide* categorizes these essential skills and knowledge into six categories. You can think of these categories as building blocks that you bring to each of your projects when you put on your business analysis hat, roll up your sleeves, and start working. The underlying competencies include:

- Analytical thinking and problem-solving skills
- Behavioral characteristics
- Business knowledge
- Software knowledge
- Interaction skills
- Communication skills

This chapter of the book steps you through these core skills. A strong and balanced set of these underlying competencies provides you with tremendous value when performing your project's business analysis tasks. The Underlying Competencies knowledge area is found in Chapter 8 of the *BABOK® Guide*.

Exam Spotlight

Although the *BABOK® Guide* says that the underlying competencies form a knowledge area, you will not find a specific percentage of questions about this knowledge area on your certification exam. Instead, you will find questions within the other six knowledge areas that check your skills in and your knowledge of these underlying competencies. Be sure to study this chapter thoroughly because it is all considered testable content.

Of course, the skills and knowledge discussed here are not confined just to performing business analysis work. They are fundamental skills required to perform almost any role in any organization. Project managers, subject matter experts, and senior managers are expected to possess a solid set of these underlying competencies.

When Are the Underlying Competencies Used?

> Even if you are on the right track, you will get run over if you just sit there.
>
> —*Will Rogers*

The knowledge and skills found in the underlying competencies are used by business analysts across the project life cycle as well as in their day-to-day work that is not related to a specific project. You might find yourself selecting a project approach by facilitating a meeting of key stakeholders and reaching agreement on the best way to get the project underway and completed. You might be called on to resolve a conflict between two opposing stakeholder groups about the relative priorities of solution requirements. You might build and deliver training on new solution capabilities to your end users.

Remember the Six Knowledge Areas

Be sure you know the six knowledge areas and the work you perform when you are using them. These knowledge areas and their tasks are where you apply the underlying competencies.

Business Analysis Planning and Monitoring This knowledge area is where you plan how to approach your project's business analysis effort. The approach is a set of processes, templates, and activities used to perform business analysis in a specific context. The tasks govern and monitor the performance of all other business analysis tasks. These planning and monitoring activities take place throughout the project life cycle. The results

---

of this knowledge area govern the tasks found in the remaining five knowledge areas and set the performance metrics to be used to evaluate all business analysis work.

Elicitation   Elicitation defines how business analysts work with stakeholders to identify and gather requirements and understand their needs and concerns. A tremendous amount of interaction with people occurs in this knowledge area. You will find yourself working with the project team and the stakeholders to gather requirements information, record the elicitation results, and confirm those results with your stakeholders.

Requirements Management and Communication   This knowledge area defines how you approach communicating your project requirements to your stakeholders. You will find yourself managing changes, conflicts, and issues related to the project requirements across the project life cycle.

Enterprise Analysis   Enterprise Analysis focuses on identifying the business needs that drive a project and defining a feasible solution scope that can be implemented by the business. This knowledge area includes developing the business requirements for a project that define the high-level goals, objectives, and needs of the organization and the high-level business functionality needed in the resulting solution.

Requirements Analysis   Requirements Analysis steps you progressively through elaborating and prioritizing the stakeholder and solution requirements for a project. Stakeholder requirements define the needs of stakeholders and how they interact with a solution. Stakeholder requirements act as a bridge between high-level business requirements and more-detailed solution requirements. In turn, the more-detailed solution requirements describe the solution characteristics that will be needed to meet the higher-level business and stakeholder requirements.

Solution Assessment and Validation   Solution Assessment and Validation assesses and validates the proposed, in-progress, and implemented solutions before, during, and after the project life cycle. This is also where the project's transition requirements are defined. Transition requirements define the solution capabilities required to transition from the current state to a future state and are no longer needed once the transition is complete.

The key skills and knowledge found here may be used to perform any task or technique found in any of the six knowledge areas. Let's take a look at the first set of core skills—analytical thinking and problem solving.

Analytical Thinking and Problem-Solving Skills

Facilitating solutions to business problems would be impossible without a structured approach for addressing the problem at hand. Analytical thinking and problem-solving skills enable you to assess and understand a situation. Once that situation is fully understood, you can assess and recommend one or more potential solutions to address the business need, problem, or opportunity at hand. The *BABOK*® *Guide* breaks the essential analytical thinking and problem-solving skills into five more detailed areas:

- Creative thinking
- *Decision making*
- Learning
- Problem solving
- *Systems thinking*

Let's take a look at each of these areas that add up to an effective skill set in analytical thinking and problem solving. First up are your creative thinking skills.

Creative Thinking

Creative thinkers are able to generate new ideas, concepts, and alternative solutions when solving business problems. Many times, the new ideas and concepts being generated are innovative and new ways to get the job done. It isn't just about your creative thinking skills. You also need to ask questions and challenge assumptions in order to foster creative thinking in your other team members and stakeholders.

 Real World Scenario

Palmer Divide Vineyards: An Unexpected Freeze

Divide Vineyards recently reaped the benefits of creative thinking and problem solving. Even though the weather at the vineyard is fairly temperate, every now and then winter brings a freeze. There was an unexpected freeze recently, and the vineyard watering systems suffered no ill effects because the agriculture team quickly reacted to the cold temperatures. Several years ago, the vineyard installed a new watering system for the terraces of grapes they grow. The design of the new watering system was a bit backward—starting with the water supply at the top of the vineyard terraces and ending at ground level. Due to this creative organization, staff members were able to turn a few knobs to drain the watering system when the freeze hit instead of trying to find a company to come and blow pressurized air to clear water out of the system. Using gravity to drain the system from the terraces was both creative and practical.

Creative thinking is just one piece of the puzzle. It is one thing to generate innovative ideas and possible solutions to a problem and quite another thing to decide what actually should be done in a particular situation. With that in mind, let's move on and talk a bit about business analysts and approaches to effective decision making.

Decision Making

You should take a two-pronged approach to your decision making. You must understand what is involved in making a good decision and be able to help other project team members and stakeholders make good decisions. Decisions need to be made in situations where you are faced with multiple ways of doing things. You might be selecting between possible solutions to solve a business problem or deciding which supplier will provide your project with goods or services. Your decision analysis activities should include:

- Gathering and breaking down relevant information
- Making comparisons and evaluating tradeoffs between options
- Identifying the option that is most desirable

Part of your decision-making process is assessing the impacts of uncertainty and of any new information. Remember, *risk* is defined as an uncertain event or condition on your project. There are always risks associated with making decisions. Your job is to minimize those risks by making the best decision possible given what you know at the time.

The *BABOK® Guide* warns about several potential traps you might encounter during decision-making activities. The first trap is accepting the initial framing of a problem without questioning whether it is complete or correct. The second trap is the *sunk cost fallacy*, where you look at what the organization already has and how much time and money have been invested in those solutions. Based on that information, organizations often continue on in the same vein. Another phrase used to describe the sunk cost fallacy is "escalation of commitment to a failing course of action." The third potential trap is a tendency to place greater weight on evidence confirming existing impressions instead of thinking out of the box and looking for more information.

Effective decision making is a key element for the business analyst. However, there is more to doing your job well than just making decisions. You need to learn from your experiences and be able to apply them to the work at hand. Let's take a closer look at how learning fits into our creative thinking and problem-solving skills.

Learning

Dynamic project environments encourage business analysts to learn new things. As you develop requirements for different parts of the business, you should absorb new business information so you can translate that information into your requirements and their resulting solution.

It isn't enough just to learn and remember data and raw facts. Experienced business analysts apply their understanding of the information to determine what is required for a given situation. This application is also known as *analysis*. You should also be able to synthesize what you have learned in order to identify opportunities to create new solutions. After new solutions are in place, you are also responsible for evaluating them to make sure that the resulting new solutions are effective.

One key application of learning new business domain information is being able to apply it properly to the business analysis tasks in your project. Let's take a look now at the problem-solving skills of effective business analysts.

Problem Solving

Business analysts are frequently asked to evaluate and select solutions that meet defined business objectives. Your project's selected solution targets solving an underlying problem, meeting a business need in the organization, or both. Your primary goal when addressing a business problem is solving that problem. You get this done through a combination of *problem definition*, *alternatives identification*, and decision making. Let's have a look at each item.

Problem Definition   You need to make sure that the problem or business need being addressed is clearly defined and understood by your stakeholders. Any issues related to the problem or need should be identified and shared with the group. All conflicts between stakeholders relative to the problem or need should also be addressed.

Alternatives Identification   Often there are many ways to solve a problem or address a business need. Solution options are developed, analyzed, and evaluated by the group. Remember that the solution options under consideration should meet the defined objectives and actually solve the problem and/or meet the business need.

Decision Making   Once your problem or need is clearly defined and the solution alternatives are identified, it is time to make or recommend a decision. Tradeoff decision making may be required to select the best solution to the problem or need. You want to avoid selecting a sub-optimal solution due to *politics* or preconceived notions.

Making good decisions during your project's business analysis work requires having the right information and involving the right people. Your ability to put together all the pieces, what your organization does, what is known about the problem at hand, and who needs to be involved, supports your skills in structured problem solving and decision making. This takes us right into the next area of competency, systems thinking.

Systems Thinking

Systems thinking looks at your ability to put all of the pieces together and understand the properties, behaviors, and characteristics of the system as a whole—across people, processes, and technology. This information is a moving target and can be quite unpredictable. You need to recognize that systems are not just information technology systems. You are looking at systems in the broader sense, consisting of not just the technology components but the people, the processes, and almost any other factors that come into play.

Projects and their resulting solutions are like puzzles; they possess many pieces and parts. Changes to one part of the puzzle can impact other parts, as well as the whole puzzle. You need to be aware of the complex systems that make up your business operations and keep an eye out for impacts within your new solution, as well as to the business itself, as work is being performed and decisions are being made.

Let's move on to the next category in the underlying competencies knowledge area, the behavioral characteristics of the business analyst. Your success and effectiveness on projects is not based totally on how well you solve problems or make decisions. It is also impacted by the behaviors and personal values you bring to the work you do.

Behavioral Characteristics

Effective business analysts should apply personal integrity and strength of character when dealing with people. This includes dealing with your business analysis team, your project team, and your internal and external project stakeholders. Your ability to build strong, lasting working relationships serves you and your project well. The *BABOK® Guide* breaks the key behavioral characteristics into three areas:

- Ethics
- Trustworthiness
- Personal organization

Let's take a look at each of these essential behaviors you should exhibit in the workplace. Our first stop is a quick look at ethics and ethical behavior.

Ethics

In order to be respected and trusted by your team and your stakeholders, you must behave ethically. That's easy enough to say, but what exactly does it mean? Ethical people know the difference between moral and immoral behavior and understand the standards that govern their own behavior. They act in a moral way to meet those behavioral standards.

 Real World Scenario

Surprise Status

During lunch, Ginger overhears information that concerns her regarding the current status of an important business continuity study program she is working on for a large financial services firm. One of the new technical team members sitting at the next table is talking loudly to a group of his friends. He brings up a piece of information regarding the project's status that is inconsistent with the current status that he just reported to the Ginger and Kim, the program manager, on an area that he is responsible for in the project plan.

"Guys, I've only been here six months, and I'm working on something that is leading edge and important. I just found out from my buddy in IT that the set of records that tracks which staff members were trained and cross trained on critical plant operations is gone. The data got erased in a failed server transfer. Poof! No backup files. How weird is that? Hope they have hard copies somewhere. But it's cool. They'll find what we need eventually."

Ginger leans across the table and asks, "Wait a minute; have you told the rest of our team about this?"

He replies, "No way, Ginger. Tomorrow someone will find the hard copies in somebody's cube, and I'll look like an idiot. I just sent in my status report anyway. I'm not revising that thing unless I absolutely have to."

Ginger gets to her feet and collects her things.

"Come on, let's find Kim and give him this update. That missing data affects our results tremendously and this can't wait. Grab your sandwich and come with me."

Withholding critical project information and issues is neither good nor ethical project team behavior. You should always be straightforward in sharing important information so problems can be identified and addressed as early as possible.

Your ethical behavior often comes into play during business analysis work. You may find yourself recognizing that a proposed solution or a particular requirement presents ethical difficulties. Ethical business analysts consider the interests of all stakeholders when making decisions and are sure to clearly articulate the basis of their decisions so everyone understands. Any conflicts of interest should be promptly and fully disclosed.

Ethical behavior generates trust and respect in the workplace. Trustworthiness is another area in our key behavioral characteristics that you need to review. Let's do that right now.

Trustworthiness

Behaving ethically and performing your business analysis work effectively generates trust between you and your stakeholders. They trust you to do the right thing at the right time on the project and to keep their interests front and center in your decision-making process. This allows you to engage with your stakeholder's needs and act in their best interests at all times.

Earning the trust of key stakeholders is a linchpin of successful business analysis. It is difficult to develop requirements when folks won't tell you what you need to know to define the best solution to meet their needs. Respect and trust can also be earned by exhibiting effective time management skills. Let's have a quick look at personal organization and see how it enhances your behavior and how you are perceived as a business analyst.

Personal Organization

Experienced business analysts can quickly locate needed information. Your ability to effectively managing your time, tasks, and information has an impact on how your team members and other stakeholders perceive you. A disorganized business analyst is not viewed as an effective business analyst. You should set your work priorities, be clear about what needs to be done, and get that work done quickly and well.

Let's move on to the next category in our underlying competencies knowledge area, business knowledge. Your effectiveness as a business analyst is defined not just by what you do but also by what you know.

Business Knowledge

It is impossible to be a liaison between the business and the technology stakeholders on your projects if you have no understanding of the business. Skilled business analysts understand the internal and external business environment surrounding their projects. They use that knowledge to make good decisions and recommendations about what should be done to define and deliver a solution that addresses business needs. The *BABOK® Guide* breaks your business knowledge into four areas:

- Business principles and practices
- Industry knowledge
- *Organization knowledge*
- *Solution knowledge*

Let's take a look at each of these areas, starting with assessing your knowledge of the business principles and practices in your organization.

Business Principles and Practices

Effective business analysts are aware of the *business principles* and *business practices* in their organizations. This is important because you need to incorporate and support these principles and practices in your solutions. Business principles are defined as the characteristics common to organizations of similar purpose and structure, such as human resources, finance, and information technology functions. In contrast, business practices or processes vary based on what an organization does and the size of that organization.

Business principles for a large pharmaceutical organization are very different from the principles found at a large retail organization. However, there may be many similarities in how their business practices work for hiring their people and getting those folks paid every two weeks. Business practices and principles are one aspect of the business knowledge you need to master. There is also knowledge of the industry that your organization is in. Let's have a quick look at your expected level of industry knowledge.

Industry Knowledge

Do you have good knowledge and understanding of the industry of which your organization is a part? If not, you should. Understanding what is taking place in your industry can have positive impacts on your projects and their solutions. You should be aware of your major competitors, partners, and customer segments. Your knowledge should also encompass your organization's common products and product types.

 Real World Scenario

Case Study: Palmer Divide Vineyards

The project team was meeting about the Research Study project effort that was underway at Palmer Divide Vineyards. The effort had been scoped out, and more detailed solution requirements were being developed. The key stakeholders and team members disagreed about whether the project should build a new software application using existing technology or purchase a customizable software package containing the capabilities the organization needed. Everyone was concerned about making sure that the new system accommodated the alcoholic beverage licensing requirements.

Taylor, the IT Director, was facilitating a meeting where people could not agree on a course of action. Prior to developing the detailed solution requirements, she felt that a decision needed to be made about the project approach. The requirements that the group would build for a vendor selection effort were significantly different from the more technical requirements they would write if the development work was to be done by the internal IT team.

Luckily, Taylor was prepared for this meeting and brought some additional research data for the group to review. A recent issue of *American Vineyard Magazine* contained a study that evaluated a number of software applications targeting operations for smaller, regional vineyards. Among the evaluation criterion for these packages was the requirement for meeting alcoholic beverage licensing requirements. As the group reviewed this information relative to the new capabilities already agreed upon for the new system, they quickly discovered that purchasing a package would provide them with more capabilities than they were looking for at a higher cost than they had been planning to pay.

Using their own research and the software study, the group was able to put together a business case and impact analysis for the two options for review and selection by the senior management team and the vineyard owners. The industry knowledge was invaluable in preparing their business case without taking the time to reinvent the wheel and research each vendor product in detail.

The Organizational Process Assets you use during your business analysis work might include industry focused resource and process documents, standard processes, methodologies, and information pertaining to any regulatory environment where work is done. Possessing some basic knowledge of the industry where you do business adds great context to your project efforts. Industry and business knowledge should be supplemented by organization knowledge. Let's have a look at that subject right now.

Organization Knowledge

Understanding your organization and how things get done enables you to get your own work done and make good decisions within that organization. Your organization provides the primary context for your work efforts. This definition of organization includes the entire business architecture: business models, organizational structure, business unit relationships, and your key project stakeholders.

Organization knowledge includes recognizing the informal lines of communication, authority, and internal politics that are in play relative to your project. It is very important that you speak the organizational language, using the right terminology or jargon during your work efforts. Organization, industry, and business knowledge should be supplemented by more technical solution knowledge as well. Let's get just a little bit technical for the next area.

Solution Knowledge

Experienced business analysts are familiar with existing solutions and their capabilities within the organization. This allows them to effectively identify, assess, and implement changes to those solutions. These changes can range from simple alterations to complex replacement projects. Your solution knowledge often reduces the time you spend developing project requirements or assisting with solution design activities on your project. This can lead to reduced implementation time and/or cost on a project.

That sums up the key knowledge required of effective business analysts. This is a lot of information about your business principles, business practices, industry, organization, and existing solutions. As previously mentioned, you don't have to be an expert in everything, but a little knowledge in each of these areas can be of great assistance on your projects. Let's move on and look at your knowledge and skills when using software applications and tools in your role as a business analyst.

Software Applications

Software applications are typically used by business analysts to develop and manage requirements. This can range from using a word processor to document project scope to using a requirements management tool to developing detailed user and system requirements. Although using a requirements management tool is not a required skill, the ability to master and apply requirements management, word processing, and spreadsheet tools are considered desirable traits in experienced business analysts.

You need proficiency in two types of software applications: general purpose and specialized. Table 8.1 defines and summarizes each of these types.

TABLE 8.1   Software Applications

Type	Definition	Examples
General purpose software applications	Office productivity tools used to store, capture, and distribute information	Word processing Spreadsheets Presentation software tools Document repositories Wikis Discussion forums Email and instant messaging
Specialized software applications	Requirements development tools used to develop, validate, and implement formal models, and build/manage requirements documentation	Diagramming tools Modeling tools Requirements management tools Change control Traceability Configuration management

Diagramming tools are viewed as low-cost options that support the rapid drawing and documentation of graphical models by providing a set of templates for the notation being used. In contrast, modeling tools tend to be more of a medium- to high-cost tool. They convert graphical models into an executable form either by using a proprietary engine or by generating actual application code.

While proficiency with software applications is appreciated on your projects, proficiency in many forms of communication is even more crucial to your project's success. Let's look at the communication skills that effective business analysts bring to their projects.

Communication Skills

A major reason for project failures is poor communication. Business analysts must have excellent communication skills in order to develop project requirements that correctly and completely state what the new solution will do for its users and the business. Communication has several dimensions that are addressed by the *BABOK® Guide*:

- Oral communications
- Teaching
- Written communications

Let's dig a little deeper into each of these areas, starting with your proficiency in communicating verbally.

Oral Communications

Experienced business analysts are experts at making themselves understood. One way to do this is by verbal communications. This means that you transfer ideas or information verbally to your target audience. This exchange of information between a sender and receiver involves more than just speaking the words. Your words are accompanied by emotional and other nonverbal cues that can add positive reinforcement to what is being said.

Lines of Communication

Communication becomes more complex as the number of people involved increases. Network models are used to explain the complexity of communications. They consist of nodes with lines between the nodes indicating communication. You need to be able to calculate the lines of communication in a network as part of your preparations for taking your certification exam.

The calculation for the number of lines of communication in a network is

$(n \times (n-1))$ divided by 2,

where n = the number of people or nodes in the network. So for a project network containing five stakeholders, the number of lines of communication = (5 × 4)/2 = 20/2 = 10.

The next illustration graphically depicts these 10 lines of communication between the five nodes in the network.

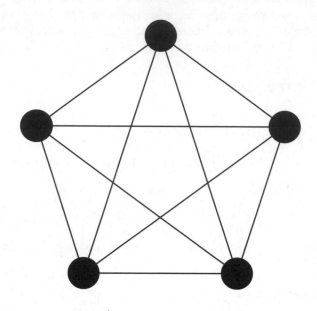

Another aspect of effective oral communication is your ability to use your active listening skills. Active listeners stay focused on the speaker and are not distracted from what is being said. Your ability to maintain your focus on the speaker allows you to understand, interpret, and evaluate what is being said in a calm, systematic fashion. Often, active listeners paraphrase statements back to the speaker to ensure that the listener understands what is being said.

In addition to active listening, good communicators are able to facilitate meetings and deliver presentations and briefings. Oral communication is also used when you are sharing your knowledge and teaching others about your project. Let's move on and talk a little bit about the teaching skills found in effective business analysts.

Teaching

Teaching is closely related to communicating with your project stakeholders. You may find yourself operating in a teaching mode as you communicate project issues and requirements to your stakeholders, making sure they are understood and agreed upon. Many times, business analysts find themselves facilitating the learning experiences of their project stakeholders, teaching them about the new capabilities, describing a new solution, or leading a meeting to determine what a set of requirements might be.

Effective teachers are aware of the different learning styles found in their students and alter their teaching approach to accommodate those preferences. There is also a feedback loop in teaching, very much like the sender-receiver model of effective communications. It isn't enough to deliver your information to the stakeholders. For example, you might find yourself teaching stakeholders about a new graphical modeling technique. Whenever you are teaching, you must confirm that your audience has learned what was needed and can apply what they have learned.

You typically encounter three types of learners. They include *visual learners* who learn best by seeing something done. Next up are the *auditory learners* who learn best by hearing or reading things. *Kinesthetic (tactile) learners* are those who learn best by doing something for themselves. Your training materials can be designed to facilitate learning for all three types of learners.

The need to apply effective communication and teaching skills is not limited to times when you are talking to people. There is a strong written component, as well. Let's look at that now.

Written Communications

As a business analyst, you will find yourself spending much time documenting and recording your elicitation results, project requirements, and other relevant information. This work takes place across the project life cycle. If you are not a good technical and business writer, you will need to master those skills quickly. You must be able to write effectively for different contexts and audiences on your projects. The *BABOK® Guide* recommends that effective business analysts possess the following written communications attributes:

- Broad vocabulary
- Strong grasp of grammar and style
- Understanding of idioms and terms

Exam Spotlight

Be sure you are comfortable explaining the basics of information exchange using the sender-receiver model. This model governs both written and oral communications on your projects. Senders package or encode messages that are sent to the receivers. The receivers then unpack or decode the messages. Transmitting gets information from the sender to the receiver for both spoken and written forms of communication. Decoding of the received message is performed by the receiver. This is where the receiver converts the message to a form that they understand.

Your communication skills are closely linked to your interaction skills. Effective business analysts play well with others. Let's move on and explore those interaction skills in greater detail.

Interaction Skills

Strong business analysts tend to be team players. In large part, this is due to their ability to interact and work well with other members of the team. Leadership and facilitation skills play a key part in defining and agreeing to a solution to a business problem or need. The *BABOK® Guide* breaks the necessary interaction skills into several components:

- Facilitation and negotiation
- Leadership and influencing
- Teamwork

Let's look closer at each of these components, starting with your facilitation and negotiation skills.

Facilitation and Negotiation

Strong facilitation skills serve multiple purposes for business analysts. You may find yourself facilitating many different types of interactions between stakeholders, such as resolving disagreements regarding the priority and nature of requirements during requirements development. You will moderate any number of group discussions and meetings, making sure that all participants get to share their views and opinions on the topics being discussed. Good facilitators must ensure that there is recognition and appreciation of differing viewpoints across the project life cycle.

Negotiation is often a facet of facilitation. People don't always agree on things, and that needs to be worked out. Effective negotiators are able to identify the underlying interests of involved parties, distinguish those interests from their stated positions, and ultimately identify solutions that satisfy the underlying interests while still keeping the business need and objectives in mind.

Effective facilitation and negotiation on your projects must be accompanied by leadership and influencing skills. Let's look at this next component of interaction skills required for a good business analyst.

Leadership and Influencing

Managing is primarily concerned with consistently producing the key results expected by your stakeholders. Good leaders and good managers are not necessarily the same thing. Leadership is not quite so tangible. It establishes the vision and direction to a desired future state and enables people to work together to get to that future state. Good leaders motivate and align people to work toward a vision. They communicate that vision through their own words and deeds.

You will fill many formal and informal leadership roles as a business analyst. You are responsible for developing requirements and getting your project stakeholders on board with the vision for a desired future state—the new solution and its capabilities. You are an agent of change, since your new solution will change the way people do their jobs.

Your leadership skills are directly related to your ability to influence people in order to get things done. You must have a solid understanding of the formal and informal organizational structure where you are working. You must be able to apply the mechanics of *power* and politics to get things done, even when you have no formal power in a given situation.

Power is the potential ability to influence behavior and change the course of events. Power allows you to overcome resistance and get people to do what they would not do otherwise. In comparison, politics is all about getting collective action from people who may have different interests. Sometimes, you will find yourself using conflict and disorder creatively in order to get things accomplished in your organization.

There are five levels of power. Of these levels, punishment power is the least desirable technique for obvious reasons. Although the *BABOK Guide* does not discuss the levels of power directly, they have been known to show up in certification exam questions. Here they are for your review as part of your study preparations.

Reward Power   Reward power allows you to provide people with incentives or bonuses in order to get things done. Rewards don't have to be money. They can be comp time for working over a weekend or movie tickets for a team member and their family.

Punishment Power   Punishment power is not a recommended type of power for collaborative team environments. Punishment power involves threatening people with negative consequences (penalties) if they do not do as you say.

Expert Power   Expert power allows you to influence others based on your knowledge or abilities. In addition to your role as a business analyst, you might also be a specialist or Subject Matter Expert (SME) in a particular industry area.

Legitimate Power   Legitimate power is associated with the formal job position that you occupy and should be exercised carefully. You can always demand that things be done based on your power of position. However, it is better to collaborate with your team members and reach consensus about how everyone will perform their work.

Referent Power   Referent power is a positive source of power for you. It is given to you by your subordinates based on their respect and regard for you. This earned power can be used to influence and motivate your team members to perform at a high level.

In addition to your leadership and influencing skills, you must be able to work well in a team environment. Let's talk a bit more about your essential teamwork skills.

Teamwork

Business analysts must work closely with other project team members to effectively define and implement new solutions. You have a role in creating the team environment, as well as contributing to that environment where everyone shares the ownership of the team goals for the project. Experienced business analysts are quite good at building effective working relationships with others in order to enhance the quality of team communications and reduce conflicts.

Modeling Team Development

The *Tuckman Model of Team Development* breaks team development into four or five stages. Each stage has distinct characteristics. Be sure you are familiar with this model and its stages for your certification exam.

Forming   Forming is the earliest stage of team development where the team members meet and are introduced to one another and to the project. Team members working together in this phase tend to exhibit reserved and more formal behavior to one another.

Storming   This stage is characterized by confrontations as team members vie for position and control within the group. Everyone is jockeying for status within the group and things can be a bit chaotic.

Norming   This is the stage where team members have adjusted to one another. They can now focus on project issues and objectives. There is cooperation and collaboration between folks on the team and work is getting done.

Performing   In this stage of team development, the planets are in alignment and the team members work effectively and productively together. The group shares a high level of trust and achievement.

Adjourning or Mourning   Some sources added a fifth stage of this model where the team is broken apart as work is completed and folks move on to their next project effort.

Another key aspect of teamwork is the ability to motivate yourself and other members of the team. You will often find yourself using your motivation skills to energize your fellow team members and project stakeholders in order to achieve a high level of performance and to overcome any barriers to change.

There are several common motivational theories that you, as a business analyst, might bring into play. The *BABOK® Guide* does not address them in detail, but they are known to occur occasionally in a question or two on your certification exam. They are listed here for your review.

Achievement Theory   People are motivated by a need for achievement, power, and affiliation. Teams populated by achievement-motivated team members are a dream come true. Many folks work hard and motivate themselves because it is important to them that they do a good job. Other folks may be motivated by more tangible things, like compensation, bonuses, and possibilities of advancement.

Frederic Herzberg's Motivational-Hygiene Theory   Herzberg's theory of motivation is fascinating. There are two sides to the theory. The first side contains the hygiene factors. Hygiene factors are things that prevent people from becoming dissatisfied (such as pay, benefits, work conditions, and working relationships). The funny thing about these factors is that in and of themselves they don't motivate people. The second side contains the motivation factors. These factors lead to work satisfaction and motivation and are quite different from the hygiene factors. They include opportunities for advancement, learning, challenges, and the work itself.

Expectancy Theory   Expectancy theory is a little bit like the carrot and the stick—well, at least the carrot portion of the situation. The basis of this theory is that expecting a positive outcome creates motivation in people. This is because the expectancy and the likelihood of a reward are linked to people's behavior. The rewards don't have to be tangible things, such as money. They can be less tangible things, such as recognition for a job well done.

Theory X and Theory Y   This motivation theory has been around for quite some time. Theory X tells us that people are inherently lazy and need to be threatened in order to be motivated. In contrast, Theory Y states that people seek out responsibility and respond to proper expectations in the workplace. Theory Y is more commonly found in today's workplace, especially among knowledge workers.

Contingency Theory   Contingency theory puts forth that the effectiveness of a leader is dependent on the characteristics of that leader, the situation they find themselves in, and the group in which they are a part. There is no one ideal leader, so your management style and your methods to motivate your team should be appropriate to the situation that is at hand. This is a more situational approach to motivating people.

Working in teams also requires you to manage and address conflict. The basic types of conflict are emotional and cognitive. Emotional conflict stems from personal interactions, while cognitive conflicts are based on disagreements on matters of substantive value or impact on the project or organization. Resolution of cognitive conflict requires the team to focus on examining the premises, assumptions, observations, and expectations of the team members. Working through such problems can have the beneficial effect of strengthening the foundation of the analysis and the solution. Many conflict situations encompass both emotional and cognitive elements.

 Real World Scenario

Increasing Your Space

Russ, a project manager, was walking down the office hallway one day when he noticed something odd. One of the cube walls situated between the cubes of his project's top two systems architects had come loose from the floor. The wall had moved over into one person's cube and looked as though it would require a bit of repair. It was the end of a very busy day, so Russ made a mental note to follow up about the mysterious moving cube wall the next morning.

The next morning, Russ was walking by with his coffee and he noticed that the traveling cube wall had moved yet again. Today, the wall was occupying space in the other team member's cube. Shaking his head, Russ decided to do a little investigating right after the morning project status meeting.

Russ didn't have to wait very long after the meeting to discover what was happening with the moving cube wall. As he exited the meeting and turned down the hallway, he was treated to a full exhibition of how the cube wall was moving back and forth. The systems architect in the space-limited cube was sitting on the floor, pushing the cube wall back into the other team member's cube with his feet.

"How interesting," Russ thought. "I wonder what happens next."

What happened over the next few days was a conflict in motion. Each team member took turns shoving the cube wall into his teammate's space. After observing the phenomenon, Russ decided to intervene. Calling both team members into his office, he asked them what was up with the cube wall.

"He unbolted it and started this," complained one team member. "It was right after the project approach meeting where my approach to solution technology and infrastructure was selected as the solution approach for the project."

"My approach was the better one," replied the other team member. "Yours was chosen because you have worked here longer, not because it had any technical merit."

They continued to bicker for a short time, until Russ interrupted them.

"Since you two are obviously in need of some togetherness," Russ said, "Let me tell you what we are going to do. The moving cube wall will be removed, and the two of you can share the office space for a time to see if you can work out your differences."

And that's exactly what happened. Russ, knowing the men's fast friendship, confronted the problem and offered up a compromise solution where each team member gave up their private space for a time. The good news is that after a few days, the team members' differences were resolved, and they asked Russ to put their cubes back the way they were. The missing cube wall was reinstalled (and bolted down with a few extra bolts) the following week.

Although it was risky to exercise a mild form of punishment power by combining the cubes, Russ used the situation as an opportunity to stress that the team members needed to work together. The underlying problem was a battle of technical egos, and moving the wall was a convenient way for each team member to be (at least temporarily) the king of the hill with the larger cube. The two team members involved were actually good friends. Moving the cube wall had started out as a joke and somehow escalated into a larger conflict that was beginning to polarize the remaining team members by implying that they should take sides.

Luckily, there was more than enough technical work to go around on this project. The friendship was stronger than the conflict between the two architects. Everyone discovered that the project results and the general work environment were much better when these two systems architects were pulling in tandem instead of pulling against one another. Russ took a calculated risk with this approach, and he solved his problem.

There are a number of conflict resolution techniques you may choose to apply in a given situation. Be sure you are familiar with them as you may see them mentioned on your certification exam even though they are not specifically outlined in the *BABOK® Guide*. Table 8.2 contains a summary of these techniques and their outcomes for you to use in your studies.

TABLE 8.2 Summary of Conflict Resolution Techniques

Technique	Outcome	Description
Forcing	Win–Lose	People often force others in order to resolve conflicts. They can do this if they have power and demand a particular outcome.
Smoothing	Lose–Lose	This technique results in a temporary reduction in the perceived severity of a conflict but provides no permanent solution.
Compromise	Lose–Lose	Each party reluctantly complies and gives up something to reach a solution. Can lead to a permanent solution if commitments are kept even, although all parties lose something in this situation.
Confrontation	Win–Win	Addressing the conflict using problem-solving methods where an analysis of facts leads to the best solution that becomes a permanent solution.
Withdrawal	Lose–Lose	This occurs when one party refuses to even discuss the conflict. This approach never addresses or resolves the conflict.

You will often find yourself resolving interpersonal conflicts by using your effective interpersonal negotiation skills. Learning to manage conflict is integral to a high-performance team. It is important to recognize that not all conflicts can be resolved. Effective business analysts assess and establish their own conflict management approach and acquire skills in conflict resolution techniques and conflict modes.

Confronting a problem is considered to be the best method for conflict resolution with the highest likelihood of permanent solution. This involves laying the problem and any related information out on the table, getting the involved parties to discuss what is going on, and reaching a resolution.

That wraps up your review of the underlying competencies required for an effective business analyst. This is certainly a significant list of knowledge and skills for any business analyst to master. Remember not to try to excel in all areas all at once. Work to your strengths and slowly improve your weak areas over time. This is one situation where practice certainly strives to create perfection.

How This Applies to Your Projects

Professional detachment is another essential skill for business analysts. Your ability to remain in control of yourself will be tested regularly when people become angry or frustrated when the way things are done changes, when people don't get their way, or when your fellow team members and stakeholders have straightforward personality clashes. Being self-aware and regulating your own emotional responses in such situations will serve you well.

Mastering your professional detachment skills provides you with a new attitude toward what happens on your projects regardless of the emotional intensity. Professional detachment is about looking at the events from a distance without being too emotionally involved or taking what happens on your projects personally. Professional detachment must be nurtured to prevent embarrassment and steer you away from making uncalculated actions and reactions. People usually regret being provoked into instant emotional reactions, because those reactions must be followed by damage control. Analysts prefer to handle conflict professionally and avoid the need for the damage control.

Tolerance for others and their verbal or physical actions is the key to your own professionalism. Observe yourself and learn what your triggers are. Discover your preferred approaches to managing conflicts. Learn to be a stronger, more capable facilitator. Practice your presentation skills and remember how your mother always said to count to ten before you say anything when you are angry or irritated.

 Real World Scenario

Phil's Checklist: Dealing with the People on Your Projects

Phil, a fellow business analyst, offers up the following list of techniques that he practices faithfully and successfully. He recently presented it at a team meeting kicking off the requirements development effort for a major IT project, and everyone found his practical advice to be quite useful. You will probably like Phil's list, too.

Compartmentalize.   Focus on one task at a time. Don't let everything pile on you all at once. You don't want your mind to be thinking about what you just did or what you're going to do, only on what's in front of you.

Be proactive.   Focus on what needs to be done, and then do it. Action creates positive energy; inactivity leads to frustration. If you don't know what to do, figure it out. And don't forget that you have a business analysis team to help you figure things out.

Have real conversations.   When you talk to your clients or your team, focus on what needs to be done, not on emotions. Don't buy into your stakeholder's emotions. Rather, lead them to focus on what can be done to solve the problem or resolve an issue.

Focus on what to do next. There's nothing you can do about the past except learn from it. Lessons learned are great when applied to future situations. You never stop learning lessons when dealing with people on your projects. And remember, hindsight is always 20/20.

Build a Plan B. To become detached from the outcome, have a contingency plan or a Plan B for certain situations on your projects. Then, you don't have to worry so much about what is happening now, because you aren't as dependent on the outcome. You have a contingency plan to implement if things go astray.

It is about the business, not about you. Do not internalize the behavior and emotions of your stakeholders or business analysis team. Acknowledge their feelings, let them know that you understand, and then use your professional detachment to help them become more detached themselves so they can get beyond their emotions and make rational decisions.

Objectively assess your performance. Get a grip and resist the impulse to get down on yourself. At least half of your job is looking for desired future states and new solutions. No one's crystal ball ever operates at 100 percent.

Summary

The skills and knowledge found in the Underlying Competencies knowledge area form the basis for your work activities and people interactions on your projects. It is difficult to work on a project without possessing a core set of skills, knowledge, and capabilities that enhance how you perform your tasks and interact with the people around you on a daily basis.

The underlying competencies enable you to do your work effectively in a collaborative business environment. The skills, knowledge, and behaviors that you bring to your projects are a significant factor in your ultimate success at defining the right requirements and deploying a new solution that meets everyone's needs and expectations.

The *BABOK® Guide* recommends that you apply a subset of the underlying competencies to every business analysis task and technique that gets done on your projects. You don't need to be an expert in every skill or possess knowledge in every aspect of the business, but most experienced business analysts have a core set of skills and behaviors that serve them well as they get the job done.

Exam Essentials

Be able to list and describe the high-level skills, knowledge, and behaviors found in the Underlying Competencies knowledge area. You will see questions about high-level skills, knowledge, and behaviors found in the Underlying Competencies knowledge area throughout your certification exam questions in each of the other six knowledge areas.

You should memorize them and make sure you understand what they are all about. The six areas are

> Analytical thinking and problem-solving skills
>
> Behavioral characteristics
>
> Business knowledge
>
> Software knowledge
>
> Interaction skills
>
> Communication skills

Be able to apply the additional skills and knowledge found in this chapter that are not specifically contained in the *BABOK® Guide*.   Several topics contained in this chapter provide additional details to the contents of the *BABOK® Guide*. These topics are known to show up in certification exam questions, and they are worth learning as part of your exam preparation activities. They include:

> Lines of communication
>
> Tuckman Model of team development
>
> Conflict-resolution techniques
>
> Motivational theories
>
> The five levels of power

Be able to discuss the three types of learners.   As a teacher, you will typically encounter three types of learners. They include visual learners who learn best by seeing something done. Next up are the auditory learners who learn best by hearing or reading things. Kinesthetic or tactile learners are those who learn best by doing something themselves.

Be able to compare business principles and business practices.   Business principles are defined as the characteristics common to organizations of similar purpose and structure, such as human resources, finance, and information technology functions. Business practices or processes vary based on what an organization does and the size of that organization.

Be able to define general-purpose software applications and specialized software applications.   General-purpose software applications are office productivity tools that are used to store, capture, and distribute information. Specialized software applications consist of more sophisticated requirements development tools that are used to develop, validate, and implement formal models and build/manage requirements documentation.

Be able to break down each of the high-level areas of underlying competencies into their pieces and parts.   Your exam questions on the underlying competencies may drill down into the more detailed pieces and parts of each competency. Make sure you are familiar with each of them. Each area is decomposed for you here:

Analytical thinking and problem-solving skills consist of creative thinking, decision making, learning, problem solving, and systems thinking.

Behavioral characteristics include ethics, trustworthiness, and personal organization.

Business knowledge consists of business principles and practices, industry knowledge, organization knowledge, and solution knowledge.

Software knowledge is composed of general purpose and specialized software applications.

Interaction skills consist of facilitation and negotiation, leadership and influencing, and teamwork.

Communication skills are composed of oral communications, teaching, and written communications.

Key Terms

You have just finished stepping through the contents of the Underlying Competencies knowledge area from the *BABOK® Guide*. The skills and information found in this chapter are used by the tasks in the other six knowledge areas; they are the foundation that allows you to do your job wisely and well.

Use the skills and information found in this chapter as the basis for evaluating and improving your underlying competencies in the business analysis realm. You will need to know this knowledge area in order to be successful on the CBAP® or CCBA™ exams. Although there are no specific questions on this specific knowledge area, questions about the underlying competencies can be found throughout your exam as part of the other six task-and-technique-focused knowledge areas. The underlying competencies include:

- Analytical thinking and problem-solving skills
- Behavioral characteristics
- Business knowledge
- Software knowledge
- Interaction skills
- Communication skills

A number of new key words in Chapter 8 are related to the underlying competencies of effective business analysts. Here is a list of some of the key terms that you encountered in this chapter:

alternatives identification	power
auditory learners	problem definition
business practices	solution knowledge
business principles	sunk cost fallacy
decision making	systems thinking
kinesthetic (tactile) learners	Tuckman Model
organization knowledge	underlying competencies
politics	visual learners

Review Questions

1. Business _____ are those characteristics that are common to all organizations with a similar purpose and structure, whether or not they are in the same industry.

   A. Processes

   B. Principles

   C. Practices

   D. Rules

2. You have strong political ties with your stakeholders from previous work in the organization, enabling you to get things done. Which underlying competency will these previous relationships enhance most for your current assignment?

   A. Facilitation

   B. Negotiation

   C. Leadership

   D. Influencing

3. You understand the existing business models, structure, business unit relationships, and people. This is an example of what type of knowledge?

   A. Organization

   B. Industry

   C. Business

   D. Strategic

4. You are deciding between three solution options early in the project life cycle. Your stakeholders have trouble visualizing what these solutions contain without graphical models to support the discussions. What type of learner are they?

   A. Kinesthetic

   B. Auditory

   C. Tactile

   D. Visual

5. What four stages of team development (in the order they are experienced) would you expect your new business analysis team to go through?

   A. Collecting, Understanding, Realization, Working

   B. Norming, Storming, Forming, Performing

   C. Forming, Storming, Norming, Performing

   D. Forming, Norming, Storming, Performing

6. Confrontation as a method of conflict resolution can be referred to as a:

   A. Win-Win

   B. Win-Lose

   C. Lose-lose

   D. Lose-Win

7. The process of gaining knowledge or skills is also known as:

   A. Learning

   B. Synthesis

   C. Experience

   D. Feedback

8. You are able to effectively manage your time by clearly defining goals and expectations and prioritizing your work efforts. These abilities illustrate your skills in:

   A. Information retrieval

   B. Politics and power

   C. Time management

   D. Analytical thinking

9. You are a business analyst measuring alternatives against objectives and identifying tradeoffs to determine which possible solution is best. You are most likely engaged in what activity?

   A. Problem solving

   B. Systems thinking

   C. Creative thinking

   D. Decision making

10. Your team needs a low-cost tool that supports rapid drawing and documentation of models. What type of tool should they choose?

    A. Requirements tool

    B. Modeling tool

    C. Diagramming tool

    D. Presentation tool

11. Knowledge management and collaboration tools that may be used to capture and distribute knowledge throughout an organization include:

    A. Discussion forums, word processors, and spreadsheets

    B. Document repositories, wikis, and discussion forums

    C. Presentation software, wikis, and other web-based tools

    D. Email, instant messaging, and document repositories

12. You are focusing the business analysis team on examining the premises, assumptions, observations, and expectations of its team members. What type of conflicts are you most likely addressing?

- **A.** Interaction
- **B.** Emotional
- **C.** Cognitive
- **D.** External

13. You are developing a vision of a desired future state toward which people can be motivated to work. After it is developed, you will encourage people to work toward that future state. What business analysis competency are you exhibiting?

- **A.** Influencing
- **B.** Leadership
- **C.** Interaction
- **D.** Trustworthiness

14. The business analysis team has been working hard to meet tight deadlines on their project. The project manager offers them a bonus and some time off if they can meet their deadlines. Which motivational theory best describes what the project manager just did?

- **A.** Expectancy theory
- **B.** Herzberg's hygiene theory
- **C.** Achievement theory
- **D.** Maslow's hierarchy of needs

15. Which of the following capabilities is not part of your analytical thinking and problem-solving skills?

- **A.** Decision making
- **B.** Teaching
- **C.** Systems thinking
- **D.** Learning

16. Effective problem solving consists of what three elements?

- **A.** Alternative identification, facilitated discussion, and decision making
- **B.** Problem definition, creative thinking, and decision making
- **C.** Creative thinking, systems thinking, and problem definition
- **D.** Problem definition, alternatives identification, and decision making

17. During an elicitation interview, you find yourself paraphrasing statements back to the speaker to reinforce that you understand what is being said. What skill are you applying?

    A. Facilitation

    B. Influencing

    C. Active listening

    D. Learning

18. Your boss tells you that you should motivate your people by threatening them with additional weekend work if project deadlines are not met. What motivation theory is being suggested to you?

    A. Achievement

    B. Theory X

    C. Theory Y

    D. Expectancy

19. What method of conflict resolution offers the highest likelihood of reaching a permanent solution?

    A. Confrontation

    B. Smoothing

    C. Compromise

    D. Withdrawal

20. The business analysis team members are jockeying for status within the group. This is a symptom found in which stage of team development according to the Tuckman Model?

    A. Performing

    B. Forming

    C. Storming

    D. Norming

Answers to Review Questions

1. B. Business principles are those characteristics that are common to all organizations with a similar purpose and structure, whether or not they are in the same industry. Examples include organizational functions such as HR and finance.

2. D. Influence skills enable you to get things done.

3. A. Organization knowledge is the understanding of the business architecture of an organization, including business models, organizational structure, business unit relationships, and people in key stakeholder positions.

4. D. Visual learners learn from seeing something, such as a graphical model of a business process or a solution.

5. C. These are Tuckman's four stages of group development in the order they occur. You will not find this specific information in the standard. Several business analysis tasks require you to manage teams, and this is a well-known model for group development.

6. A. Confrontation is considered to be the best method for conflict resolution with the highest likelihood of reaching a permanent solution. It involves addressing the conflict using a problem-solving method by analyzing the facts. You will not find this specific information in the standard.

7. A. The process of gaining knowledge or skills is also known as learning.

8. C. Personal organization skills assist you in effectively managing tasks and information. One measure of personal organization is effective time management, which requires prioritization, eliminating procrastination, and clarifying goals and objectives.

9. A. Problem solving involves measuring alternatives against objectives and identifying tradeoffs to determine which possible solution is best. Evaluating tradeoffs and measurements is part of decision making.

10. C. Diagramming tools support rapid drawing and documentation of a model by providing a set of templates for a particular notation, and they are generally low cost and easy-to-use. The resulting diagrams can often be integrated into a word-processing document.

11. B. Knowledge management and collaboration tools that may be used to capture and distribute knowledge throughout an organization include document repositories that link with office productivity software, wikis allowing easy creation and linking of web pages, discussion forums, or other web-based tools.

12. C. Cognitive conflicts are based on disagreements on matters of substantive value or impact on the project or organization. Resolution of cognitive conflict requires the team to focus on examining the premises, assumptions, observations, and expectations of the team members.

13. B. Effective leadership requires that a business analyst be able to develop a vision of a desired future state that people can be motivated to work toward and the interpersonal skills needed to encourage them to do so.

14. A. Expectancy theory links the expectancy and likelihood of a reward to behavior.

15. B. Analytical thinking and problem-solving skills are divided into five more detailed areas: creative thinking, decision making, learning, problem solving, and systems thinking.

16. D. Effective problem solving is a combination of problem definition, alternatives identification, and decision making.

17. C. One aspect of effective oral communications is your ability to use your active listening skills. Active listeners maintain a focus on the speaker in order to understand, interpret, and evaluate what is being said in a calm, systematic fashion. Often, active listeners paraphrase statements back to the speaker to ensure that the listener understands what is being said.

18. B. Theory X says people are inherently lazy and need to be threatened in order to be motivated. In contrast, Theory Y states that people seek out responsibility and respond to proper expectations in the workplace.

19. A. Confronting a problem is considered to be the best method for conflict resolution with the highest likelihood of permanent solution. This involves laying the problem and any related information out on the table and getting the involved parties to discuss what is going on and reach a resolution.

20. C. The storming stage of the Tuckman Model is characterized by confrontations as team members vie for position and control within the group. Everyone is jockeying for status within the group and things can be a bit chaotic.

Appendix

A

Advice on Completing Your Exam Application

TOPICS COVERED IN THIS APPENDIX

- ✓ Discuss experience requirements for the CBAP® and CCBA™ exams.

- ✓ Calculate your hours of business analysis experience.

- ✓ Review additional exam eligibility requirements.

- ✓ Navigate the steps of the exam application process.

This appendix helps you understand the application requirements for the Certified Business Analysis Professional (CBAP®) or Certification of Competency in Business Analysis™ (CCBA™) credentials. It provides suggestions for completing your application correctly to minimize the chances of errors and application approval delays.

There are specific experience and eligibility requirements that will be used to evaluate your fitness for taking the CBAP® or CCBA™ exams. Both certifications require work experience as a business analyst. Both certifications ask you to meet or exceed the same non-work-related requirements, such as education and professional development. In this section, you will look at the unique experience requirements for each exam and then review the common set of four eligibility requirements that apply for both exams.

CBAP® Experience Requirements

The CBAP® designation is available to more-experienced business analysts. Applicants who want to take the CBAP® certification exam must meet specific experience and education requirements. During the application process, you must demonstrate your competencies across the spectrum of business analysis knowledge and skills. After your application has been reviewed and accepted, you will be eligible to take and pass your certification exam. Table A.1 summarizes the experience-specific requirements for you.

TABLE A.1 Experience Requirements for the CBAP® Certification Exam

Requirement	Description
Work Experience	Minimum of 7,500 hours of business analysis work experience aligned with the *BABOK® Guide* in the last 10 years
Knowledge Areas	Minimum of 900 hours of business analysis work each in at least four of the six knowledge areas

Let's take a closer look at the experience requirements needed to qualify for taking the CBAP® exam.

Work Experience   You must possess a minimum of 7,500 hours of business analysis work experience aligned with the *BABOK® Guide* in the last 10 years of your work life. The timeframe is measured backward from the date of your application. You can calculate that 7,500 hours of work equals about five full years of business analysis work experience during that 10-year period, or doing business analysis stuff about half of the time.

The work experience can be you directly performing the business analysis tasks (hands on) or time you spent coaching or mentoring others in performing those tasks. Conducting business analysis training and performing project management activities on your projects are not acceptable experiences to include in your application. Be very careful to select and provide experiences in your application that are aligned with the *BABOK® Guide* and that are specific business analysis tasks.

Knowledge Areas   You must demonstrate business analysis experience and expertise in four of the six knowledge areas. You must show a minimum of 900 hours of business analysis experience and expertise in each knowledge area you choose to document. This means that you engaged in tasks specifically related to the *BABOK® Guide* knowledge areas, so make sure that you review them carefully relative to the work you have performed. The 900 hours across each of four knowledge areas make up 3,600 hours of your business analysis experience.

This is a minimum requirement; it is just fine if you have experience across all six of the knowledge areas. Actually, the more experience you document in your application, the better off you will be. This approach provides a buffer in case some of your experience is disqualified during your application's review cycle, so your application process won't be jeopardized.

If the contents of your application do not support compliance with both of the two experience requirements, your application will be declined. If you don't meet the experience requirements for the CBAP® certification, you might want to consider applying for the CCBA™ credential.

CCBA™ Experience Requirements

The CCBA™ designation is available to less-experienced business analysts. Although the experience requirements are less than those required for taking the CBAP® certification exam, they are reviewed and enforced with equal vigor. Applicants who want to take the CCBA™ certification exam must meet specific experience and education requirements. During the application process, you must demonstrate your competencies across the spectrum of business analysis knowledge and skills. After your application has been reviewed and accepted, you will then be eligible to take your certification exam. Table A.2 summarizes the exam eligibility requirements.

TABLE A.2   Experience Requirements for the CCBA™ Certification Exam

Requirement	Description
Work Experience	Minimum of 3,750 hours of business analysis work experience aligned with the *BABOK® Guide* in the last seven years
Knowledge Areas	Minimum of 900 hours of business analysis work each in two of the six knowledge areas or 500 hours each across four of the knowledge areas

Let's take a closer look at the work experience required to take the CCBA™ exam.

Work Experience   You must possess a minimum of 3,750 hours of business analysis work experience aligned with the *BABOK® Guide* in the last seven years of your work life. The timeframe is measured backward from your application date. Again, you can calculate that 3,750 hours of work equals about 2.5 full years of business analysis work experience during that seven-year period, or doing business analysis stuff close to one third of the time.

Your work experience can be you directly performing the business analysis tasks (hands on) or time you spent coaching or mentoring others in performing those tasks. Conducting business analysis training and performing project management activities on your projects are not acceptable experiences to include in your application. Be very careful to select and provide experiences in your application that are aligned with the *BABOK® Guide* and that are specific business analysis tasks.

Knowledge Areas   You must demonstrate a minimum of 900 hours of business analysis experience and expertise each in two of the six knowledge areas or 500 hours each in four of the six knowledge areas. This means that you engaged in tasks specifically related to the *BABOK® Guide* knowledge areas, so make sure that you review them carefully relative to the work you have performed. The 900 hours each across two knowledge areas makes up 1,800 hours of your business analysis experience, while the 500 hours each across four areas accounts for 2,000 hours of the required 3,750 hours.

These are minimum requirements; it is just fine if you have experience across all six of the knowledge areas. Actually, the more experience you document in your application, the better off you will be. This approach will provide a buffer in case some of your experience is disqualified during your application's review cycle, so your application process won't be jeopardized.

If the contents of your application do not comply with both of the two experience requirements, your application will be declined. In addition to the work experience requirements for taking either exam, you must meet some additional requirements to qualify to take either exam. Let's review those requirements now.

Calculate Your Experience Hours

The *BABOK® Guide* provides explicit instructions about how to calculate the required hours of business analysis work experience for your application. You should use your résumé as the basis for your listed projects, the business analysis activities you performed, and the time you spent doing them. However, you cannot submit your résumé to meet the experience requirement—you must parse through its contents in detail and provide the International Institute of Business Analysis (IIBA) with a detailed list of projects, work activities, and hours spent. One helpful suggestion is to build a spreadsheet to track everything by project, knowledge area, and time. Then you can use your spreadsheet summary to complete the experience section of your application.

As previously mentioned, you need to document a minimum of 7,500 experience hours for your CBAP® application and 3,750 hours for your CCBA™ application. These totals are the minimum experience requirements. It is a really good idea to document additional hours above the minimum requirement (if you have them). If the IIBA reviewers disapprove part of your experience hours, the additional hours can prevent the disapproval from impacting your application process.

You need to list your projects in chronological order, starting with the most recent project you worked on or are working on as of your application date and then working backward. If you performed business analysis activities on a bunch of small projects during any particular year, combine them into one project and make sure to point out that you did this in the description of the large project that encompassed the smaller ones.

If you are completing an online application, you will be able to select from a set of business analysis tasks that you performed to achieve the stated number of work hours. Read the tasks you are selecting from carefully. Do not select tasks from the lists that are project management tasks or general management work. Everything you enter for work experience must be business analysis work and align with the contents of version 2 of the *BABOK® Guide* (the current version on which you will be tested). If you select tasks that are not business analysis tasks within the scope of the *BABOK® Guide,* those tasks and their associated hours will be deducted from your total hours.

CBAP® applicants must also meet the minimum requirement of 900 experience hours each in four of the six knowledge areas. CCBA™ applicants have a lesser experience requirement, and they can slice and dice their business analysis experience in one of two ways, showing either:

- A minimum of 900 hours of business analysis work each in two of the six knowledge areas
- A minimum of 500 hours of business analysis work each in four of the six knowledge areas

For each project, from the list of tasks in the table, check off the tasks you have completed that are aligned with the *BABOK® Guide* v2.0. Do this for each of the knowledge areas. You can select a task when you have either performed the task yourself or coached/mentored another business analyst in performing the task. For each knowledge area, indicate the percentage of the total business analysis hours you spent on the tasks you selected. The percentages across all of the knowledge areas must total 100 within a project.

Several steps need to be taken to calculate your experience hours for each of your documented projects and each knowledge area. For each knowledge area specified for a particular project, the percentage of time you say that you spent on that knowledge area is multiplied by the total business analysis hours you entered for the project. Likewise, the percentage of invalid experience you selected from the list of tasks for your project is calculated and deducted. The tasks you select from are provided by the IIBA for you in your application form.

Once the experience hours for each knowledge area are calculated for each project, they are summarized in two ways:

- By knowledge area across all of your projects to see if you meet the minimum knowledge area requirements for the exam
- Total hours across all projects to see if you meet the experience minimum requirement to take the exam

Both the total experience hours and the knowledge area experience hours must be met for your application to be considered. If one or both of these requirements falls short, your application will be declined. You will not be allowed to apply again for another three months.

Additional Exam Eligibility Requirements

In order to apply for and be approved to take either the CBAP® or CCBA™ certification exams, applicants must meet four additional requirements relating to education, professional development, professional references, and code of conduct. Table A.3 contains a summary of these additional requirements.

TABLE A.3   Additional Exam Eligibility Requirements

Requirement	Description
Education	A high school or equivalent level of education
Professional Development	Minimum of 21 hours of professional development, such as attending a training course, in the past four years
References	Two references from a career manager, client (internal or external), or a CBAP® recipient
Code of Conduct	A signed Code of Conduct

Education You must possess a high school education or its equivalent in order to take the CBAP® or CCBA™ exam. If you have one or more college or university degrees, you can document them as well. Unlike other professional certification exams, there is no reduction in your work experience requirements for any additional post-secondary education.

Professional Development You also have a requirement to document 21 hours of professional development in the last four years. The professional development must be directly related to business analysis, such as one or more instructor-led training courses. Each hour of class time counts toward 1 hour of professional development time. This professional development must be completed prior to your application date, so if you are planning to take a training course on business analysis as part of your exam preparations, finish that course before you apply.

References As part of your application, you must provide two professional references. One of those references needs to be current. These references might be from a career manager, a client (internal or external), or a CBAP® recipient. Be aware that a project manager can only be used as a reference if they were also the career manager responsible for completing your annual performance review. You must have known each of these individuals for a minimum of six months.

You will be asking your references to indicate that you are a suitable candidate for the CBAP® or CCBA™ certification. Each reference will receive an email message containing a recipient-specific link for them to use to complete a CBAP® or CCBA™ Candidate Reference form online.

Signed Code of Conduct You will be asked to complete and sign a Code of Conduct form in order to apply to take the CBAP® or CCBA™ exam. This is the same form you are asked to complete when you become a member of the IIBA®. This form contains your agreement to act ethically, responsibly, and professionally in your business analysis work.

Exam Spotlight

Review the current CBAP® or CCBA™ handbooks located on the IIBA website for complete and up-to-date information on application criteria, fees, and specific details on how to apply. This information can change without warning, and the data provided to you here may no longer be up-to-date.

Review your application contents thoroughly before submitting your application. Aligning your business analysis work experience with the contents of the *BABOK® Guide* in your application is one small step in starting your exam preparation. Completing the application can be quite time-consuming, so plan to put your materials together in several sittings over a number of days. You can complete your online application contents incrementally and save your work as you go.

Prepare your application content as if your data were going to be audited—it just might be. Many exam candidates are randomly audited to verify and validate their work experience and any other information that they provided in their application.

Now that you have reviewed the experience requirements for applying to sit the CBAP® or CCBA™ certification exams, let's review the exam application process.

The Exam Application Process

There are three distinct steps for you to navigate as you apply for and seek approval to take the CBAP® or CCBA™ certification exam. Remember that you must meet all of the requirements in either the CCBA™ Handbook or CBAP® Handbook to be eligible for the exam. The steps of the application process are

1. Apply and pay for CBAP® or CCBA™ certification.

2. Pay for the exam.

3. Register for the exam.

Let's have a more detailed look at each of these steps right now.

Applying and Paying for Certification   You will be asked to pay two fees to the IIBA in order to complete the application process. The first fee is submitted with your completed application and supporting information. Please check the IIBA website for the latest application and examination fee information. The application fee is the same for IIBA members and nonmembers. The fee will not be refunded if your application is denied. Your certification application package should contain the following items:

- Your completed application form

- Your two professional references

- Your agreement to adhere to the Code of Ethical Conduct and Professional Standards

- Your certification application fee

After you submit everything, the IIBA will send you an email message indicating your application has been successfully submitted. Your application will be reviewed and either approved or denied within 21 business days of its receipt. If your application is approved, you are eligible to take your exam within a one-year window from the date of exam eligibility approval.

Exam Spotlight

Remember to print a paper copy of your completed online application for your own records.

If your application is denied, you are not eligible to take the exam at this time. You will be notified of the reason why your application was declined. In many cases, applicants have had work experience disallowed and have fallen below the minimum experience requirement threshold. You may reapply to take the exam after a three-month delay if your reason for denial can be remedied.

Paying for the Exam　　The exam fee pays for your initial exam sitting after your application has been approved. This fee is not reimbursed if you fail the exam. You can include your exam fee with your application package, or you can wait until you receive the results of your application and pay at that time. Please check the IIBA website for the latest examination fee information. In order to receive the IIBA member rate for your exam fee, you must be a member at the time you submit your exam fee.

Registering for the Exam　　Once your exam fee has been processed by the IIBA, you can register to take your exam at a dedicated test center or as part of a hosted group. At the time of this writing, the test center exams are administered by Castle Worldwide. Check the IIBA website for a current list of test center locations. Castle Worldwide will send you an exam registration letter with instructions for registering online for your exam. After you register for your selected location, date, and time, you will receive a confirmation letter that is your admission ticket to take the exam.

If you fail your exam on your first attempt, you may pay a retake fee and can retake the exam after a three-month waiting period. This waiting period must fall within your original year of exam eligibility. You may retake the exam twice during your eligible testing year. If you fail both retake attempts or your eligibility expires, you must reapply to take the exam and pay the full fee again.

Appendix

B

Knowledge Areas, Tasks, and Elements

TOPICS COVERED IN APPENDIX B

✓ Define the terms knowledge area, task, and element.

✓ Review the six knowledge areas.

✓ Outline the tasks and elements of each knowledge area.

Appendix B contains an outline of the six *BABOK® Guide* knowledge areas, their tasks, and the elements making up those tasks. This appendix is intended to be used as an orientation device and a study aid as you prepare for your CBAP® or CCBA™ certification exam. Appendix B also summarizes the intent of each knowledge area so you can refresh your memory and practice describing them.

Review the Six Knowledge Areas

Knowledge areas divide what business analysts need to know and how they perform their tasks into six common buckets. The business analyst can dip into one or more buckets at any time—in any order—to select a deliverable or perform a necessary task. The knowledge areas are not a road map or a methodology; they simply break business analysis materials and information into common areas. The six knowledge areas defined in the *BABOK® Guide* are

- Business Analysis Planning and Monitoring
- Enterprise Analysis
- Requirements Management and Communication
- Elicitation
- Requirements Analysis
- Solution Assessment and Validation

Each knowledge area is decomposed into the more-detailed tasks performed by the business analyst. Each task has a particular purpose and adds value to the overall business analysis effort on your project when the task is performed.

Tasks are broken down further into elements. Elements are the detailed concepts that are necessary to perform a particular task. For some tasks, the elements are categories of things to be considered. For other tasks, the elements are subtasks performed by the business analyst.

Business Analysis Planning and Monitoring The Business Analysis Planning and Monitoring knowledge area is where a business analyst plans how to approach the business analysis effort. The approach is a set of processes, templates, and activities used to perform business analysis in a specific context. The tasks govern and monitor the performance of all other business analysis tasks. These planning and monitoring activities take place throughout the project life cycle. The results of this knowledge area govern the tasks found in the remaining five knowledge areas and set the performance metrics to be used to evaluate all business analysis work.

Enterprise Analysis   Enterprise Analysis focuses on how the business analyst identifies the business needs driving a project by performing problem definition and analysis. In addition to defining and refining these driving needs, a business analyst is responsible for defining a feasible solution scope that can be implemented by the business. This work may also include developing a business case or feasibility study for a proposed project. Typically, the tasks in this knowledge area occur prior to or early in the project life cycle.

Requirements Management and Communication   The Requirements Management and Communication knowledge area defines how a business analyst approaches communicating requirements to stakeholders. Tasks and techniques for managing changes, conflicts, and issues related to requirements are also described.

Elicitation   Elicitation defines how business analysts work with stakeholders to identify and gather requirements and understand their needs and concerns.

Requirements Analysis   Requirements Analysis describes how the business analyst progressively elaborates and prioritizes stakeholder and solution requirements. In essence, the business analyst is taking the elicited information and making sense of it to derive the real requirements for the project. This knowledge area also focuses on graphically modeling the requirements as well as documenting them. When performing these tasks, a business analyst should ensure the feasibility of the requirements while defining, describing, and refining the characteristics of an acceptable solution.

Solution Assessment and Validation   The Solution Assessment and Validation knowledge area focuses on assessing and validating proposed, in-progress, and implemented solutions before, during, and after the project life cycle. While many tasks in this knowledge area take place later in the project life cycle, some solution-focused activities might occur quite early.

Let's decompose each knowledge area into its tasks and elements. You can use these outlines to help you prepare to take your certification exam. You will need this level of knowledge to successfully prepare for and pass the certification exams. You will also need this level of knowledge to be an effective business analysis practitioner in your organization.

Knowledge Areas, Tasks, and Elements

The following outline decomposes each knowledge area into its pieces and parts—the tasks and elements that provide you with more detailed direction as to what you should be doing.

Business Analysis Planning and Monitoring

Plan business analysis approach

Timing of BA work

Formality and level of detail of BA deliverables

Requirements prioritization approach

Change management

BA planning process

Communication with stakeholders

Requirements analysis and management tools

Project complexity considerations

Conduct stakeholder analysis

Identify stakeholders

Determine complexity of stakeholder group

Assess attitude and influence

Define authority levels for business analysis work

Plan business analysis activities

Look at geographic distribution of stakeholders

Type of project or initiative

Determine business analysis deliverables and activities

Plan business analysis communications

Geography

Culture

Project type

Communication frequency

Communication formality

Plan requirements management process

Repository

Traceability

Select requirements attributes

Define requirements prioritization process

Change management

Manage business analysis performance

Define performance measures

Performance reporting

Preventive and corrective action

Enterprise Analysis

Define business need

Business goals and objectives

Business problem or opportunity

Desired outcome

Assess capability gaps

Current capability analysis

Assessment of new capability requirements

Assumptions

Determine solution approach

Alternative generation

Assumptions and constraints

Ranking and selection of approaches

Define solution scope

Solution scope definition

Implementation approach

Dependencies

Define business case

Benefits

Costs

Risk assessment

Results measurement

Requirements Management and Communication

Manage solution scope and requirements

Solution scope management

Conflict and issue management

Presenting requirements for review

Approval

Manage requirements traceability

Relationships

Impact analysis

Configuration Management System

Maintain requirements for reuse

Ongoing requirements

Satisfied requirements

Prepare requirements package

    Work products and deliverables

    Format

Communicate requirements

    General communication

    Presentations—formal and informal

Elicitation

Prepare for elicitation

    Clarify scope for selected elicitation technique

    Schedule all resources

    Notify parties of the plan

Conduct elicitation activity

    Tracing requirements

    Capturing requirements attributes

    Metrics

Document elicitation results

Confirm elicitation results

Requirements Analysis

Prioritize requirements

    Basis for prioritization

    Challenges

Organize requirements

    Levels of abstraction

    Model selection

Specify and model requirements

    Text

    Matrix documentation

    Models

    Capture requirements attributes

    Improvement opportunities

Define assumptions and constraints

    Assumptions

    Business constraints

    Technical constraints

Verify requirements

    Characteristics of requirements quality

    Verification activities

Validate requirements

    Identify assumptions

    Define measurable evaluation criteria

    Determine business value

    Determine dependencies for benefits realization

    Evaluate alignment with business case and opportunity cost

Solution Assessment and Validation

Assess proposed solution

    Ranking of solution options

    Identification of additional potential capabilities

Allocate requirements

    Solution components

    Release planning

Assess organizational readiness

    Cultural assessment

    Operational or technical assessment

    Stakeholder impact analysis

Define transition requirements

    Data

    Ongoing work

    Organizational change

Validate solution

    Investigate defective solution outputs

    Assess defects and issues

Evaluate solution performance

    Understand value delivered by solution

    Validate solution metrics

    Solution replacement or elimination

Appendix
C

Mapping Techniques, Stakeholders, and Deliverables to Knowledge Areas and Tasks

---

TOPICS COVERED IN APPENDIX C

✓ Mapping techniques to knowledge area tasks

✓ Mapping stakeholders to knowledge area tasks

✓ Mapping deliverables to knowledge area tasks

Appendix C provides you with a coverage matrix that maps the business analysis techniques, deliverables, and stakeholders to the knowledge area tasks that use them in some way. You can use this matrix to keep yourself oriented during your exam preparation studies as you work through the knowledge areas and tasks. These relationships can also be used to help you determine whether or not to use a specific deliverable or apply a certain technique when performing a business analysis task at work.

Techniques

The tables in this section (Tables C.1 through C.6) map the business analysis techniques to the knowledge area tasks that might use them. The references being used are the knowledge area chapter and the task section numbers of the *BABOK® Guide*. An X indicates that a specific technique might be used by a business analyst performing a particular task.

For example, column header 2.1 references the first task in Chapter 2, "Plan the Business Analysis Approach (Section 1)," as part of the Business Analysis Planning and Monitoring knowledge area (Chapter 2). The far-left column in the table provides you with the chapter and section number for locating the details about a specific technique.

For a more comprehensive view of this data, see the Techniques sheet in the BABOKTechniquesMap.xlsx file, available for download from the book web page at www.sybex.com/go/cbap.

TABLE C.1 Business Analysis Planning and Monitoring Techniques

Section	Technique	2.1	2.2	2.3	2.4	2.5	2.6
9.1	Acceptance and Evaluation Criteria Definition		x				
9.3	Brainstorming		x				
9.8	Decision Analysis	x				x	
9.10	Estimation			x			
9.12	Functional Decomposition			x			

Section	Technique	2.1	2.2	2.3	2.4	2.5	2.6
9.14	Interviews		x				x
9.15	Lessons Learned Process						x
9.16	Metrics and KPIs						x
9.19	Organization Modeling		x				
9.20	Problem Tracking					x	x
9.21	Process Modeling	x	x				x
9.23	Requirements Workshops		x				
9.24	Risk Analysis		x	x		x	
9.25	Root Cause Analysis						x
9.26	Scenarios and Use Cases		x				
9.27	Scope Modeling		x				
9.30	Structured Walkthrough	x			x		
9.31	Survey/Questionnaire		x				x
9.33	User Stories		x				
2.2	RACI Matrix		x				
2.2	Stakeholder Map		x				
2.6	Variance Analysis						x

TABLE C.2 Elicitation Techniques

Section	Technique	3.1	3.2	3.3	3.4
9.3	Brainstorming	x	x	x	
9.5	Data Dictionary and Glossary		x		
9.9	Document Analysis	x	x	x	

TABLE C.2 Elicitation Techniques *(continued)*

Section	Technique	3.1	3.2	3.3	3.4
9.11	Focus Groups	x	x	x	
9.13	Interface Analysis	x	x	x	
9.14	Interviews	x	x	x	x
9.18	Observation	x	x	x	x
9.20	Problem Tracking			x	
9.22	Prototyping	x	x	x	
9.23	Requirements Workshops	x	x	x	
9.31	Survey/Questionnaire	x	x	x	

TABLE C.3 Requirements Management and Communication Techniques

Section	Technique	4.1	4.2	4.3	4.4	4.5
9.20	Problem Tracking	x				
9.23	Requirements Workshops					x
9.30	Structured Walkthrough					x
4.1	Baselining	x				
4.1	Signoff	x				
4.2	Coverage Matrix		x			
4.4	Requirements Documentation				x	
4.4	Requirements for Vendor Selection				x	

TABLE C.4 Enterprise Analysis Techniques

Section	Technique	5.1	5.2	5.3	5.4	5.5
9.2	Benchmarking	x		x		
9.3	Brainstorming	x		x		
9.4	Business Rules Analysis	x				
9.8	Decision Analysis			x		x
9.9	Document Analysis		x			
9.10	Estimation			x		x
9.11	Focus Groups	x				
9.12	Functional Decomposition	x			x	
9.13	Interface Analysis				x	
9.16	Metrics and KPIs					x
9.24	Risk Analysis					x
9.25	Root Cause Analysis	x				
9.27	Scope Modeling				x	
9.32	SWOT Analysis		x	x		x
9.33	User Stories				x	
9.34	Vendor Assessment					x
5.3	Feasibility Analysis			x		
5.4	Problem or Vision Statement				x	

TABLE C.5   Requirements Analysis Techniques

Section	Technique	6.1	6.2	6.3	6.4	6.5	6.6
9.1	Acceptance and Evaluation Criteria Definition			x		x	x
9.4	Business Rules Analysis		x	x			
9.5	Data Dictionary and Glossary			x			
9.6	Data Flow Diagrams		x	x			
9.7	Data Modeling		x	x			
9.8	Decision Analysis	x					
9.12	Functional Decomposition		x	x			
9.13	Interface Analysis			x			
9.16	Metrics and KPIs			x			x
9.17	Non-functional Requirements Analysis			x			
9.19	Organization Modeling		x	x			
9.20	Problem Tracking				x	x	
9.21	Process Modeling		x	x			
9.22	Prototyping			x			x
9.24	Risk Analysis	x			x		x
9.26	Scenarios and Use Cases		x	x			
9.27	Scope Modeling		x				
9.28	Sequence Diagrams			x			
9.29	State Diagrams			x			
9.30	Structured Walkthrough					x	x

Section	Technique	6.1	6.2	6.3	6.4	6.5	6.6
9.33	User Stories		x	x			
6.1	MoSCoW Analysis	x					
6.1	Timeboxing/Budgeting	x					
6.1	Voting	x					
6.5	Checklists					x	

TABLE C.6   Solution Assessment and Validation Techniques

Section	Technique	7.1	7.2	7.3	7.4	7.5	7.6
9.1	Acceptance and Evaluation Criteria Definition	x	x	x		x	
9.4	Business Rules Analysis		x		x		
9.6	Data Flow Diagrams			x	x		
9.7	Data Modeling				x		
9.8	Decision Analysis	x	x				x
9.11	Focus Groups			x			x
9.12	Functional Decomposition		x				
9.14	Interviews			x			
9.18	Observation						x
9.19	Organization Modeling			x	x		
9.20	Problem Tracking			x		x	
9.21	Process Modeling		x	x	x		
9.24	Risk Analysis			x			

TABLE C.6   Solution Assessment and Validation Techniques *(continued)*

Section	Technique	7.1	7.2	7.3	7.4	7.5	7.6
9.25	Root Cause Analysis					x	
9.26	Scenarios and Use Cases		x				
9.31	Survey/Questionnaire				x		x
9.32	SWOT Analysis				x		
9.34	Vendor Assessment	x					
7.3	Force Field Analysis				x		

Stakeholders

The tables in this section (Tables C.7 through C.12) map the business analysis stakeholders to the knowledge area tasks in which they might participate. The references being used are the knowledge area chapter and the task section numbers of the *BABOK® Guide*. An X indicates that a specific stakeholder role may participate in a particular task.

The tables map the business analyst role to every business analysis task in the *BABOK® Guide*. The business analysts' level of involvement (whether formal or informal) is not explicitly stated in the list of stakeholders for each and every task.

The task is identified by its chapter and section number. For example, the column header 2.1 references the first task in Chapter 2, "Plan the Business Analysis Approach (Section 1)," as part of the Business Analysis Planning and Monitoring knowledge area (Chapter 2).

For a more comprehensive view, see the Stakeholders sheet in the BABOKTechniquesMap .xlsx file, available for download from the book web page at www.sybex.com/go/cbap.

TABLE C.7   Business Analysis Planning and Monitoring Stakeholders

Stakeholder	2.1	2.2	2.3	2.4	2.5	2.6
Business Analyst	x	x	x	x	x	x
Customer	x		x	x		
Domain SME	x	x	x	x	x	x

Stakeholder	2.1	2.2	2.3	2.4	2.5	2.6
End User	x		x	x	x	x
Implementation SME	x	x	x	x	x	x
Operational Support			x	x	x	x
Project Manager	x	x	x	x	x	x
Tester	x	x	x	x	x	x
Regulator	x	x		x		
Sponsor	x	x	x	x	x	x
Supplier	x		x	x		

TABLE C.8   Elicitation Stakeholders

Stakeholder	3.1	3.2	3.3	3.4
Business Analyst	x	x	x	x
Customer	x	x		x
Domain SME	x	x		x
End User	x	x		x
Implementation SME	x	x		x
Developers/Software Engineers	x			x
Operational Support	x	x		x
Org. Change Mgmt. Professionals	x			x
System Architects	x			x
Trainers	x			x
Usability Professionals	x			x

TABLE C.8   Elicitation Stakeholders *(continued)*

Stakeholder	3.1	3.2	3.3	3.4
Project Manager	x	x		x
Tester	x	x		x
Regulator	x	x		x
Sponsor	x	x		x
Supplier	x	x		x

TABLE C.9   Requirements Management and Communication Stakeholders

Stakeholder	4.1	4.2	4.3	4.4	4.5
Business Analyst	x	x	x	x	x
Customer					x
Domain SME	x		x	x	x
End User				x	x
Implementation SME	x	x	x	x	x
Developers/Software Engineers					x
Operational Support					x
Org. Change Mgmt. Professionals					x
System Architects					x
Trainers					x
Usability Professionals					x
Project Manager	x	x		x	x
Tester		x		x	x

Stakeholder	4.1	4.2	4.3	4.4	4.5
Regulator				x	x
Sponsor	x			x	x
Supplier					x

TABLE C.10 Enterprise Analysis Stakeholders

Stakeholder	5.1	5.2	5.3	5.4	5.5
Business Analyst	x	x	x	x	x
Customer	x	x	x		
Domain SME	x	x	x	x	x
End User	x	x	x		
Implementation SME	x	x	x	x	x
Project Manager				x	x
Regulator	x				
Sponsor	x	x	x	x	x
Supplier	x	x	x		

TABLE C.11 Requirements Analysis Stakeholders

Stakeholder	6.1	6.2	6.3	6.4	6.5	6.6
Business Analyst	x	x	x	x	x	x
Customer			x	x	x	x
Domain SME	x	x	x	x	x	x
End User		x	x	x	x	x

TABLE C.11 Requirements Analysis Stakeholders *(continued)*

Stakeholder	6.1	6.2	6.3	6.4	6.5	6.6
Implementation SME	x	x	x	x	x	x
Developers/Software Engineers			x	x	x	x
Operational Support			x	x	x	x
Org. Change Mgmt. Professionals			x	x	x	x
System Architects			x	x	x	x
Trainers			x	x	x	x
Usability Professionals			x	x	x	x
Project Manager	x	x	x	x	x	x
Tester			x	x	x	x
Regulator			x	x	x	x
Sponsor	x	x	x	x	x	x
Supplier			x	x	x	x

TABLE C.12 Solution Assessment and Validation Stakeholders

Stakeholder	7.1	7.2	7.3	7.4	7.5	7.6
Business Analyst	x	x	x	x	x	x
Customer		x		x		x
Domain SME	x	x	x	x	x	x
End User		x		x	x	x
Implementation SME	x	x	x	x	x	
Developers/Software Engineers						
Operational Support	x	x	x	x	x	x
Org. Change Mgmt. Professionals			x			

Stakeholder	7.1	7.2	7.3	7.4	7.5	7.6
Trainers			x			
Usability Professionals			x			
Project Manager	x	x	x	x	x	
Tester			x		x	x
Regulator				x	x	x
Sponsor	x	x	x	x	x	x
Supplier	x	x				x

Deliverables

The tables in this section (Tables C.13 through C.18) map the business analysis deliverables to the knowledge area tasks that use them as inputs or produce them as outputs. Some of the deliverables are out of the scope of the *BABOK® Guide* and may be generated by the organization or by the project's technical team members during design and development. The references being used are the knowledge area chapter and the task section numbers of the *BABOK® Guide*. An I indicates that a specific deliverable is used by a particular task as an input. An O indicates that a specific deliverable is produced as an output by a task.

These tables map the business analysis plan or plans to each knowledge area task in the *BABOK® Guide* except for the tasks in Business Analysis Planning and Monitoring. By definition in the introduction to each knowledge area, the business analysis plan or plans govern the performance of all activities in the Elicitation, Enterprise Analysis, Requirements Management and Communication, Requirements Analysis, and Solution Assessment and Validation knowledge areas. For them to do so, the business analysis plan or plans must be an implied input to these tasks so people can reference what was planned to be done.

Each task is identified by its chapter and section number. For example, column header 2.1 references the first task in Chapter 2 of the *BABOK® Guide*, "Plan the Business Analysis Approach (Section 1)," as part of the Business Analysis Planning and Monitoring knowledge area (Chapter 2).

For a more comprehensive view, see the Deliverables sheet in the BABOKTechniquesMap .xlsx file, available for down load from the book web page at www.sybex.com/go/cbap.

TABLE C.13   Business Analysis Planning and Monitoring Inputs and Outputs

Deliverables	2.1	2.2	2.3	2.4	2.5	2.6
BA Communication Plan				O		
BA Performance Assessment			I			O
BA Process Assets						O
Business Analysis Approach	O		I	I	I	
Business Analysis Performance Metrics						I
Business Analysis Plan(s)			O	I	I	I
Business Need	I	I				
Enterprise Architecture		I				
Expert Judgment	I	I				
Organizational Performance Standards						I
Organizational Process Assets (OPAs)	I	I	I	I	I	
Requirements Management Plan					O	I
Stakeholder List, Roles, and Responsibilities		O	I	I		

TABLE C.14   Elicitation Inputs and Outputs

Deliverables	3.1	3.2	3.3	3.4
Business Analysis Plan(s)		I	I	I	I
Business Case		I	I	
Business Need		I	I	
Elicitation Results			O	I
Organizational Process Assets (OPAs)			I	

Deliverables	3.1	3.2	3.3	3.4
Requirements (Stated)			O	
Requirements (Stated, Confirmed)				O
Requirements (Stated, Unconfirmed)				I
Requirements Management Plan		I		
Scheduled Resources		I		
Scheduled Resources	O			
Solution Scope	I	I		
Stakeholder Concerns			O	
Stakeholder Concerns (Confirmed)				O
Stakeholder Concerns (Unconfirmed)				I
Stakeholder List, Roles, and Responsibilities	I			
Supporting Materials	O	I		

TABLE C.15 Requirements Management and Communication Inputs and Outputs

Deliverables	4.1	4.2	4.3	4.4	4.5
BA Communication Plan				I	I
Business Analysis Plan(s)	I	I	I	I	I
Organizational Process Assets (OPAs)			I	I	
Requirements (Any)		I	I	I	I
Requirements (Approved)	O				
Requirements (Communicated)	I				O
Requirements (Maintained and Reusable)			O		
Requirements (Traced)	I	O			

TABLE C.15   Requirements Management and Communication Inputs and
Outputs *(continued)*

Deliverables	4.1	4.2	4.3	4.4	4.5
Requirements Management Plan	I	I			
Requirements Package				O	I
Requirements Structure				I	
Solution Scope	I				
Stakeholder List, Roles, and Responsibilities	I				

TABLE C.16   Enterprise Analysis Inputs and Outputs

Deliverables	5.1	5.2	5.3	5.4	5.5
Assumptions and Constraints				I	I
Business Analysis Plan(s)	I	I	I	I	I
Business Case					O
Business Goals and Objectives	I				
Business Need	O	I	I	I	I
Enterprise Architecture		I			
Organizational Process Assets (OPAs)			I		
Required Capabilities		O	I	I	
Requirements (Stated)	I				
Solution Approach			O	I	
Solution Options					
Solution Performance Assessment		I			
Solution Scope				O	I
Stakeholder Concerns					I

TABLE C.17 Requirements Analysis Inputs and Outputs

Deliverables	6.1	6.2	6.3	6.4	6.5	6.6
Assumptions and Constraints				O		
Business Analysis Plan(s)	I	I	I	I	I	I
Business Case	I					I
Business Need	I					
Organizational Process Assets (OPAs)		I				
Requirements (Analyzed)			O		I	
Requirements (Any)	I				I	
Requirements (Approved)					I	
Requirements (Communicated)					I	
Requirements (Maintained and Reusable)					I	
Requirements (Prioritized)	O				O	
Requirements (Stated)		I	I			
Requirements (Stated, Confirmed)					I	
Requirements (Validated)						O
Requirements (Verified)						I
Requirements Management Plan	I					
Requirements Structure		O	I			
Solution Scope		I				
Stakeholder Concerns				I		
Stakeholder List, Roles, and Responsibilities	I					

TABLE C.18 Solution Assessment and Validation Inputs and Outputs

Deliverables	7.1	7.2	7.3	7.4	7.5	7.6
Assessment of Proposed Solution	O					
Assumptions and Constraints	I					
Business Analysis Plan(s)	I	I	I	I	I	I
Business Requirements						I
Enterprise Architecture			I			
Identified Defects					O	I
Mitigating Actions					O	
Organizational Readiness Assessment			O	I		
Requirements (Allocated)		O				
Requirements (Prioritized and Validated)					I	
Requirements (Prioritized and Approved)	I	I				
Requirements (Stated)				I		
Solution (Constructed)					I	
Solution (Deployed)				I		I
Solution (Designed)		I	I	I		
Solution Options	I					
Solution Performance Assessment						O
Solution Performance Metrics						I
Solution Scope		I	I			
Solution Validation Assessment					O	
Stakeholder Concerns			I			
Transition Requirements				O		

Appendix

D

Quick Summary of Business Analysis Techniques

TOPICS COVERED IN APPENDIX D

- ✓ Define a business analysis technique.

- ✓ Differentiate between general and task-specific techniques.

- ✓ Review brief descriptions of the *BABOK® Guide* techniques.

Appendix D reviews the definition of a technique and differentiates between the two types of techniques you will encounter—general techniques and task-specific techniques. This appendix also provides a table containing brief descriptions of each technique found in the *BABOK® Guide*. This should refresh your memory about the high-level descriptions of each business analysis technique you might see on your certification exam or use at work.

Business Analysis Techniques

The *BABOK® Guide* has a total of 49 business analysis techniques. These techniques are considered to be the best practices used by many business analysts. They offer you options for how business analysis tasks might be performed. Experienced business analysts are expected to be skilled in many of these techniques. Although it is not essential to be proficient in all of them, you should master a decent subset of business analysis techniques that work for you. The *BABOK® Guide* identifies 16 of these techniques as essential for all business analysts. They are discussed throughout the book and covered in detail. The 16 essential techniques include:

- Acceptance and Evaluation Criteria Definition
- Brainstorming
- Business Rules Analysis
- Data Dictionary and Glossary
- Data Flow Diagrams
- Data Modeling
- Decision Analysis
- Document Analysis
- Interviews
- Metrics and Key Performance Indicators
- Nonfunctional Requirements Analysis
- Organization Modeling
- Problem Tracking
- Process Modeling

- Requirements Workshops
- Scenarios and Use Cases

Two types of techniques are found in the *BABOK® Guide:* general and knowledge-area-specific. General techniques can be used by any task at any time, and many general techniques are used by more than one task. Knowledge-area-specific techniques are defined as part of the knowledge area task that uses them. They are used only by a single task. The knowledge-area-specific techniques were discussed when you looked at the single, specific tasks that used them.

The 34 General Techniques

Table D.1 lists and defines the 34 general business analysis techniques found in the *BABOK® Guide.* They are defined for you in much more detail in Chapter 9 of the *BABOK® Guide.*

TABLE D.1 The General Business Analysis Techniques

Technique	Description
Acceptance and Evaluation Criteria Definition	Acceptance criteria define a set of requirements that must be met for a new solution to be acceptable to its stakeholders. Evaluation criteria are metrics and indicators used to assess how an operational solution meets its objectives over time.
Benchmarking	Comparing organizational practices or processes against best in-class practices or processes of peer organizations to identify opportunities for improvement.
Brainstorming	Generating creative ideas and options to solve a problem or meet a business need in a noncritical group environment.
Business Rules Analysis	Modeling and analyzing the business principles and processes that define, constrain, and/or enable business operations.
Data Dictionary and Glossary	Collections of definitions used to explain the terminology used by the business and the data relevant to each business domain.
Data Flow Diagrams	Drawings used to visually represent how information moves through a system by showing the external entities, processes, data storage, and data flow.
Data Modeling	Describing and diagramming the concepts relevant to a business area, the relationships between these concepts, and information associated with them.
Decision Analysis	Examining and modeling the possible consequences of different decisions to make the optimal decision under uncertain conditions.

TABLE D.1   The General Business Analysis Techniques *(continued)*

Technique	Description
Document Analysis	Eliciting the requirements for an existing system by studying available documentation and identifying any other relevant information.
Estimation	Developing the possible range of costs and effort associated with business analysis work on your project.
Focus Groups	Collections of people used to elicit ideas and attitudes about a specific product, service, or opportunity in an interactive environment.
Functional Decomposition	Decomposing business processes, functional areas, or deliverables into smaller parts in order to analyze the parts independently.
Interface Analysis	Clarifying the boundaries and interfaces between solutions and solution components and defining the requirements describing how they will interact with one another.
Interviews	Conversations used to elicit information from a person or group of people in an informal or formal setting by asking questions and documenting the responses.
Lessons Learned Process	Learning about and improving a project or process by compiling and documenting successes, opportunities for improvement, failures, and recommendations for improving performance.
Metrics and Key Performance Indicators	Measurements used to indicate the performance of solutions, solution components, and other matters of interest to your stakeholders.
Nonfunctional Requirements Analysis	Describing qualities and characteristics of a system or solution, such as usability and performance.
Observation	Eliciting requirements by conducting an assessment of the stakeholder's work environment.
Organization Modeling	Describing roles, responsibilities, and reporting structures that exist within an organization.
Problem Tracking	Formally tracking the management and resolution of defects, issues, problems, and risks throughout the project life cycle.
Process Modeling	Visually modeling the sequential flow and control logic of a set of related activities or actions.
Prototyping	Building a partial or preliminary version of a system or solution as part of your requirements development activities.

Technique	Description
Requirements Workshops	Structured and facilitated meetings for a carefully selected group of stakeholders to collaborate and define/refine requirements.
Risk Analysis	Assessing an identified risk and deciding on a response to that risk.
Root Cause Analysis	Performing a structured examination of an identified problem to understand the underlying causes of that problem.
Scenarios and Use Cases	Stories used to describe the tasks a system or solution will perform for actors and the goals that the system will achieve for those actors.
Scope Modeling	Defining the boundaries of a business domain or solution.
Sequence Diagrams	Drawings used to show how objects interact during a scenario and the messages they exchange with one another.
State Diagrams	Drawings used to show the life cycle of a data entity or class.
Structured Walkthrough	An organized peer review of a deliverable, looking for errors and omissions.
Survey/Questionnaire	A set of written questions to stakeholders to collect responses from a large group in a relatively short period of time.
SWOT Analysis	An evaluation of the influencing factors and how they affect a project by looking at strengths, weaknesses, opportunities, and threats.
User Stories	High-level, informal, and short descriptions of a solution capability for a stakeholder in one or two sentences.
Vendor Assessment	An evaluation of the ability of a potential vendor to meet commitments regarding providing you with a product or service.

The 15 Knowledge-Area-Specific Techniques

Table D.2 lists and defines the 15 knowledge-area-specific techniques in the *BABOK®* *Guide*. So that you can easily find them if you need more information, they are defined as part of the knowledge area tasks that use them.

TABLE D.2   Knowledge-Area-Specific Business Analysis Techniques

Technique	Brief Description	Knowledge Area	Task
Baselining	Taking a snapshot of requirements at a specific point in time and using it as a basis for further development.	Requirements Management and Communication	Manage solution scope and requirements
Checklists	Lists used to verify that important items are included in your final requirements deliverables to ensure consistent project approaches and outcomes.	Requirements Analysis	Verify requirements
Coverage Matrix	Using a table or spreadsheet to trace your requirements and track the relationships between them.	Requirements Management and Communication	Manage requirements traceability
Feasibility Analysis	Evaluating proposed solution alternatives to see if they are technically feasible for the organization and if they deliver the desired business benefits.	Enterprise Analysis	Determine solution approach
Force Field Analysis	Graphically depicting and analyzing the forces that support and oppose an organizational change, such as implementation of a new solution.	Solution Assessment and Validation	Assess organizational readiness
MoSCoW Analysis	Prioritizing requirements by dividing the requirements into four categories: must, should, could, and won't.	Requirements Analysis	Prioritize requirements
Problem or Vision Statement	A document that describes the problems found in the current state of the organization and clarifies what a successful solution will do about those problems.	Enterprise Analysis	Define solution scope
RACI Matrix	Describing roles and responsibilities of people performing business analysis work by showing if they are responsible, accountable, consulted, and/or informed about specific tasks and deliverables.	Business Analysis Planning and Monitoring	Conduct stakeholder analysis

Technique	Brief Description	Knowledge Area	Task
Requirements Documentation	Capturing your project requirements in a formal requirements document or a set of requirements documents.	Requirements Management and Communication	Prepare requirements package
Requirements for Vendor Selection	Capturing requirements to use for vendor evaluation and selection purposes by using a Request for Information (RFI), Request for Quote (RFQ), or Request for Proposal (RFP).	Requirements Management and Communication	Prepare requirements package
Signoff	A requirements signoff formalizes agreement by project stakeholders that the content and presentation of documented requirements are accurate and complete.	Requirements Management and Communication	Manage solution scope and requirements
Stakeholder Map	A drawing that visually depicts the relationships of stakeholders to the solution and to one another, using either a matrix or an onion diagram.	Business Analysis Planning and Monitoring	Conduct stakeholder analysis
Timeboxing/ Budgeting	Prioritizing requirements based on allocation of a fixed resource— timeboxing prioritizes based on the work that can be done in a set period of time, while budgeting prioritizes based upon a fixed amount of money.	Requirements Analysis	Prioritize requirements
Variance Analysis	Analyzing the differences between planned and actual performance of work activities to see if corrective or preventive actions are required while business analysis work is being done.	Business Analysis Planning and Monitoring	Manage business analysis performance
Voting	Prioritizing requirements by allocating a fixed amount of resources for your stakeholders to distribute across a set of proposed features or requirements.	Requirements Analysis	Prioritize requirements

Appendix E

Quick Summary of Business Analysis Deliverables

TOPICS COVERED IN APPENDIX E

✓ Define a business analysis deliverable.

✓ List and briefly describe the BABOK® Guide deliverables.

Appendix E reviews the definition of a business analysis deliverable and provides a table containing brief descriptions of each deliverable found in the *BABOK® Guide*. This should refresh your memory about the high-level descriptions of each business analysis deliverable that you might see on your certification exam or use back at work.

Business Analysis Deliverables

The *BABOK® Guide* recommends and defines a set of deliverables that you can tailor and use when planning for, defining, and managing your project's business analysis efforts. These deliverables are not always documents; they can also be information sets that you use to measure business analysis performance, take action, and make the right decisions at the right time. These deliverables evolve over the project life cycle and are often reviewed and updated as the project and its associated business analysis efforts progress.

Table E.1 lists and defines the deliverables produced as outputs by the tasks found in the *BABOK® Guide*. It also provides the knowledge area and task where each output is produced. Deliverables used as task inputs that are produced outside of the scope of the *BABOK® Guide* and its tasks are not addressed here.

TABLE E.1 Summary of Business Analysis Deliverables

Deliverable	Brief Description	Knowledge Area	Task
Assessment of Proposed Solution	Evaluates the value delivered by each proposed solution and recommends the best option of multiple options, including termination of the initiative	Solution Assessment and Validation	Assess proposed solution
Assumptions and Constraints	Limits and boundary conditions that constrain the solution options and the new solution capabilities	Requirements Analysis	Define assumptions and constraints

Deliverable	Brief Description	Knowledge Area	Task
Business Analysis Approach	Defines the set of processes, templates, techniques, and activities used to perform business analysis on a project or initiative	Business Analysis Planning and Monitoring	Plan business analysis approach
Business Analysis Communication Plan	Describes how, when, and why the business analyst will communicate directly with stakeholders	Business Analysis Planning and Monitoring	Plan business analysis communication
Business Analysis Performance Assessment	Compares planned versus actual estimates for business analysis activities to determine the level of effort required to complete the work	Business Analysis Planning and Monitoring	Manage business analysis performance
Business Analysis Plan(s)	Contains the planned and scheduled business analysis activities that will be done on the project	Business Analysis Planning and Monitoring	Plan business analysis activities
Business Analysis Process Assets	Documents the processes and templates used for business analysis deliverables and lessons learned	Business Analysis Planning and Monitoring	Manage business analysis performance
Business Case	Presents the information necessary to make a go/no go decision to Invest and move forward with a proposed project	Enterprise Analysis	Define business case
Business Need	Describes the problem or opportunity faced by the organization and the desired outcome	Enterprise Analysis	Define business need
Elicitation Results	Documented requirements information provided by the stakeholders	Elicitation	Conduct elicitation activity
Identified Defects	Known problems that exist in a solution which are reviewed, assessed, and addressed	Solution Assessment and Validation	Validate solution

TABLE E.1   Summary of Business Analysis Deliverables *(continued)*

Deliverable	Brief Description	Knowledge Area	Task
Mitigating Actions	Steps that can be taken to reduce or eliminate the impact of an identified defect on the stakeholders	Solution Assessment and Validation	Validate solution
Organizational Readiness Assessment	Assesses if stakeholders are prepared to accept a change associated with a solution	Solution Assessment and Validation	Assess organizational readiness
Required Capabilities	Provides an understanding of the current capabilities of the organization and the new capabilities that may be needed to meet the business need	Enterprise Analysis	Assess capability gaps
Requirements (allocated)	Requirements associated with the solution component that will implement them	Solution Assessment and Validation	Allocate requirements
Requirements (analyzed)	Specified and modeled stakeholder or solution requirements	Requirements Analysis	Specify and model requirements
Requirements (approved)	Requirements agreed to by stakeholders and ready for use in subsequent business analysis activities	Requirements Management and Communication	Manage solution scope and requirements
Requirements (communicated)	Requirements that have been communicated to the stakeholders to ensure common understanding	Requirements Management and Communication	Communicate requirements
Requirements (maintained and reusable)	Requirements formatted for long-term use by the organization	Requirements Management and Communication	Maintain requirements for reuse
Requirements (prioritized)	Requirements prioritized relative to one another based on relative importance to stakeholders and the organization	Requirements Analysis	Prioritize requirements
Requirements (stated)	Requirements described from the stakeholder's point of view during elicitation	Elicitation	Document elicitation results Confirm elicitation results

Deliverable	Brief Description	Knowledge Area	Task
Requirements (traced)	Requirements with clearly defined relationships to other requirements within the solution scope	Requirements Management and Communication	Manage requirements traceability
Requirements (validated)	Requirements that deliver value to stakeholders and align with business goals and objectives	Requirements Analysis	Validate requirements
Requirements (verified)	Requirements of sufficient quality to allow further work based on those requirements to be performed	Requirements Analysis	Verify requirements
Requirements Management Plan	Describes the approach to be taken for traceability, requirements attributes, prioritization, and change management on a project	Business Analysis Planning and Monitoring	Plan requirements management process
Requirements Package	Requirements document, presentation, or a package of requirements for stakeholder review	Requirements Management and Communication	Prepare requirements package
Requirements Structure	Provides the organized structure for documenting your requirements in the requirements document(s)	Requirements Analysis	Organize requirements
Scheduled Resources	Participants, location, and materials used for an elicitation activity	Elicitation	Prepare for elicitation
Solution Approach	Describes the approach that will be taken to implement a new set of capabilities, including the solution components that will be delivered and the methodology to be used	Enterprise Analysis	Determine solution approach
Solution Performance Assessment	Measures how the solution is performing relative to the business goals and objectives based on the solution performance metrics	Solution Assessment and Validation	Evaluate solution performance

TABLE E.1 Summary of Business Analysis Deliverables *(continued)*

Deliverable	Brief Description	Knowledge Area	Task
Solution Scope	Defines the set of capabilities that must be delivered to meet the business need and the effect the capabilities will have on business and technology operations and infrastructure	Enterprise Analysis	Define solution scope
Solution Validation Assessment	Assesses if the solution is able to meet the business need at an acceptable level of quality	Solution Assessment and Validation	Validate solution
Stakeholder Concerns	Issues, risks, assumptions, and constraints identified by stakeholders during elicitation	Elicitation	Document elicitation results Confirm elicitation results
Stakeholder List, Roles, and Responsibilities	Lists and describes the business analysis stakeholders and their roles/responsibilities on your project	Business Analysis Planning and Monitoring	Conduct stakeholder analysis
Supporting Materials	Any materials required to explain or perform the techniques being used in an elicitation activity	Elicitation	Prepare for elicitation
Transition Requirements	Describe capabilities that must be developed in order to transition from the existing solution to the new solution	Solution Assessment and Validation	Define transition requirements

Appendix
F

About the Companion CD

TOPICS IN THIS APPENDIX:

✓ What you'll find on the CD

✓ System requirements

✓ Using the CD

✓ Troubleshooting

What You'll Find on the CD

The following sections are arranged by category and summarize the software and other goodies you'll find on the CD. If you need help with installing the items provided on the CD, refer to the installation instructions in the "Use the CD" section of this appendix.

Sybex Test Engine

The CD contains the Sybex test engine, the assessment test, all the chapter review questions, and four bonus exams: two each for the CBAP® and CCBA™ exams.

Electronic Flashcards

These handy electronic flashcards are just what they sound like. One side contains a question, and the other side shows the answer.

PDF of the Glossary of Terms

We have included an electronic version of the Glossary in .pdf format. You can view the electronic version of the book with Adobe Reader.

Adobe Reader

We've also included a copy of Adobe Reader so you can view PDF files that accompany the book's content. For more information on Adobe Reader or to check for a newer version, visit Adobe's website at www.adobe.com/products/reader/.

System Requirements

Make sure your computer meets the minimum system requirements shown in the following list. If your computer doesn't match up to most of these requirements, you may have problems using the software and files on the companion CD. For the latest and greatest information, please refer to the ReadMe file located at the root of the CD-ROM.

- A PC running Microsoft Windows 98, Windows 2000, Windows NT4 (with SP4 or later), Windows Me, Windows XP, Windows Vista, or Windows 7
- An Internet connection
- A CD-ROM drive

Using the CD

To install the items from the CD to your hard drive, follow these steps:

1. Insert the CD into your computer's CD-ROM drive. The license agreement appears.

Windows users: The interface won't launch if autorun is disabled. If that is the case, click Start ➢ Run (for Windows Vista or Windows 7, Start ➢ All Programs ➢ Accessories ➢ Run). In the dialog box that appears, type **D:\Start.exe**. (Replace *D* with the proper letter if your CD drive uses a different letter. If you don't know the letter, see how your CD drive is listed under My Computer.) Click OK.

2. Read the license agreement, and then click the Accept button if you want to use the CD.

The CD interface appears. The interface allows you to access the content with just one or two clicks.

Troubleshooting

Wiley has attempted to provide programs that work on most computers with the minimum system requirements. Alas, your computer may differ, and some programs may not work properly for some reason.

The two likeliest problems are that you don't have enough memory (RAM) for the programs you want to use or you have other programs running that are affecting installation or running of a program. If you get an error message such as "Not enough memory" or "Setup cannot continue," try one or more of the following suggestions and then try using the software again:

Turn off any antivirus software running on your computer. Installation programs sometimes mimic virus activity and may make your computer incorrectly believe that it's being infected by a virus.

Close all running programs. The more programs you have running, the less memory is available to other programs. Installation programs typically update files and programs; so if you keep other programs running, installation may not work properly.

Have your local computer store add more RAM to your computer. This is, admittedly, a drastic and somewhat expensive step. However, adding more memory can really help the speed of your computer and allow more programs to run at the same time.

Customer Care

If you have trouble with the book's companion CD-ROM, please call the Wiley Product Technical Support phone number at (800) 762-2974.

Index

Index

Note to the Reader: Throughout this index **boldfaced** page numbers indicate primary discussions of a topic. *Italicized* page numbers indicate illustrations.

E

F

K

S

T

The Best Certified Business Analysis Book/CD Package on the Market!

Get ready for your Certified Business Analysis Professional (CBAP®) or Certification of Competency in Business Analysis (CCBA™) certifications with the most comprehensive and challenging sample tests anywhere!

The Sybex Test Engine features:

- All the review questions, as covered in each chapter of the book

- Challenging questions representative of those you'll find on the real exam

- A total of four bonus practice exams available only on the CD, two each for the CBAP and CCBA exams

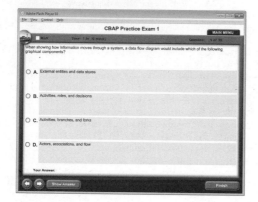

- An Assessment Test to narrow your focus to certain objective groups

A Glossary to use for instant reference

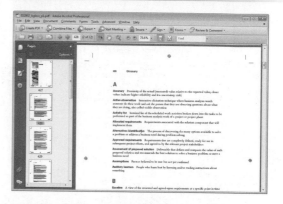

Use the Electronic Flashcards to jog your memory and prep last-minute for the exam!

- Reinforce your understanding of key concepts with these hardcore flashcard-style questions.

- Now you can study for Certified Business Analysis exams anytime, anywhere.

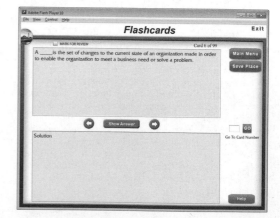